Louis B. Wright,

director of the Folger Shakespeare Library, has devoted more than thirty years to the study of the Elizabethan period. In 1926 he completed a doctoral thesis on "Vaudeville Elements in Elizabethan Drama" and subsequently published many articles on stagecraft and theatre in the Elizabethan era. He is the author of many books and essays, the most recent of which is **SHAKESPEARE FOR EVERYMAN** (1964), and is coeditor of The Folger Library General Reader's Shakespeare series. He has taught at the University of North Carolina, the University of Michigan, the University of Minnesota, and other American institutions. From 1932 to 1948 he was instrumental in developing the research program of the Henry E. Huntington Library and Art Gallery. Since 1948 he has been director of the Folger Shakespeare Library in Washington, D.C., which in that time has become one of the leading research institutions of the world for the study of the backgrounds of Anglo-American civilization.

Virginia A. LaMar

is executive secretary of the Folger Shakespeare Library and research assistant to the director. From 1941 to 1946 Miss LaMar was a secretary in the British Admiralty Delegation in Washington, D.C., and in 1945 she received the King's Medal for her services. She was coeditor of the **HISTORIE OF TRAVELL INTO VIRGINIA BRITANIA** by William Strachey (1953), and is presently coeditor of The Folger Library General Reader's Shakespeare series.

The Folger Shakespeare Library of Washington, D.C., is a research institution, founded and endowed by Henry Clay Folger and administered by the Trustees of Amherst College. It contains one of the world's most important collections of Shakespeareana. Its materials include extraordinary resources for the study of varied aspects of Western civilization from 1485 to 1715, and are not confined to Shakespeare.

Although the Folger Library's primary purpose is to encourage advanced research in history and literature, it also has a profound concern in stimulating a popular interest in the literature of the Tudor and Stuart periods. This edition is designed to provide the general reader with a modern text that is clear and understandable, with such notes and explanations as may be needed to clarify obscure words and passages.

GENERAL EDITOR
LOUIS B. WRIGHT
Director, Folger Shakespeare Library

ASSISTANT EDITOR
VIRGINIA A. LaMAR
Executive Secretary, Folger Shakespeare Library

FOUR GREAT RESTORATION PLAYS

ALL FOR LOVE
John Dryden

THE BEAUX' STRATAGEM
George Farquhar

THE WAY OF THE WORLD
William Congreve

THE COUNTRY WIFE
William Wycherley

Edited and with an Introduction by
Louis B. Wright
and Virginia A. LaMar

WASHINGTON SQUARE PRESS, INC. • NEW YORK

FOUR GREAT RESTORATION PLAYS

A *Washington Square Press* edition

1st printing.........................June, 1964

The first edition of *The Country Wife* was printed for Thomas Dring, 1675, London; *All for Love* was printed by Thomas Newcomb for Henry Herringman, 1678, London; *The Way of the World* was printed for Jacob Tonson, 1700, London; *The Beaux' Stratagem* was printed for B. Lintott, 1707, London.

L

Published by
Washington Square Press, Inc., 630 Fifth Avenue, New York, N.Y.

WASHINGTON SQUARE PRESS editions are distributed in the U.S. by Affiliated Publishers, a division of Pocket Books, Inc., 630 Fifth Avenue, New York 20, N.Y.

Preface

In preparing the texts of these four Restoration plays, we have gone back to the earliest printed versions. We have modernized spelling, punctuation, and capitalization to conform to present-day usage. Any material interpolated by the editors is placed within square brackets. We have made a minimum number of emendations where the early versions showed obvious printing errors or corruption of the texts. We have kept notes to the minimum needed to explain obscure passages or allusions.

L. B. W.
V. A. L.

March 11, 1963

Table of Contents

Introduction   ix

William Wycherley. *The Country Wife*   1

John Dryden. *All for Love*   135

William Congreve. *The Way of the World*   251

George Farquhar. *The Beaux' Stratagem*   371

Restoration Drama, Wicked and Witty

Few periods in our history have produced such witty plays with so little moral purpose or with such utter disregard of conventional morality as the Restoration. The comedies of William Wycherley, John Dryden, John Vanbrugh, or William Congreve excite our risibilities and set us to laughing at situations and dialogue that cannot pass any test of moral virtue. The wicked do not get their deserts in Restoration comedy, and we find ourselves laughing at, if not approving, the discomfiture of cuckolded husbands and wronged wives. Squeamish admirers of Restoration comedy have sometimes been troubled in their consciences by the delight that they have taken in literature obviously immoral, and they have sought some rationalization of their own attitudes. The classic effort to rationalize Restoration comedy to comport with an attitude that a well-behaved modern reader ought to have was made by Charles Lamb in a famous essay, "On the Artificial Comedy of the Last Century," which he published in the *London Magazine* in 1822. Lamb believed that his age had been spoiled for witty drama by "the exclusive and all-devouring drama of common life, where the moral point is everything." "We carry our fireside concerns to the theatre with us," he continued. "We do not go thither like our ancestors, to escape from the pressure of reality, so much as to confirm our experience of it, to make assurance double and take a bond of fate. We must live our toilsome lives twice over, as it was the mournful privilege of Ulysses to descend twice to the shades."

But in Restoration comedy, Lamb discovered, he could escape into another world, a fairyland, peopled by characters who did not offend his moral sense because "they do not appeal to it at all." And he found escape from purposeful drama a comfort. "I confess for myself that (with no great delinquencies to answer for) I am glad for a season to take an airing beyond the diocese of strict conscience. . . . I am the gayer, at least, for it; and I could never connect those sports of a witty fancy in any shape with any result to be drawn from them to imitation in real life."

Those amusing characters of Restoration comedy, Lamb asserted, all "seem engaged in their proper element. They break through no laws or conscientious restraints. They know of none. They have got out of Christendom into the land—what shall I call it?—of cuckoldry—the Utopia of gallantry, where pleasure is duty and the manners perfect freedom. . . . No good person can be justly offended, because no good person suffers on the stage. Judged morally, every character in these plays . . . is alike essentially vain and worthless. The great art of Congreve is especially shown in this, that he has entirely excluded from his scenes . . . not only anything like a faultless character but any pretensions to goodness or good feelings whatsoever."

Lamb could enjoy the witty byplay of clever rogues, rascals, seducers, and strumpets by convincing himself that they dwelt in a world of unreality, that they were a fiction of writers whose brilliant lines he could relish without bringing any moral judgment to bear. Our own age, less concerned than Lamb's, perhaps, to justify our taste on moral grounds, can find amusing the wit of the Restoration without the elaborate justification that Lamb created for himself. We know better now than to deny that the Restoration dramatists reflected at least some of the attitudes found about the court of that "merry monarch" Charles II.

Victorian writers took it upon themselves to refute the Lamb interpretation of Restoration drama. The most famous essay correcting this point of view is Lord Macaulay's review of Leigh Hunt's edition of the dramatic works of Wycherley, Congreve, Vanbrugh, and Farquhar, published in 1840. Although Macaulay admitted that he thought Hunt's edition "perfectly justifiable," he hastened to assert that "this part of our literature is a disgrace to our language and our national character. It is clever, indeed, and very entertaining; but it is, in the most emphatic sense of the words, 'earthly, sensual, devilish.' Its indecency . . . is not, in our opinion, so disgraceful a fault as its singularly inhuman spirit."

Today we may read Restoration drama as a relic of the taste of another age, and we would do well to consider for a moment some of the aspects of that age and to compare the spirit of the Restoration with the great age of Elizabeth, which saw the performance of some of the greatest plays in the English language.

Charles II's return to London on May 29, 1660, ended the Interregnum, which had begun with the execution of his father, Charles I, on January 30, 1649. The iron rule of the Puritans had created a godly commonwealth, but it had brought little joy to England. With Charles II's return, the country threw off many of its restraints, and some portions of the populace gave themselves over to an orgy of

licentiousness. Charles II set the tone for the behavior of his courtiers. The sovereign maintained a
veritable seraglio of mistresses, and his insatiable
interest in every pretty face that met his gaze was
imitated by the young noblemen who surrounded
him. The pursuit of sexual pleasure by both king
and courtiers became an obsession cynically ac-
cepted as the way of the aristocratic world in the
period after 1660. It is this world that the dramatists
reflected.

But one should remember that England was not
completely altered by the return of Charles II; that
not all Englishmen suddenly reversed their behavior
in 1660. The rank and file of Englishmen continued
to behave as they had before the Restoration. A
large Puritan element that strongly disapproved of
the licentious behavior of the courtier class domi-
nated the city of London and much of the rest of
England. Although a fashionable group took delight in the cynical and ribald comedies of the Restoration dramatists, a much larger number of Englishmen read with appreciation and approval John
Milton's *Paradise Lost* and John Bunyan's *Pilgrim's
Progress*. If the small world of fashion, as represented by the court, brooked no restraints on their
appetites and pleasures, a much larger group ac-
cepted Puritan prohibitions as their normal way of
life. Since the drama of the time was written ex-
clusively for the courtly group, it pandered to their
tastes and reflected not at all the attitudes of the
substantial citizens of the day.

Never before or since in England has the theatre
been so completely the monopoly of a special class
as it was in Restoration London. With few exceptions, the only people who went to the theatre were
courtiers, hangers-on about the court, their wives,

and women of dubious reputation. The rank and file of citizens, who had gone to the theatre in great numbers in the age of Elizabeth, now stayed away. If such citizens went to the theatre, they were likely to find themselves objects of ridicule. A merchant's wife, for example, was represented as the object of a courtier's seduction and as eagerly anticipating that hoped-for occasion. Even if the plays did not positively satirize ordinary citizens, their themes were not likely to entertain anyone except those familiar with the intrigues of the court and its denizens.

The broad interest in drama that had prevailed in Shakespeare's time had died out in the barren years of Puritan rule. The Puritans, even in Shakespeare's day, had looked upon the theatre as the Devil's schoolhouse and had inveighed against it. In 1632, that arch-Puritan William Prynne published a vast indictment of stage plays entitled *Histriomastix*— and had his ears cropped for some fancied reflections on the Queen and her ladies. When the Puritans were finally in control, the Long Parliament on September 2, 1642, decreed that henceforth "public stage plays shall cease and be forborne." For the next eighteen years no theatre opened its doors for play performance in London. Although a few plays were written, a few were privately performed, and many were reprinted, the tradition of theatregoing died.

When the Restoration of Charles II cancelled the ban on theatres, the way was open for a return of actors and playwrights to their normal professions, but new conditions had arisen. The theatres would not be the same again. For one thing, courtiers who had spent years of exile in France brought back ideas of playhouse design and playhouse practices that were unfamiliar to the earlier London stage. One of the simplest but most significant changes was the substitution of women actors for the boys who had taken women's parts on the English stage up to the time of the closing of the theatres in 1642. Shakespeare's Cleopatra was a boy; Dryden's was an enticing female. This change made a subtle—and sometimes a not so subtle—difference in the writing and presentation of a play. Shakespeare contrived to avoid much physical contact in his love scenes, which concentrated upon the poetic imagery of love-making; the Restoration dramatists let their characters make love more realistically—to the greater titillation of the jaded appetites of the spectators.

Another change was in the physical construction of the stage and the use of scenery. Englishmen familiar with Continental stagecraft were no longer content with the bare apron stage that Shakespeare and his contemporaries had used. Restoration stage designers gradually adopted something more nearly approaching the modern proscenium stage, with a curtain that could drop to cut off the scene. Some elements of the old platform stage were retained, but the Restoration stage was soon well on its evolution toward the modern proscenium stage with footlights in front and movable scenery behind. The development, however, was not sudden. Restoration stages still used a rather prominent apron front to which the actors advanced in many scenes to achieve an intimacy with the audience lost on later stages. Gallants still sat on the edges of this apron stage and made nuisances of themselves, ogling the actresses or talking among themselves to the disturbance of others.

Charles II, who had such an interest in the theatre that he would sometimes lend his royal robes for the actors' use, was determined that control of the stage would be a royal prerogative. Consequently, he saw to it that only acting companies licensed by his own authority should have the right to perform stage plays. On August 21, 1660, he issued letters patent to Thomas Killigrew and Sir William Davenant to "erect" two companies of players. Killigrew's company was to be known as the players of the Theatre Royal and Davenant's as the players of the Duke of York. After using various sites, Killigrew established the Theatre Royal in Drury Lane. Davenant's company acted in two of the Duke's houses, in Lincoln's Inn Fields and Dorset Gardens. This monopoly was made all the more restricted in 1682, when the two companies amalgamated, a condition that prevailed for the next thirteen years. From 1695, when the companies again separated, until the end of the century, London had two theatres.

The literary quality of the drama written for the Restoration stage reflected the changed tastes of the later seventeenth century. Partly under the influence of French pseudo-classical fashion, partly as a result of the growing classical emphasis among English poets of the second half of the seventeenth century, Restoration dramatists for a time abandoned blank verse in favor of rhymed heroic couplets as the medium for expressing tragic sentiments. For a period of nearly twenty years, a curious dramatic form called heroic tragedy was popular. These plays, written in heroic couplets, were characterized by high-flown sentiments expressed in bombastic verbiage. The heroes and heroines of these plays struggled with an inner conflict between love and honor amidst various external sensations. John Dryden, collaborating with Sir Robert Howard, set the fashion for this type of heroic nonsense with *The Indian Queen,* first acted in 1664; he followed this tragedy with several others equally tiresome to the modern reader. But Restoration theatregoers found these rhyming plays, filled with artificial sentiments and faked passions, delightful. The height of absurdity was reached in Elkanah Settle's *The Empress of Morocco* (1673).

At length, even Restoration taste rebelled against too much bombast, and George Villiers, second Duke of Buckingham, with several collaborators, brought out in 1673 a satire of the "love-and-honor" tragedies called *The Rehearsal,* which was frequently performed in various revisions. In its final form it satirized Dryden and the absurdities in some of his heroic tragedies. In Act III, Sc. v, one of the heroes, Prince Volscius, engages in a great debate with himself as to whether he will pull on his boots and follow Mars or leave off his boots and remain with Venus.

> How has my passion made me Cupid's scoff!
> This hasty boot is on, the other off,
> And sullen lies, with amorous design
> To quit loud fame and make that beauty mine.
>
> . . . .
>
> My legs, the emblem of my various thought,
> Show to what distraction I am brought.
> Sometimes with stubborn honor, like this boot,
> My mind is guarded and resolved to do't.
> Sometimes, again, that very mind, by love
> Disarmed, like this other leg does prove.
> Shall I to Honor or to Love give way?
> "Go on," cries Honor; tender Love says, "Nay."
> Honor aloud commands: "Pluck both boots on";
> But softer Love does whisper, "Put on none."

What shall I do? what conduct shall I find
To lead me through this twilight of my mind?

In the end Prince Volscius, as the stage direction signifies, "Goes out hopping with one boot on and the other off." Some of the debates in the rhyming love-and-honor tragedies were only a little less ridiculous than this burlesque.

Not all the tragedies of the Restoration followed the fashion of rhyme. Dryden himself, in his best effort at tragedy, *All for Love*, first acted in 1677, returned to blank verse.

Restoration comedy has a greater interest for the modern reader and spectator in the theatre than Restoration tragedy. That is merely to say that a few Restoration comedies are sufficiently witty to entertain us today. The vast majority of the comedies of intrigue of this period are so keyed to topical events and forgotten scandals that they are of little concern to anyone except a specialist in the period.

Restoration comedy began with obvious imitations of Ben Jonson's comedies of humors—plays like *Every Man in His Humor* and *Bartholomew Fair*—and eventually evolved into comedies of manners. From the French stage Restoration writers also took plots and situations from Molière and adapted them to the milieu of London. Although rhyming couplets found their place in the comic drama of the period, the dramatists discovered that prose was better adapted to the purposes of witty dialogue, and we have in the best of Restoration comedy excellent examples of repartee in a new type of realistic prose. Some comedies depended for their effectiveness upon farcical situations, and some utilized spectacle, dance, and comic song to hold the attention of jaded audiences.

William Wycherley and *The Country Wife*

William Wycherley, born about 1640 in Shropshire, came of a substantial family. At the age of fifteen, during the Puritan Revolution, he was sent to France and made the acquaintance of Madame de Montausier (better known as Mademoiselle de Rambouillet) and other great ladies of the French court circle. Wycherley always had an affinity for ladies of the court. Madame de Montausier is said to have converted him to the Catholic faith. After the Restoration of Charles II, he returned to England, again became a Protestant, and was for a time a "gentleman commoner" of Queen's College, Oxford, but left the university without a degree. He became a member of the Inner Temple and soon took his place among the fashionable literary set of London.

Wycherley's first play was *Love in a Wood, or St. James's Park*, acted in 1671. One of the King's mistresses, the Duchess of Cleveland, was much taken with the play and was fascinated by the author, upon whom she showered her favors. If the King was aware that he was sharing his mistress with a writer whom he admired, he showed no jealousy. The Duke of Buckingham, however, who also shared the Duchess of Cleveland's favors, was a little more concerned, but was persuaded by the Earl of Rochester, another literary wit, that the Duchess had enough love for them all. To show his good will toward Wycherley, Buckingham made him a lieutenant in his own regiment, an honorary position requiring no military service.

Wycherley's second play, *The Gentleman Dancing Master*, acted late in 1671 or early in 1672, like his first play was a comedy of intrigue, filled with witty and amusing commentary on the manners and morals of the time. During the Dutch War in 1672, Wycherley appears to have gone to sea in some naval vessel, but the record of his service is obscure. Wycherley's third play, *The Country Wife*, acted sometime between 1673 and 1675 at Lincoln's Inn Fields, was followed soon afterward by his last play, *The Plain Dealer*.

In the winter of 1678, when Wycherley came down with a fever, the King visited him, gave him a gift of £500, and told him to take a holiday abroad. When Wycherley returned to London, the King offered him the post of tutor to his illegitimate son, the Duke of Richmond, born to the Duchess of Portsmouth. Before this arrangement was completed, however, Wycherley went to Tunbridge Wells, where he met and married the wealthy Countess of Drogheda, who, like the Duchess of Cleveland, had been attracted to the author by reading one of his plays, in this case, *The Plain Dealer*.

Wycherley's marriage to the Countess proved anything but happy. The King regarded it as an affront, since Wycherley turned down the offered tutorship. The Countess was exceedingly jealous and would not let Wycherley out of her sight. And when she died, her estate was in such litigation that Wycherley found himself facing debtors' prison. After James II's accession, Wycherley was reconverted to the Roman Church. King James offered him a pension of £200 per year and sought to help pay his debts. At length he inherited an estate from his father. Realizing late in life that his property at his death would go to an ungrateful nephew, he married a second wife eleven days before his death in 1716 in order that she might inherit the property that he wanted to keep from this nephew.

Wycherley was the typical Restoration wit and man about town, a writer who illustrated by his own life qualities that characters in his plays exemplified. Yet his contemporaries regarded his comedies as satires on the times. Dryden and others praised him for his satirical approach. Of *The Plain Dealer* Dryden commented that it was "one of the most bold, most general, and most useful satires which has ever been presented in the English theatre." And the editor of Wycherley's *Posthumous Works* (1728) remarked that "his plays are an excellent satire upon the vices and follies of the age in which he lived."

The Country Wife was a popular success when it first appeared and enjoyed a long life in the theatre. It was acted at frequent intervals until the middle of the eighteenth century. David Garrick made an adaptation of Wycherley's play, *The Country Girl* (1766), which was supposed to be less coarse and more to the taste of Garrick's age. This version had a number of performances in the nineteenth century, which regarded Wycherley's play as too broad for public performance. During the present less squeamish century, Wycherley's original play has had a number of revivals.

The Country Wife is an extended treatment of the theme of cuckoldry, in which the seventeenth century found a morbid fascination. Every allusion to horns, the symbol of the cuckold, for some reason inexplicable to the modern reader, provoked gales of laughter. But Wycherley's play goes beyond this. In the creation of his characters, he achieved genuine comic effects and he managed to convey an impression of the follies, vanities, and stupidities of the circle of the court wits who are represented. The play also emphasized the Restoration adoration of town life as opposed to the barbarities of the country, a view that held supreme in fashionable circles until the time of Doctor Johnson. Mrs. Pinchwife is a notable creation. Her artless naïveté has been a delight to audiences, and this part has been a favored role for many actresses.

John Dryden and *All for Love*

John Dryden (1631-1700), the most distinguished man of letters of the Restoration period, was a graduate of Westminster School and of Trinity College, Cambridge. He came of a good family and married Lady Elizabeth Howard, daughter of the Earl of Berkshire and sister of Sir Robert Howard, with whom he collaborated in *The Indian Queen.* Later, in his *Essay on Dramatic Poesy,* Dryden gave a sharp answer to criticism that Howard had made of his use of rhyme in the play *The Rival Ladies,* but this literary controversy did not permanently estrange them.

Ironically, one of Dryden's early literary efforts was an elegiac poem lamenting the death of Oliver Cromwell, which he contributed in 1658 to a volume containing verses by Edmund Waller and others. As a hopeful professional writer and a royalist at heart, Dryden found it easy two years later to write two poems exulting in the Restoration and glorifying King Charles. From this time forward one of Dryden's most notable characteristics was the desire to stand in the good graces of those in power. To that end he applied his pen.

Since, as the husband of an expensive wife, Dryden needed money, he directed his literary efforts to the theatre. During a long and diligent career he turned out more than a score of plays of various sorts, sometimes in collaboration with other dramatists. His first dramatic piece was a comedy, *The Wild Gallant* (1663), which was followed the next year by the tragicomedy *The Rival Ladies.* His collaborative heroic tragedy *The Indian Queen* was followed by another heroic tragedy, *The Indian Emperor*, and from this time onward until 1694 a steady stream of plays, comedies, tragedies, and operatic pieces flowed from Dryden's pen. An opera called *The State of Innocence* (1674), which went unacted, was based on Milton's *Paradise Lost*. John Aubrey, in his *Brief Lives*, said that Dryden went to Milton, whom he very much admired, to ask permission, and that "Mr. Milton received him civilly and told him he would give him leave to tag his verses."

In 1670, Dryden was appointed poet laureate, succeeding Davenant. The laureateship was combined with the post of historiographer. His emoluments from the two offices were to be £200 and a butt of canary wine, a potation believed good for poetic inspiration. A few years later his salary was increased by another £100, but, like most officials of the day, he could not count on regularity in his pay and consequently had to continue to write for the stage.

Dryden reached the height of his literary reputation with the publication of *Absalom and Achitophel* (1681), a satiric poem ridiculing, among other things, the Earl of Shaftesbury's espousal of the cause of the King's illegitimate son, the Duke of Monmouth. Using his satiric skill in behalf of the sovereign, he brought out another attack on Shaftesbury entitled *The Medal*. When Thomas Shadwell wrote a reply to *The Medal*, Dryden annihilated him in the satiric poem *MacFlecknoe*, which Pope later imitated in *The Dunciad*. Under the title of *Religio Laici*, Dryden also wrote a reasoned statement of a layman's acceptance of the doctrines of the Church of England. After the death of Charles

II and the accession of James II, who had turned Catholic, Dryden too became a Catholic and in 1687 wrote a defense of the Roman Church under the title of *The Hind and the Panther*. The Glorious Revolution of 1688 and the accession of William and Mary left Dryden without a royal patron, for he could not change faiths again. He lost his pension and other sinecures and once more had to turn to the theatre and to professional writing for a livelihood. During his later years he made translations from Vergil, Horace, Ovid, and other classical writers.

Dryden became a sort of literary dictator in his late years and occupied a position somewhat similar to that of Ben Jonson earlier and Samuel Johnson later. At Will's or Button's Coffee House, the great man of letters could be found, and there he handed down his opinions on the literary merits of his contemporaries, opinions that carried an enormous weight of authority in the small literary circle of London in the last years of the seventeenth century.

Dryden was an admirer of Shakespeare, and his best play, *All for Love*, set out deliberately to imitate the great Elizabethan. In his preface, Dryden asserts that "in my style, I have professed to imitate the divine Shakespeare; which that I might perform more freely I have disencumbered myself from rhyme. Not that I condemn my former way, but that this is more proper to my present purpose." Hence he utilized blank verse, as his master Shakespeare had done. To the Restoration and the early eighteenth century, Shakespeare was a wild genius, almost barbaric in his disregard of the "rules" of dramatic composition. Consequently, Dryden set out to improve upon Shakespeare by making his own play conform to the classical unities of time, place, and action. The result is a far more compact and unified play than Shakespeare had written, with fewer scenes and more concentration upon the two protagonists, Antony and Cleopatra. Although Shakespeare gave many good lines to Cleopatra, interest was focussed primarily upon Antony; in Dryden, the emphasis shifts to Cleopatra. Perhaps the fact that Dryden had a beautiful female to play the part instead of the "squeaking boy" who had taken the role in Shakespeare's theatre helped to make the difference. At any rate, Cleopatra in Dryden's play holds the center of the stage and begins that concentration of interest upon the siren of Egypt that lingers still in the motion-picture world.

Although Dryden's interpretation of this famous love story lacks the depth of emotion and the poetic passion that Shakespeare achieved, it is nevertheless one of the great dramatic treatments of the theme. Dryden's simplification of the plot and his skill in revealing the action make for easy reading. Some of the qualities of the heroic tragedy remain. For example, Ventidius, personifying duty and honor, and Alexas, as the messenger of Cleopatra, representing love, convey to the play the familiar struggle between love and honor for the soul of the hero.

All for Love, first produced at the Theatre Royal in Drury Lane in December, 1677, long remained popular upon the English stage. It was frequently revived in the public theatres, and from time to time its performance was commanded at court. On Candlemas Day, 1704, for example, a remarkable performance took place at St. James's Palace with Thomas Betterton, the greatest actor of the day, in the role of Antony, Elizabeth Barry as Cleopatra,

and Anne Bracegirdle as Octavia. Throughout the
eighteenth century the play was frequently revived.
Cleopatra was one of Peg Woffington's most popular roles. In the nineteenth century, Shakespeare's
version of the story, sometimes with additions from
Dryden, regained the stage at infrequent intervals.
In the twentieth century, Dryden's play has had a
few revivals, usually by academic or amateur
groups.

William Congreve and *The Way of the World*

Although later chronologically than Wycherley and Dryden, William Congreve is spiritually a typical Restoration wit and man of letters, who illustrates the qualities of the Restoration as few others do. He was born in 1670 near Leeds, in Yorkshire. His father was an army officer who was soon ordered to the command of the garrison of Youghal in Ireland. Young William was sent to Kilkenny School, where he had as a schoolmate Jonathan Swift. When Congreve a little later went to Trinity College, Dublin, he was again an associate and friend of Swift's.

From Trinity College, Congreve went to London and entered the Middle Temple, but he had little appetite for the law as a profession and, like Wycherley, soon transferred his interests to the world of letters. His first published work was an indifferent novel, *Incognita* (1692), which was soon followed by a comedy, *The Old Bachelor*, acted in 1693 at Drury Lane. This play was a great success and encouraged Congreve to make other contributions to the theatre. When a new theatre was opened in 1695 by Thomas Betterton and associates in Lincoln's Inn Fields, Congreve's *Love for Love* was chosen for the first performance. He next tried his hand at a tragedy, *The Mourning Bride,* which ran for thirteen days without interruption in 1697, a phenomenal run by the standards of the day. Though popular, this tragedy did not represent Congreve's genius so well as his comedies. Congreve's last play was *The Way of the World,* produced at Lincoln's Inn Fields in 1700 before an audience that received it without enthusiasm, a reception that induced Congreve to declare that he did not intend to write any more plays.

In the meantime, Congreve had held a number of small government sinecures: commissioner for licensing hackney coaches, commissioner of wine licenses, and similar appointments that required few duties and brought in a certain amount of revenue. Congreve early developed a greed for money and in his old age was accused of avarice.

As a wit and a popular writer, Congreve became a favorite of the leaders of fashion. He was a friend of Lady Mary Wortley Montagu, who declared that she "never knew anybody that had so much wit as Congreve" and addressed to him a poem entitled "The Lover" with one line reading "Take, Congreve, at once, the inside of my breast." When Lady Mary returned from travels abroad she was distressed to find that Henrietta, second Duchess of Marlborough, had superseded her in Congreve's affections. Indeed, the Duchess of Marlborough was so taken with Congreve that after his death she had a statue made of him which she kept at her table and served meals like a living guest.

Congreve wrote some of his best parts for the actress Anne Bracegirdle. She had such a reputation for chastity that the Dukes of Dorset and Devonshire made up a purse of 800 guineas and presented it to her in consideration of her virtue, because few like her could be found. Whether her virtue held out against the importunities of Congreve has been a matter of argument from Congreve's time to ours. Gossips of the day said they were married—or ought to have been.

Congreve died in 1729, full of honors, the pet of

society, and a well-to-do man, thanks to his avarice. He left £10,000 to the Duchess of Marlborough and £200 to Mrs. Bracegirdle.

The Way of the World, though unfavorably received when first performed, gained in popularity later and has come to typify the characteristic comedy of manners of this period. At intervals throughout the eighteenth century the comedy was revived with considerable success, and it had occasional revivals in the nineteenth century. It has enjoyed a certain amount of popularity in the present century.

The somewhat devious plot of *The Way of the World* makes the action hard to follow, but the merit of the comedy lies in its brilliant dialogue and the wit combats, particularly between Millamant and Mirabell. Like all the Restoration comedies that preceded it, it is cynical and without a glimmer of illusion about the goodness of human nature, but nevertheless it has gaiety and lightness that make it delightful reading. It is essentially a comedy of conversation rather than situation.

Congreve came under attack from Jeremy Collier, who published a famous philippic against the theatres of his day, *A Short View of the Immorality and Profaneness of the English Stage* (1698). Three months after the appearance of this diatribe, Congreve replied with *Amendments of Mr. Collier's False and Imperfect Citations,* which attempted, not too successfully, to refute Collier's charges. Although Collier did not succeed in reforming the stage, his attack made a deep impression, and drama henceforth rarely descended to the depths of coarseness that characterized the typical plays of the Restoration wits.

George Farquhar and *The Beaux' Stratagem*

Whether George Farquhar was influenced by the attack on the stage for its immorality and profaneness, or whether he was reflecting a slight change in the tone of life around him, *The Beaux' Stratagem* has less coarseness and less of the tone of complete cynicism than the characteristic comedies of the Restoration.

The early life of Farquhar is somewhat obscure. He was born in Londonderry, Ireland, in 1678, probably the son of a clergyman. For a time he attended Trinity College, Dublin, but left to try his skill as an actor, playing the part of Othello in a Dublin theatre. This experience brought him into contact with an actor named Robert Wilks, who became his friend and later took leading roles in Farquhar's comedies.

Because of an accident in which he stabbed a fellow actor nearly to death, Farquhar gave up the stage, went to London, and turned to writing for the theatre. His first play was *Love and a Bottle,* a not very original comedy, acted at the Theatre Royal in Drury Lane in 1698. The play proved popular and induced Farquhar to write *The Constant Couple* (1699), which had an extraordinary reception. It is said to have run for fifty-three nights in London and twenty-three in Dublin. Farquhar's reputation as a dramatist was made. The most important of his later comedies were *The Inconstant* (1702), *The Twin Rivals* (1702), *The Recruiting Officer* (1706), and his last play, *The Beaux' Stratagem* (1707), acted a few months before Farquhar's death in May, 1707.

Farquhar did not have the good fortune to win influential friends as Congreve did, nor did he succeed in procuring sinecures that paid him a profit. He was poor all his life. For a time he served as an army officer, going on recruiting missions that gave him a knowledge of the country and an eye for local scenes and characters that his plays reflect. Farquhar is said to have married a woman who fell in love with him and in order to win him pretended to be an heiress, a situation beloved of the dramatists of the day. At any rate, his marriage about 1703 does not appear to have brought him any great satisfaction, and on his deathbed he wrote his friend Wilks begging him to look after his two daughters, who were about to be orphaned with nothing to support them. His widow died in want. Indeed, it is said that Farquhar's worry and distress over his poverty brought on the "settled illness" that ended in death. Although he realized that he was dying, he drove himself to finish *The Beaux' Stratagem,* his greatest play.

This play has a freshness not found in the preceding comedies. It is a sort of anticipation of the kind of comedy that Richard Steele was presently to write, a comedy that treated love as a genuine sentiment instead of the passing pleasure of a libertine. It also reflects a new interest in the country, which is no longer pictured as a region of barbarians alien to the cultivation and sophistication of fashionable London.

The Beaux' Stratagem has had a long popularity in the theatre. It was frequently acted in the eighteenth century and enjoyed some popularity in the nineteenth. Of the so-called Restoration genre, it has been one of the most frequently revived in modern times. Its witty dialogue and comic situations provide excellent entertainment.

REFERENCES FOR FURTHER READING

A detailed account of the theatre and drama of this period will be found in Allardyce Nicoll, *A History of Restoration Drama, 1660-1700* (Cambridge, 1923). The same author's *British Drama* (New York, 1925) provides a briefer treatment of the drama and theatre of the period. Still a useful survey is G. H. Nettleton, *English Drama of the Restoration and Eighteenth Century* (New York, 1923). Alwin Thaler, *Shakspere to Sheridan* (Cambridge, Mass., 1922) provides valuable stage history. Bonamy Dobreé's *Restoration Comedy, 1660-1700* (Oxford, 1924) and Joseph Wood Krutch, *Comedy and Conscience after the Restoration* (New York, 1924; 1949), throw much light on this period. Other useful titles are Montague Summers, *The Restoration Theatre* (London, 1934) and *Restoration Comedies* (London, 1921), and Leslie Hotson, *The Commonwealth and Restoration Stage* (Cambridge, Mass., 1928). A multivolume calendar of plays and other entertainments for the period 1660-1800, entitled *The London Stage*, contains a wealth of information about theatrical conditions. For the Restoration period see the first volume of Part 2 (1700-1729), edited by Emmett L. Avery (Carbondale, Ill., 1960). Volumes for 1660-1700 are still in preparation.

For individual dramatists see:

Wycherley: Willard Connely, *Brawny Wycherley* (New York & London, 1930), and *The Complete Works of William Wycherley,* edited by Montague Summers (4 vols., London, 1924).

Dryden: Louis I. Bredvold, *The Intellectual Milieu of John Dryden* (Ann Arbor, 1934), Bonamy Dobreé, *John Dryden* (London, 1956), Richard Garnett, *The Age of Dryden* (London, 1895), Christopher Hollis, *Dryden* (London, 1933). There are numerous editions of Dryden's works. The dramatic works alone have been edited by Montague Summers (6 vols., London, 1931-32). A definitive scholarly edition of all of Dryden's works is being prepared under the general editorship of H. T. Swedenberg, Jr., for publication by the University of California Press. Two volumes have been published: *Poems, 1649-1680* (1956) and *Plays: Wild Gallant, Rival Ladies, Indian Queen* (1962).

Congreve: John C. Hodges, *William Congreve the Man* (New York & London, 1941), and *The Complete Works,* edited by Montague Summers (4 vols., London, 1923).

Farquhar: There is little literature on George Farquhar, but editions of his plays provide what biographical details are known. The most recent edition of selected plays, including *The Beaux' Stratagem,* was prepared by William Archer for the Mermaid Series (London, 1949).

THE COUNTRY WIFE

A Comedy by William Wycherley

Indignior quicquam reprehendi, non quia crasse
Compositum illepideve putetur, sed quia nuper:
Nec veniam antiquis, sed honorem et praemia posci.

HORAT.

INDIGNIOR . . . POSCI: I am impatient that anything should be censured not because it is considered coarse and rude but because it is new; and that for the ancients is demanded not indulgence but honor and distinction (Horace *Epis.*ii.1.76-78).

PROLOGUE

Spoken by Mr. Hart [Horner]

Poets, like cudgeled bullies, never do
At first or second blow submit to you;
But will provoke you still, and ne'er have done,
Till you are weary first with laying on.
The late so baffled scribbler of this day,   5
Though he stands trembling, bids me boldly say
What we before most plays are used to do;
For poets out of fear first draw on you,
In a fierce prologue the still pit defy,
And, ere you speak, like Kastrill give the lie.   10
But though our Bayes's battles oft I've fought,
And with bruised knuckles their dear conquests
    bought;
Nay, never yet feared odds upon the stage,
In prologue dare not hector with the age,   15
But would take quarter from your saving hands,
Though Bayes within all yielding countermands,
Says you confed'rate wits no quarter give,
Therefore his play shan't ask your leave to live.
Well, let the vain, rash fop, by huffing so,   20
Think to obtain the better terms of you;

(Prologue)
   5. LATE . . . SCRIBBLER: i.e., lately disgraced author, presumably
referring to the failure of Wycherley's recent play, *The Gentleman
Dancing Master*.
   10. KASTRILL: Jonson's *The Alchemist*, Act IV, Sc. ii.
   11. BAYES: John Dryden, satirized in the character BAYES in Buckingham's *The Rehearsal*. The Prologue was spoken by an actor who had
appeared in many of Dryden's plays.

But we, the actors, humbly will submit,
Now, and at any time, to a full pit;
Nay, often we anticipate your rage,
And murder poets for you on our stage;   25
We set no guards upon our tiring room,
But when with flying colors there you come,
We patiently, you see, give up to you
Our poets, virgins, nay, our matrons too.

Persons [of the Play]

	[By]
Mr. Horner.	Mr. Hart.
Mr. Harcourt.	Mr. Kynaston.
Mr. Dorilant.	Mr. Lydal.
Mr. Pinchwife.	Mr. Mohun.
Mr. Sparkish.	Mr. Haines.
Sir Jasper Fidget.	Mr. Cartwright.
A Boy.	
A Quack.	Mr. Shotterell.
Mrs. Margery Pinchwife.	Mrs. Boutell.
Mrs. Alithea.	Mrs. James.
Lady Fidget.	Mrs. Knepp.
Mrs. Dainty Fidget.	Mrs. Corbet.
Mrs. Squeamish.	Mrs. Wyatt.
Old Lady Squeamish.	Mrs. Rutter.
Lucy, Alithea's maid.	Mrs. Corey.

Waiters, Servants, and Attendants.

THE SCENE: *London.*

(Persons of the Play)
MRS. ALITHEA: MRS. is "Mistress" abbreviated, the designation of unmarried women.

ACT I

‖‖‖

Scene I

Enter Horner, and Quack, following him at a distance.

Horn. (*Aside*) A quack is as fit for a pimp as a midwife for a bawd; they are still but in their way both
helpers of nature.—Well, my dear Doctor, hast thou
done what I desired?

Quack. I have undone you forever with the women   5
and reported you throughout the whole town as bad
as an eunuch, with as much trouble as if I had made
you one in earnest.

Horn. But have you told all the midwives you
know, the orange wenches at the playhouses, the city   10
husbands, and old fumbling keepers of this end of the
town? for they'll be the readiest to report it.

Quack. I have told all the chambermaids, waiting
women, tirewomen, and old women of my acquaintance; nay, and whispered it as a secret to 'em and   15
to the whisperers of Whitehall; so that you need not
doubt 'twill spread and you will be as odious to the
handsome young women as—

Horn. As the smallpox. Well—

Quack. And to the married women of this end of   20
the town as—

Horn. As the great ones; nay, as their own husbands.

9

Quack. And to the city dames as aniseed Robin, of
filthy and contemptible memory; and they will 25
frighten their children with your name, especially
their females.

Horn. And cry, "Horner's coming to carry you
away." I am only afraid 'twill not be believed. You
told 'em 'twas by an English-French disaster and an 30
English-French chirurgeon, who has given me at once
not only a cure but an antidote for the future against
that damned malady and that worse distemper, love,
and all other women's evils?

Quack. Your late journey into France has made it 35
the more credible, and your being here a fortnight
before you appeared in public looks as if you appre-
hended the shame, which I wonder you do not. Well,
I have been hired by young gallants to belie 'em
t'other way, but you are the first would be thought a 40
man unfit for women.

Horn. Dear Mr. Doctor, let vain rogues be contented only to be thought abler men than they are;
generally 'tis all the pleasure they have, but mine lies
another way. 45

Quack. You take, methinks, a very preposterous
way to it, and as ridiculous as if we operators in
physic should put forth bills to disparage our medica-
ments, with hopes to gain customers.

Horn. Doctor, there are quacks in love as well as 50
physic, who get but the fewer and worse patients for
their boasting; a good name is seldom got by giving it
one's self; and women no more than honor are com-
passed by bragging. Come, come, Doctor, the wisest
lawyer never discovers the merits of his cause till the 55
trial; the wealthiest man conceals his riches and the
cunning gamester his play. Shy husbands and keepers,

(I.i.)
24. ANISEED ROBIN: a notorious hermaphrodite of the period.

like old rooks, are not to be cheated but by a new
unpracticed trick: false friendship will pass now no
more than false dice upon 'em; no, not in the city. 60

Enter Boy.

Boy. There are two ladies and a gentleman coming
up.   *Exit.*
Horn. A pox! some unbelieving sisters of my former
acquaintance, who, I am afraid, expect their sense
should be satisfied of the falsity of the report. No—this 65
formal fool and women!

*Enter Sir Jasper Fidget, Lady Fidget, and Mrs.
Dainty Fidget.*

Quack. His wife and sister.
Sir Jasp. My coach breaking just now before your
door, sir, I look upon as an occasional reprimand to
me, sir, for not kissing your hands, sir, since your com- 70
ing out of France, sir; and so my disaster, sir, has been
my good fortune, sir; and this is my wife and sister,
sir.
Horn. What then, sir?
Sir Jasp. My lady, and sister, sir.—Wife, this is Mas- 75
ter Horner.
Lady Fid. Master Horner, husband!
Sir Jasp. My lady, my Lady Fidget, sir.
Horn. So, sir.
Sir Jasp. Won't you be acquainted with her, sir?— 80
(*Aside*) So, the report is true, I find, by his coldness
or aversion to the sex; but I'll play the wag with him.
—Pray salute my wife, my lady, sir.
Horn. I will kiss no man's wife, sir, for him, sir; I
have taken my eternal leave, sir, of the sex already, 85
sir.

Sir Jasp. (*Aside*) Ha! ha! ha! I'll plague him yet.—
Not know my wife, sir?

Horn. I do not know your wife, sir; she's a woman,
sir, and consequently a monster, sir, a greater monster   90
than a husband, sir.

Sir Jasp. A husband! How, sir?

Horn. So, sir; but I make no more cuckolds, sir.

                              Makes horns.

Sir Jasp. Ha! ha! ha! Mercury! Mercury!

Lady Fid. Pray, Sir Jasper, let us be gone from this   95
rude fellow.

Mrs. Dain. Who, by his breeding, would think he
had ever been in France?

Lady Fid. Foh! he's but too much a French fellow,
such as hate women of quality and virtue for their   100
love to their husbands, Sir Jasper; a woman is hated
by 'em as much for loving her husband as for loving
their money. But pray, let's be gone.

Horn. You do well, madam, for I have nothing that
you came for: I have brought over not so much as a   105
bawdy picture, no new postures, nor the second part
of the *Escole des Filles*; nor—

Quack. (*Apart to Horner*) Hold, for shame, sir!
What d'ye mean? You'll ruin yourself forever with
the sex—   110

Sir Jasp. Ha! ha! ha! he hates women perfectly, I
find.

Mrs. Dain. What pity 'tis he should!

Lady Fid. Ay, he's a base rude fellow for't. But
affectation makes not a woman more odious to them   115
than virtue.

---

93. CUCKOLDS: men with unfaithful wives, who were figuratively
said to have acquired horns.

107. ESCOLE DES FILLES: a book described by Samuel Pepys in his
Diary, January 13, 1668, as "the most bawdy, lewd book that ever I
saw, . . . so that I was ashamed of reading in it."

Horn. Because your virtue is your greatest affectation, madam.

Lady Fid. How, you saucy fellow! would you wrong my honor?   120

Horn. If I could.

Lady Fid. How d'ye mean, sir?

Sir Jasp. Ha! ha! ha! No, he can't wrong your Ladyship's honor, upon my honor; he, poor man—hark you in your ear—a mere eunuch.   125

Lady Fid. O filthy French beast! foh! foh! why do we stay? let's be gone: I can't endure the sight of him.

Sir Jasp. Stay but till the chairs come; they'll be here presently.

Lady Fid. No, no.   130

Sir Jasp. Nor can I stay longer. 'Tis—let me see, a quarter and a half quarter of a minute past eleven. The council will be sat; I must away. Business must be preferred always before love and ceremony with the wise, Mr. Horner.   135

Horn. And the impotent, Sir Jasper.

Sir Jasp. Ay, ay, the impotent, Master Horner; ha! ha! ha!

Lady Fid. What, leave us with a filthy man alone in his lodgings?   140

Sir Jasp. He's an innocent man now, you know. Pray stay, I'll hasten the chairs to you.—Mr. Horner, your servant; I should be glad to see you at my house. Pray come and dine with me and play at cards with my wife after dinner; you are fit for women at that game 145 yet, ha! ha!—(*Aside*) 'Tis as much a husband's prudence to provide innocent diversion for a wife as to hinder her unlawful pleasures; and he had better employ her than let her employ herself.—Farewell.

Horn. Your servant, Sir Jasper.   *Exit Sir Jasper.* 150

Lady Fid. I will not stay with him, foh!

Horn. Nay, madam, I beseech you stay, if it be but

to see I can be as civil to ladies yet as they would
desire.

Lady Fid. No, no, foh! you cannot be civil to ladies. 155

Mrs. Dain. You as civil as ladies would desire?

Lady Fid. No, no, no, foh! foh! foh!

   Exeunt Lady Fidget and Mrs. Dainty Fidget.

Quack. Now, I think, I, or you yourself, rather, have
done your business with the women.

Horn. Thou art an ass. Don't you see already, upon 160
the report and my carriage, this grave man of business
leaves his wife in my lodgings, invites me to his house
and wife, who before would not be acquainted with
me out of jealousy?

Quack. Nay, by this means you may be the more 165
acquainted with the husbands, but the less with the
wives.

Horn. Let me alone; if I can but abuse the husbands, I'll soon disabuse the wives. Stay—I'll reckon
you up the advantages I am like to have by my 170
stratagem. First, I shall be rid of all my old acquaint-
ances, the most insatiable sorts of duns, that invade
our lodgings in a morning; and next to the pleasure
of making a new mistress is that of being rid of an old
one and of all old debts. Love, when it comes to be 175
so, is paid the most unwillingly.

Quack. Well, you may be so rid of your old ac-
quaintances; but how will you get any new ones?

Horn. Doctor, thou wilt never make a good chemist,
thou art so incredulous and impatient. Ask but all the 180
young fellows of the town if they do not lose more
time, like huntsmen, in starting the game than in running it down. One knows not where to find 'em, who
will or will not. Women of quality are so civil you can
hardly distinguish love from good breeding, and a 185

---

188. RIGHT: slang for "libidinous."
210. VIZARD MASK: whore.

man is often mistaken: but now I can be sure she that
shows an aversion to me loves the sport, as those
women that are gone, whom I warrant to be right.
And then the next thing is, your women of honor, as
you call 'em, are only chary of their reputations, not 190
their persons; and 'tis scandal they would avoid, not
men. Now may I have, by the reputation of an eunuch,
the privileges of one, and be seen in a lady's chamber
in a morning as early as her husband; kiss virgins before their parents or lovers; and may be, in short, the 195
passe-partout of the town. Now, Doctor.

Quack. Nay, now you shall be the doctor, and your
process is so new that we do not know but it may succeed.

Horn. Not so new neither; *probatum est*, Doctor.   200

Quack. Well, I wish you luck, and many patients,
whilst I go to mine.   *Exit.*

Enter Harcourt and Dorilant to Horner.

Har. Come, your appearance at the play yesterday
has, I hope, hardened you for the future against the
women's contempt and the men's raillery; and now 205
you'll abroad as you were wont.

Horn. Did I not bear it bravely?

Dor. With a most theatrical impudence, nay, more
than the orange wenches show there, or a drunken
vizard mask, or a great-bellied actress; nay, or the 210
most impudent of creatures, an ill poet; or what is yet
more impudent, a second-hand critic.

Horn. But what say the ladies? Have they no pity?

Har. What! ladies? The vizard masks, you know,
never pity a man when all's gone, though in their 215
service.

Dor. And for the women in the boxes, you'd never
pity them when 'twas in your power.

Har. They say 'tis pity but all that deal with common women should be served so.   220

Dor. Nay, I dare swear they won't admit you to
play at cards with them, go to plays with 'em, or do
the little duties which other shadows of men are wont
to do for 'em.

Horn. What do you call shadows of men?   225

Dor. Half-men.

Horn. What, boys?

Dor. Ay, your old boys, old *beaux garçons,* who, like
superannuated stallions, are suffered to run, feed, and
whinny with the mares as long as they live, though   230
they can do nothing else.

Horn. Well, a pox on love and wenching! Women
serve but to keep a man from better company. Though
I can't enjoy them, I shall you the more. Good fellow-
ship and friendship are lasting, rational, and manly   235
pleasures.

Har. For all that, give me some of those pleasures
you call effeminate too; they help to relish one another.

Horn. They disturb one another.   240

Har. No, mistresses are like books. If you pore upon
them too much, they doze you and make you unfit
for company; but if used discreetly you are the fitter
for conversation by 'em.

Dor. A mistress should be like a little country re- 245
treat near the town: not to dwell in constantly, but
only for a night and away, to taste the town the better
when a man returns.

Horn. I tell you, 'tis as hard to be a good fellow, a
good friend, and a lover of women, as 'tis to be a good   250
fellow, a good friend, and a lover of money. You cannot follow both; then choose your side. Wine gives
you liberty; love takes it away.

Dor. Gad, he's in the right on't.

Horn. Wine gives you joy; love, grief and tortures, 255
besides the chirurgeon's. Wine makes us witty; love,
only sots. Wine makes us sleep; love breaks it.

Dor. By the world, he has reason, Harcourt.

Horn. Wine makes—

Dor. Ay, wine makes us—makes us princes; love 260
makes us beggars, poor rogues, egad; and wine—

Horn. So, there's one converted.—No, no, love and
wine, oil and vinegar.

Har. I grant it; love will still be uppermost.

Horn. Come, for my part, I will have only those 265
glorious manly pleasures of being very drunk and very
slovenly.

Enter Boy.

Boy. Mr. Sparkish is below, sir.   *Exit.*

Har. What, my dear friend! a rogue that is fond of
me only, I think, for abusing him.   270

Dor. No, he can no more think the men laugh at
him than that women jilt him, his opinion of himself
is so good.

Horn. Well, there's another pleasure by drinking I
thought not of: I shall lose his acquaintance, because 275
he cannot drink; and you know 'tis a very hard thing
to be rid of him, for he's one of those nauseous offerers
at wit, who, like the worst fiddlers, run themselves
into all companies.

Har. One that, by being in the company of men of 280
sense, would pass for one.

Horn. And may so to the short-sighted world, as a
false jewel amongst true ones is not discerned at a
distance. His company is as troublesome to us as
a cuckold's when you have a mind to his wife's.   285

Har. No, the rogue will not let us enjoy one another,
but ravishes our conversation, though he signifies no

more to't than Sir Martin Mar-all's gaping and awkward thrumming upon the lute does to his man's voice
and music.   290

Dor. And to pass for a wit in town shows himself a
fool every night to us, that are guilty of the plot.

Horn. Such wits as he are, to a company of reasonable men, like rooks to the gamesters, who only fill a
room at the table, but are so far from contributing to 295
the play that they only serve to spoil the fancy of
those that do.

Dor. Nay, they are used like rooks too, snubbed,
checked, and abused; yet the rogues will hang on.

Horn. A pox on 'em and all that force Nature and 300
would be still what she forbids 'em! Affectation is her
greatest monster.

Har. Most men are the contraries to that they would
seem. Your bully, you see, is a coward with a long
sword; the little humbly fawning physician, with his 305
ebony cane, is he that destroys men.

Dor. The usurer a poor rogue possessed of moldy
bonds and mortgages; and we they call spendthrifts
are only wealthy who lay out his money upon daily
new purchases of pleasure.   310

Horn. Ay, your arrantest cheat is your trustee or
executor; your jealous man the greatest cuckold; your
churchman the greatest atheist; and your noisy pert
rogue of a wit the greatest fop, dullest ass, and worst
company, as you shall see, for here he comes.   315

Enter Sparkish to them.

Spark. How is't, sparks? how is't? Well, faith, Harry,
I must rally thee a little, ha! ha! ha! upon the report in

---

288. SIR MARTIN MAR-ALL: reference to Dryden's play, specifically
Act V, Sc. i.
294. ROOKS: dupes.
341. CROWD: fiddle.

town of thee, ha! ha! ha! I can't hold i'faith; shall I
speak?

Horn. Yes; but you'll be so bitter then.   320

Spark. Honest Dick and Frank here shall answer for
me, I will not be extreme bitter, by the universe.

Har. We will be bound in a ten-thousand-pound
bond he shall not be bitter at all.

Dor. Nor sharp, nor sweet.   325

Horn. What, not downright insipid?

Spark. Nay, then, since you are so brisk and
provoke me, take what follows. You must know, I was
discoursing and rallying with some ladies yesterday,
and they happened to talk of the fine new signs in   330
town.

Horn. Very fine ladies, I believe.

Spark. Said I, "I know where the best new sign is."
—"Where?" says one of the ladies.—"In Covent Garden," I replied.—Said another, "In what street?"—"In   335
Russell Street," answered I.—"Lord," says another,
"I'm sure there was ne'er a fine new sign there yesterday."—"Yes, but there was," said I again, "and it came
out of France and has been there a fortnight."

Dor. A pox! I can hear no more, prithee.   340

Horn. No, hear him out; let him tune his crowd a
while.

Har. The worst music, the greatest preparation.

Spark. Nay, faith, I'll make you laugh.—"It cannot
be," says a third lady.—"Yes, yes," quoth I again.—Says   345
a fourth lady—

Horn. Look to't, we'll have no more ladies.

Spark. No—then mark, mark, now. Said I to the
fourth, "Did you never see Mr. Horner? he lodges in
Russell Street, and he's a sign of a man, you know,   350
since he came out of France; ha! ha! ha!"

Horn. But the Devil take me if thine be the sign of
a jest.

Spark. With that they all fell a-laughing, till they bepissed themselves. What, but it does not move you, 355 methinks? Well, I see one had as good go to law without a witness as break a jest without a laugher on one's side.—Come, come, sparks, but where do we dine? I have left at Whitehall an earl to dine with you.   360

Dor. Why, I thought thou hadst loved a man with a title better than a suit with a French trimming to't.

Har. Go to him again.

Spark. No, sir, a wit to me is the greatest title in the world.   365

Horn. But go dine with your earl, sir; he may be exceptious. We are your friends and will not take it ill to be left, I do assure you.

Har. Nay, faith, he shall go to him.

Spark. Nay, pray, gentlemen.   370

Dor. We'll thrust you out, if you won't; what, disappoint anybody for us?

Spark. Nay, dear gentlemen, hear me.

Horn. No, no, sir, by no means; pray go, sir.

Spark. Why, dear rogues—   375

Dor. No, no.   *They all thrust him out of the room.*

All. Ha! ha! ha!

Sparkish returns.

Spark. But, sparks, pray hear me. What, d'ye think I'll eat then with gay shallow fops and silent coxcombs? I think wit as necessary at dinner as a glass of 380 good wine, and that's the reason I never have any stomach when I eat alone.—Come, but where do we dine?

Horn. Even where you will.

Spark. At Chateline's?   385

Dor. Yes, if you will.

Spark. Or at the Cock?

Dor. Yes, if you please.

Spark. Or at the Dog and Partridge?

Horn. Ay, if you have a mind to't; for we shall dine 390
at neither.

Spark. Pshaw! with your fooling we shall lose the
new play; and I would no more miss seeing a new
play the first day than I would miss sitting in the wits'
row. Therefore I'll go fetch my mistress and away. 395
Exit.

*Manent Horner, Harcourt, Dorilant: enter to them
Mr. Pinchwife.*

Horn. Who have we here? Pinchwife?

Pinch. Gentlemen, your humble servant.

Horn. Well, Jack, by thy long absence from the
town, the grumness of thy countenance, and the
slovenliness of thy habit, I should give thee joy, 400
should I not, of marriage?

Pinch. (*Aside*) Death! does he know I'm married
too? I thought to have concealed it from him at least.
—My long stay in the country will excuse my dress;
and I have a suit of law that brings me up to town 405
that puts me out of humor. Besides, I must give
Sparkish tomorrow five thousand pound to lie with
my sister.

Horn. Nay, you country gentlemen, rather than not
purchase, will buy anything; and he is a cracked title, 410
if we may quibble. Well, but am I to give thee joy?
I heard thou wert married.

Pinch. What then?

Horn. Why, the next thing that is to be heard is
thou'rt a cuckold.   415

Pinch. (*Aside*) Insupportable name!

Horn. But I did not expect marriage from such a

whoremaster as you, one that knew the town so much
and women so well.

Pinch. Why, I have married no London wife.   420

Horn. Pshaw! that's all one. That grave circum-
spection in marrying a country wife is like refusing
a deceitful, pampered, Smithfield jade to go and be
cheated by a friend in the country.

Pinch. (*Aside*) A pox on him and his simile!—At   425
least we are a little surer of the breed there, know
what her keeping has been, whether foiled or un-
sound.

Horn. Come, come, I have known a clap gotten in
Wales; and there are cozens, justices' clerks, and   430
chaplains in the country; I won't say coachmen. But
she's handsome and young?

Pinch. (*Aside*) I'll answer as I should do.—No, no;
she has no beauty but her youth, no attraction but
her modesty: wholesome, homely, and huswifely;   435
that's all.

Dor. He talks as like a grazier as he looks.

Pinch. She's too awkward, ill-favored, and silly to
bring to town.

Har. Then methinks you should bring her to be   440
taught breeding.

Pinch. To be taught! No, sir, I thank you. Good
wives and private soldiers should be ignorant—I'll
keep her from your instructions, I warrant you.

Har. (*Aside*) The rogue is as jealous as if his wife   445
were not ignorant.

Horn. Why, if she be ill-favored, there will be less
danger here for you than by leaving her in the coun-

---

423. SMITHFIELD JADE: nag purchased at Smithfield Market.
427. FOILED: smirched.
430. COZENS: probably, cheats.
437. GRAZIER: cattle-breeder.
451–52. SWINGEING: huge.

try. We have such variety of dainties that we are seldom hungry.   450

Dor. But they have always coarse, constant, swingeing stomachs in the country.

Har. Foul feeders indeed!

Dor. And your hospitality is great there.

Har. Open house; every man's welcome.   455

Pinch. So, so, gentlemen.

Horn. But prithee, why wouldst thou marry her?
If she be ugly, ill-bred, and silly, she must be rich
then.

Pinch. As rich as if she brought me twenty thou-   460
sand pound out of this town; for she'll be as sure not
to spend her moderate portion as a London baggage
would be to spend hers, let it be what it would: so
'tis all one. Then, because she's ugly, she's the like-
lier to be my own; and, being ill-bred, she'll hate con-   465
versation; and, since silly and innocent, will not know
the difference betwixt a man of one-and-twenty and
one of forty.

Horn. Nine—to my knowledge. But if she be silly,
she'll expect as much from a man of forty-nine as   470
from him of one-and-twenty. But methinks wit is more
necessary than beauty; and I think no young woman
ugly that has it and no handsome woman agreeable
without it.

Pinch. 'Tis my maxim he's a fool that marries; but   475
he's a greater that does not marry a fool. What is wit
in a wife good for but to make a man a cuckold?

Horn. Yes, to keep it from his knowledge.

Pinch. A fool cannot contrive to make her husband
a cuckold.   480

Horn. No; but she'll club with a man that can: and
what is worse, if she cannot make her husband a
cuckold, she'll make him jealous and pass for one;
and then 'tis all one.

Pinch. Well, well, I'll take care for one. My wife 485
shall make me no cuckold, though she had your help,
Mr. Horner. I understand the town, sir.

Dor. (*Aside*) His help!

Har. (*Aside*) He's come newly to town, it seems,
and has not heard how things are with him. 490

Horn. But tell me, has marriage cured thee of
whoring, which it seldom does?

Har. 'Tis more than age can do.

Horn. No, the word is I'll marry and live honest:
but a marriage vow is like a penitent gamester's oath 495
and entering into bonds and penalties to stint himself
to such a particular small sum at play for the future,
which makes him but the more eager; and, not being
able to hold out, loses his money again and his forfeit
to boot. 500

Dor. Ay, ay, a gamester will be a gamester whilst
his money lasts, and a whoremaster whilst his vigor.

Har. Nay, I have known 'em, when they are broke
and can lose no more, keep a-fumbling with the box
in their hands to fool with only and hinder other 505
gamesters.

Dor. That had wherewithal to make lusty stakes.

Pinch. Well, gentlemen, you may laugh at me; but
you shall never lie with my wife: I know the town.

Horn. But prithee, was not the way you were in 510
better? Is not keeping better than marriage?

Pinch. A pox on't! The jades would jilt me; I could
never keep a whore to myself.

Horn. So, then, you only married to keep a whore
to yourself. Well, but let me tell you, women, as you 515
say, are like soldiers, made constant and loyal by

520–21. EIGHTEENPENNY PLACE: section of the playhouse frequented
by harlots.
551. CHEAPSIDE . . . WIFE: i.e., a rich merchant who keeps a young
mistress. Although it was a fashionable residential district, Covent Garden had many brothels and independent harlots.

good pay rather than by oaths and covenants. Therefore I'd advise my friends to keep rather than marry,
since, too, I find by your example it does not serve
one's turn; for I saw you yesterday in the eighteen-   520
penny place with a pretty country wench.

Pinch. (Aside) How the Devil! Did he see my wife
then? I sat there that she might not be seen. But she
shall never go to a play again.

Horn. What! dost thou blush at nine-and-forty for   525
having been seen with a wench?

Dor. No, faith, I warrant 'twas his wife, which he
seated there out of sight; for he's a cunning rogue
and understands the town.

Har. He blushes. Then 'twas his wife; for men are   530
now more ashamed to be seen with them in public
than with a wench.

Pinch. (Aside) Hell and damnation! I'm undone,
since Horner has seen her and they know 'twas she.

Horn. But prithee, was it thy wife? She was exceed-   535
ingly pretty: I was in love with her at that distance.

Pinch. You are like never to be nearer to her. Your
servant, gentlemen.   *Offers to go.*

Horn. Nay, prithee stay.

Pinch. I cannot; I will not.   540

Horn. Come, you shall dine with us.

Pinch. I have dined already.

Horn. Come, I know thou hast not: I'll treat thee,
dear rogue; thou shalt spend none of thy Hampshire
money today.   545

Pinch. (Aside) Treat me! So, he uses me already
like his cuckold.

Horn. Nay, you shall not go.

Pinch. I must; I have business at home.   *Exit.*

Har. To beat his wife. He's as jealous of her as a   550
Cheapside husband of a Covent Garden wife.

Horn. Why, 'tis as hard to find an old whoremaster without jealousy and the gout as a young one without fear or the pox.

As gout in age from pox in youth proceeds, 555
So, wenching past, then jealousy succeeds:
The worst disease that love and wenching breeds.

[*Exeunt.*]

(II.i.)
4. CLOSE: secret.
5. NEW EXCHANGE: an arcade of fashionable shops, a popular place for clandestine meetings.

ACT II

Scene I

*[Enter] Mrs. Margery Pinchwife and Alithea; Pinch-
wife peeping behind at the door.*

Mrs. Pinch. Pray, sister, where are the best fields
and woods to walk in in London?

Alith. A pretty question! Why, sister, Mulberry
Garden and St. James's Park; and, for close walks, the
New Exchange. 5

Mrs. Pinch. Pray, sister, tell me why my husband
looks so grum here in town and keeps me up so close,
and will not let me go a-walking nor let me wear my
best gown yesterday.

Alith. O, he's jealous, sister. 10

Mrs. Pinch. Jealous! what's that?

Alith. He's afraid you should love another man.

Mrs. Pinch. How should he be afraid of my loving
another man, when he will not let me see any but
himself? 15

Alith. Did he not carry you yesterday to a play?

Mrs. Pinch. Ay; but we sat amongst ugly people.
He would not let me come near the gentry, who sat
under us, so that I could not see 'em. He told me none
but naughty women sat there, whom they toused and 20
moused. But I would have ventured for all that.

Alith. But how did you like the play?

Mrs. Pinch. Indeed I was aweary of the play, but
I liked hugeously the actors. They are the goodliest,
properest men, sister! 25

Alith. O, but you must not like the actors, sister.

27

Mrs. Pinch. Ay, how should I help it, sister? Pray, sister, when my husband comes in, will you ask leave for me to go a-walking?

Alith. (*Aside*) A-walking! ha! ha! Lord, a country 30
gentlewoman's leisure is the drudgery of a footpost; and she requires as much airing as her husband's horses.—But here comes your husband; I'll ask, though I'm sure he'll not grant it.

Mrs. Pinch. He says he won't let me go abroad for 35
fear of catching the pox.

Alith. Fie! the smallpox you should say.

Enter Pinchwife to them.

Mrs. Pinch. O my dear, dear bud, welcome home!
Why dost thou look so froppish? Who has nangered thee? 40

Pinch. You're a fool.

> *Mrs. Pinchwife goes aside, and cries.*

Alith. Faith, so she is, for crying for no fault, poor tender creature!

Pinch. What, you would have her as impudent as yourself, as arrant a jillflirt, a gadder, a magpie; and 45
to say all, a mere notorious town woman?

Alith. Brother, you are my only censurer; and the honor of your family shall sooner suffer in your wife there than in me, though I take the innocent liberty of the town. 50

Pinch. Hark you, mistress, do not talk so before my wife.—The innocent liberty of the town!

Alith. Why, pray, who boasts of any intrigue with me? What lampoon has made my name notorious? What ill women frequent my lodgings? I keep no 55
company with any women of scandalous reputations.

---
39. FROPPISH: peevish.

Pinch. No, you keep the men of scandalous reputations company.

Alith. Where? Would you not have me civil? answer 'em in a box at the plays, in the drawing room at Whitehall, in St. James's Park, Mulberry Garden, or— 60

Pinch. Hold, hold! Do not teach my wife where the men are to be found: I believe she's the worse for your town documents already. I bid you keep her in ignorance, as I do. 65

Mrs. Pinch. Indeed, be not angry with her, bud, she will tell me nothing of the town, though I ask her a thousand times a day.

Pinch. Then you are very inquisitive to know, I find? 70

Mrs. Pinch. Not I, indeed, dear; I hate London. Our placehouse in the country is worth a thousand of't: would I were there again!

Pinch. So you shall, I warrant. But were you not talking of plays and players when I came in?—You are her encourager in such discourses. 75

Mrs. Pinch. No, indeed, dear; she chid me just now for liking the player-men.

Pinch. (*Aside*) Nay, if she be so innocent as to own to me her liking them, there is no hurt in't.—Come, my poor rogue, but thou likest none better than me? 80

Mrs. Pinch. Yes, indeed, but I do. The player-men are finer folks.

Pinch. But you love none better than me? 85

Mrs. Pinch. You are mine own dear bud, and I know you. I hate a stranger.

Pinch. Ay, my dear, you must love me only and not be like the naughty town women, who only hate their husbands and love every man else; love plays, visits, fine coaches, fine clothes, fiddles, balls, treats, and so lead a wicked town life. 90

Mrs. Pinch. Nay, if to enjoy all these things be a town life, London is not so bad a place, dear.

Pinch. How! If you love me, you must hate London. 95

Alith. (*Aside*) The fool has forbid me discovering to her the pleasures of the town, and he is now setting her agog upon them himself.

Mrs. Pinch. But, husband, do the town women love the player-men too? 100

Pinch. Yes, I warrant you.

Mrs. Pinch. Ay, I warrant you.

Pinch. Why, you do not, I hope?

Mrs. Pinch. No, no, bud. But why have we no player-men in the country? 105

Pinch. Ha!—Mrs. Minx, ask me no more to go to a play.

Mrs. Pinch. Nay, why, love? I did not care for going; but when you forbid me, you make me, as 'twere, desire it. 110

Alith. (*Aside*) So 'twill be in other things, I warrant.

Mrs. Pinch. Pray let me go to a play, dear.

Pinch. Hold your peace, I wo' not.

Mrs. Pinch. Why, love? 115

Pinch. Why, I'll tell you.

Alith. (*Aside*) Nay, if he tell her, she'll give him more cause to forbid her that place.

Mrs. Pinch. Pray why, dear?

Pinch. First, you like the actors; and the gallants 120 may like you.

Mrs. Pinch. What, a homely country girl! No, bud, nobody will like me.

Pinch. I tell you yes, they may.

Mrs. Pinch. No, no, you jest—I won't believe you; I 125 will go.

Pinch. I tell you, then, that one of the lewdest fel-

lows in town, who saw you there, told me he was in
love with you.

Mrs. Pinch. Indeed! Who, who, pray who was't?   130

Pinch. (*Aside*) I've gone too far and slipped before I was aware; how overjoyed she is!

Mrs. Pinch. Was it any Hampshire gallant, any of
our neighbors? I promise you, I am beholding to him.

Pinch. I promise you, you lie; for he would but ruin   135
you, as he has done hundreds. He has no other love
for women but that; such as he look upon women like
basilisks, but to destroy 'em.

Mrs. Pinch. Ay, but if he loves me, why should he
ruin me? answer me to that. Methinks he should not;   140
I would do him no harm.

Alith. Ha! ha! ha!

Pinch. 'Tis very well; but I'll keep him from doing
you any harm, or me either. But here comes company; get you in, get you in.   145

Mrs. Pinch. But, pray, husband, is he a pretty gentleman that loves me?

Pinch. In, baggage, in.

                    Thrusts her in, shuts the door.

Enter Sparkish and Harcourt.

What, all the lewd libertines of the town brought
to my lodging by this easy coxcomb! 'Sdeath, I'll not   150
suffer it.

Spark. Here, Harcourt, do you approve my choice?
—Dear little rogue, I told you I'd bring you acquainted with all my friends, the wits and—

                    Harcourt salutes her.

Pinch. Ay, they shall know her, as well as you your-   155
self will, I warrant you.

Spark. This is one of those, my pretty rogue, that
are to dance at your wedding tomorrow; and him you

must bid welcome ever to what you and I have.

Pinch. (*Aside*) Monstrous!   160

Spark. Harcourt, how dost thou like her, faith?
Nay, dear, do not look down; I should hate to have a
wife of mine out of countenance at anything.

Pinch. (*Aside*) Wonderful!

Spark. Tell me, I say, Harcourt, how dost thou like   165
her? Thou hast stared upon her enough to resolve me.

Har. So infinitely well that I could wish I had a
mistress too, that might differ from her in nothing but
her love and engagement to you.

Alith. Sir, Master Sparkish has often told me that   170
his acquaintance were all wits and railleurs, and now
I find it.

Spark. No, by the universe, madam, he does not
rally now; you may believe him. I do assure you, he is
the honestest, worthiest, true-hearted gentleman—a   175
man of such perfect honor he would say nothing to a
lady he does not mean.

Pinch. (*Aside*) Praising another man to his mistress!

Har. Sir you are so beyond expectation obliging   180
that—

Spark. Nay, egad, I am sure you do admire her extremely; I see't in your eyes.—He does admire you,
madam.—By the world, don't you?

Har. Yes, above the world or, the most glorious part   185
of it, her whole sex; and till now I never thought I
should have envied you or any man about to marry,
but you have the best excuse for marriage I ever
knew.

Alith. Nay, now, sir, I'm satisfied you are of the so-   190
ciety of the wits and railleurs, since you cannot spare
your friend, even when he is but too civil to you; but
the surest sign is, since you are an enemy to marriage,

for that, I hear, you hate as much as business or bad
wine.   195

Har. Truly, madam, I never was an enemy to marriage till now, because marriage was never an enemy
to me before.

Alith. But why, sir, is marriage an enemy to you
now? Because it robs you of your friend here? For   200
you look upon a friend married as one gone into a
monastery, that is, dead to the world.

Har. 'Tis, indeed, because you marry him; I see,
madam, you can guess my meaning. I do confess
heartily and openly I wish it were in my power to   205
break the match; by Heavens I would.

Spark. Poor Frank!

Alith. Would you be so unkind to me?

Har. No, no, 'tis not because I would be unkind to
you.   210

Spark. Poor Frank! No gad, 'tis only his kindness
to me.

Pinch. (*Aside*) Great kindness to you indeed! Insensible fop, let a man make love to his wife to his
face!   215

Spark. Come, dear Frank, for all my wife, there,
that shall be, thou shalt enjoy me sometimes, dear
rogue. By my honor, we men of wit condole for our
deceased brother in marriage as much as for one
dead in earnest: I think that was prettily said of me,   220
ha, Harcourt?—But come, Frank, be not melancholy
for me.

Har. No, I assure you, I am not melancholy for you.

Spark. Prithee, Frank, dost think my wife that shall
be, there, a fine person?   225

Har. I could gaze upon her till I became as blind
as you are.

Spark. How as I am? How?

Har. Because you are a lover, and true lovers are
blind, stock-blind.   230

Spark. True, true; but by the world, she has wit
too, as well as beauty. Go, go with her into a corner
and try if she has wit; talk to her anything; she's bashful before me.

Har. Indeed, if a woman wants wit in a corner, she   235
has it nowhere.

Alith. (*Aside to Sparkish*) Sir, you dispose of me
a little before your time—

Spark. Nay, nay, madam, let me have an earnest of
your obedience, or—go, go, madam—   240
                    Harcourt courts Alithea aside.

Pinch. How, sir! if you are not concerned for the
honor of a wife, I am for that of a sister; he shall not
debauch her. Be a pander to your own wife! Bring
men to her! Let 'em make love before your face!
Thrust 'em into a corner together, then leave 'em in   245
private! Is this your town wit and conduct?

Spark. Ha! ha! ha! a silly wise rogue would make
one laugh more than a stark fool, ha! ha! I shall burst.
Nay, you shall not disturb 'em; I'll vex thee, by the
world.   *Struggles with Pinchwife to keep him from* 250
                    Harcourt and Alithea.

Alith. The writings are drawn, sir, settlements
made; 'tis too late, sir, and past all revocation.

Har. Then so is my death.

Alith. I would not be unjust to him.

Har. Then why to me so?   255

Alith. I have no obligation to you.

Har. My love.

Alith. I had his before.

---

283. CIT: tradesman.

Har. You never had it; he wants, you see, jealousy, the only infallible sign of it.   260

Alith. Love proceeds from esteem; he cannot distrust my virtue; besides, he loves me or he would not marry me.

Har. Marrying you is no more sign of his love than bribing your woman, that he may marry you, is a sign 265 of his generosity. Marriage is rather a sign of interest than love; and he that marries a fortune covets a mistress, not loves her. But if you take marriage for a sign of love, take it from me immediately.

Alith. No, now you have put a scruple in my head; 270 but in short, sir, to end our dispute, I must marry him; my reputation would suffer in the world else.

Har. No; if you do marry him, with your pardon, madam, your reputation suffers in the world, and you would be thought in necessity for a cloak.   275

Alith. Nay, now you are rude, sir.—Mr. Sparkish, pray come hither; your friend here is very troublesome and very loving.

Har. (*Aside to Alithea*) Hold! hold!—

Pinch. D'ye hear that?   280

Spark. Why, d'ye think I'll seem to be jealous, like a country bumpkin?

Pinch. No, rather be a cuckold, like a credulous cit.

Har. Madam, you would not have been so little generous as to have told him.   285

Alith. Yes, since you could be so little generous as to wrong him.

Har. Wrong him! No man can do't, he's beneath an injury: a bubble, a coward, a senseless idiot, a wretch so contemptible to all the world but you that—   290

Alith. Hold, do not rail at him, for since he is like to be my husband, I am resolved to like him: nay, I think I am obliged to tell him you are not his friend.— Master Sparkish, Master Sparkish!

Spark. What, what?—Now, dear rogue, has not she 295
wit?

Har. Not so much as I thought and hoped she had.

                                      Speaks surlily.

Alith. Mr. Sparkish, do you bring people to rail at
you?

Har. Madam— 300

Spark. How! No; but if he does rail at me, 'tis but in
jest, I warrant: what we wits do for one another and
never take any notice of it.

Alith. He spoke so scurrilously of you I had no patience to hear him; besides, he has been making love 305
to me.

Har. (*Aside*) True, damned telltale woman!

Spark. Pshaw! to show his parts—we wits rail and
make love often but to show our parts; as we have no
affections, so we have no malice, we— 310

Alith. He said you were a wretch, below an injury—

Spark. Pshaw!

Har. [*Aside*] Damned, senseless, impudent, virtuous
jade! Well, since she won't let me have her, she'll do
as good; she'll make me hate her. 315

Alith. A common bubble—

Spark. Pshaw!

Alith. A coward—

Spark. Pshaw, pshaw!

Alith. A senseless, driveling idiot— 320

Spark. How! Did he disparage my parts? Nay,
then, my honor's concerned, I can't put up that, sir,
by the world—brother, help me to kill him.—(*Aside*)
I may draw now, since we have the odds of him; 'tis
a good occasion, too, before my mistress— 325

                                      Offers to draw.

Alith. Hold, hold!

Spark. What, what?

Alith. (*Aside*) I must not let 'em kill the gentleman

neither, for his kindness to me: I am so far from hating him that I wish my gallant had his person and un- 330
derstanding. Nay, if my honor—

Spark. I'll be thy death.

Alith. Hold, hold! Indeed, to tell the truth, the gentleman said after all that what he spoke was but out
of friendship to you.   335

Spark. How! say, I am—I am a fool, that is, no wit,
out of friendship to me?

Alith. Yes, to try whether I was concerned enough
for you; and made love to me only to be satisfied of
my virtue, for your sake.   340

Har. (*Aside*) Kind, however.

Spark. Nay, if it were so, my dear rogue, I ask thee
pardon; but why would not you tell me so, faith?

Har. Because I did not think on't, faith.

Spark. Come, Horner does not come; Harcourt, let's 345
be gone to the new play.—Come, madam.

Alith. I will not go, if you intend to leave me alone
in the box and run into the pit, as you use to do.

Spark. Pshaw! I'll leave Harcourt with you in the
box to entertain you, and that's as good; if I sat in the 350
box, I should be thought no judge but of trimmings.—
Come away, Harcourt, lead her down.

> *Exeunt Sparkish, Harcourt, and Alithea.*

Pinch. Well, go thy ways for the flower of the true
town fops, such as spend their estates before they
come to 'em and are cuckolds before they're married.   355
But let me go look to my own freehold.—How!

*Enter My Lady Fidget, Mrs. Dainty Fidget, and
Mrs. Squeamish.*

Lady Fid. Your servant, sir; where is your lady? We
are come to wait upon her to the new play.

Pinch. New play!

Lady Fid. And my husband will wait upon you 360
presently.

Pinch. (*Aside*) Damn your civility.—Madam, by no
means; I will not see Sir Jasper here till I have waited
upon him at home; nor shall my wife see you till she
has waited upon your Ladyship at your lodgings. 365

Lady Fid. Now we are here, sir—

Pinch. No, madam.

Mrs. Dain. Pray, let us see her.

Mrs. Squeam. We will not stir till we see her.

Pinch. (*Aside*) A pox on you all!—(*Goes to the* 370
door, and returns) She has locked the door and is
gone abroad.

Lady Fid. No, you have locked the door and she's
within.

Mrs. Dain. They told us below she was here. 375

Pinch. (*Aside*) Will nothing do?—Well, it must out
then. To tell you the truth, ladies, which I was afraid
to let you know before lest it might endanger your
lives, my wife has just now the smallpox come out
upon her. Do not be frightened, but pray be gone, 380
ladies; you shall not stay here in danger of your lives;
pray get you gone, ladies.

Lady Fid. No, no, we have all had 'em.

Mrs. Squeam. Alack, alack!

Mrs. Dain. Come, come, we must see how it goes 385
with her; I understand the disease.

Lady Fid. Come!

Pinch. (*Aside*) Well, there is no being too hard for
women at their own weapon, lying; therefore I'll quit
the field. *Exit.* 390

Mrs. Squeam. Here's an example of jealousy!

Lady Fid. Indeed, as the world goes, I wonder
there are no more jealous, since wives are so neglected.

Mrs. Dain. Pshaw! as the world goes, to what end 395
should they be jealous?

Lady Fid. Foh! 'tis a nasty world.

Mrs. Squeam. That men of parts, great acquaintance, and quality should take up with and spend
themselves and fortunes in keeping little playhouse 400
creatures, foh!

Lady Fid. Nay, that women of understanding, great
acquaintance, and good quality should fall a-keeping,
too, of little creatures, foh!

Mrs. Squeam. Why, 'tis the men of quality's fault; 405
they never visit women of honor and reputation as
they used to do and have not so much as common
civility for ladies of our rank, but use us with the same
indifference and ill breeding as if we were all married to 'em. 410

Lady Fid. She says true; 'tis an arrant shame wom-
en of quality should be so slighted; methinks birth—
birth should go for something. I have known men admired, courted, and followed for their titles only.

Mrs. Squeam. Ay, one would think men of honor 415
should not love, no more than marry, out of their own
rank.

Mrs. Dain. Fie, fie, upon 'em! They are come to
think cross breeding for themselves best, as well as
for their dogs and horses. 420

Lady Fid. They are dogs and horses for't.

Mrs. Squeam. One would think, if not for love, for
vanity a little.

Mrs. Dain. Nay, they do satisfy their vanity upon
us sometimes and are kind to us in their report, tell all 425
the world they lie with us.

Lady Fid. Damned rascals, that we should be only
wronged by 'em! To report a man has had a person,
when he has not had a person, is the greatest wrong
in the whole world that can be done to a person. 430

Mrs. Squeam. Well, 'tis an arrant shame noble persons should be so wronged and neglected.

Lady Fid. But still 'tis an arranter shame for a noble person to neglect her own honor and defame her own noble person with little inconsiderable fellows, foh!

Mrs. Dain. I suppose the crime against our honor is the same with a man of quality as with another.

Lady Fid. How! No, sure; the man of quality is likest one's husband, and therefore the fault should be the less.

Mrs. Dain. But then the pleasure should be the less.

Lady Fid. Fie, fie, fie, for shame, sister! Whither shall we ramble? Be continent in your discourse, or I shall hate you.

Mrs. Dain. Besides, an intrigue is so much the more notorious for the man's quality.

Mrs. Squeam. 'Tis true; nobody takes notice of a private man, and therefore with him 'tis more secret; and the crime's the less when 'tis not known.

Lady Fid. You say true; i'faith, I think you are in the right on't: 'tis not an injury to a husband till it be an injury to our honors; so that a woman of honor loses no honor with a private person; and to say truth—

Mrs. Dain. (*Apart to Mrs. Squeamish*) So, the little fellow is grown a private person—with her—

Lady Fid. But still my dear, dear honor—

Enter Sir Jasper, Horner, and Dorilant.

Sir Jasp. Ay, my dear, dear of honor, thou hast still so much honor in thy mouth—

---

478. MR. TATTLE . . . LIMBERHAM: types of the harmless gallant, not to be feared by jealous husbands.

Horn. (*Aside*) That she has none elsewhere.

Lady Fid. O, what d'ye mean to bring in these upon us?

Mrs. Dain. Foh! these are as bad as wits.   465

Mrs. Squeam. Foh!

Lady Fid. Let us leave the room.

Sir Jasp. Stay, stay; faith, to tell you the naked truth—

Lady Fid. Fie, Sir Jasper! do not use that word   470 "naked."

Sir Jasp. Well, well, in short, I have business at Whitehall and cannot go to the play with you, therefore would have you go—

Lady Fid. With those two to a play?   475

Sir Jasp. No, not with t'other, but with Mr. Horner; there can be no more scandal to go with him than with Mr. Tattle or Master Limberham.

Lady Fid. With that nasty fellow! No—no.

Sir Jasp. Nay, prithee, dear, hear me.   480

> *Whispers to Lady Fidget.*

Horn. Ladies—

> *Horner, Dorilant drawing near Mrs. Squeamish*
> *and Mrs. Dainty Fidget.*

Mrs. Dain. Stand off.

Mrs. Squeam. Do not approach us.

Mrs. Dain. You herd with the wits; you are obscenity all over.   485

Mrs. Squeam. And I would as soon look upon a picture of Adam and Eve without fig-leaves as any of you, if I could help it; therefore keep off, and do not make us sick.

Dor. What a Devil are these?   490

Horn. Why, these are pretenders to honor, as critics to wit, only by censuring others; and as every raw, peevish, out-of-humored, affected, dull, tea-drinking, arithmetical fop sets up for a wit by railing at men of

sense, so these for honor by railing at the court and 495
ladies of as great honor as quality.

Sir Jasp. Come, Mr. Horner, I must desire you to
go with these ladies to the play, sir.

Horn. I, sir?

Sir Jasp. Ay, ay, come, sir. 500

Horn. I must beg your pardon, sir, and theirs; I will
not be seen in women's company in public again for
the world.

Sir Jasp. Ha, ha, strange aversion!

Mrs. Squeam. No, he's for women's company in 505
private.

Sir Jasp. He—poor man—he—ha! ha! ha!

Mrs. Dain. 'Tis a greater shame amongst lewd fellows to be seen in virtuous women's company than for
the women to be seen with them. 510

Horn. Indeed, madam, the time was I only hated
virtuous women, but now I hate the other too; I beg
your pardon, ladies.

Lady Fid. You are very obliging, sir, because we
would not be troubled with you. 515

Sir Jasp. In sober sadness, he shall go.

Dor. Nay, if he wo' not, I am ready to wait upon
the ladies, and I think I am the fitter man.

Sir Jasp. You, sir! no, I thank you for that. Master
Horner is a privileged man amongst the virtuous 520
ladies; 'twill be a great while before you are so; he!
he! he! he's my wife's gallant; he! he! he! No, pray
withdraw, sir; for, as I take it, the virtuous ladies have
no business with you.

Dor. And I am sure he can have none with them. 525
'Tis strange a man can't come amongst virtuous wom-

529. OMBRE: popular card game.
544. MORTIFIED: dead.
545. WETHER: eunuch.
556. CRAZY: infirm.
556–57. GENTLEMAN-USHER: escort.

en now but upon the same terms as men are admitted
into the Great Turk's seraglio. But Heavens keep me
from being an ombre player with 'em!—But where is
Pinchwife?   *Exit.*   530

Sir Jasp. Come, come, man; what, avoid the sweet
society of womankind? that sweet, soft, gentle, tame,
noble creature, woman, made for man's companion—

Horn. So is that soft, gentle, tame, and more noble
creature a spaniel, and has all their tricks; can fawn,   535
lie down, suffer beating, and fawn the more; barks at
your friends when they come to see you, makes your
bed hard, gives you fleas, and the mange sometimes.
And all the difference is the spaniel's the more faithful animal and fawns but upon one master.   540

Sir Jasp. He! he! he!

Mrs. Squeam. O, the rude beast!

Mrs. Dain. Insolent brute!

Lady Fid. Brute! stinking, mortified, rotten French
wether, to dare—   545

Sir Jasp. Hold, an't please your Ladyship.—For
shame, Master Horner! your mother was a woman—
(*Aside*) Now shall I never reconcile 'em.—Hark you,
madam, take my advice in your anger. You know you
often want one to make up your drolling pack of om-   550
bre players, and you may cheat him easily, for he's an
ill gamester and consequently loves play. Besides, you
know you have but two old civil gentlemen (with
stinking breaths too) to wait upon you abroad; take
in the third into your service. The others are but   555
crazy; and a lady should have a supernumerary gentleman-usher as a supernumerary coach-horse, lest
sometimes you should be forced to stay at home.

Lady Fid. But are you sure he loves play and has
money?   560

Sir Jasp. He loves play as much as you, and has
money as much as I.

Lady Fid. Then I am contented to make him pay for his scurrility. Money makes up in a measure all other wants in men.—Those whom we cannot make 565 hold for gallants, we make fine.

Sir Jasp. (*Aside*) So, so; now to mollify, to wheedle him.—(*Aside*) Master Horner, will you never keep civil company? Methinks 'tis time now, since you are only fit for them. Come, come, man, you must e'en fall 570 to visiting our wives, eating at our tables, drinking tea with our virtuous relations after dinner, dealing cards to 'em, reading plays and gazettes to 'em, picking fleas out of their shocks for 'em, collecting receipts, new songs, women, pages, and footmen for 'em. 575

Horn. I hope they'll afford me better employment, sir.

Sir Jasp. He! he! he! 'Tis fit you know your work before you come into your place. And since you are unprovided of a lady to flatter and a good house to 580 eat at, pray frequent mine and call my wife mistress, and she shall call you gallant, according to the custom.

Horn. Who, I?

Sir Jasp. Faith, thou shalt for my sake; come, for 585 my sake only.

Horn. For your sake—

Sir Jasp. Come, come, here's a gamester for you; let him be a little familiar sometimes; nay, what if a little rude? Gamesters may be rude with ladies, you know. 590

Lady Fid. Yes; losing gamesters have a privilege with women.

Horn. I always thought the contrary, that the winning gamester had most privilege with women; for when you have lost your money to a man, you'll lose 595 anything you have, all you have, they say, and he may use you as he pleases.

---

566. MAKE FINE: force to pay a fine.
574. SHOCKS: poodles.

Sir Jasp. He! he! he! Well, win or lose, you shall have your liberty with her.

Lady Fid. As he behaves himself; and for your sake 600 I'll give him admittance and freedom.

Horn. All sorts of freedom, madam?

Sir Jasp. Ay, ay, ay, all sorts of freedom thou canst take. And so go to her, begin thy new employment; wheedle her, jest with her, and be better acquainted 605 one with another.

Horn. (*Aside*) I think I know her already; therefore may venture with her my secret for hers.

           Horner and Lady Fidget whisper.

Sir Jasp. Sister, cuz, I have provided an innocent playfellow for you there.   610

Mrs. Dain. Who, he?

Mrs. Squeam. There's a playfellow indeed!

Sir Jasp. Yes, sure. What, he is good enough to play at cards, blindman's-buff, or the fool with, sometimes!   615

Mrs. Squeam. Foh! we'll have no such playfellows.

Mrs. Dain. No, sir; you shan't choose playfellows for us, we thank you.

Sir Jasp. Nay, pray hear me.   *Whispering to them.*

Lady Fid. But, poor gentleman, could you be so 620 generous, so truly a man of honor, as for the sakes of us women of honor, to cause yourself to be reported no man? No man! and to suffer yourself the greatest shame that could fall upon a man, that none might fall upon us women by your conversation? But, in- 625 deed, sir, as perfectly, perfectly the same man as before your going into France, sir? as perfectly, perfectly, sir?

Horn. As perfectly, perfectly, madam. Nay, I scorn you should take my word; I desire to be tried only, 630 madam.

Lady Fid. Well, that's spoken again like a man of

honor: all men of honor desire to come to the test.
But, indeed, generally you men report such things of
yourselves one does not know how or whom to be- 635
lieve; and it is come to that pass we dare not take
your words no more than your tailor's, without some
staid servant of yours be bound with you. But I have
so strong a faith in your honor, dear, dear, noble sir,
that I'd forfeit mine for yours, at any time, dear sir. 640

Horn. No, madam, you should not need to forfeit it
for me; I have given you security already to save you
harmless, my late reputation being so well known in
the world, madam.

Lady Fid. But if upon any future falling-out, or 645
upon a suspicion of my taking the trust out of your
hands to employ some other, you yourself should betray your trust, dear sir? I mean, if you'll give me
leave to speak obscenely, you might tell, dear sir.

Horn. If I did, nobody would believe me. The repu- 650
tation of impotency is as hardly recovered again in
the world as that of cowardice, dear madam.

Lady Fid. Nay, then, as one may say, you may do
your worst, dear, dear sir.

Sir Jasp. Come, is your Ladyship reconciled to him 655
yet? Have you agreed on matters? For I must be gone
to Whitehall.

Lady Fid. Why, indeed, Sir Jasper, Master Horner is
a thousand, thousand times a better man than I
thought him. Cousin Squeamish, Sister Dainty, I can 660
name him now. Truly, not long ago, you know, I
thought his very name obscenity; and I would as soon
have lain with him as have named him.

Sir Jasp. Very likely, poor madam.

Mrs. Dain. I believe it.   665

Mrs. Squeam. No doubt on't.

---

649. OBSCENELY: openly (literally, "before the scene").
651. RECOVERED: i.e., overcome.

Sir Jasp. Well, well—that your Ladyship is as virtuous as any she, I know, and him all the town knows —he! he! he! Therefore, now you like him, get you gone to your business together; go, go to your business, I say, pleasure; whilst I go to my pleasure, business.

Lady Fid. Come, then, dear gallant.

Horn. Come away, my dearest mistress.

Sir Jasp. So, so; why, 'tis as I'd have it.   *Exit.* 675

Horn. And as I'd have it.

Lady Fid.

Who for his business from his wife will run,
Takes the best care to have her business done.

                                        Exeunt omnes.

ACT III

<hr>

Scene I

[Enter] Alithea and Mrs. Pinchwife.

Alith. Sister, what ails you? You are grown melancholy.

Mrs. Pinch. Would it not make anyone melancholy to see you go every day fluttering about abroad, whilst I must stay at home like a poor, lonely, sullen 5
bird in a cage?

Alith. Ay, sister, but you came young, and just from the nest to your cage, so that I thought you liked it and could be as cheerful in't as others that took their flight themselves early and are hopping abroad in the 10
open air.

Mrs. Pinch. Nay, I confess I was quiet enough till my husband told me what pure lives the London ladies live abroad, with their dancing, meetings, and junketings, and dressed every day in their best gowns; 15
and I warrant you, play at ninepins every day of the week, so they do.

Enter Pinchwife.

Pinch. Come, what's here to do? You are putting the town pleasures in her head and setting her a-longing. 20

Alith. Yes, after ninepins. You suffer none to give her those longings, you mean, but yourself.

Pinch. I tell her of the vanities of the town, like a confessor.

Alith. A confessor! Just such a confessor as he that 25
by forbidding a silly ostler to grease the horse's teeth
taught him to do't.

Pinch. Come, Mistress Flippant, good precepts are
lost when bad examples are still before us: the liberty
you take abroad makes her hanker after it and out of 30
humor at home. Poor wretch! She desired not to come
to London; I would bring her.

Alith. Very well.

Pinch. She has been this week in town and never
desired till this afternoon to go abroad. 35

Alith. Was she not at a play yesterday?

Pinch. Yes, but she ne'er asked me; I was myself the
cause of her going.

Alith. Then if she ask you again, you are the cause
of her asking, and not my example. 40

Pinch. Well, tomorrow night I shall be rid of you;
and the next day, before 'tis light, she and I'll be rid
of the town and my dreadful apprehensions.—Come,
be not melancholy, for thou shalt go into the country
after tomorrow, dearest. 45

Alith. Great comfort!

Mrs. Pinch. Pish! what d'ye tell me of the country
for?

Pinch. How's this! What, pish at the country?

Mrs. Pinch. Let me alone; I am not well. 50

Pinch. O, if that be all—what ails my dearest?

Mrs. Pinch. Truly, I don't know; but I have not
been well since you told me there was a gallant at the
play in love with me.

Pinch. Ha!— 55

Alith. That's by my example too!

Pinch. Nay, if you are not well, but are so concerned because a lewd fellow chanced to lie and say
he liked you, you'll make me sick too.

Mrs. Pinch. Of what sickness? 60

Pinch. O, of that which is worse than the plague, jealousy.

Mrs. Pinch. Pish, you jeer! I'm sure there's no such disease in our receipt-book at home.

Pinch. No, thou never met'st with it, poor innocent. 65
—(*Aside*) Well, if thou cuckold me, 'twill be my own fault, for cuckolds and bastards are generally makers of their own fortune.

Mrs. Pinch. Well, but pray, bud, let's go to a play tonight. 70

Pinch. 'Tis just done, she comes from it. But why are you so eager to see a play?

Mrs. Pinch. Faith, dear, not that I care one pin for their talk there; but I like to look upon the player-men, and would see, if I could, the gallant you say 75 loves me: that's all, dear bud.

Pinch. Is that all, dear bud?

Alith. This proceeds from my example!

Mrs. Pinch. But if the play be done, let's go abroad however, dear bud. 80

Pinch. Come, have a little patience and thou shalt go into the country on Friday.

Mrs. Pinch. Therefore I would see first some sights to tell my neighbors of. Nay, I will go abroad, that's once. 85

Alith. I'm the cause of this desire too!

Pinch. But now I think on't, who, who was the cause of Horner's coming to my lodgings today? That was you.

Alith. No, you, because you would not let him see 90 your handsome wife out of your lodging.

Mrs. Pinch. Why, O Lord! did the gentleman come hither to see me indeed?

Pinch. No, no. You are not cause of that damned question too, Mistress Alithea?—(*Aside*) Well, she's 95 in the right of it. He is in love with my wife—and

comes after her—'tis so—but I'll nip his love in the
bud, lest he should follow us into the country and
break his chariot-wheel near our house, on purpose
for an excuse to come to't. But I think I know the 100
town.

Mrs. Pinch. Come, pray, bud, let's go abroad before
'tis late; for I will go, that's flat and plain.

Pinch. (*Aside*) So! the obstinacy already of the
town wife; and I must, whilst she's here, humor her 105
like one.—Sister, how shall we do, that she may not be
seen or known?

Alith. Let her put on her mask.

Pinch. Pshaw! a mask makes people but the more
inquisitive and is as ridiculous a disguise as a stage- 110
beard: her shape, stature, habit will be known. And if
we should meet with Horner, he would be sure to take
acquaintance with us, must wish her joy, kiss her, talk
to her, leer upon her, and the Devil and all. No, I'll
not use her to a mask, 'tis dangerous, for masks have 115
made more cuckolds than the best faces that ever
were known.

Alith. How will you do then?

Mrs. Pinch. Nay, shall we go? The Exchange will be
shut, and I have a mind to see that.   120

Pinch. So—I have it—I'll dress her up in the suit we
are to carry down to her brother, little Sir James; nay,
I understand the town tricks. Come, let's go dress her.
A mask! No—a woman masked, like a covered dish,
gives a man curiosity and appetite; when, it may be, 125
uncovered 'twould turn his stomach: no, no.

Alith. Indeed your comparison is something a
greasy one; but I had a gentle gallant used to say, "A
beauty masked, like the sun in eclipse, gathers together more gazers than if it shined out."   130

                                        Exeunt.

[Scene II.] The scene changes to the New Exchange.

Enter Horner, Harcourt, Dorilant.

Dor. Engaged to women, and not sup with us!

Horn. Ay, a pox on 'em all!

Har. You were much a more reasonable man in the morning, and had as noble resolutions against 'em as a widower of a week's liberty.   5

Dor. Did I ever think to see you keep company with women in vain?

Horn. In vain: no—'tis, since I can't love 'em, to be revenged on 'em.

Har. Now your sting is gone, you looked in the box   10
amongst all those women like a drone in the hive, all upon you; shoved and ill used by 'em all, and thrust from one side to t'other.

Dor. Yet he must be buzzing amongst 'em still, like other old beetle-headed, lickerish drones. Avoid 'em,   15
and hate 'em, as they hate you.

Horn. Because I do hate 'em, and would hate 'em yet more, I'll frequent 'em. You may see by marriage, nothing makes a man hate a woman more than her constant conversation. In short, I converse with 'em, as   20
you do with rich fools, to laugh at 'em and use 'em ill.

Dor. But I would no more sup with women unless I could lie with 'em than sup with a rich coxcomb unless I could cheat him.

(III.ii.)
15. BEETLE-HEADED: stupid; LICKERISH: lecherous.
26. SET OUT . . . HAND: i.e., give you a chance to display your superiority.
30. TOSSES . . . MARKER: uses a counter to practice tossing coins; URE: practice.
41. CIVIL: respectable.
47. LEWIS': a London tavern.

Horn. Yes, I have known thee sup with a fool for 25
his drinking; if he could set out your hand that way
only, you were satisfied, and if he were a wine-swal-
lowing mouth, 'twas enough.

Har. Yes, a man drinks often with a fool, as he
tosses with a marker, only to keep his hand in ure. 30
But do the ladies drink?

Horn. Yes, sir; and I shall have the pleasure at least
of laying 'em flat with a bottle and bring as much
scandal that way upon 'em as formerly t'other.

Har. Perhaps you may prove as weak a brother 35
amongst 'em that way as t'other.

Dor. Foh! drinking with women is as unnatural as
scolding with 'em. But 'tis a pleasure of decayed
fornicators and the basest way of quenching love.

Har. Nay, 'tis drowning love, instead of quenching 40
it. But leave us for civil women too!

Dor. Ay, when he can't be the better for 'em. We
hardly pardon a man that leaves his friend for a
wench, and that's a pretty lawful call.

Horn. Faith, I would not leave you for 'em, if they 45
would not drink.

Dor. Who would disappoint his company at Lewis'
for a gossiping?

Har. Foh! Wine and women, good apart, together
as nauseous as sack and sugar. But hark you, sir, be- 50
fore you go, a little of your advice; an old, maimed
general, when unfit for action, is fittest for counsel.
I have other designs upon women than eating and
drinking with them; I am in love with Sparkish's mistress, whom he is to marry tomorrow: now how shall I 55
get her?

Enter Sparkish, looking about.

Horn. Why, here comes one will help you to her.

Har. He! He, I tell you, is my rival, and will hinder
my love.

Horn. No; a foolish rival and a jealous husband   60
assist their rival's designs, for they are sure to make
their women hate them, which is the first step to their
love for another man.

Har. But I cannot come near his mistress but in his
company.   65

Horn. Still the better for you; for fools are most
easily cheated when they themselves are accessories,
and he is to be bubbled of his mistress as of his
money, the common mistress, by keeping him company.   70

Spark. Who is that that is to be bubbled? Faith, let
me snack; I han't met with a bubble since Christmas.
Gad, I think bubbles are like their brother woodcocks,
go out with the cold weather.

Har. (*Apart to Horner*) A pox! he did not hear all, 75
I hope.

Spark. Come, you bubbling rogues you, where do
we sup?—O, Harcourt, my mistress tells me you have
been making fierce love to her all the play long: ha!
ha! But I—   80

Har. I make love to her!

Spark. Nay, I forgive thee, for I think I know thee,
and I know her; but I am sure I know myself.

Har. Did she tell you so? I see all women are like
these of the Exchange; who, to enhance the price of 85
their commodities, report to their fond customers
offers which were never made 'em.

Horn. Ay, women are as apt to tell before the intrigue as men after it, and so show themselves the

---

68. BUBBLED: hoodwinked.
72. SNACK: partake; A BUBBLE: a piece of trickery.
73. BUBBLES . . . WOODCOCKS: dupes . . . fools.
86. FOND: foolish.
124–25. HICTIUS DOCTIUS: juggler's phrase, similar to "hocus-pocus."

vainer sex. But hast thou a mistress, Sparkish? 'Tis as   90
hard for me to believe it as that thou ever hadst a
bubble, as you bragged just now.

Spark. O, your servant, sir; are you at your raillery,
sir? But we were some of us beforehand with you
today at the play. The wits were something bold with   95
you, sir; did you not hear us laugh?

Horn. Yes; but I thought you had gone to plays to
laugh at the poet's wit, not at your own.

Spark. Your servant, sir; no, I thank you. Gad, I go
to a play as to a country treat; I carry my own wine   100
to one and my own wit to t'other, or else I'm sure I
should not be merry at either. And the reason why we
are so often louder than the players is because we
think we speak more wit and so become the poet's
rivals in his audience; for to tell you the truth, we   105
hate the silly rogues, nay, so much that we find fault
even with their bawdy upon the stage, whilst we talk
nothing else in the pit as loud.

Horn. But why shouldst thou hate the silly poets?
Thou hast too much wit to be one; and they, like   110
whores, are only hated by each other; and thou dost
scorn writing, I'm sure.

Spark. Yes, I'd have you to know I scorn writing;
but women, women, that make men do all foolish
things, make 'em write songs too. Everybody does it.   115
'Tis even as common with lovers as playing with fans;
and you can no more help rhyming to your Phyllis
than drinking to your Phyllis.

Har. Nay, poetry in love is no more to be avoided
than jealousy.   120

Dor. But the poets damned your songs, did they?

Spark. Damn the poets! They turned 'em into burlesque, as they call it. That burlesque is a hocus-pocus
trick they have got, which, by the virtue of *Hictius
doctius*, topsy turvy, they make a wise and witty man   125

in the world a fool upon the stage, you know not how;
and 'tis therefore I hate 'em too, for I know not but it
may be my own case, for they'll put a man into a play
for looking asquint. Their predecessors were contented to make servingmen only their stage fools; but   130
these rogues must have gentlemen, with a pox to 'em,
nay, knights; and, indeed, you shall hardly see a fool
upon the stage but he's a knight. And to tell you the
truth, they have kept me these six years from being
a knight in earnest, for fear of being knighted in a   135
play and dubbed a fool.

Dor. Blame 'em not, they must follow their copy,
the age.

Har. But why shouldst thou be afraid of being in a
play, who expose yourself every day in the playhouses   140
and at public places?

Horn. 'Tis but being on the stage, instead of standing on a bench in the pit.

Dor. Don't you give money to painters to draw you
like? and are you afraid of your pictures at length in   145
a playhouse, where all your mistresses may see you?

Spark. A pox! Painters don't draw the smallpox or
pimples in one's face. Come, damn all your silly authors whatever, all books and booksellers, by the
world, and all readers, courteous or uncourteous!   150

Har. But who comes here, Sparkish?

*Enter Mr. Pinchwife and his wife, in man's clothes,
Alithea, Lucy her maid.*

Spark. O, hide me! There's my mistress too.
          Sparkish hides himself behind Harcourt.

---

171. CLASP: presumably a vendor of books and ballads, whose name
does not appear in the author's list of "Persons."

172. COVENT GARDEN DROLLERY: a collection of songs, etc., from
dramatic pieces, compiled by Alexander Brome and printed in 1672.

173–74. TARUGO'S WILES: a comic drama by Sir Thomas Sydserff,
produced 1667 and printed 1668; THE SLIGHTED MAIDEN: a play by Sir
Robert Stapleton, printed 1663.

Har. She sees you.

Spark. But I will not see her. 'Tis time to go to Whitehall, and I must not fail the drawing room.   155

Har. Pray, first carry me and reconcile me to her.

Spark. Another time. Faith, the King will have supped.

Har. Not with the worse stomach for thy absence. Thou art one of those fools that think their attendance   160 at the King's meals as necessary as his physicians', when you are more troublesome to him than his doctors or his dogs.

Spark. Pshaw! I know my interest, sir. Prithee hide me.   165

Horn. Your servant, Pinchwife.—What, he knows us not!

Pinch. (*To his wife aside*) Come along.

Mrs. Pinch. Pray, have you any ballads? Give me sixpenny worth.   170

Clasp. We have no ballads.

Mrs. Pinch. Then give me *Covent Garden Drollery*, and a play or two—O, here's *Tarugo's Wiles*, and *The Slighted Maiden*; I'll have them.

Pinch. (*Apart to her*) No; plays are not for your   175 reading. Come along; will you discover yourself?

Horn. Who is that pretty youth with him, Sparkish?

Spark. I believe, his wife's brother, because he's something like her; but I never saw her but once.

Horn. Extremely handsome; I have seen a face like   180 it too. Let us follow 'em.

 Exeunt Pinchwife, Mrs. Pinchwife, Alithea, Lucy;
    Horner, Dorilant following them.

Har. Come, Sparkish, your mistress saw you and will be angry you go not to her. Besides, I would fain be reconciled to her, which none but you can do, dear friend.   185

Spark. Well, that's a better reason, dear friend. I

would not go near her now for hers or my own sake,
but I can deny you nothing; for though I have known
thee a great while, never go if I do not love thee as
well as a new acquaintance.   190

Har. I am obliged to you indeed, dear friend. I
would be well with her only to be well with thee still;
for these ties to wives usually dissolve all ties to
friends. I would be contented she should enjoy you
a-nights, but I would have you to myself a-days as I   195
have had, dear friend.

Spark. And thou shalt enjoy me a-days, dear, dear
friend, never stir; and I'll be divorced from her sooner
than from thee. Come along.

Har. (*Aside*) So, we are hard put to't when we   200
make our rival our procurer; but neither she nor her
brother would let me come near her now. When all's
done, a rival is the best cloak to steal to a mistress
under without suspicion; and when we have once got
to her as we desire, we throw him off like other cloaks. 205
        Exit Sparkish, and Harcourt following him.

Re-enter Pinchwife, Mrs. Pinchwife in man's clothes.

Pinch. (*To Alithea*) Sister, if you will not go, we
must leave you.—(*Aside*) The fool her gallant and she
will muster up all the young saunterers of this place,
and they will leave their dear seamstresses to follow
us. What a swarm of cuckolds and cuckold-makers are   210
here!—Come, let's be gone, Mistress Margery.

Mrs. Pinch. Don't you believe that; I han't half my
bellyfull of sights yet.

Pinch. Then walk this way.

Mrs. Pinch. Lord, what a power of brave signs are   215
here! stay— the Bull's Head, the Ram's Head, and the
Stag's Head, dear—

218. EVERY HUSBAND'S . . . SIGN: the cuckold's horns.

Pinch. Nay, if every husband's proper sign here were visible, they would be all alike.

Mrs. Pinch. What d'ye mean by that, bud?   220

Pinch. 'Tis no matter—no matter, bud.

Mrs. Pinch. Pray tell me; nay, I will know.

Pinch. They would be all Bulls', Stags', and Rams' heads.   *Exeunt Mr. Pinchwife and Mrs. Pinchwife.*

Re-enter Sparkish, Harcourt, Alithea, Lucy, at t'other door.

Spark. Come, dear madam, for my sake you shall be   225 reconciled to him.

Alith. For your sake I hate him.

Har. That's something too cruel, madam, to hate me for his sake.

Spark. Ay, indeed, madam, too, too cruel to me, to   230 hate my friend for my sake.

Alith. I hate him because he is your enemy; and you ought to hate him too, for making love to me, if you love me.

Spark. That's a good one! I hate a man for loving   235 you! If he did love you, 'tis but what he can't help; and 'tis your fault, not his, if he admires you. I hate a man for being of my opinion? I'll ne'er do't, by the world!

Alith. Is it for your honor, or mine, to suffer a man   240 to make love to me, who am to marry you tomorrow?

Spark. Is it for your honor, or mine, to have me jealous? That he makes love to you is a sign you are handsome; and that I am not jealous is a sign you are virtuous. That, I think, is for your honor.   245

Alith. But 'tis your honor, too, I am concerned for.

Har. But why, dearest madam, will you be more concerned for his honor than he is himself? Let his

honor alone, for my sake and his. He! he has no   250
honor—

   Spark. How's that?

   Har. But what my dear friend can guard himself.

   Spark. Oho—that's right again.

   Har. Your care of his honor argues his neglect of it,
which is no honor to my dear friend here. Therefore,   255
once more, let his honor go which way it will, dear
madam.

   Spark. Ay, ay; were it for my honor to marry a
woman whose virtue I suspected and could not trust
her in a friend's hands?   260

   Alith. Are you not afraid to lose me?

   Har. He afraid to lose you, madam! No, no; you
may see how the most estimable and most glorious
creature in the world is valued by him. Will you not
see it?   265

   Spark. Right, honest Frank; I have that noble value
for her that I cannot be jealous of her.

   Alith. You mistake him. He means, you care not for
me nor who has me.

   Spark. Lord, madam, I see you are jealous! Will you 270
wrest a poor man's meaning from his words?

   Alith. You astonish me, sir, with your want of
jealousy.

   Spark. And you make me giddy, madam, with your
jealousy and fears, and virtue and honor. Gad, I see   275
virtue makes a woman as troublesome as a little reading or learning.

   Alith. Monstrous!

   Lucy. (*Behind*) Well, to see what easy husbands
these women of quality can meet with! A poor cham-   280
bermaid can never have such ladylike luck. Besides,
he's thrown away upon her. She'll make no use of her
fortune, her blessing; none to a gentleman for a pure
cuckold, for it requires good breeding to be a cuckold.

Alith. I tell you, then, plainly: he pursues me to 285
marry me.

Spark. Pshaw!

Har. Come, madam, you see you strive in vain to
make him jealous of me. My dear friend is the kindest
creature in the world to me. 290

Spark. Poor fellow!

Har. But his kindness only is not enough for me,
without your favor, your good opinion, dear madam:
'tis that must perfect my happiness. Good gentleman,
he believes all I say; would you would do so! Jealous 295
of me! I would not wrong him nor you for the world.

Spark. Look you there. Hear him, hear him, and do
not walk away so. *Alithea walks carelessly to and fro.*

Har. I love you, madam, so—

Spark. How's that? Nay, now you begin to go too 300
far indeed.

Har. So much, I confess, I say, I love you, that I
would not have you miserable and cast yourself away
upon so unworthy and inconsiderable a thing as what
you see here. 305

Clapping his hand on his breast, points at Sparkish.

Spark. No, faith, I believe thou wouldst not: now
his meaning is plain; but I knew before thou wouldst
not wrong me nor her.

Har. No, no. Heavens forbid the glory of her sex
should fall so low as into the embraces of such a con- 310
temptible wretch, the last of mankind—my dear friend
here—I injure him!   *Embracing Sparkish.*

Alith. Very well.

Spark. No, no, dear friend, I knew it.—Madam, you
see he will rather wrong himself than me, in giving 315
himself such names.

Alith. Do not you understand him yet?

Spark. Yes; how modestly he speaks of himself, poor
fellow!

Alith. Methinks he speaks impudently of yourself, 320
since—before yourself too; insomuch that I can no
longer suffer his scurrilous abusiveness to you, no
more than his love to me.   *Offers to go.*

Spark. Nay, nay, madam, pray stay—his love to you!
Lord, madam, has he not spoke yet plain enough? 325

Alith. Yes, indeed, I should think so.

Spark. Well then, by the world, a man can't speak
civilly to a woman now but presently she says he
makes love to her. Nay, madam, you shall stay, with
your pardon, since you have not yet understood him, 330
till he has made an *éclaircissement* of his love to you,
that is, what kind of love it is. Answer to thy
catechism, friend; do you love my mistress here?

Har. Yes, I wish she would not doubt it.

Spark. But how do you love her? 335

Har. With all my soul.

Alith. I thank him, methinks he speaks plain enough
now.

Spark. (*To Alithea*) You are out still.—But with
what kind of love, Harcourt? 340

Har. With the best and the truest love in the world.

Spark. Look you there then, that is with no matrimonial love, I'm sure.

Alith. How's that? Do you say matrimonial love is
not best? 345

Spark. Gad, I went too far ere I was aware. But
speak for thyself, Harcourt; you said you would not
wrong me nor her.

Har. No, no, madam, e'en take him for Heaven's
sake— 350

Spark. Look you there, madam.

339. OUT: mistaken.
378. SALUTED: kissed.

Har. Who should in all justice be yours, he that
loves you most.   *Claps his hand on his breast.*

Alith. Look you there, Mr. Sparkish, who's that?

Spark. Who should it be?—Go on, Harcourt.   355

Har. Who loves you more than women titles or
Fortune fools.   *Points at Sparkish.*

Spark. Look you there, he means me still, for he
points at me.

Alith. Ridiculous!   360

Har. Who can only match your faith and constancy
in love.

Spark. Ay.

Har. Who knows, if it be possible, how to value so
much beauty and virtue.   365

Spark. Ay.

Har. Whose love can no more be equaled in the
world than that heavenly form of yours.

Spark. No.

Har. Who could no more suffer a rival than your 370
absence, and yet could no more suspect your virtue
than his own constancy in his love to you.

Spark. No.

Har. Who, in fine, loves you better than his eyes,
that first made him love you.   375

Spark. Ay—Nay, madam, faith, you shan't go till—

Alith. Have a care, lest you make me stay too long.

Spark. But till he has saluted you; that I may be
assured you are friends, after his honest advice and
declaration. Come, pray, madam, be friends with him. 380

Enter Master Pinchwife, Mrs. Pinchwife.

Alith. You must pardon me, sir, that I am not yet so
obedient to you.

Pinch. What, invite your wife to kiss men? Monstrous! Are you not ashamed? I will never forgive you.

Spark. Are you not ashamed that I should have 385
more confidence in the chastity of your family than
you have? You must not teach me; I am a man of
honor, sir, though I am frank and free; I am frank,
sir—

Pinch. Very frank, sir, to share your wife with your 390
friends.

Spark. He is an humble, menial friend, such as
reconciles the differences of the marriage bed; you
know man and wife do not always agree; I design him
for that use, therefore would have him well with my 395
wife.

Pinch. A menial friend!—you will get a great many
menial friends by showing your wife as you do.

Spark. What then? It may be I have a pleasure in't,
as I have to show fine clothes at a playhouse the first 400
day and count money before poor rogues.

Pinch. He that shows his wife or money will be in
danger of having them borrowed sometimes.

Spark. I love to be envied and would not marry a
wife that I alone could love; loving alone is as dull as 405
eating alone. Is it not a frank age? and I am a frank
person. And to tell you the truth, it may be I love to
have rivals in a wife; they make her seem to a man
still but as a kept mistress. And so good night, for I
must to Whitehall.—Madam, I hope you are now 410
reconciled to my friend; and so I wish you a good
night, madam, and sleep if you can, for tomorrow, you
know, I must visit you early with a canonical gentleman. Good night, dear Harcourt.   *Exit Sparkish.*

Har. Madam, I hope you will not refuse my visit to- 415
morrow, if it should be earlier with a canonical gentleman than Mr. Sparkish's.

Pinch. This gentlewoman is yet under my care,

390. VERY FRANK: very liberal.

therefore you must yet forbear your freedom with her, sir.   *Coming between Alithea and Harcourt.* 420

Har. Must, sir?

Pinch. Yes, sir, she is my sister.

Har. 'Tis well she is, sir—for I must be her servant, sir.—Madam—

Pinch. Come away, sister, we had been gone, if it 425 had not been for you, and so avoided these lewd rakehells, who seem to haunt us.

Enter Horner, Dorilant to them.

Horn. How now, Pinchwife!

Pinch. Your servant.

Horn. What! I see a little time in the country makes 430 a man turn wild and unsociable and only fit to converse with his horses, dogs, and his herds.

Pinch. I have business, sir, and must mind it; your business is pleasure; therefore you and I must go different ways. 435

Horn. Well, you may go on, but this pretty young gentleman—   *Takes hold of Mrs. Pinchwife.*

Har. The lady—

Dor. And the maid—

Horn. Shall stay with us; for I suppose their busi- 440 ness is the same with ours, pleasure.

Pinch. (*Aside*) 'Sdeath, he knows her, she carries it so sillily! Yet if he does not, I should be more silly to discover it first.

Alith. Pray, let us go, sir. 445

Pinch. Come, come—

Horn. (*To Mrs. Pinchwife*) Had you not rather stay with us?—Prithee, Pinchwife, who is this pretty young gentleman?

Pinch. One to whom I'm a guardian.—(*Aside*) I 450 wish I could keep her out of your hands.

Horn. Who is he? I never saw anything so pretty in all my life.

Pinch. Pshaw! do not look upon him so much, he's a poor bashful youth; you'll put him out of countenance. 455 —Come away, brother.   *Offers to take her away.*

Horn. O, your brother!

Pinch. Yes, my wife's brother.—Come, come, she'll stay supper for us.

Horn. I thought so, for he is very like her I saw you 460 at the play with, whom I told you I was in love with.

Mrs. Pinch. (*Aside*) O jeminy! is this he that was in love with me? I am glad on't, I vow, for he's a curious fine gentleman, and I love him already, too.—(*To Pinchwife*) Is this he, bud?   465

Pinch. (*To his wife*) Come away, come away.

Horn. Why, what haste are you in? Why won't you let me talk with him?

Pinch. Because you'll debauch him; he's yet young and innocent, and I would not have him debauched 470 for anything in the world.—(*Aside*) How she gazes on him! The Devil!

Horn. Harcourt, Dorilant, look you here, this is the likeness of that dowdy he told us of, his wife; did you ever see a lovelier creature? The rogue has reason to 475 be jealous of his wife, since she is like him, for she would make all that see her in love with her.

Har. And, as I remember now, she is as like him here as can be.

Dor. She is indeed very pretty, if she be like him. 480

Horn. Very pretty? a very pretty commendation!— she is a glorious creature, beautiful beyond all things I ever beheld.

Pinch. So, so.

463. CURIOUS: remarkably.

Har. More beautiful than a poet's first mistress of 485
imagination.

Horn. Or another man's last mistress of flesh and
blood.

Mrs. Pinch. Nay, now you jeer, sir; pray don't jeer
me. 490

Pinch. Come, come.—(*Aside*) By Heavens, she'll
discover herself!

Horn. I speak of your sister, sir.

Pinch. Ay, but saying she was handsome, if like him,
made him blush.—(*Aside*) I am upon a rack! 495

Horn. Methinks he is so handsome he should not be
a man.

Pinch. (*Aside*) O, there 'tis out! he has discovered
her! I am not able to suffer any longer.—(*To his wife*)
Come, come away, I say. 500

Horn. Nay, by your leave, sir, he shall not go yet.—
(*Aside to them*) Harcourt, Dorilant, let us torment
this jealous rogue a little.

Har., Dor. How?

Horn. I'll show you. 505

Pinch. Come, pray let him go, I cannot stay fooling
any longer; I tell you his sister stays supper for us.

Horn. Does she? Come then, we'll all go sup with
her and thee.

Pinch. No, now I think on't, having stayed so long 510
for us, I warrant she's gone to bed.—(*Aside*) I wish
she and I were well out of their hands.—Come, I must
rise early tomorrow, come.

Horn. Well then, if she be gone to bed, I wish her
and you a good night. But pray, young gentleman, 515
present my humble service to her.

Mrs. Pinch. Thank you heartily, sir.

Pinch. (*Aside*) 'Sdeath! she will discover herself yet
in spite of me.—He is something more civil to you, for
your kindness to his sister, than I am, it seems. 520

Horn. Tell her, dear sweet little gentleman, for all
your brother there, that you have revived the love I
had for her at first sight in the playhouse.

Mrs. Pinch. But did you love her indeed and in-
deed?   525

Pinch. (*Aside*) So, so.—Away, I say.

Horn. Nay, stay.—Yes, indeed and indeed; pray do
you tell her so and give her this kiss from me.

Kisses her.

Pinch. (*Aside*) O Heavens! what do I suffer? Now
'tis too plain he knows her, and yet—   530

Horn. And this, and this—   *Kisses her again.*

Mrs. Pinch. What do you kiss me for? I am no
woman.

Pinch. (*Aside*) So, there, 'tis out.—Come, I cannot,
nor will, stay any longer.   535

Horn. Nay, they shall send your lady a kiss too.
Here, Harcourt, Dorilant, will you not? *They kiss her.*

Pinch. (*Aside*) How! do I suffer this? Was I not
accusing another just now for this rascally patience in
permitting his wife to be kissed before his face? Ten   540
thousand ulcers gnaw away their lips.—Come, come.

Horn. Good night, dear little gentleman; madam,
good night; farewell, Pinchwife.—(*Apart to Harcourt
and Dorilant*) Did not I tell you I would raise his
jealous gall? *Exeunt Horner, Harcourt, and Dorilant.* 545

Pinch. So, they are gone at last; stay, let me see first
if the coach be at this door.   *Exit.*

Horner, Harcourt, and Dorilant return.

Horn. What, not gone yet? Will you be sure to do
as I desired you, sweet sir?

Mrs. Pinch. Sweet sir, but what will you give me 550
then?

Horn. Anything. Come away into the next walk.
                    Exit, haling away Mrs. Pinchwife.
Alith. Hold! hold! what d'ye do?
Lucy. Stay, stay, hold—
Har. Hold, madam, hold, let him present him—he'll 555
come presently; nay, I will never let you go till you
answer my question.
Alithea, Lucy, struggling with Harcourt and Dorilant.
Lucy. For God's sake, sir, I must follow 'em.
Dor. No, I have something to present you with too,
you shan't follow them.   560

            Pinchwife returns.

Pinch. Where?—how—what's become of?—gone!—
whither?
Lucy. He's only gone with the gentleman, who will
give him something, an't please your Worship.
Pinch. Something!—give him something, with a pox! 565
—Where are they?
Alith. In the next walk only, brother.
Pinch. Only, only! where, where?
                    *Exit Pinchwife and returns presently,
                        then goes out again.*
Har. What's the matter with him? Why so much
concerned? But, dearest madam—   570
Alith. Pray let me go, sir; I have said and suffered
enough already.
Har. Then you will not look upon, nor pity, my
sufferings?
Alith. To look upon 'em, when I cannot help 'em, 575
were cruelty, not pity; therefore, I will never see you
more.
Har. Let me then, madam, have my privilege of a
banished lover, complaining or railing, and giving you
but a farewell reason why, if you cannot condescend 580

to marry me, you should not take that wretch, my rival.

Alith. He only, not you, since my honor is engaged
so far to him, can give me a reason why I should not
marry him; but if he be true and what I think him to
me, I must be so to him. Your servant, sir.   585

Har. Have women only constancy when 'tis a vice
and, like Fortune, only true to fools?

Dor. Thou shalt not stir, thou robust creature; you
see I can deal with you, therefore you should stay the
rather and be kind.   590

To Lucy, who struggles to get from him.

Enter Pinchwife.

Pinch. Gone, gone, not to be found! quite gone! Ten
thousand plagues go with 'em! Which way went they?

Alith. But into t'other walk, brother.

Lucy. Their business will be done presently sure,
an't please your Worship; it can't be long in doing,   595
I'm sure on't.

Alith. Are they not there?

Pinch. No, you know where they are, you infamous
wretch, eternal shame of your family, which you do
not dishonor enough yourself, you think, but you must   600
help her to do it too, thou legion of bawds!

Alith. Good brother—

Pinch. Damned, damned sister!

Alith. Look you here, she's coming.

*Enter Mrs. Pinchwife in man's clothes, running, with
her hat under her arm, full of oranges and dried fruit,
Horner following.*

Mrs. Pinch. O dear bud, look you here what I have   605
got, see!

Pinch. (*Aside, rubbing his forehead*) And what I have got here too, which you can't see.

Mrs. Pinch. The fine gentleman has given me better things yet.

Pinch. Has he so?—(*Aside*) Out of breath and colored!—I must hold yet.

Horn. I have only given your little brother an orange, sir.

Pinch. (*To Horner*) Thank you, sir.—(*Aside*) You have only squeezed my orange, I suppose, and given it me again; yet I must have a city patience.—(*To his wife*) Come, come away.

Mrs. Pinch. Stay, till I have put up my fine things, bud.

Enter Sir Jasper Fidget.

Sir Jasp. O Master Horner, come, come, the ladies stay for you; your mistress, my wife, wonders you make not more haste to her.

Horn. I have stayed this half hour for you here, and 'tis your fault I am not now with your wife.

Sir Jasp. But, pray, don't let her know so much; the truth on't is, I was advancing a certain project to His Majesty about—I'll tell you.

Horn. No, let's go, and hear it at your house. Good night, sweet little gentleman; one kiss more. You'll remember me now, I hope.   *Kisses her.*

Dor. What, Sir Jasper, will you separate friends? He promised to sup with us, and if you take him to your house, you'll be in danger of our company too.

Sir Jasp. Alas! gentlemen, my house is not fit for you; there are none but civil women there, which are not for your turn. He, you know, can bear with the society of civil women now, ha! ha! ha! besides, he's one of my family—he's—he! he! he!

Dor. What is he? 640

Sir Jasp. Faith, my eunuch, since you'll have it; he!
he! he! *Exeunt Sir Jasper Fidget and Horner.*

Dor. I rather wish thou wert his or my cuckold.
Harcourt, what a good cuckold is lost there for want
of a man to make him one! Thee and I cannot have 645
Horner's privilege, who can make use of it.

Har. Ay, to poor Horner 'tis like coming to an estate
at threescore, when a man can't be the better for't.

Pinch. Come.

Mrs. Pinch. Presently, bud. 650

Dor. Come, let us go too.—(*To Alithea*) Madam,
your servant.—(*To Lucy*) Good night, strapper.

Har. Madam, though you will not let me have a
good day or night, I wish you one; but dare not name
the other half of my wish. 655

Alith. Good night, sir, forever.

Mrs. Pinch. I don't know where to put this here,
dear bud, you shall eat it; nay, you shall have part of
the fine gentleman's good things, or treat, as you call
it, when we come home. 660

Pinch. Indeed, I deserve it, since I furnished the
best part of it. *Strikes away the orange.*

The gallant treats, presents, and gives the ball,
But 'tis the absent cuckold pays for all.

[*Exeunt.*]

(IV.i.)
3. PULVILLIO: sachet powder.

ACT IV

Scene I. In Pinchwife's house in the morning.

[*Enter*] *Lucy, Alithea, dressed in new clothes.*

Lucy. Well, madam,—now have I dressed you and
set you out with so many ornaments and spent upon
you ounces of essence and pulvillio; and all this for no
other purpose but as people adorn and perfume a
corpse for a stinking secondhand grave: such, or as   5
bad, I think Master Sparkish's bed.

Alith. Hold your peace.

Lucy. Nay, madam, I will ask you the reason why
you would banish poor Master Harcourt forever from
your sight; how could you be so hard-hearted?   10

Alith. 'Twas because I was not hard-hearted.

Lucy. No, no; 'twas stark love and kindness, I warrant.

Alith. It was so; I would see him no more because
I love him.   15

Lucy. Heyday, a very pretty reason!

Alith. You do not understand me.

Lucy. I wish you may yourself.

Alith. I was engaged to marry, you see, another
man, whom my justice will not suffer me to deceive   20
or injure.

Lucy. Can there be a greater cheat or wrong done
to a man than to give him your person without your
heart? I should make a conscience of it.

Alith. I'll retrieve it for him after I am married a   25
while.

Lucy. The woman that marries to love better will be as much mistaken as the wencher that marries to live better. No, madam, marrying to increase love is like gaming to become rich; alas! you only lose what 30 little stock you had before.

Alith. I find by your rhetoric you have been bribed to betray me.

Lucy. Only by his merit, that has bribed your heart, you see, against your word and rigid honor. But what 35 a Devil is this honor! 'Tis sure a disease in the head, like the megrim or falling sickness, that always hurries people away to do themselves mischief. Men lose their lives by it; women, what's dearer to 'em, their love, the life of life. 40

Alith. Come, pray talk you no more of honor nor Master Harcourt; I wish the other would come to secure my fidelity to him and his right in me.

Lucy. You will marry him then?

Alith. Certainly; I have given him already my word 45 and will my hand too, to make it good, when he comes.

Lucy. Well, I wish I may never stick pin more if he be not an arrant natural to t'other fine gentleman.

Alith. I own he wants the wit of Harcourt, which 50 I will dispense withal for another want he has, which is want of jealousy, which men of wit seldom want.

Lucy. Lord, madam, what should you do with a fool to your husband? You intend to be honest, don't you? Then that husbandly virtue, credulity, is thrown away 55 upon you.

Alith. He only that could suspect my virtue should have cause to do it; 'tis Sparkish's confidence in my truth that obliges me to be so faithful to him.

Lucy. You are not sure his opinion may last. 60

---

49. NATURAL: idiot.

Alith. I am satisfied 'tis impossible for him to be jealous after the proofs I have had of him. Jealousy in a husband—Heaven defend me from it! It begets a thousand plagues to a poor woman, the loss of her honor, her quiet, and her—   65

Lucy. And her pleasure.

Alith. What d'ye mean, impertinent?

Lucy. Liberty is a great pleasure, madam.

Alith. I say, loss of her honor, her quiet, nay, her life, sometimes; and what's as bad almost, the loss of 70 this town; that is, she is sent into the country, which is the last ill-usage of a husband to a wife, I think.

Lucy. (*Aside*) O, does the wind lie there?—Then of necessity, madam, you think a man must carry his wife into the country, if he be wise. The country is as 75 terrible, I find, to our young English ladies, as a monastery to those abroad; and, on my virginity, I think they would rather marry a London jailer than a high sheriff of a county, since neither can stir from his employment. Formerly, women of wit married fools for 80 a great estate, a fine seat, or the like; but now 'tis for a pretty seat only in Lincoln's Inn Fields, St. James's Fields, or the Pall Mall.

*Enter to them Sparkish, and Harcourt, dressed like
a Parson.*

Spark. Madam, your humble servant, a happy day to you and to us all.   85

Har. Amen.

Alith. Who have we here?

Spark. My chaplain, faith—O madam, poor Harcourt remembers his humble service to you; and, in obedience to your last commands, refrains coming 90 into your sight.

Alith. Is not that he?

Spark. No, fie, no; but to show that he ne'er intended to hinder our match has sent his brother here to
join our hands. When I get me a wife, I must get 95
her a chaplain, according to the custom; this is his
brother and my chaplain.

Alith. His brother!

Lucy. (*Aside*) And your chaplain, to preach in your
pulpit then— 100

Alith. His brother!

Spark. Nay, I knew you would not believe it.—I
told you, sir, she would take you for your brother
Frank.

Alith. Believe it! 105

Lucy. (*Aside*) His brother! ha! ha! he! He has a
trick left still, it seems.

Spark. Come, my dearest, pray let us go to church
before the canonical hour is past.

Alith. For shame! you are abused still. 110

Spark. By the world, 'tis strange, now, you are so
incredulous.

Alith. 'Tis strange you are so credulous.

Spark. Dearest of my life, hear me. I tell you this is
Ned Harcourt of Cambridge, by the world; you see 115
he has a sneaking college look. 'Tis true he's something like his brother Frank; and they differ from
each other no more than in their age, for they were
twins.

Lucy. Ha! ha! he! 120

Alith. Your servant, sir; I cannot be so deceived,
though you are. But come, let's hear, how do you
know what you affirm so confidently?

Spark. Why, I'll tell you all. Frank Harcourt coming to me this morning to wish me joy and present 125

109. CANONICAL HOUR: period during which marriage ceremonies
could be performed.
110. ABUSED: deceived.

his service to you, I asked him if he could help me to a parson. Whereupon he told me he had a brother in town who was in orders; and he went straight away and sent him you see there to me.

Alith. Yes, Frank goes and puts on a black coat, 130 then tells you he is Ned; that's all you have for't.

Spark. Pshaw! pshaw! I tell you, by the same token, the midwife put her garter about Frank's neck to know 'em asunder, they were so like.

Alith. Frank tells you this too? 135

Spark. Ay, and Ned there too; nay, they are both in a story.

Alith. So, so; very foolish.

Spark. Lord, if you won't believe one, you had best try him by your chambermaid there; for cham- 140 bermaids must needs know chaplains from other men, they are so used to 'em.

Lucy. Let's see: nay, I'll be sworn he has the ca-nonical smirk and the filthy, clammy palm of a chap-lain. 145

Alith. Well, most reverend Doctor, pray let us make an end of this fooling.

Har. With all my soul, divine heavenly creature, when you please.

Alith. He speaks like a chaplain indeed. 150

Spark. Why, was there not soul, divine, heavenly, in what he said?

Alith. Once more, most impertinent blackcoat, cease your persecution, and let us have a conclusion of this ridiculous love. 155

Har. (*Aside*) I had forgot; I must suit my style to my coat, or I wear it in vain.

Alith. I have no more patience left; let us make once an end of this troublesome love, I say.

Har. So be it, seraphic lady, when your honor shall 160 think it meet and convenient so to do.

Spark. Gad, I'm sure none but a chaplain could speak so, I think.

Alith. Let me tell you, sir, this dull trick will not serve your turn; though you delay our marriage, you 165 shall not hinder it.

Har. Far be it from me, munificent patroness, to delay your marriage; I desire nothing more than to marry you presently, which I might do, if you yourself would; for my noble, good-natured, and thrice 170 generous patron here would not hinder it.

Spark. No, poor man, not I, faith.

Har. And now, madam, let me tell you plainly, nobody else shall marry you, by Heavens! I'll die first, for I'm sure I should die after it. 175

Lucy. How his love has made him forget his function, as I have seen it in real parsons!

Alith. That was spoken like a chaplain too? Now you understand him, I hope.

Spark. Poor man, he takes it heinously to be re- 180 fused. I can't blame him, 'tis putting an indignity upon him not to be suffered; but you'll pardon me, madam, it shan't be; he shall marry us. Come away, pray, madam.

Lucy. Ha! ha! he! more ado! 'tis late. 185

Alith. Invincible stupidity! I tell you, he would marry me as your rival, not as your chaplain.

Spark. Come, come, madam.   *Pulling her away.*

Lucy. I pray, madam, do not refuse this reverend divine the honor and satisfaction of marrying you; 190 for I dare say he has set his heart upon't, good doctor.

Alith. What can you hope or design by this?

Har. (*Aside*) I could answer her, a reprieve for a day only often revokes a hasty doom. At worst, if she will not take mercy on me and let me marry her, I 195 have at least the lover's second pleasure, hindering my rival's enjoyment, though but for a time.

Spark. Come, madam, 'tis e'en twelve o'clock, and
my mother charged me never to be married out of the
canonical hours. Come, come. Lord, here's such a 200
deal of modesty, I warrant, the first day.

Lucy. Yes, an't please your Worship, married wom-
en show all their modesty the first day, because married men show all their love the first day.

Exeunt Sparkish, Alithea, Harcourt, and Lucy.

[Scene II.] The scene changes to a bedchamber,
where appear *Pinchwife* and *Mrs. Pinchwife.*

Pinch. Come, tell me, I say.

Mrs. Pinch. Lord! han't I told it an hundred times
over?

Pinch. (*Aside*) I would try if in the repetition of the
ungrateful tale I could find her altering it in the least 5
circumstance; for if her story be false, she is so too.—
Come, how was't, baggage?

Mrs. Pinch. Lord, what pleasure you take to hear
it, sure!

Pinch. No, you take more in telling it, I find; but 10
speak, how was't?

Mrs. Pinch. He carried me up into the house next
to the Exchange.

Pinch. So, and you two were only in the room!

Mrs. Pinch. Yes, for he sent away a youth that was 15
there for some dried fruit and China oranges.

Pinch. Did he so? Damn him for it—and for—

Mrs. Pinch. But presently came up the gentlewoman of the house.

Pinch. O, 'twas well she did; but what did he do 20
whilst the fruit came?

Mrs. Pinch. He kissed me an hundred times and
told me he fancied he kissed my fine sister, meaning

me, you know, whom he said he loved with all his
soul, and bid me be sure to tell her so, and to desire 25
her to be at her window by eleven of the clock this
morning and he would walk under it at that time.

Pinch. (*Aside*) And he was as good as his word,
very punctual; a pox reward him for't.

Mrs. Pinch. Well, and he said if you were not with- 30
in he would come up to her, meaning me, you know,
bud, still.

Pinch. (*Aside*) So—he knew her certainly; but for
this confession I am obliged to her simplicity.—But
what, you stood very still when he kissed you? 35

Mrs. Pinch. Yes, I warrant you; would you have
had me discover myself?

Pinch. But you told me he did some beastliness to
you, as you call it; what was't?

Mrs. Pinch. Why, he put— 40

Pinch. What?

Mrs. Pinch. Why, he put the tip of his tongue between my lips, and so mousled me—and I said I'd
bite it.

Pinch. An eternal canker seize it, for a dog! 45

Mrs. Pinch. Nay, you need not be so angry with
him, neither, for to say truth, he has the sweetest
breath I ever knew.

Pinch. The Devil! You were satisfied with it then
and would do it again? 50

Mrs. Pinch. Not unless he should force me.

Pinch. Force you, changeling! I tell you, no woman
can be forced.

Mrs. Pinch. Yes, but she may sure by such a one
as he, for he's a proper, goodly, strong man; 'tis hard, 55
let me tell you, to resist him.

Pinch. (*Aside*) So, 'tis plain she loves him, yet she
has not love enough to make her conceal it from me;
but the sight of him will increase her aversion for

me and love for him; and that love instruct her how   60
to deceive me and satisfy him, all idiot as she is.
Love! 'twas he gave women first their craft, their art
of deluding. Out of Nature's hands they came plain,
open, silly, and fit for slaves, as she and Heaven intended 'em; but damned Love—well—I must strangle   65
that little monster whilst I can deal with him.—Go
fetch pen, ink, and paper out of the next room.

Mrs. Pinch. Yes, bud.   *Exit.*

Pinch. Why should women have more invention in
love than men? It can only be because they have   70
more desires, more soliciting passions, more lust, and
more of the Devil.

Mrs. Pinchwife returns.

Come, minx, sit down and write.

Mrs. Pinch. Ay, dear bud, but I can't do't very well.

Pinch. I wish you could not at all.   75

Mrs. Pinch. But what should I write for?

Pinch. I'll have you write a letter to your lover.

Mrs. Pinch. O Lord, to the fine gentleman a letter!

Pinch. Yes, to the fine gentleman.

Mrs. Pinch. Lord, you do but jeer; sure you jest.   80

Pinch. I am not so merry; come, write as I bid you.

Mrs. Pinch. What, do you think I am a fool?

Pinch. (*Aside*) She's afraid I would not dictate any
love to him, therefore she's unwilling.—But you had
best begin.   85

Mrs. Pinch. Indeed and indeed but I won't, so I
won't.

Pinch. Why?

Mrs. Pinch. Because he's in town; you may send
for him if you will.   90

Pinch. Very well, you would have him brought to
you; is it come to this? I say, take the pen and write,
or you'll provoke me.

Mrs. Pinch. Lord, what d'ye make a fool of me for? Don't I know that letters are never writ but from the 95 country to London and from London into the country? Now he's in town, and I am in town too; therefore I can't write to him, you know.

Pinch. (*Aside*) So, I am glad it is no worse; she is innocent enough yet.—Yes, you may, when your hus- 100 band bids you, write letters to people that are in town.

Mrs. Pinch. O, may I so? Then I'm satisfied.

Pinch. Come, begin (*Dictates*)—"Sir"—

Mrs. Pinch. Shan't I say, "Dear Sir"? You know one 105 says always something more than bare "Sir."

Pinch. Write as I bid you, or I will write "whore" with this penknife in your face.

Mrs. Pinch. Nay, good bud (*She writes.*)—"Sir"—

Pinch. "Though I suffered last night your nauseous, 110 loathed kisses and embraces"—Write!

Mrs. Pinch. Nay, why should I say so? You know I told you he had a sweet breath.

Pinch. Write!

Mrs. Pinch. Let me but put out "loathed." 115

Pinch. Write, I say!

Mrs. Pinch. Well then.   *Writes.*

Pinch. Let's see, what have you writ?—(*Takes the paper and reads*) "Though I suffered last night your kisses and embraces"—Thou impudent creature! where 120 is "nauseous" and "loathed"?

Mrs. Pinch. I can't abide to write such filthy words.

Pinch. Once more write as I'd have you and question it not, or I will spoil thy writing with this. I will stab out those eyes that cause my mischief. 125

                    Holds up the penknife.

Mrs. Pinch. O Lord! I will.

Pinch. So—so—let's see now.—(*Reads*) "Though I

suffered last night your nauseous, loathed kisses and
embraces"—go on—"yet I would not have you presume that you shall ever repeat them"—so—   130
                                              She writes.

Mrs. Pinch. I have writ it.
Pinch. On, then—"I then concealed myself from
your knowledge, to avoid your insolencies."—
                                              She writes.

Mrs. Pinch. So—
Pinch. "The same reason, now I am out of your   135
hands"—   *She writes.*
Mrs. Pinch. So—
Pinch. "Makes me own to you my unfortunate,
though innocent, frolic of being in man's clothes"—
                                              She writes.

Mrs. Pinch. So—   140
Pinch. "That you may forevermore cease to pursue
her who hates and detests you."—   *She writes on.*
Mrs. Pinch. So—h—   *Sighs.*
Pinch. What, do you sigh?—"detests you—as much
as she loves her husband and her honor."   145
Mrs. Pinch. I vow, husband, he'll ne'er believe I
should write such a letter.
Pinch. What, he'd expect a kinder from you? Come,
now your name only.
Mrs. Pinch. What, shan't I say "Your most faithful,   150
humble servant till death"?
Pinch. No, tormenting fiend!— (*Aside*) Her style,
I find, would be very soft.—Come, wrap it up now,
whilst I go fetch wax and a candle; and write on the
backside, "For Mr. Horner."   *Exit Pinchwife.* 155
Mrs. Pinch. "For Mr. Horner."—So, I am glad he
has told me his name. Dear Mr. Horner! But why
should I send thee such a letter that will vex thee and
make thee angry with me?—Well, I will not send
it.—Ay, but then my husband will kill me—for I see   160

plainly he won't let me love Mr. Horner—but what
care I for my husband? I won't, so I won't, send poor
Mr. Horner such a letter—But then my husband—
but O, what if I writ at bottom my husband made me
write it?—Ay, but then my husband would see't— 165
Can one have no shift? Ah, a London woman would
have had a hundred presently. Stay—what if I should
write a letter, and wrap it up like this, and write
upon't too? Ay, but then my husband would see't—I
don't know what to do.—But yet, ivads, I'll try, so I 170
will; for I will not send this letter to poor Mr. Horner,
come what will on't.

"Dear, sweet Mr. Horner"—(*She writes and repeats
what she hath writ.*)—so—"my husband would have
me send you a base, rude, unmannerly letter; but I 175
won't"—so—"and would have me forbid you loving
me; but I won't"—so—"and would have me say to you
I hate you, poor Mr. Horner; but I won't tell a lie for
him"—there—"for I'm sure if you and I were in the
country at cards together"—so—"I could not help 180
treading on your toe under the table"—so—"or rubbing knees with you and staring in your face till you
saw me"—very well—"and then looking down and
blushing for an hour together"—so—"but I must make
haste before my husband come: and now he has 185
taught me to write letters, you shall have longer ones
from me, who am, dear, dear, poor, dear Mr. Horner,
your most humble friend and servant to command till
death,—Margery Pinchwife."

Stay, I must give him a hint at bottom—so—now 190
wrap it up just like t'other—so—now write "For Mr.
Horner"—But, O, now, what shall I do with it? for
here comes my husband.

(IV.ii.)
170. IVADS: in faith.
209. CURIOUSLY: cleverly.

Enter Pinchwife.

Pinch. (*Aside*)I have been detained by a sparkish
coxcomb, who pretended a visit to me; but I fear 195
'twas to my wife—What, have you done?

Mrs. Pinch. Ay, ay, bud, just now.

Pinch. Let's see't: what d'ye tremble for? What,
you would not have it go?

Mrs. Pinch. Here—(*Aside*) No, I must not give him 200
that; so I had been served if I had given him this.

> *He opens and reads the first letter.*

Pinch. Come, where's the wax and seal?

Mrs. Pinch. (*Aside*) Lord, what shall I do now?
Nay, then I have it—Pray let me see't. Lord, you
think me so arrant a fool I cannot seal a letter; I will 205
do't, so I will.

> *Snatches the letter from him, changes it for the
> other, seals it, and delivers it to him.*

Pinch. Nay, I believe you will learn that, and other
things too, which I would not have you.

Mrs. Pinch. So, han't I done it curiously?—(*Aside*)
I think I have; there's my letter going to Mr. Horner, 210
since he'll needs have me send letters to folks.

Pinch. 'Tis very well; but I warrant you would not
have it go now?

Mrs. Pinch. Yes, indeed, but I would, bud, now.

Pinch. Well, you are a good girl then. Come, let me 215
lock you up in your chamber till I come back; and be
sure you come not within three strides of the window
when I am gone, for I have a spy in the street.

> *Exit Mrs. Pinchwife, Pinchwife locks the door.*

At least, 'tis fit she think so. If we do not cheat wom-
en, they'll cheat us, and fraud may be justly used with 220
secret enemies, of which a wife is the most dangerous; and he that has a handsome one to keep and a

frontier town must provide against treachery rather
than open force. Now I have secured all within, I'll
deal with the foe without, with false intelligence.   225

Holds up the letter. Exit Pinchwife.

[Scene III.] The scene changes to Horner's lodging.

[*Enter*] *Quack and Horner.*

Quack. Well, sir, how fadges the new design? Have
you not the luck of all your brother projectors, to deceive only yourself at last?

Horn. No, good domine Doctor, I deceive you, it
seems, and others too; for the grave matrons and old,   5
rigid husbands think me as unfit for love as they are;
but their wives, sisters, and daughters know, some
of 'em, better things already.

Quack. Already!

Horn. Already, I say. Last night I was drunk with   10
half-a-dozen of your civil persons, as you call 'em,
and people of honor, and so was made free of their
society and dressing rooms forever hereafter; and am
already come to the privileges of sleeping upon their
pallets, warming smocks, tying shoes and garters, and   15
the like, Doctor, already, already, Doctor.

Quack. You have made use of your time, sir.

Horn. I tell thee, I am now no more interruption
to 'em when they sing or talk bawdy than a little
squab French page who speaks no English.   20

Quack. But do civil persons and women of honor
drink and sing bawdy songs?

Horn. O, amongst friends, amongst friends. For
your bigots in honor are just like those in religion:

(IV.iii.)
1. FADGES: succeeds.
20. SQUAB: immature.

they fear the eye of the world more than the eye of   25
Heaven and think there is no virtue but railing at vice
and no sin but giving scandal. They rail at a poor little kept player and keep themselves some young
modest pulpit comedian to be privy to their sins in
their closets, not to tell 'em of them in their chapels.   30

Quack. Nay, the truth on't is priests, amongst the
women now, have quite got the better of us lay con-
fessors, physicians.

Horn. And they are rather their patients; but—

Enter My Lady Fidget, looking about her.

Now we talk of women of honor, here comes one.   35
Step behind the screen there and but observe if I
have not particular privileges with the women of
reputation already, Doctor, already.

[*Quack retires.*]

Lady Fid. Well, Horner, am not I a woman of
honor? You see I'm as good as my word.   40

Horn. And you shall see, madam, I'll not be be-
hindhand with you in honor; and I'll be as good as
my word too, if you please but to withdraw into the
next room.

Lady Fid. But first, my dear sir, you must promise   45
to have a care of my dear honor.

Horn. If you talk a word more of your honor, you'll
make me incapable to wrong it. To talk of honor in
the mysteries of love is like talking of Heaven or the
Deity in an operation of witchcraft: just when you are   50
employing the Devil, it makes the charm impotent.

Lady Fid. Nay, fie! let us not be smutty. But you
talk of mysteries and bewitching to me; I don't understand you.

Horn. I tell you, madam, the word "money" in a   55
mistress's mouth, at such a nick of time, is not a more

disheartening sound to a younger brother than that of
honor to an eager lover like myself.

Lady Fid. But you can't blame a lady of my reputation to be chary.   60

Horn. Chary! I have been chary of it already, by
the report I have caused of myself.

Lady Fid. Ay, but if you should ever let other
women know that dear secret, it would come out.
Nay, you must have a great care of your conduct;   65
for my acquaintance are so censorious (O, 'tis a
wicked, censorious world, Mr. Horner!), I say, are so
censorious and detracting, that perhaps they'll talk to
the prejudice of my honor, though you should not let
them know the dear secret.   70

Horn. Nay, madam, rather than they shall prejudice
your honor, I'll prejudice theirs; and, to serve you,
I'll lie with 'em all, make the secret their own, and
then they'll keep it. I am a Machiavel in love, madam.

Lady Fid. O, no, sir, not that way.   75

Horn. Nay, the Devil take me if censorious women
are to be silenced any other way.

Lady Fid. A secret is better kept, I hope, by a single person than a multitude; therefore, pray do not
trust anybody else with it, dear, dear Mr. Horner.   80
                                    Embracing him.

Enter Sir Jasper Fidget.

Sir Jasp. How now!

Lady Fid. (*Aside*) O my husband!—prevented—and
what's almost as bad, found with my arms about another man—that will appear too much—what shall I
say?—Sir Jasper, come hither: I am trying if Mr.   85
Horner were ticklish, and he's as ticklish as can be. I

---
100. HACKNEY: common.
---

love to torment the confounded toad; let you and I
tickle him.

Sir Jasp. No, your Ladyship will tickle him better
without me, I suppose. But is this your buying china? 90
I thought you had been at the china house.

Horn. (*Aside*) China house! That's my cue, I must
take it.—A pox! can't you keep your impertinent
wives at home? Some men are troubled with the husbands, but I with the wives; but I'd have you to 95
know, since I cannot be your journeyman by night,
I will not be your drudge by day, to squire your wife
about and be your man of straw or scarecrow only
to pies and jays that would be nibbling at your for-
bidden fruit. I shall be shortly the hackney gentle- 100
man-usher of the town.

Sir Jasp. (*Aside*) He! he! he! poor fellow, he's in
the right on't, faith. To squire women about for other
folks is as ungrateful an employment as to tell money
for other folks.—He! he! he! be'n't angry, Horner. 105

Lady Fid. No, 'tis I have more reason to be angry,
who am left by you to go abroad indecently alone;
or, what is more indecent, to pin myself upon such
ill-bred people of your acquaintance as this is.

Sir Jasp. Nay, prithee, what has he done? 110

Lady Fid. Nay, he has done nothing.

Sir Jasp. But what d'ye take ill, if he has done nothing?

Lady Fid. Ha! ha! ha! faith, I can't but laugh, however; why, d'ye think the unmannerly toad would 115
come down to me to the coach? I was fain to come
up to fetch him or go without him, which I was resolved not to do; for he knows china very well, and
has himself very good, but will not let me see it lest
I should beg some; but I will find it out and have 120
what I came for yet.

Horn. (*Apart to Lady Fidget*) Lock the door, madam.—

> *Exit Lady Fidget, and locks the door, followed by Horner to the door.*

—So, she has got into my chamber and locked me out. O the impertinency of womankind! Well, Sir Jasper, 125 plain-dealing is a jewel; if ever you suffer your wife to trouble me again here, she shall carry you home a pair of horns, by my lord mayor she shall. Though I cannot furnish you myself, you are sure, yet I'll find a way. 130

Sir Jasp. Ha! ha! he!—(*Aside*) At my first coming in and finding her arms about him, tickling him it seems, I was half jealous, but now I see my folly.— He! he! he! poor Horner.

Horn. Nay, though you laugh now, 'twill be my turn 135 ere long. O women, more impertinent, more cunning, and more mischievous than their monkeys, and to me almost as ugly!—Now is she throwing my things about and rifling all I have; but I'll get in to her the back way, and so rifle her for it. 140

Sir Jasp. Ha! ha! ha! poor angry Horner.

Horn. Stay here a little, I'll ferret her out to you presently, I warrant. *Exit at t'other door.*

> *Sir Jasper calls through the door to his wife; she answers from within.*

Sir Jasp. Wife! My Lady Fidget! wife! He is coming in to you the back way. 145

Lady Fid. Let him come and welcome, which way he will.

Sir Jasp. He'll catch you and use you roughly, and be too strong for you.

Lady Fid. Don't you trouble yourself, let him if he 150 can.

---

177. TOMRIG: hoyden.

Quack. (*Behind*) This, indeed, I could not have believed from him, nor any but my own eyes.

Enter Mrs. Squeamish.

Mrs. Squeam. Where's this woman-hater, this toad, this ugly, greasy, dirty sloven?   155

Sir Jasp. (*Aside*) So, the women all will have him ugly. Methinks he is a comely person, but his wants make his form contemptible to 'em; and 'tis e'en as my wife said yesterday, talking of him, that a proper handsome eunuch was as ridiculous a thing as a   160 gigantic coward.

Mrs. Squeam. Sir Jasper, your servant; where is the odious beast?

Sir Jasp. He's within in his chamber with my wife; she's playing the wag with him.   165

Mrs. Squeam. Is she so? And he's a clownish beast; he'll give her no quarter; he'll play the wag with her again, let me tell you. Come, let's go help her.—What, the door's locked?

Sir Jasp. Ay, my wife locked it.   170

Mrs. Squeam. Did she so? Let's break it open then.

Sir Jasp. No, no; he'll do her no hurt.

Mrs. Squeam. No.—(*Aside*) But is there no other way to get in to 'em? Whither goes this? I will disturb 'em.   *Exit Mrs. Squeamish at another door.*   175

Enter Old Lady Squeamish.

Lady Squeam. Where is this harlotry, this impudent baggage, this rambling tomrig? O Sir Jasper, I'm glad to see you here; did you not see my vile grandchild come in hither just now?

Sir Jasp. Yes.   180

Lady Squeam. Ay, but where is she then? Where
is she? Lord, Sir Jasper, I have e'en rattled myself to
pieces in pursuit of her; but can you tell what she
makes here? They say below, no woman lodges here.

Sir Jasp. No.   185

Lady Squeam. No! What does she here then? Say,
if it be not a woman's lodging, what makes she here?
But are you sure no woman lodges here?

Sir Jasp. No, nor no man neither; this is Mr.
Horner's lodging.   190

Lady Squeam. Is it so, are you sure?

Sir Jasp. Yes, yes.

Lady Squeam. So; then there's no hurt in't, I hope.
But where is he?

Sir Jasp. He's in the next room with my wife.   195

Lady Squeam. Nay, if you trust him with your wife,
I may with my Biddy. They say he's a merry harmless man now, e'en as harmless a man as ever came
out of Italy with a good voice, and as pretty, harmless company for a lady as a snake without his teeth. 200

Sir Jasp. Ay, ay, poor man.

Enter Mrs. Squeamish.

Mrs. Squeam. I can't find 'em.—O, are you here,
grandmother? I followed, you must know, My Lady
Fidget hither; 'tis the prettiest lodging, and I have
been staring on the prettiest pictures—   205

*Enter Lady Fidget with a piece of china in her hand,
and Horner following.*

Lady Fid. And I have been toiling and moiling for
the prettiest piece of china, my dear.

226. ROLL WAGON: truck or van.

Horn. Nay, she has been too hard for me, do what I could.

Mrs. Squeam. O Lord, I'll have some china too. 210 Good Mr. Horner, don't think to give other people china and me none; come in with me too.

Horn. Upon my honor, I have none left now.

Mrs. Squeam. Nay, nay, I have known you deny your china before now, but you shan't put me off so. 215 Come.

Horn. This lady had the last there.

Lady Fid. Yes, indeed, madam, to my certain knowledge, he has no more left.

Mrs. Squeam. O, but it may be he may have some 220 you could not find.

Lady Fid. What, d'ye think if he had had any left I would not have had it too? For we women of quality never think we have china enough.

Horn. Do not take it ill I cannot make china for you 225 all, but I will have a roll wagon for you too, another time.

Mrs. Squeam. Thank you, dear toad.

Lady Fid. (*To Horner aside*) What do you mean by that promise?   230

Horn. (*Apart to Lady Fidget*) Alas, she has an innocent, literal understanding.

Lady Squeam. Poor Mr. Horner! He has enough to do to please you all, I see.

Horn. Ay, madam, you see how they use me.   235

Lady Squeam. Poor gentleman, I pity you.

Horn. I thank you, madam: I could never find pity but from such reverend ladies as you are; the young ones will never spare a man.

Mrs. Squeam. Come, come, beast, and go dine with 240 us; for we shall want a man at ombre after dinner.

Horn. That's all their use of me, madam, you see.

Mrs. Squeam. Come, sloven, I'll lead you, to be
sure of you.   *Pulls him by the cravat.*

Lady Squeam. Alas, poor man, how she tugs him! 245
Kiss, kiss her; that's the way to make such nice wom-
en quiet.

Horn. No, madam, that remedy is worse than the
torment. They know I dare suffer anything rather
than do it. 250

Lady Squeam. Prithee kiss her, and I'll give you
her picture in little that you admired so last night;
prithee do.

Horn. Well, nothing but that could bribe me. I love
a woman only in effigy and good painting, as much as 255
I hate them. I'll do't, for I could adore the Devil well
painted.   *Kisses Mrs. Squeamish.*

Mrs. Squeam. Foh, you filthy toad! Nay, now I've
done jesting.

Lady Squeam. Ha! ha! ha! I told you so. 260

Mrs. Squeam. Foh! a kiss of his—

Sir Jasp. Has no more hurt in't than one of my
spaniel's.

Mrs. Squeam. Nor no more good neither.

Quack. (*Behind*) I will now believe anything he 265
tells me.

Enter Pinchwife.

Lady Fid. O Lord, here's a man! Sir Jasper, my mask,
my mask! I would not be seen here for the world.

Sir Jasp. What, not when I am with you?

Lady Fid. No, no, my honor—let's be gone. 270

Mrs. Squeam. O grandmother, let us be gone; make

286. DIFFIDE IN: distrust.
305. LOCKET'S: a London tavern.

haste, make haste, I know not how he may censure
us.

Lady Fid. Be found in the lodging of anything like
a man!—Away.   *Exeunt Sir Jasper Fidget, Lady* 275
    Fidget, Old Lady Squeamish, Mrs. Squeamish.
Quack. (*Behind*) What's here? Another cuckold?
He looks like one, and none else, sure, have any business with him.

Horn. Well, what brings my dear friend hither?

Pinch. Your impertinency.   280

Horn. My impertinency!—Why, you gentlemen that
have got handsome wives think you have a privilege
of saying anything to your friends and are as brutish
as if you were our creditors.

Pinch. No, sir, I'll ne'er trust you any way.   285

Horn. But why not, dear Jack? Why diffide in me
thou know'st so well?

Pinch. Because I do know you so well.

Horn. Han't I been always thy friend, honest Jack,
always ready to serve thee, in love or battle, before 290
thou wert married, and am so still?

Pinch. I believe so; you would be my second, now,
indeed.

Horn. Well then, dear Jack, why so unkind, so
grum, so strange to me? Come, prithee, kiss me, dear 295
rogue. Gad, I was always, I say, and am still, as much
thy servant as—

Pinch. As I am yours, sir. What, you would send a
kiss to my wife, is that it?

Horn. So, there 'tis—a man can't show his friend- 300
ship to a married man but presently he talks of his
wife to you. Prithee let thy wife alone, and let thee
and I be all one, as we were wont. What, thou art as
shy of my kindness as a Lombard Street alderman of
a courtier's civility at Locket's!   305

Pinch. But you are overkind to me, as kind as if I
were your cuckold already; yet I must confess you
ought to be kind and civil to me, since I am so kind,
so civil, to you as to bring you this: look you there,
sir.   *Delivers him a letter.* 310

Horn. What is't?

Pinch. Only a love letter, sir.

Horn. From whom?—How! this is from your wife
—hum—and hum—   *Reads.*

Pinch. Even from my wife, sir. Am I not wondrous 315
kind and civil to you now too?—(*Aside*) But you'll
not think her so.

Horn. (*Aside*) Ha! is this a trick of his or hers?

Pinch. The gentleman's surprised I find.—What, you
expected a kinder letter?   320

Horn. No faith, not I, how could I?

Pinch. Yes, yes, I'm sure you did. A man so well
made as you are must needs be disappointed if the
women declare not their passion at first sight or opportunity.   325

Horn. (*Aside*) But what should this mean? Stay,
the postscript.—(*Reads aside*) "Be sure you love me,
whatsoever my husband says to the contrary, and let
him not see this, lest he should come home and pinch
me or kill my squirrel."—It seems he knows not what 330
the letter contains.

Pinch. Come, ne'er wonder at it so much.

Horn. Faith, I can't help it.

Pinch. Now, I think I have deserved your infinite
friendship and kindness, and have showed myself 335
sufficiently an obliging kind friend and husband; am
I not so, to bring a letter from my wife to her gallant?

Horn. Ay, the Devil take me, art thou, the most
obliging, kind friend and husband in the world, ha!
ha!   340

Pinch. Well, you may be merry, sir; but in short I
must tell you, sir, my honor will suffer no jesting.

Horn. What dost thou mean?

Pinch. Does the letter want a comment? Then, know, sir, though I have been so civil a husband as to 345 bring you a letter from my wife, to let you kiss and court her to my face, I will not be a cuckold, sir, I will not.

Horn. Thou art mad with jealousy. I never saw thy wife in my life but at the play yesterday, and I know 350 not if it were she or no. I court her, kiss her!

Pinch. I will not be a cuckold, I say; there will be danger in making me a cuckold.

Horn. Why, wert thou not well cured of thy last clap? 355

Pinch. I wear a sword.

Horn. It should be taken from thee, lest thou shouldst do thyself a mischief with it; thou art mad, man.

Pinch. As mad as I am, and as merry as you are, I 360 must have more reason from you ere we part. I say again, though you kissed and courted last night my wife in man's clothes, as she confesses in her letter—

Horn. (*Aside*) Ha!

Pinch. Both she and I say you must not design it 365 again, for you have mistaken your woman, as you have done your man.

Horn. (*Aside*) O—I understand something now— Was that thy wife! Why wouldst thou not tell me 'twas she? Faith, my freedom with her was your fault, 370 not mine.

Pinch. (*Aside*) Faith, so 'twas.

Horn. Fie! I'd never do't to a woman before her husband's face, sure.

Pinch. But I had rather you should do't to my wife 375 before my face than behind my back; and that you shall never do.

Horn. No—you will hinder me.

Pinch. If I would not hinder you, you see by her letter she would.   380

Horn. Well, I must e'en acquiesce, then, and be contented with what she writes.

Pinch. I'll assure you 'twas voluntarily writ; I had no hand in't, you may believe me.

Horn. I do believe thee, faith.   385

Pinch. And believe her too, for she's an innocent creature, has no dissembling in her. And so fare you well, sir.

Horn. Pray, however, present my humble service to her, and tell her I will obey her letter to a tittle 390 and fulfill her desires, be what they will or with what difficulty soever I do't; and you shall be no more jealous of me, I warrant her and you.

Pinch. Well, then, fare you well; and play with any man's honor but mine, kiss any man's wife but mine, 395 and welcome.   *Exit Mr. Pinchwife.*

Horn. Ha! ha! ha! Doctor.

Quack. It seems he has not heard the report of you or does not believe it.

Horn. Ha! ha!—Now, Doctor, what think you? 400

Quack. Pray let's see the letter—hum—(*Reads the letter*)—"for—dear—love you—"

Horn. I wonder how she could contrive it! What say'st thou to't? 'Tis an original.

Quack. So are your cuckolds, too, originals, for they 405 are like no other common cuckolds, and I will henceforth believe it not impossible for you to cuckold the Grand Seignior amidst his guards of eunuchs, that I say.

Horn. And I say, for the letter, 'tis the first love let- 410 ter that ever was without flames, darts, fates, destinies, lying and dissembling in't.

Enter Sparkish pulling in Mr. Pinchwife.

Spark. Come back, you are a pretty brother-in-law, neither go to church nor to dinner with your sister bride! 415

Pinch. My sister denies her marriage and you see is gone away from you dissatisfied.

Spark. Pshaw! upon a foolish scruple that our parson was not in lawful orders and did not say all the common prayer; but 'tis her modesty only, I believe. 420 But let women be never so modest the first day, they'll be sure to come to themselves by night, and I shall have enough of her then. In the meantime, Harry Horner, you must dine with me. I keep my wedding at my aunt's in the Piazza. 425

Horn. Thy wedding! What stale maid has lived to despair of a husband, or what young one of a gallant?

Spark. O, your servant, sir—this gentleman's sister then,—no stale maid.

Horn. I'm sorry for't. 430

Pinch. (*Aside*) How comes he so concerned for her?

Spark. You sorry for't? Why, do you know any ill by her?

Horn. No, I know none but by thee; 'tis for her sake, not yours, and another man's sake that might have 435 hoped, I thought.

Spark. Another man! another man! What is his name?

Horn. Nay, since 'tis past, he shall be nameless.— (*Aside*) Poor Harcourt! I am sorry thou hast missed 440 her.

Pinch. (*Aside*) He seems to be much troubled at the match.

Spark. Prithee, tell me—Nay, you shan't go, brother.

Pinch. I must of necessity, but I'll come to you to 445
dinner.   *Exit Pinchwife.*

Spark. But, Harry, what, have I a rival in my wife
already? But with all my heart, for he may be of use
to me hereafter; for though my hunger is now my
sauce, and I can fall on heartily without, the time will 450
come when a rival will be as good sauce for a married
man to a wife as an orange to veal.

Horn. O thou damned rogue! Thou hast set my
teeth on edge with thy orange.

Spark. Then let's to dinner—there I was with you 455
again. Come.

Horn. But who dines with thee?

Spark. My friends and relations, my brother Pinchwife, you see, of your acquaintance.

Horn. And his wife?   460

Spark. No, gad, he'll ne'er let her come amongst us
good fellows. Your stingy country coxcomb keeps his
wife from his friends as he does his little firkin of ale
for his own drinking, and a gentleman can't get a
smack on't; but his servants, when his back is turned, 465
broach it at their pleasures and dust it away, ha! ha!
ha!—Gad, I am witty, I think, considering I was married today, by the world; but come—

Horn. No, I will not dine with you unless you can
fetch her too.   470

Spark. Pshaw! What pleasure canst thou have with
women now, Harry?

Horn. My eyes are not gone; I love a good prospect
yet and will not dine with you unless she does too.
Go fetch her, therefore, but do not tell her husband 475
'tis for my sake.

Spark. Well, I'll go try what I can do; in the mean-

---

466. DUST . . . AWAY: drink it up.
482. PALE: fence.

time, come away to my aunt's lodging; 'tis in the way
to Pinchwife's.

Horn. The poor woman has called for aid and 480
stretched forth her hand, Doctor; I cannot but help
her over the pale out of the briers.

Exeunt Sparkish, Horner, Quack.

[Scene IV.] The scene changes to Pinchwife's house.

[*Enter*] *Mrs. Pinchwife alone, leaning on her elbow.
A table, pen, ink, and paper.*

Mrs. Pinch. Well, 'tis e'en so, I have got the London
disease they call love; I am sick of my husband and
for my gallant. I have heard this distemper called a
fever, but methinks 'tis liker an ague; for when I
think of my husband, I tremble and am in a cold 5
sweat and have inclinations to vomit; but when I
think of my gallant, dear Mr. Horner, my hot fit comes
and I am all in a fever indeed; and, as in other fevers,
my own chamber is tedious to me and I would fain
be removed to his, and then methinks I should be 10
well. Ah, poor Mr. Horner! Well, I cannot, will not,
stay here; therefore I'll make an end of my letter to
him, which shall be a finer letter than my last, because I have studied it like anything. O, sick, sick!

Takes the pen and writes.

*Enter Pinchwife, who, seeing her writing, steals softly
behind her, and, looking over her shoulder, snatches
the paper from her.*

Pinch. What, writing more letters? 15
Mrs. Pinch. O Lord, bud, why d'ye fright me so?

She offers to run out; he stops her, and reads.

Pinch. How's this? Nay, you shall not stir, madam:
—"Dear, dear, dear Mr. Horner"—very well—I have

taught you to write letters to good purpose—but let's
see't. "First, I am to beg your pardon for my boldness   20
in writing to you, which I'd have you to know I would
not have done had not you said first you loved me so
extremely, which if you do, you will never suffer me
to lie in the arms of another man whom I loathe,
nauseate, and detest."—Now you can write these filthy   25
words. But what follows?—"Therefore, I hope you
will speedily find some way to free me from this unfortunate match, which was never, I assure you, of
my choice, but I'm afraid 'tis already too far gone;
however, if you love me, as I do you, you will try   30
what you can do; but you must help me away before
tomorrow, or else, alas! I shall be forever out of your
reach, for I can defer no longer our—our—" (*The letter concludes.*) what is to follow "our"?—Speak, what?
Our journey into the country I suppose—O woman,   35
damned woman! and Love, damned Love, their old
tempter! For this is one of his miracles; in a moment
he can make those blind that could see and those see
that were blind, those dumb that could speak and
those prattle who were dumb before; nay, what is   40
more than all, make these dough-baked, senseless,
indocile animals, women, too hard for us, their politic
lords and rulers, in a moment. But make an end of
your letter, and then I'll make an end of you, thus,
and all my plagues together.   *Draws his sword.*   45

Mrs. Pinch. O Lord, O Lord, you are such a passionate man, bud!

Enter Sparkish.

Spark. How now, what's here to do?

Pinch. This fool here now!

Spark. What! drawn upon your wife? You should 50
never do that but at night in the dark, when you can't
hurt her. This is my sister-in-law, is it not? Ay, faith,
e'en our country Margery (*Pulls aside her handker-
chief*); one may know her. Come, she and you must
go dine with me; dinner's ready, come. But where's 55
my wife? Is she not come home yet? Where is she?

Pinch. Making you a cuckold; 'tis that they all do,
as soon as they can.

Spark. What, the wedding day? No, a wife that designs to make a cully of her husband will be sure to 60
let him win the first stake of love, by the world. But
come, they stay dinner for us; come, I'll lead down
our Margery.

Mrs. Pinch. No—sir, go, we'll follow you.

Spark. I will not wag without you. 65

Pinch. (*Aside*) This coxcomb is a sensible torment
to me amidst the greatest in the world.

Spark. Come, come, Madam Margery.

Pinch. No; I'll lead her my way: what, would you
treat your friends with mine, for want of your own 70
wife?—(*Leads her to t'other door, and locks her in
and returns.*) I am contented my rage should take
breath—

Spark. (*Aside*) I told Horner this.

Pinch. Come now. 75

Spark. Lord, how shy you are of your wife! But let
me tell you, brother, we men of wit have amongst us
a saying that cuckolding, like the smallpox, comes
with a fear; and you may keep your wife as much as
you will out of danger of infection, but if her constitu- 80
tion incline her to't, she'll have it sooner or later, by
the world, say they.

Pinch. (*Aside*) What a thing is a cuckold, that
every fool can make him ridiculous!—Well, sir—but

let me advise you, now you are come to be concerned 85
because you suspect the danger, not to neglect the
means to prevent it, especially when the greatest
share of the malady will light upon your own head,
for

Hows'e'er the kind wife's belly comes to swell, 90
The husband breeds for her and first is ill.

[*Exeunt.*]

ACT V

Scene I. Mr. Pinchwife's house.

Enter Mr. Pinchwife and Mrs. Pinchwife.
A table and candle.

Pinch. Come, take the pen and make an end of the
letter, just as you intended; if you are false in a tittle,
I shall soon perceive it and punish you with this as
you deserve.—(*Lays his hand on his sword.*) Write
what was to follow—let's see—"You must make haste   5
and help me away before tomorrow, or else I shall be
forever out of your reach, for I can defer no longer
our"—What follows "our"?

Mrs. Pinch. Must all out, then, bud?—Look you
there, then.   10

       Mrs. Pinchwife takes the pen and writes.

Pinch. Let's see—"For I can defer no longer our—
wedding—Your slighted Alithea."—What's the meaning of this? My sister's name to't? Speak; unriddle.

Mrs. Pinch. Yes, indeed, bud.

Pinch. But why her name to't? Speak—speak, I say. 15

Mrs. Pinch. Ay, but you'll tell her then again. If
you would not tell her again—

Pinch. I will not—I am stunned, my head turns
round.—Speak.

Mrs. Pinch. Won't you tell her, indeed and indeed? 20

Pinch. No; speak, I say.

Mrs. Pinch. She'll be angry with me; but I had
rather she should be angry with me than you, bud;
and, to tell you the truth, 'twas she made me write the
letter and taught me what I should write.   25

Pinch. (*Aside*) Ha! I thought the style was somewhat better than her own.— But how could she come
to you to teach you, since I had locked you up alone?

Mrs. Pinch. O, through the keyhole, bud.

Pinch. But why should she make you write a letter   30
for her to him, since she can write herself?

Mrs. Pinch. Why, she said because—for I was unwilling to do it—

Pinch. Because what—because?

Mrs. Pinch. Because, lest Mr. Horner should be   35
cruel and refuse her; or vain afterwards and show the
letter, she might disown it, the hand not being hers.

Pinch. (*Aside*) How's this? Ha!—then I think I shall
come to myself again. This changeling could not invent this lie; but if she could, why should she? she   40
might think I should soon discover it.—Stay—now I
think on't too, Horner said he was sorry she had married Sparkish; and her disowning her marriage to me
makes me think she has evaded it for Horner's sake.
Yet why should she take this course? But men in love   45
are fools; women may well be so—But hark you,
madam, your sister went out in the morning and I
have not seen her within since.

Mrs. Pinch. Alackaday, she has been crying all day
above, it seems, in a corner.   50

Pinch. Where is she? Let me speak with her.

Mrs. Pinch. (*Aside*) O Lord, then he'll discover all!
— Pray hold, bud; what, d'ye mean to discover me?
She'll know I have told you then. Pray, bud, let me
talk with her first.   55

Pinch. I must speak with her, to know whether
Horner ever made her any promise and whether she
be married to Sparkish or no.

(V.i.)
39. CHANGELING: simpleton.

Mrs. Pinch. Pray, dear bud, don't, till I have spoken with her and told her that I have told you all; for she'll kill me else.   60

Pinch. Go then, and bid her come out to me.

Mrs. Pinch. Yes, yes, bud.

Pinch. Let me see—

Mrs. Pinch. (*Aside*) I'll go, but she is not within to   65
come to him. I have just got time to know of Lucy her maid, who first set me on work, what lie I shall tell next, for I am e'en at my wit's end.

> *Exit Mrs. Pinchwife.*

Pinch. Well, I resolve it, Horner shall have her. I'd rather give him my sister than lend him my wife; and   70
such an alliance will prevent his pretensions to my wife, sure. I'll make him of kin to her, and then he won't care for her.

Mrs. Pinchwife returns.

Mrs. Pinch. O Lord, bud! I told you what anger you would make me with my sister.   75

Pinch. Won't she come hither?

Mrs. Pinch. No, no. Alackaday, she's ashamed to look you in the face; and she says, if you go in to her, she'll run away downstairs and shamefully go herself to Mr. Horner, who has promised her marriage, she   80
says, and she will have no other, so she won't.

Pinch. Did he so?—promise her marriage!—then she shall have no other. Go tell her so; and if she will come and discourse with me a little concerning the means, I will about it immediately. Go.—   85

> *Exit Mrs. Pinchwife.*

His estate is equal to Sparkish's, and his extraction as much better than his as his parts are; but my chief reason is I'd rather be of kin to him by the name of brother-in-law than that of cuckold.

Enter Mrs. Pinchwife.

Well, what says she now?   90

Mrs. Pinch. Why, she says she would only have you
lead her to Horner's lodging, with whom she first will
discourse the matter before she talks with you, which
yet she cannot do; for alack, poor creature, she says
she can't so much as look you in the face, therefore   95
she'll come to you in a mask. And you must excuse
her if she make you no answer to any question of
yours till you have brought her to Mr. Horner; and
if you will not chide her nor question her she'll come
out to you immediately.   100

Pinch. Let her come; I will not speak a word to her
nor require a word from her.

Mrs. Pinch. O, I forgot; besides, she says she cannot look you in the face, though through a mask,
therefore would desire you to put out the candle.   105

Pinch. I agree to all. Let her make haste.—There,
'tis out.   *Puts out the candle. Exit Mrs. Pinchwife.*
My case is something better: I'd rather fight with
Horner for not lying with my sister than for lying with
my wife; and of the two, I had rather find my sister 110
too forward than my wife. I expected no other from
her free education, as she calls it, and her passion
for the town. Well, wife and sister are names which
make us expect love and duty, pleasure and comfort;
but we find 'em plagues and torments, and are equal- 115
ly, though differently, troublesome to their keeper;
for we have as much ado to get people to lie with our
sisters as to keep 'em from lying with our wives.

*Enter Mrs. Pinchwife, masked and in hoods and
scarfs, and a nightgown and petticoat of Alithea's, in
the dark.*

What, are you come, sister? let us go then.—But first, let me lock up my wife. Mrs. Margery, where are 120 you?

Mrs. Pinch. Here, bud.

Pinch. Come hither, that I may lock you up. Get you in.—(*Locks the door.*) Come, sister, where are you now? 125

Mrs. Pinchwife gives him her hand; but when he lets her go, she steals softly on t'other side of him and is led away by him for his sister, Alithea.

[Scene II.] The scene changes to Horner's lodging.

[*Enter*] *Quack, Horner.*

Quack. What, all alone? Not so much as one of your cuckolds here, nor one of their wives! They use to take their turns with you as if they were to watch you.

Horn. Yes, it often happens that a cuckold is but his wife's spy and is more upon family duty when he is 5 with her gallant abroad, hindering his pleasure, than when he is at home with her, playing the gallant. But the hardest duty a married woman imposes upon a lover is keeping her husband company always.

Quack. And his fondness wearies you almost as 10 soon as hers.

Horn. A pox! Keeping a cuckold company after you have had his wife is as tiresome as the company of a country squire to a witty fellow of the town when he has got all his money. 15

Quack. And as at first a man makes a friend of the husband to get the wife, so at last you are fain to fall out with the wife to be rid of the husband.

Horn. Ay, most cuckold-makers are true courtiers; when once a poor man has cracked his credit for 'em, 20 they can't abide to come near him.

Quack. But at first, to draw him in, are so sweet, so kind, so dear! Just as you are to Pinchwife. But what becomes of that intrigue with his wife?

Horn. A pox! He's as surly as an alderman that has been bit; and since he's so coy, his wife's kindness is in vain, for she's a silly innocent. 25

Quack. Did she not send you a letter by him?

Horn. Yes; but that's a riddle I have not yet solved. Allow the poor creature to be willing, she is silly too, and he keeps her up so close— 30

Quack. Yes, so close that he makes her but the more willing and adds but revenge to her love; which two, when met, seldom fail of satisfying each other one way or other. 35

Horn. What! Here's the man we are talking of, I think.

Enter Mr. Pinchwife, leading in his wife, masked, muffled, and in her sister's gown.

Pshaw!

Quack. Bringing his wife to you is the next thing to bringing a love letter from her. 40

Horn. What means this?

Pinch. The last time, you know, sir, I brought you a love letter; now, you see, a mistress. I think you'll say I am a civil man to you.

Horn. Ay, the Devil take me, will I say thou art the 45 civilest man I ever met with; and I have known some. I fancy I understand thee now better than I did the letter. But, hark thee in thy ear—

Pinch. What?

Horn. Nothing but the usual question, man: is she 50 sound, on thy word?

(V.ii.)
54. PAW: improper.

Pinch. What, you take her for a wench and me for a pimp?

Horn. Pshaw! wench and pimp, paw words; I know thou art an honest fellow and hast a great acquaintance among the ladies, and perhaps hast made love for me, rather than let me make love to thy wife.

Pinch. Come, sir; in short, I am for no fooling.

Horn. Nor I neither; therefore, prithee, let's see her face presently. Make her show, man; art thou sure I don't know her?

Pinch. I am sure you do know her.

Horn. A pox! Why dost thou bring her to me then?

Pinch. Because she's a relation of mine—

Horn. Is she, faith, man? Then thou art still more civil and obliging, dear rogue.

Pinch. Who desired me to bring her to you.

Horn. Then she is obliging, dear rogue.

Pinch. You'll make her welcome for my sake, I hope.

Horn. I hope she is handsome enough to make herself welcome. Prithee let her unmask.

Pinch. Do you speak to her; she would never be ruled by me.

Horn. Madam—(*Mrs. Pinchwife whispers to Horner.*) She says she must speak with me in private. Withdraw, prithee.

Pinch. (*Aside*) She's unwilling, it seems, I should know all her undecent conduct in this business.—Well then, I'll leave you together and hope when I am gone, you'll agree; if not, you and I shan't agree, sir.

Horn. What means the fool? If she and I agree, 'tis no matter what you and I do.

> *Whispers to Mrs. Pinchwife, who makes signs with her hand for him to be gone.*

Pinch. In the meantime, I'll fetch a parson, and find out Sparkish and disabuse him. You would have me fetch a parson, would you not? Well then—[*Aside*]

Now I think I am rid of her and shall have no more
trouble with her. Our sisters and daughters, like
usurers' money, are safest when put out; but our
wives, like their writings, never safe but in our closets
under lock and key.   *Exit Mr. Pinchwife.* 90

Enter Boy.

Boy. Sir Jasper Fidget, sir, is coming up.   *Exit.*
Horn. Here's the trouble of a cuckold, now, we are
talking of. A pox on him! Has he not enough to do to
hinder his wife's sport, but he must other women's
too?—Step in here, madam.   *Exit Mrs. Pinchwife.* 95

Enter Sir Jasper.

Sir Jasp. My best and dearest friend.
Horn. (*Aside to Quack*) The old style, Doctor.—
Well, be short, for I am busy. What would your impertinent wife have now?
Sir Jasp. Well guessed, i'faith; for I do come from 100
her.
Horn. To invite me to supper! Tell her, I can't
come: go.
Sir Jasp. Nay, now you are out, faith; for my lady
and the whole knot of the virtuous gang, as they call 105
themselves, are resolved upon a frolic of coming to
you tonight in masquerade, and are all dressed already.
Horn. I shan't be at home.
Sir Jasp. (*Aside*) Lord, how churlish he is to wom- 110
en—Nay, prithee don't disappoint' em; they'll think
'tis my fault: prithee don't. I'll send in the banquet
and the fiddles. But make no noise on't; for the poor
virtuous rogues would not have it known for the

world that they go a-masquerading; and they would 115
come to no man's ball but yours.

Horn. Well, well—get you gone; and tell 'em, if they
come, 'twill be at the peril of their honor and yours.

Sir Jasp. He! he! he!—we'll trust you for that: farewell.   *Exit Sir Jasper.* 120

Horn.   Doctor, anon you too shall be my guest,
            But now I'm going to a private feast.
                                                  Exeunt.

[Scene III.] The scene changes to the Piazza
            of Covent Garden.

[*Enter*] *Sparkish, Pinchwife.*

Spark. (*With the letter in his hand*) But who would
have thought a woman could have been false to me?
By the world, I could not have thought it.

Pinch. You were for giving and taking liberty: she
has taken it only, sir, now you find in that letter. You 5
are a frank person, and so is she, you see there.

Spark. Nay, if this be her hand—for I never saw it.

Pinch. 'Tis no matter whether that be her hand or
no; I am sure this hand, at her desire, led her to Mr.
Horner, with whom I left her just now to go fetch a 10
parson to 'em at their desire too, to deprive you of
her forever; for it seems yours was but a mock marriage.

Spark. Indeed, she would needs have it that 'twas
Harcourt himself, in a parson's habit, that married us; 15
but I'm sure he told me 'twas his brother Ned.

Pinch. O, there 'tis out; and you were deceived, not
she: for you are such a frank person. But I must be
gone.—You'll find her at Mr. Horner's. Go, and believe
your eyes.   *Exit Mr. Pinchwife.* 20

Spark. Nay, I'll to her and call her as many croco-
diles, sirens, harpies, and other heathenish names as
a poet would do a mistress who had refused to hear
his suit, nay more, his verses on her.—But stay, is not
that she following a torch at t'other end of the Piazza? 25
and from Horner's certainly—'tis so.

Enter Alithea, following a torch, and Lucy behind.

You are well met, madam, though you don't think so.
What, you have made a short visit to Mr. Horner!
But I suppose you'll return to him presently; by that
time the parson can be with him.   30

Alith. Mr. Horner and the parson, sir!

Spark. Come, madam, no more dissembling, no
more jilting; for I am no more a frank person.

Alith. How's this?

Lucy. (*Aside*) So, 'twill work, I see.   35

Spark. Could you find out no easy country fool to
abuse? none but me, a gentleman of wit and pleasure
about the town? But it was your pride to be too hard
for a man of parts, unworthy, false woman! false as a
friend that lends a man money to lose; false as dice, 40
who undo those that trust all they have to 'em.

Lucy. (*Aside*) He has been a great bubble, by his
similes, as they say.

Alith. You have been too merry, sir, at your wedding dinner, sure.   45

Spark. What, d'ye mock me too?

Alith. Or you have been deluded.

Spark. By you.

Alith. Let me understand you.

Spark. Have you the confidence—I should call it 50
something else, since you know your guilt—to stand
my just reproaches? You did not write an impudent
letter to Mr. Horner? who I find now has clubbed

with you in deluding me with his aversion for women, that I might not, forsooth, suspect him for my rival.   55

Lucy. (*Aside*) D'ye think the gentleman can be jealous now, madam?

Alith. I write a letter to Mr. Horner!

Spark. Nay, madam, do not deny it. Your brother showed it me just now; and told me likewise he left   60 you at Horner's lodging to fetch a parson to marry you to him: and I wish you joy, madam, joy, joy; and to him, too, much joy; and to myself more joy, for not marrying you.

Alith. (*Aside*) So, I find my brother would break   65 off the match; and I can consent to't, since I see this gentleman can be made jealous.— O Lucy, by his rude usage and jealousy he makes me almost afraid I am married to him. Art thou sure 'twas Harcourt himself, and no parson, that married us?   70

Spark. No, madam, I thank you. I suppose that was a contrivance too of Mr. Horner's and yours, to make Harcourt play the parson; but I would as little as you have him one now, no, not for the world. For shall I tell you another truth? I never had any passion for   75 you till now, for now I hate you. 'Tis true, I might have married your portion, as other men of parts of the town do sometimes: and so, your servant. And to show my unconcernedness, I'll come to your wedding and resign you with as much joy as I would a stale   80 wench to a new cully; nay, with as much joy as I would after the first night, if I had been married to you. There's for you; and so, your servant, servant.

Exit Sparkish.

Alith. How was I deceived in a man!

Lucy. You'll believe, then, a fool may be made jeal-   85 ous now? For that easiness in him that suffers him to be led by a wife will likewise permit him to be persuaded against her by others.

Alith. But marry Mr. Horner! My brother does not
intend it, sure: if I thought he did, I would take thy   90
advice and Mr. Harcourt for my husband. And now I
wish that if there be any overwise woman of the town,
who, like me, would marry a fool for fortune, liberty,
or title, first, that her husband may love play and be
a cully to all the town but her, and suffer none but   95
Fortune to be mistress of his purse; then, if for liberty,
that he may send her into the country under the conduct of some huswifely mother-in-law; and if for title,
may the world give 'em none but that of cuckold.

Lucy. And for her greater curse, madam, may he   100
not deserve it.

Alith. Away, impertinent! Is not this my old Lady
Lanterlu's?

Lucy. Yes, madam.—(*Aside*) And here I hope we
shall find Mr. Harcourt.   105

                                                Exeunt.

[Scene IV.] The scene changes again
to Horner's lodging.

[*Enter*] *Horner, Lady Fidget, Mrs. Dainty Fidget,
Mrs. Squeamish. A table, banquet, and bottles.*

Horn. (*Aside*) A pox! They are come too soon—
before I have sent back my new mistress. All I have
now to do is to lock her in, that they may not see her.

Lady Fid. That we may be sure of our welcome,
we have brought our entertainment with us and are   5
resolved to treat thee, dear toad.

Mrs. Dain. And that we may be merry to purpose,
have left Sir Jasper and my old Lady Squeamish quarreling at home at backgammon.

Mrs. Squeam. Therefore, let us make use of our   10
time, lest they should chance to interrupt us.

Lady Fid. Let us sit, then.

Horn. First, that you may be private, let me lock this door and that, and I'll wait upon you presently.

Lady Fid. No, sir, shut 'em only, and your lips for- 15
ever; for we must trust you as much as our women.

Horn. You know, all vanity's killed in me; I have no occasion for talking.

Lady Fid. Now, ladies, supposing we had drank each of us our two bottles, let us speak the truth of 20
our hearts.

Mrs. Dain. & Mrs. Squeam. Agreed.

Lady Fid. By this brimmer, for truth is nowhere else to be found—(*Aside to Horner*) not in thy heart, false man! 25

Horn. (*Aside to Lady Fidget*) You have found me a true man, I'm sure.

Lady Fid. (*Aside to Horner*) Not every way.—But let us sit and be merry.   *Sings.*

Why should our damned tyrants oblige us to live   30
On the pittance of pleasure which they only give?
             We must not rejoice
             With wine and with noise.
In vain we must wake in a dull bed alone,
Whilst to our warm rival, the bottle, they're gone. 35
             Then lay aside charms,
             And take up these arms.*

'Tis wine only gives 'em their courage and wit;
Because we live sober, to men we submit.
             If for beauties you'd pass,   40
             Take a lick of the glass;
'Twill mend your complexions, and when they are
       gone,

-----
*The glasses.

The best red we have is the red of the grape;
Then, sisters, lay't on,   45
And damn a good shape.

Mrs. Dain. Dear brimmer! Well, in token of our
openness and plain dealing, let us throw our masks
over our heads.

Horn. So, 'twill come to the glasses anon.   50

Mrs. Squeam. Lovely brimmer! Let me enjoy him
first.

Lady Fid. No, I never part with a gallant till I've
tried him. Dear brimmer! that makest our husbands
short-sighted.   55

Mrs. Dain. And our bashful gallants bold.

Mrs. Squeam. And, for want of a gallant, the butler
lovely in our eyes.—Drink, eunuch.

Lady Fid. Drink, thou representative of a husband.
—Damn a husband!   60

Mrs. Dain. And, as it were a husband, an old
keeper.

Mrs. Squeam. And an old grandmother.

Horn. And an English bawd, and a French chirurgeon.   65

Lady Fid. Ay, we have all reason to curse 'em.

Horn. For my sake, ladies?

Lady Fid. No, for our own; for the first spoils all
young gallants' industry.

Mrs. Dain. And the other's art makes 'em bold only   70
with common women.

Mrs. Squeam. And rather run the hazard of the vile
distemper amongst them than of a denial amongst us.

Mrs. Dain. The filthy toads choose mistresses now
as they do stuffs, for having been fancied and worn   75
by others.

Mrs. Squeam. For being common and cheap.

(V.iv.)
85–6. DRUGGETS: fabrics of silk and wool combined.

Lady Fid. Whilst women of quality, like the richest stuffs, lie untumbled and unasked for.

Horn. Ay, neat, and cheap, and new, often they 80 think best.

Mrs. Dain. No, sir, the beasts will be known by a mistress longer than by a suit.

Mrs. Squeam. And 'tis not for cheapness neither.

Lady Fid. No, for the vain fops will take up drug- 85 gets and embroider 'em. But I wonder at the depraved appetites of witty men; they use to be out of the common road and hate imitation. Pray tell me, beast, when you were a man, why you rather chose to club with a multitude in a common house for an 90 entertainment than to be the only guest at a good table.

Horn. Why, faith, ceremony and expectation are unsufferable to those that are sharp bent. People always eat with the best stomach at an ordinary, where 95 every man is snatching for the best bit.

Lady Fid. Though he get a cut over the fingers.— But I have heard people eat most heartily of another man's meat, that is, what they do not pay for.

Horn. When they are sure of their welcome and 100 freedom; for ceremony in love and eating is as ridiculous as in fighting; falling on briskly is all should be done on those occasions.

Lady Fid. Well, then, let me tell you, sir, there is nowhere more freedom than in our houses; and we 105 take freedom from a young person as a sign of good breeding; and a person may be as free as he pleases with us, as frolic, as gamesome, as wild as he will.

Horn. Han't I heard you all declaim against wild men? 110

Lady Fid. Yes; but for all that, we think wildness in a man as desirable a quality as in a duck or rabbit: a tame man! foh!

Horn. I know not, but your reputations frightened me as much as your faces invited me. 115

Lady Fid. Our reputation! Lord, why should you not think that we women make use of our reputation, as you men of yours, only to deceive the world with less suspicion? Our virtue is like the statesman's religion, the Quaker's word, the gamester's oath, and the 120 great man's honor—but to cheat those that trust us.

Mrs. Squeam. And that demureness, coyness, and modesty that you see in our faces in the boxes at plays is as much a sign of a kind woman as a vizard mask in the pit. 125

Mrs. Dain. For, I assure you, women are least masked when they have the velvet vizard on.

Lady Fid. You would have found us modest women in our denials only.

Mrs. Squeam. Our bashfulness is only the reflection 130 of the men's.

Mrs. Dain. We blush when they are shamefaced.

Horn. I beg your pardon, ladies, I was deceived in you devilishly. But why that mighty pretense to honor? 135

Lady Fid. We have told you; but sometimes 'twas for the same reason you men pretend business often, to avoid ill company, to enjoy the better and more privately those you love.

Horn. But why would you ne'er give a friend a 140 wink then?

Lady Fid. Faith, your reputation frightened us as much as ours did you, you were so notoriously lewd.

Horn. And you so seemingly honest.

Lady Fid. Was that all that deterred you? 145

Horn. And so expensive—you allow freedom, you say—

---

144. HONEST: chaste.

Lady Fid. Ay, ay.

Horn. That I was afraid of losing my little money, as well as my little time, both which my other pleas- 150 ures required.

Lady Fid. Money! foh! you talk like a little fellow now. Do such as we expect money?

Horn. I beg your pardon, madam; I must confess, I have heard that great ladies, like great merchants, 155 set but the higher prices upon what they have be- cause they are not in necessity of taking the first offer.

Mrs. Dain. Such as we make sale of our hearts?

Mrs. Squeam. We bribed for our love? foh!

Horn. With your pardon, ladies, I know, like great 160 men in offices, you seem to exact flattery and attend- ance only from your followers; but you have receivers about you and such fees to pay a man is afraid to pass your grants. Besides, we must let you win at cards or we lose your hearts; and if you make an assigna- 165 tion, 'tis at a goldsmith's, jeweler's, or china house, where for your honor you deposit to him he must pawn his to the punctual cit, and so, paying for what you take up, pays for what he takes up.

Mrs. Dain. Would you not have us assured of our 170 gallants' love?

Mrs. Squeam. For love is better known by liberality than by jealousy.

Lady Fid. For one may be dissembled, the other not.—(*Aside*) But my jealousy can be no longer dis- 175 sembled, and they are telling ripe.—Come, here's to our gallants in waiting, whom we must name, and I'll begin. This is my false rogue.

Claps him on the back.

Mrs. Squeam. How!

Horn. So, all will out now.   180

Mrs. Squeam. (*Aside to Horner*) Did you not tell

me 'twas for my sake only you reported yourself no
man?

   Mrs. Dain. (*Aside to Horner*) O wretch! Did you
not swear to me 'twas for my love and honor you 185
passed for that thing you do?

   Horn. So, so.

   Lady Fid. Come, speak, ladies: this is my false
villain.

   Mrs. Squeam. And mine too. 190

   Mrs. Dain. And mine.

   Horn. Well then, you are all three my false rogues
too, and there's an end on't.

   Lady Fid. Well, then, there's no remedy; sister
sharers, let us not fall out but have a care of our 195
honor. Though we get no presents, no jewels of him,
we are savers of our honor, the jewel of most value
and use, which shines yet to the world unsuspected,
though it be counterfeit.

   Horn. Nay, and is e'en as good as if it were true, 200
provided the world think so; for honor, like beauty
now, only depends on the opinion of others.

   Lady Fid. Well, Harry Common, I hope you can be
true to three. Swear—but 'tis to no purpose to require
your oath, for you are as often forsworn as you swear 205
to new women.

   Horn. Come, faith, madam, let us e'en pardon one
another; for all the difference I find betwixt we men
and you women: we forswear ourselves at the begin-
ning of an amour, you as long as it lasts. 210

Enter Sir Jasper Fidget, and Old Lady Squeamish.

   Sir Jasp. O my Lady Fidget, was this your cunning,
to come to Mr. Horner without me? But you have
been nowhere else, I hope.

   Lady Fid. No, Sir Jasper.

Lady Squeam. And you came straight hither, Biddy? 215

Mrs. Squeam. Yes, indeed, lady grandmother.

Sir Jasp. 'Tis well, 'tis well; I knew when once they were thoroughly acquainted with poor Horner they'd ne'er be from him. You may let her masquerade it with my wife and Horner, and I warrant her reputa- 220 tion safe.

Enter Boy.

Boy. O sir, here's the gentleman come whom you bid me not suffer to come up without giving you notice, with a lady too, and other gentlemen.

Horn. Do you all go in there, whilst I send 'em 225 away; and, boy, do you desire 'em to stay below till I come, which shall be immediately.

Exeunt Sir Jasper, Lady Squeamish, Lady Fidget,
Mrs. Dainty, Mrs. Squeamish.

Boy. Yes, sir. *Exit.*

Exit Horner at t'other door, and returns with Mrs.
Pinchwife.

Horn. You would not take my advice to be gone home before your husband came back; he'll now dis- 230 cover all. Yet pray, my dearest, be persuaded to go home, and leave the rest to my management; I'll let you down the back way.

Mrs. Pinch. I don't know the way home, so I don't.

Horn. My man shall wait upon you. 235

Mrs. Pinch. No, don't you believe that I'll go at all; what, are you weary of me already?

Horn. No, my life, 'tis that I may love you long, 'tis to secure my love and your reputation with your husband; he'll never receive you again else. 240

Mrs. Pinch. What care I? D'ye think to frighten me with that? I don't intend to go to him again; you shall be my husband now.

Horn. I cannot be your husband, dearest, since you are married to him. 245

Mrs. Pinch. O, would you make me believe that? Don't I see every day, at London here, women leave their first husbands and go and live with other men as their wives? Pish, pshaw! You'd make me angry, but that I love you so mainly. 250

Horn. So, they are coming up—In again, in, I hear 'em.—(*Exit Mrs. Pinchwife.*) Well, a silly mistress is like a weak place, soon got, soon lost, a man has scarce time for plunder. She betrays her husband first to her gallant, and then her gallant to her husband. 255

Enter Pinchwife, Alithea, Harcourt, Sparkish, Lucy, and a Parson.

Pinch. Come, madam, 'tis not the sudden change of your dress, the confidence of your asseverations, and your false witness there, shall persuade me I did not bring you hither just now. Here's my witness, who cannot deny it, since you must be confronted.— 260 Mr. Horner, did not I bring this lady to you just now?

Horn. (*Aside*) Now must I wrong one woman for another's sake, but that's no new thing with me, for in these cases I am still on the criminal's side against the innocent. 265

Alith. Pray speak, sir.

Horn. (*Aside*) It must be so. I must be impudent and try my luck; impudence uses to be too hard for truth.

Pinch. What, you are studying an evasion or excuse 270 for her! Speak, sir.

Horn. No, faith, I am something backward, only, to speak in women's affairs or disputes.

Pinch. She bids you speak.

Alith. Ah, pray, sir, do: pray satisfy him. 275

Horn. Then truly, you did bring that lady to me just now.

Pinch. Oho!

Alith. How, sir?

Har. How, Horner?   280

Alith. What mean you, sir? I always took you for a man of honor.

Horn. (*Aside*) Ay, so much a man of honor that I must save my mistress, I thank you, come what will on't.   285

Spark. So, if I had had her, she'd have made me believe the moon had been made of a Christmas pie.

Lucy. (*Aside*) Now could I speak, if I durst, and solve the riddle, who am the author of it.

Alith. O unfortunate woman! A combination against 290 my honor! which most concerns me now, because you share in my disgrace, sir, and it is your censure, which I must now suffer, that troubles me, not theirs.

Har. Madam, then have no trouble, you shall now see 'tis possible for me to love too, without being 295 jealous; I will not only believe your innocence myself but make all the world believe it.—(*Apart to Horner*) Horner, I must now be concerned for this lady's honor.

Horn. And I must be concerned for a lady's honor 300 too.

Har. This lady has her honor, and I will protect it.

Horn. My lady has not her honor but has given it me to keep, and I will preserve it.

Har. I understand you not.   305

Horn. I would not have you.

Mrs. Pinch. (*Peeping in behind*) What's the matter with 'em all?

Pinch. Come, come, Mr. Horner, no more disputing. Here's the parson, I brought him not in vain. 310

Har. No, sir, I'll employ him, if this lady please.

Pinch. How! what d'ye mean?

Spark. Ay, what does he mean?

Horn. Why, I have resigned your sister to him; he has my consent. 315

Pinch. But he has not mine, sir. A woman's injured honor, no more than a man's, can be repaired or satisfied by any but him that first wronged it; and you shall marry her presently, or—

Lays his hand on his sword.

Enter to them Mrs. Pinchwife.

Mrs. Pinch. (*Aside*) O Lord, they'll kill poor Mr. 320 Horner! Besides, he shan't marry her whilst I stand by and look on; I'll not lose my second husband so.

Pinch. What do I see?

Alith. My sister in my clothes!

Spark. Ha! 325

Mrs. Pinch. (*To Mr. Pinchwife*) Nay, pray now, don't quarrel about finding work for the parson: he shall marry me to Mr. Horner; for now, I believe, you have enough of me.

Horn. (*Aside*) Damned, damned, loving change- 330 ling!

Mrs. Pinch. Pray, sister, pardon me for telling so many lies of you.

Horn. I suppose the riddle is plain now.

Lucy. No, that must be my work.— Good sir, hear 335 me. *Kneels to Mr. Pinchwife, who stands doggedly with his hat over his eyes.*

Pinch. I will never hear woman again but make 'em all silent thus— *Offers to draw upon his wife.*

Horn. No, that must not be.

Pinch. You, then, shall go first; 'tis all one to me. 340

368. FETCH . . . OFF: rescue.

Offers to draw on Horner; stopped by Harcourt.

Har. Hold!

Enter Sir Jasper Fidget, Lady Fidget, Lady Squeamish, Mrs. Dainty Fidget, Mrs. Squeamish.

Sir Jasp. What's the matter? what's the matter? pray, what's the matter, sir? I beseech you communicate, sir.

Pinch. Why, my wife has communicated, sir, as 345 your wife may have done too, sir, if she knows him, sir.

Sir Jasp. Pshaw, with him! ha! ha! he!

Pinch. D'ye mock me, sir? A cuckold is a kind of a wild beast; have a care, sir. 350

Sir Jasp. No, sure, you mock me, sir. He cuckold you! It can't be, ha! ha! he! why, I'll tell you, sir—

Offers to whisper.

Pinch. I tell you again, he has whored my wife, and yours too, if he knows her, and all the women he comes near. 'Tis not his dissembling, his hypocrisy, 355 can wheedle me.

Sir Jasp. How! Does he dissemble? Is he a hypocrite? Nay, then—how—wife—sister, is he a hypocrite?

Lady Squeam. An hypocrite! a dissembler! Speak, young harlotry, speak, how? 360

Sir Jasp. Nay, then—O my head too!—O thou libidinous lady!

Lady Squeam. O thou harloting harlotry! Hast thou done't then?

Sir Jasp. Speak, good Horner, art thou a dissembler, 365 a rogue? hast thou—

Horn. Soh!

Lucy. (*Apart to Horner*) I'll fetch you off, and her too, if she will but hold her tongue.

Horn. (*Apart to Lucy*) Canst thou? I'll give thee— 370

Lucy. (*To Mr. Pinchwife*) Pray have but patience
to hear me, sir, who am the unfortunate cause of
all this confusion. Your wife is innocent, I only cul-
pable; for I put her upon telling you all these lies
concerning my mistress in order to the breaking off 375
the match between Mr. Sparkish and her, to make
way for Mr. Harcourt.

Spark. Did you so, eternal rotten tooth? Then, it
seems, my mistress was not false to me, I was only
deceived by you. Brother, that should have been, now 380
man of conduct, who is a frank person now, to bring
your wife to her lover, ha?

Lucy. I assure you, sir, she came not to Mr. Horner
out of love, for she loves him no more—

Mrs. Pinch. Hold, I told lies for you, but you shall 385
tell none for me, for I do love Mr. Horner with all my
soul, and nobody shall say me nay; pray, don't you
go to make poor Mr. Horner believe to the contrary;
'tis spitefully done of you, I'm sure.

Horn. (*Aside to Mrs. Pinchwife*) Peace, dear idiot. 390

Mrs. Pinch. Nay, I will not peace.

Pinch. Not till I make you.

Enter Dorilant, Quack.

Dor. Horner, your servant. I am the doctor's guest,
he must excuse our intrusion.

Quack. But what's the matter, gentlemen? For 395
Heaven's sake, what's the matter?

Horn. O, 'tis well you are come. 'Tis a censorious
world we live in. You may have brought me a reprieve, or else I had died for a crime I never committed and these innocent ladies had suffered with 400
me; therefore, pray satisfy these worthy, honorable,
jealous gentlemen that— *Whispers.*

Quack. O, I understand you; is that all?—Sir Jas-

per, by Heavens, and upon the word of a physician,
sir—   *Whispers to Sir Jasper.* 405

Sir Jasp. Nay, I do believe you truly.—Pardon me,
my virtuous lady and dear of honor.

Lady Squeam. What, then all's right again?

Sir Jasp. Ay, ay, and now let us satisfy him too.
              They whisper with Mr. Pinchwife.

Pinch. An eunuch! Pray, no fooling with me. 410

Quack. I'll bring half the chirurgeons in town to
swear it.

Pinch. They!—they'll swear a man that bled to death
through his wounds died of an apoplexy.

Quack. Pray hear me, sir—why, all the town has 415
heard the report of him.

Pinch. But does all the town believe it?

Quack. Pray inquire a little, and, first, of all these.

Pinch. I'm sure, when I left the town, he was the
lewdest fellow in't. 420

Quack. I tell you, sir, he has been in France since;
pray ask but these ladies and gentlemen, your friend
Mr. Dorilant. Gentlemen and ladies, han't you all
heard the late sad report of poor Mr. Horner?

All the Ladies. Ay, ay, ay. 425

Dor. Why, thou jealous fool, dost thou doubt it?
He's an arrant French capon.

Mrs. Pinch. 'Tis false, sir, you shall not disparage
poor Mr. Horner, for to my certain knowledge—

Lucy. O, hold! 430

Mrs. Squeam. (*Aside to Lucy*) Stop her mouth!

Lady Fid. (*To Pinchwife*) Upon my honor, sir, 'tis
as true—

Mrs. Dain. D'ye think we would have been seen in
his company? 435

Mrs. Squeam. Trust our unspotted reputations with
him?

Lady Fid. (*Aside to Horner*) This you get, and we too, by trusting your secret to a fool.

Horn. Peace, madam.—(*Aside to Quack*) Well, 440 Doctor, is not this a good design, that carries a man on unsuspected and brings him off safe?

Pinch. (*Aside*) Well, if this were true—but my wife—   *Dorilant whispers with Mrs. Pinchwife.*

Alith. Come, brother, your wife is yet innocent, 445 you see; but have a care of too strong an imagination, lest, like an overconcerned timorous gamester, by fancying an unlucky cast it should come. Women and Fortune are truest still to those that trust 'em.

Lucy. And any wild thing grows but the more fierce 450 and hungry for being kept up, and more dangerous to the keeper.

Alith. There's doctrine for all husbands, Mr. Harcourt.

Har. I edify, madam, so much, that I am impatient 455 till I am one.

Dor. And I edify so much by example I will never be one.

Spark. And because I will not disparage my parts, I'll ne'er be one.   460

Horn. And I, alas! can't be one.

Pinch. But I must be one—against my will—to a country wife, with a country murrain to me!

Mrs. Pinch. (*Aside*) And I must be a country wife still too, I find; for I can't, like a city one, be rid of 465 my musty husband and do what I list.

Horn. Now, sir, I must pronounce your wife innocent, though I blush whilst I do it; and I am the only man by her now exposed to shame, which I will straight drown in wine, as you shall your suspicion; 470

----

457. EDIFY: am edified.
463. MURRAIN: plague.

and the ladies' troubles we'll divert with a ballad.—
Doctor, where are your maskers?

Lucy. Indeed, she's innocent, sir, I am her witness;
and her end of coming out was but to see her sister's
wedding; and what she has said to your face of her   475
love to Mr. Horner was but the usual innocent revenge on a husband's jealousy—was it not, madam,
speak?

Mrs. Pinch. (*Aside to Lucy and Horner*) Since
you'll have me tell more lies—Yes, indeed, bud.   480

Pinch.

For my own sake fain I would all believe;
Cuckolds, like lovers, should themselves deceive.
But—(*Sighs*) his honor is least safe (too late I
   find)
Who trusts it with a foolish wife or friend.   485

                  A dance of cuckolds.

Horn.

Vain fops but court and dress and keep a
   pother,
To pass for women's men with one another;
But he who aims by women to be prized,
First by the men, you see, must be despised.   490

EPILOGUE

Spoken by Mrs. Knepp [My Lady Fidget]

Now you, the vigorous, who daily here
O'er vizard mask in public domineer,
And what you'd do to her, if in place where;
Nay, have the confidence to cry, "Come out!"
Yet when she says, "Lead on!" you are not stout;   5
But to your well-dressed brother straight turn round
And cry, "Pox on her, Ned, she can't be sound!"
Then slink away, a fresh one to engage,
With so much seeming heat and loving rage,
You'd frighten listening actress on the stage;   10
Till she at last has seen you huffing come,
And talk of keeping in the tiring room,
Yet cannot be provoked to lead her home.
Next, you Falstaffs of fifty, who beset
Your buckram maidenheads, which your friends get;   15
And whilst to them you of achievements boast,
They share the booty and laugh at your cost.
In fine, you essenced boys, both old and young,
Who would be thought so eager, brisk, and strong,
Yet do the ladies, not their husbands, wrong;   20
Whose purses for your manhood make excuse,
And keep your Flanders mares for show, not use;
Encouraged by our woman's man today,
A Horner's part may vainly think to play;
And may intrigues so bashfully disown,   25
That they may doubted be by few or none;
May kiss the cards at picquet, ombre, loo,

(Epilogue)
33. COZENING: cheating.

And so be thought to kiss the lady too;
But, gallants, have a care, faith, what you do.
The world, which to no man his due will give,   30
You by experience know you can deceive;
And men may still believe you vigorous,
But then we women—there's no cozening us.

FINIS

ALL FOR LOVE
or
THE WORLD WELL LOST

A Tragedy by John Dryden

WRITTEN IN IMITATION OF SHAKESPEARE'S STYLE

Facile est verbum aliquod ardens (ut ita dicam)
notare: idque restinctis animorum incendiis irridere.

FACILE . . . IRRIDERE: It is easy to censure some fiery word, so to
speak, and to laugh at it when the fire of passion is extinguished
(Cicero *Orator* viii.27).

The death of Antony and Cleopatra is a subject which has been treated by the greatest wits of our nation, after Shakespeare; and by all so variously that their example has given me the confidence to try myself in this bow of Ulysses amongst the crowd 5 of suitors; and, withal, to take my own measures in aiming at the mark. I doubt not but the same motive has prevailed with all of us in this attempt, I mean the excellency of the moral; for the chief persons represented were famous patterns of unlawful love, 10 and their end accordingly was unfortunate. All reasonable men have long since concluded that the hero of the poem ought not to be a character of perfect virtue, for then he could not, without injustice, be made unhappy; nor yet altogether wicked, be- 15 cause he could not then be pitied. I have therefore steered the middle course and have drawn the character of Antony as favorably as Plutarch, Appian, and Dion Cassius would give me leave; the like I have observed in Cleopatra. That which is wanting 20 to work up the pity to a greater height was not afforded me by the story; for the crimes of love which they both committed were not occasioned by any necessity or fatal ignorance but were wholly voluntary, since our passions are, or ought to be, within 25 our power. The fabric of the play is regular enough, as to the inferior parts of it; and the unities of time, place, and action more exactly observed than, perhaps, the English theatre requires. Particularly, the

---

(Preface)
5. BOW . . . ULYSSES: i.e., like the suitors of Penelope in the *Odyssey*, who were required to attempt the bending of Ulysses' bow. Dryden proposes to show what he can do with a theme attempted by many other writers in emulation of Shakespeare's play.
18, 19. APPIAN . . . DION CASSIUS: both writers on Roman history.

action is so much one that it is the only of the kind   30
without episode or underplot, every scene in the
tragedy conducing to the main design, and every
act concluding with a turn of it. The greatest error
in the contrivance seems to be in the person of
Octavia; for, though I might use the privilege of a   35
poet to introduce her into Alexandria, yet I had not
enough considered that the compassion she moved
to herself and children was destructive to that which
I reserved for Antony and Cleopatra, whose mutual
love, being founded upon vice, must lessen the favor   40
of the audience to them when virtue and innocence
were oppressed by it. And, though I justified Antony
in some measure, by making Octavia's departure to
proceed wholly from herself, yet the force of the
first machine still remained; and the dividing of pity,   45
like the cutting of a river into many channels, abated
the strength of the natural stream. But this is an
objection which none of my critics have urged against
me; and therefore I might have let it pass if I could
have resolved to have been partial to myself. The   50
faults my enemies have found are rather cavils concerning little and not essential decencies, which a
master of the ceremonies may decide betwixt us.
The French poets, I confess, are strict observers of
these punctilios. They would not, for example, have   55
suffered Cleopatra and Octavia to have met; or, if
they had met, there must only have passed betwixt
them some cold civilities but no eagerness of repartee, for fear of offending against the greatness of

---

81–93. NOUS . . . CROIT: We are nothing but ceremony, ceremony
carries us away and we leave the substance of things. We catch hold of
the branches and abandon the trunk and body. We have taught women
to blush at hearing only the name of that which they do not fear to do.
We dare not call our limbs by their right names; and we are not afraid
to use them in all kinds of debauchery. Ceremony prohibits us from
expressing in words permissible and natural things, and we obey it;
reason forbids our doing anything illicit and wicked, and no one obeys
it (Essais, II, 17, "De la presumption").

their characters and the modesty of their sex. This 60
objection I foresaw and at the same time contemned;
for I judged it both natural and probable that Octavia, proud of her new-gained conquest, would
search out Cleopatra to triumph over her; and that
Cleopatra, thus attacked, was not of a spirit to shun 65
the encounter. And 'tis not unlikely that two exas-
perated rivals should use such satire as I have put
into their mouths; for, after all, though the one were
a Roman and the other a queen, they were both
women. 'Tis true, some actions, though natural, are 70
not fit to be represented; and broad obscenities in
words ought in good manners to be avoided: ex-
pressions therefore are a modest clothing of our
thoughts, as breeches and petticoats are of our
bodies. If I have kept myself within the bounds of 75
modesty, all beyond it is but nicety and affectation,
which is no more but modesty depraved into a vice:
they betray themselves who are too quick of apprehension in such cases, and leave all reasonable men
to imagine worse of them than of the poet. 80

Honest Montaigne goes yet farther: *Nous ne
sommes que cérémonie; la cérémonie nous emporte,
et laissons la substance des choses. Nous nous tenons
aux branches, et abandonnons le tronc et le corps.
Nous avons appris aux dames de rougir, oyans seule-* 85
*ment nommer ce qu'elles ne craignent aucunement
à faire. Nous n'osons appeller à droit nos membres,
et ne craignons pas de les employer à toute sorte de
débauche. La cérémonie nous défend d'exprimer
par paroles les choses licites et naturelles, et nous* 90
*l'en croyons; la raison nous défend de n'en faire
point d'illicites et mauvaises, et personne ne l'en
croit.* My comfort is that by this opinion my enemies
are but sucking critics, who would fain be nibbling
ere their teeth are come. 95

Yet, in this nicety of manners does the excellency
of French poetry consist; their heroes are the most
civil people breathing; but their good breeding seldom extends to a word of sense. All their wit is in
their ceremony; they want the genius which ani-   100
mates our stage; and therefore 'tis but necessary,
when they cannot please, that they should take care
not to offend. But as the civilest man in the company is commonly the dullest, so these authors, while
they are afraid to make you laugh or cry, out of   105
pure good manners make you sleep. They are so
careful not to exasperate a critic that they never
leave him any work; so busy with the broom, and
make so clean a riddance, that there is little left
either for censure or for praise: for no part of a   110
poem is worth our discommending where the whole
is insipid; as when we have once tasted of palled
wine, we stay not to examine it glass by glass. But
while they affect to shine in trifles, they are often
careless in essentials. Thus, their Hippolytus is so   115
scrupulous in point of decency that he will rather
expose himself to death than accuse his stepmother
to his father; and my critics, I am sure, will commend him for it: but we of grosser apprehensions
are apt to think that this excess of generosity is not   120
practicable but with fools and madmen. This was
good manners with a vengeance; and the audience
is like to be much concerned at the misfortunes of
this admirable hero: but take Hippolytus out of his
poetic fit and I suppose he would think it a wiser   125
part to set the saddle on the right horse and choose
rather to live with the reputation of a plain-spoken,
honest man than to die with the infamy of an in-

115. THEIR HIPPOLYTUS: referring to the character in Racine's *Phèdre*
(1677).
126. SET . . . HORSE; i.e., place the guilt where it belongs.
140. CHEDREUX: a fashionable peruke-maker; i.e., affected.

cestuous villain. In the meantime, we may take notice that where the poet ought to have preserved 130
the character as it was delivered to us by antiquity,
when he should have given us the picture of a rough
young man, of the Amazonian strain, a jolly hunts-
man, and both by his profession and his early rising a mortal enemy to love, he has chosen to give 135
him the turn of gallantry, sent him to travel from
Athens to Paris, taught him to make love, and trans-
formed the Hippolytus of Euripides into Monsieur
Hippolyte. I should not have troubled myself thus
far with French poets but that I find our *Chedreux* 140
critics wholly form their judgments by them. But
for my part, I desire to be tried by the laws of my
own country; for it seems unjust to me that the
French should prescribe here till they have conquered. Our little sonneteers who follow them have 145
too narrow souls to judge of poetry. Poets themselves are the most proper, though I conclude not
the only, critics. But till some genius as universal as
Aristotle shall arise, one who can penetrate into all
arts and sciences without the practice of them, I shall 150
think it reasonable that the judgment of an artificer
in his own art should be preferable to the opinion
of another man; at least where he is not bribed by
interest or prejudiced by malice. And this, I suppose,
is manifest by plain induction: for, first, the crowd 155
cannot be presumed to have more than a gross instinct of what pleases or displeases them. Every man
will grant me this; but then, by a particular kindness to himself, he draws his own stake first and will
be distinguished from the multitude, of which other 160
men may think him one. But, if I come closer to
those who are allowed for witty men, either by the
advantage of their quality or by common fame, and

affirm that neither are they qualified to decide sov-
ereignly concerning poetry, I shall yet have a strong   165
party of my opinion; for most of them severally
will exclude the rest, either from the number of witty
men or at least of able judges. But here again they
are all indulgent to themselves; and everyone who
believes himself a wit, that is, every man, will pre-   170
tend at the same time to a right of judging. But to
press it yet farther, there are many witty men but
few poets; neither have all poets a taste of tragedy.
And this is the rock on which they are daily split-
ting. Poetry, which is a picture of Nature, must gen-   175
erally please; but 'tis not to be understood that all
parts of it must please every man; therefore is not
tragedy to be judged by a witty man whose taste is
only confined to comedy. Nor is every man who loves
tragedy a sufficient judge of it: he must understand   180
the excellencies of it too, or he will only prove a
blind admirer, not a critic. From hence it comes that
so many satires on poets and censures of their writings fly abroad. Men of pleasant conversation (at
least esteemed so) and endued with a trifling kind   185
of fancy, perhaps helped out with some smattering
of Latin, are ambitious to distinguish themselves from
the herd of gentlemen by their poetry

> *Rarus enim ferme sensus communis in illa*
> *Fortuna*   190

And is not this a wretched affectation, not to be
contented with what Fortune has done for them
and sit down quietly with their estates, but they
must call their wits in question and needlessly ex-

189–90. Rarus . . . Fortuna: Juvenal *Sat.* viii.73, 74. Dryden translated: "We seldom find much sense with an exalted fortune joined."
   209–10. no . . . condition: Horace *Sat.* i.1.1-3.
   222. Dionysius: Dionysius the Elder, Tyrant of Syracuse, 430-367,
who competed for the prize for tragedy at Athens.

pose their nakedness to public view? not consider- 195
ing that they are not to expect the same approbation
from sober men which they have found from their
flatterers after the third bottle? If a little glittering
in discourse has passed them on us for witty men,
where was the necessity of undeceiving the world? 200
Would a man who has an ill title to an estate, but
yet is in possession of it, would he bring it of his
own accord to be tried at Westminster? We who
write, if we want the talent yet have the excuse that
we do it for a poor subsistence; but what can be 205
urged in their defense who, not having the vocation
of poverty to scribble, out of mere wantonness take
pains to make themselves ridiculous? Horace was
certainly in the right where he said that no man is
satisfied with his own condition. A poet is not pleased 210
because he is not rich; and the rich are discontented
because the poets will not admit them of their number. Thus the case is hard with writers: if they succeed not, they must starve; and if they do, some
malicious satire is prepared to level them for daring 215
to please without their leave. But while they are so
eager to destroy the fame of others, their ambition
is manifest in their concernment: some poem of their
own is to be produced, and the slaves are to be laid
flat with their faces on the ground, that the monarch 220
may appear in the greater majesty.

Dionysius and Nero had the same longings, but
with all their power they could never bring their
business well about. 'Tis true, they proclaimed themselves poets by sound of trumpet; and poets they 225
were, upon pain of death to any man who durst
call them otherwise. The audience had a fine time
on't, you may imagine; they sate in a bodily fear
and looked as demurely as they could: for 'twas a
hanging matter to laugh unseasonably; and the ty- 230

rants were suspicious, as they had reason, that their subjects had 'em in the wind; so every man, in his own defense, set as good a face upon the business as he could. 'Twas known beforehand that the monarchs were to be crowned laureates; but when the show was over and an honest man was suffered to depart quietly, he took out his laughter which he had stifled, with a firm resolution never more to see an emperor's play, though he had been ten years a-making it. In the meantime, the true poets were they who made the best markets, for they had wit enough to yield the prize with a good grace and not contend with him who had thirty legions. They were sure to be rewarded if they confessed themselves bad writers, and that was somewhat better than to be martyrs for their reputation. Lucan's example was enough to teach them manners; and after he was put to death for overcoming Nero, the Emperor carried it without dispute for the best poet in his dominions. No man was ambitious of that grinning honor; for if he heard the malicious trumpeter proclaiming his name before his betters, he knew there was but one way with him. Maecenas took another course, and we know he was more than a great man, for he was witty too: but finding himself far gone in poetry, which Seneca assures us was not his talent, he thought it his best way to be well with Vergil and with Horace, that at least he might be a poet at the second hand; and we see how happily it has succeeded

235

240

245

250

255

232. IN THE WIND: i.e., in an exposed position.
250. GRINNING HONOR: cf. Falstaff's contempt for the dead Sir Walter Blunt (*1 Henry IV*, Act V, Sc. iii, 65).
256. SENECA: see *Epis.* cxiv.4–6.
275. CRISPINUS: a philosopher of the Stoic school, ridiculed by Horace in several of his *Satires*, here identified by Dryden with the unnamed bore Horace describes in *Sat.* i.9.
279–80. DEMETRI . . . CATHEDRAS: Demetrius, and you Tigellius, I bid you wail among the armchairs of your pupils.
286–87. SAXUM . . . ARVIS: *Aeneid* xii.897–98. Dryden translated the lines: "An antique stone he saw, the common bound/Of neighb'ring fields, and barriers of the ground."

with him, for his own bad poetry is forgotten and 260
their panegyrics of him still remain. But they who
should be our patrons are for no such expensive ways
to fame; they have much of the poetry of Maecenas
but little of his liberality. They are for persecuting
Horace and Vergil, in the persons of their successors 265
(for such is every man who has any part of their soul
and fire, though in a less degree). Some of their little
zanies yet go farther; for they are persecutors even of
Horace himself, as far as they are able, by their
ignorant and vile imitations of him; by making an 270
unjust use of his authority and turning his artillery
against his friends. But how would he disdain to be
copied by such hands! I dare answer for him he
would be more uneasy in their company than he
was with Crispinus, their forefather, in the Holy 275
Way; and would no more have allowed them a place
amongst the critics than he would Demetrius the
mimic and Tigellius the buffoon;

> *Demetri, teque, Tigelli,*
> *discipulorum inter iubeo plorare cathedras.* 280

With what scorn would he look down on such miserable translators, who make doggerel of his Latin,
mistake his meaning, misapply his censures, and often
contradict their own? He is fixed as a landmark to
set out the bound of poetry, 285

> *Saxum antiquum ingens,*
> *limes agro positus, litem ut discerneret arvis.*

But other arms than theirs, and other sinews, are
required to raise the weight of such an author; and
when they would toss him against their enemies, 290

Genua labant, gelidus concrevit frigore sanguis,
tum lapis ipse viri vacuum per inane volutus,
nec spatium evasit totum, nec pertulit ictum.

For my part, I would wish no other revenge, either
for myself or the rest of the poets, from this rhyming 295
judge of the twelvepenny gallery, this legitimate son
of Sternhold, than that he would subscribe his name
to his censure, or (not to tax him beyond his learning) set his mark: for, should he own himself pub-
licly and come from behind the lion's skin, they 300
whom he condemns would be thankful to him, they
whom he praises would choose to be condemned, and
the magistrates whom he has elected would modestly withdraw from their employment to avoid the
scandal of his nomination. The sharpness of his satire, 305
next to himself, falls most heavily on his friends,
and they ought never to forgive him for commending
them perpetually the wrong way, and sometimes by
contraries. If he have a friend whose hastiness in
writing is his greatest fault, Horace would have 310
taught him to have minced the matter and to have
called it readiness of thought and a flowing fancy;
for friendship will allow a man to christen an imper-
fection by the name of some neighbor virtue:

291–93. GENUA . . . ICTUM: *Aeneid* xii.905-7. Dryden translated:
"His knocking knees are bent beneath the load,/And shiv'ring cold con-
geals his vital blood./The stone drops from his arms, and, falling
short/For want of vigor, mocks his vain effort."

297. STERNHOLD: Thomas Sternhold, referring to his sorry rhymes
in the English version of the Psalms that he prepared with John Hopkins.

315–16. VELLEM . . . HONESTUM: Horace *Sat.* i.3.41-2: I wish that
we erred thus out of friendship and that virtue gave an honorable name
to that error.

320–23. CANIBUS . . . VIOLENTIUS: Juvenal *Sat.* viii.34-7: Lazy dogs,
hairless from long-standing mange, and licking the edges of a drained
oil-lamp, their name shall be pard, tiger, lion, or whatever rages more
violently on the earth.

326–28. NIGRA . . .: Lucretius *De natura rerum* iv.1160, 1164.
Dryden's own translation: "The sallow skin is for the swarthy put,/And
love can make a slattern of a slut; . . . She stammers; O what grace in
lisping lies!/If she says nothing, to be sure she's wise."

329. AD AETHIOPEM CYGNUM: Juvenal *Sat.* viii.33: to the point of
calling a Negro a swan.

Vellem in amicitia sic erraremus; et isti 315
errori nomen virtus posuisset honestum.

But he would never have allowed him to have called
a slow man hasty or a hasty writer a slow drudge,
as Juvenal explains it:

Canibus pigris, scabieque vetusta 320
levibus, et siccae lambentibus ora lucernae,
nomen erit pardus, tigris, leo; si quid adhuc est
quod fremit in terris violentius.

Yet Lucretius laughs at a foolish lover, even for
excusing the imperfections of his mistress: 325

Nigra μελίχροος *est, immunda et foetida* ἄκοσμος.
Balba loqui non quit, τραυλίζει; *muta pudens est,*
etc.

But to drive it *ad Aethiopem cygnum* is not to be
endured. I leave him to interpret this by the benefit 330
of his French version on the other side, and without
farther considering him than I have the rest of my
illiterate censors, whom I have disdained to answer
because they are not qualified for judges. It remains
that I acquaint the reader that I have endeavored 335
in this play to follow the practice of the ancients,
who, as Mr. Rymer has judiciously observed, are and
ought to be our masters. Horace likewise gives it for
a rule in his art of poetry.

Vos exemplaria Graeca 340
nocturna versate manu, versate diurna.

Yet, though their models are regular, they are too
little for English tragedy, which requires to be built

in a larger compass. I could give an instance in the
Oedipus Tyrannus, which was the masterpiece of 345
Sophocles; but I reserve it for a more fit occasion,
which I hope to have hereafter. In my style, I have
professed to imitate the divine Shakespeare; which
that I might perform more freely I have disencumbered myself from rhyme. Not that I condemn my 350
former way, but that this is more proper to my
present purpose. I hope I need not to explain myself,
that I have not copied my author servilely—words
and phrases must of necessity receive a change in
succeeding ages—but 'tis almost a miracle that much 355
of his language remains so pure; and that he who began dramatic poetry amongst us, untaught by any,
and as Ben Jonson tells us, without learning, should
by the force of his own genius perform so much that
in a manner he has left no praise for any who come 360
after him. The occasion is fair, and the subject would
be pleasant, to handle the difference of styles betwixt him and Fletcher, and wherein and how far
they are both to be imitated. But since I must not
be overconfident of my own performance after him, 365
it will be prudence in me to be silent. Yet I hope I
may affirm, and without vanity, that by imitating him
I have excelled myself throughout the play; and particularly, that I prefer the scene betwixt Antony and
Ventidius in the first act to anything which I have 370
written in this kind.

(Prologue)
12. BATES . . . METTLE: abates in spirit.
16. TONIES: pun on Antony's name and a slang term for "simple-
tons."

PROLOGUE

What flocks of critics hover here today,
As vultures wait on armies for their prey,
All gaping for the carcass of a play!
With croaking notes they bode some dire event,
And follow dying poets by the scent.   5
Ours gives himself for gone; y' have watched your
    time!
He fights this day unarmed, without his rhyme,
And brings a tale which often has been told,
As sad as Dido's, and almost as old.   10
His hero, whom you wits his bully call,
Bates of his mettle and scarce rants at all:
He's somewhat lewd but a well-meaning mind;
Weeps much; fights little; but is wondrous kind.
In short, a pattern and companion fit   15
For all the keeping Tonies of the pit.
I could name more: a wife and mistress too;
Both (to be plain) too good for most of you:
The wife well-natured and the mistress true.

Now, poets, if your fame has been his care,   20
Allow him all the candor you can spare.
A brave man scorns to quarrel once a day;
Like Hectors, in at every petty fray.
Let those find fault whose wit's so very small
They've need to show that they can think at all: 25
Errors like straws upon the surface flow;

151

He who would search for pearls must dive below.
Fops may have leave to level all they can,
As pygmies would be glad to lop a man.
Half-wits are fleas, so little and so light,   30
We scarce could know they live but that they bite.
But, as the rich, when tired with daily feasts,
For change, become their next poor tenant's guests;
Drink hearty draughts of ale from plain brown bowls,
And snatch the homely rasher from the coals: 35
So you, retiring from much better cheer,
For once may venture to do penance here.
And since that plenteous autumn now is past
Whose grapes and peaches have indulged your taste,
Take in good part, from our poor poet's board,   40
Such riveled fruits as winter can afford.

---

41. RIVELED: shriveled.

Persons Represented

	By
Mark Antony.	Mr. Hart.
Ventidius, his general.	Mr. Mohun.
Dolabella, his friend.	Mr. Clarke.
Alexas, the Queen's eunuch.	Mr. Goodman.
Serapion, priest of Isis.	Mr. Griffin.
[*Myris,*] another priest.	Mr. Coysh.
Servants to *Antony.*	
Cleopatra, Queen of Egypt.	Mrs. Boutell.
Octavia, Antony's wife.	Mrs. Corey.

Charmion,
Iras, } Cleopatra's maids.

Antony's two little daughters.

SCENE: *Alexandria.*

ACT I

Scene: The Temple of Isis.

Enter Serapion, Myris, priests of Isis.

Serap. Portents and prodigies are grown so frequent
That they have lost their name. Our fruitful Nile
Flowed ere the wonted season, with a torrent
So unexpected and so wondrous fierce
That the wild deluge overtook the haste   5
Ev'n of the hinds that watched it: men and beasts
Were borne above the tops of trees that grew
On th' utmost margin of the watermark.
Then, with so swift an ebb the flood drove backward,
It slipt from underneath the scaly herd.   10
Here monstrous phocae panted on the shore;
Forsaken dolphins there, with their broad tails,
Lay lashing the departing waves; hard by 'em,
Seahorses, flound'ring in the slimy mud,
Tossed up their heads and dashed the ooze about 'em.   15

Enter Alexas behind them.

Myr. Avert these omens, Heav'n!
Serap. Last night, between the hours of twelve and
        one,
In a lone aisle o' th' temple while I walked,
A whirlwind rose that, with a violent blast,   20

(I)
2. LOST . . . NAME: ceased to seem marvelous.
6. HINDS: slaves.
10. SCALY HERD: i.e., fish inhabiting the river.
11. PHOCAE: seals.
14. SEAHORSES: hippopotamuses.

155

Shook all the dome; the doors around me clapt;
The iron wicket that defends the vault
Where the long race of Ptolemies is laid
Burst open and disclosed the mighty dead.
From out each monument, in order placed,   25
An armed ghost start up; the boy-king last
Reared his inglorious head. A peal of groans
Then followed, and a lamentable voice
Cried, "Egypt is no more!" My blood ran back,
My shaking knees against each other knocked;   30
On the cold pavement down I fell entranced,
And so unfinished left the horrid scene.
     Alex. (*Showing himself*) And dreamed you this? or
          did invent the story
To frighten our Egyptian boys withal,   35
And train 'em up betimes in fear of priesthood?
     Serap. My Lord, I saw you not,
Nor meant my words should reach your ears; but
          what
I uttered was most true.   40
     Alex.   A foolish dream,
Bred from the fumes of indigested feasts
And holy luxury.
     Serap.   I know my duty:
This goes no farther.   45
     Alex.   'Tis not fit it should;
Nor would the times now bear it, were it true.
All southern, from yon hills, the Roman camp
Hangs o'er us black and threat'ning, like a storm
Just breaking on our heads.   50
     Serap. Our faint Egyptians pray for Antony;
But in their servile hearts they own Octavius.
     Myr. Why then does Antony dream out his hours,

------

26. START: started; BOY-KING: Ptolemy, the deceased brother and husband of Cleopatra.

And tempts not Fortune for a noble day
Which might redeem what Actium lost?   55
   Alex. He thinks 'tis past recovery.
   Serap.   Yet the foe
Seems not to press the siege.
   Alex.   O, there's the wonder.
Maecenas and Agrippa, who can most   60
With Caesar, are his foes. His wife Octavia,
Driv'n from his house, solicits her revenge;
And Dolabella, who was once his friend,
Upon some private grudge now seeks his ruin:
Yet still war seems on either side to sleep.   65
   Serap. 'Tis strange that Antony for some days past
Has not beheld the face of Cleopatra;
But here in Isis' temple lives retired
And makes his heart a prey to black despair.
   Alex. 'Tis true; and we much fear he hopes by ab-   70
     sence
To cure his mind of love.
   Serap.   If he be vanquished,
Or make his peace, Egypt is doomed to be
A Roman province; and our plenteous harvests   75
Must then redeem the scarceness of their soil.
While Antony stood firm, our Alexandria
Rivaled proud Rome (dominion's other seat),
And Fortune, striding like a vast Colossus,
Could fix an equal foot of empire here.   80
   Alex. Had I my wish, these tyrants of all nature
Who lord it o'er mankind should perish—perish,
Each by the other's sword; but, since our will
Is lamely followed by our pow'r, we must
Depend on one, with him to rise or fall.   85
   Serap. How stands the Queen affected?
   Alex.   O, she dotes,
She dotes, Serapion, on this vanquished man,
And winds herself about his mighty ruins,

Whom would she yet forsake, yet yield him up,   90
This hunted prey, to his pursuers' hands,
She might preserve us all; but 'tis in vain—
This changes my designs, this blasts my counsels,
And makes me use all means to keep him here,
Whom I could wish divided from her arms   95
Far as the earth's deep center. Well, you know
The state of things; no more of your ill omens
And black prognostics; labor to confirm
The people's hearts.

Enter Ventidius, talking aside with a gentleman
of Antony's.

  Serap.   These Romans will o'erhear us.   100
But who's that stranger? By his warlike port,
His fierce demeanor and erected look,
He's of no vulgar note.
  Alex.   O, 'tis Ventidius,
Our emp'ror's great lieutenant in the East,   105
Who first showed Rome that Parthia could be con-
          quered.
When Antony returned from Syria last,
He left this man to guard the Roman frontiers.
  Serap. You seem to know him well.   110
  Alex. Too well. I saw him in Cilicia first,
When Cleopatra there met Antony:
A mortal foe he was to us and Egypt.
But, let me witness to the worth I hate,
A braver Roman never drew a sword;   115
Firm to his prince, but as a friend, not slave.
He ne'er was of his pleasures, but presides
O'er all his cooler hours and morning counsels:

---

102. ERECTED LOOK: upright carriage.
134. THOUGHT: melancholy.

In short, the plainness, fierceness, rugged virtue
Of an old true-stamped Roman lives in him.   120
His coming bodes I know not what of ill
To our affairs. Withdraw, to mark him better;
And I'll acquaint you why I sought you here,
And what's our present work.

They withdraw to a corner of the stage; and Ventid-
  ius, with the other, comes forward to the front.

 Vent.   Not see him, say you? 125
I say I must and will.
 Gent.   He has commanded,
On pain of death, none should approach his presence.
 Vent. I bring him news will raise his drooping spirits,
Give him new life.   130
 Gent.   He sees not Cleopatra.
 Vent. Would he had never seen her!
 Gent. He eats not, drinks not, sleeps not, has no use
Of anything but thought; or, if he talks,
'Tis to himself, and then 'tis perfect raving: 135
Then he defies the world and bids it pass;
Sometimes he gnaws his lip and curses loud
The boy Octavius; then he draws his mouth
Into a scornful smile and cries, "Take all,
The world's not worth my care."   140
 Vent.   Just, just his nature.
Virtue's his path, but sometimes 'tis too narrow
For his vast soul, and then he starts out wide
And bounds into a vice that bears him far
From his first course and plunges him in ills: 145
But, when his danger makes him find his fault,
Quick to observe, and full of sharp remorse,
He censures eagerly his own misdeeds,
Judging himself with malice to himself,
And not forgiving what as man he did 150
Because his other parts are more than man.

He must not thus be lost.

                Alexas and the Priests come forward.

  Alex. You have your full instructions, now advance;
Proclaim your orders loudly.

  Serap. Romans, Egyptians, hear the Queen's com- 155
mand.
Thus Cleopatra bids: "Let labor cease;
To pomp and triumphs give this happy day
That gave the world a lord: 'tis Antony's."
Live, Antony; and Cleopatra live!   160
Be this the general voice sent up to Heav'n,
And every public place repeat this echo.

  Vent. (*Aside*) Fine pageantry!

  Serap.   Set out before your doors
The images of all your sleeping fathers,   165
With laurels crowned; with laurels wreathe your posts,
And strew with flow'rs the pavement; let the priests
Do present sacrifice; pour out the wine,
And call the gods to join with you in gladness.

  Vent. Curse on the tongue that bids this general joy! 170
Can they be friends of Antony who revel
When Antony's in danger? Hide, for shame,
You Romans, your great grandsires' images,
For fear their souls should animate their marbles,
To blush at their degenerate progeny.   175

  Alex. A love which knows no bounds to Antony
Would mark the day with honors when all Heaven
Labored for him, when each propitious star
Stood wakeful in his orb to watch that hour
And shed his better influence. Her own birthday   180
Our queen neglected, like a vulgar fate
That passed obscurely by.

  Vent.   Would it had slept,
Divided far from his, till some remote

---

181. VULGAR FATE: ordinary happening.
216. ENGINE: instrument.

And future age had called it out, to ruin   185
Some other prince, not him.
   Alex.   Your emperor,
Though grown unkind, would be more gentle than
T' upbraid my queen for loving him too well.
   Vent. Does the mute sacrifice upbraid the priest?   190
He knows him not his executioner.
O, she has decked his ruin with her love,
Led him in golden bands to gaudy slaughter
And made perdition pleasing; she has left him
The blank of what he was;   195
I tell thee, eunuch, she has quite unmanned him.
Can any Roman see and know him now,
Thus altered from the lord of half mankind,
Unbent, unsinewed, made a woman's toy,
Shrunk from the vast extent of all his honors,   200
And cramped within a corner of the world?
O Antony!
Thou bravest soldier, and thou best of friends!
Bounteous as nature; next to nature's god!
Couldst thou but make new worlds, so wouldst thou   205
    give 'em,
As bounty were thy being: rough in battle,
As the first Romans when they went to war;
Yet, after victory, more pitiful
Than all their praying virgins left at home!   210
   Alex. Would you could add, to those more shining
    virtues,
His truth to her who loves him.
   Vent.   Would I could not!
But wherefore waste I precious hours with thee?   215
Thou art her darling mischief, her chief engine,
Antony's other fate. Go tell thy queen
Ventidius is arrived, to end her charms.
Let your Egyptian timbrels play alone;
Nor mix effeminate sounds with Roman trumpets.   220

You dare not fight for Antony; go pray,
And keep your cowards' holy day in temples.
                              Exeunt Alexas, Serapion.

Enter [a second] gentleman of Mark Antony.

2. Gent. The emperor approaches, and commands,
On pain of death, that none presume to stay.
1. Gent. I dare not disobey him.   225
                              Going out with the other.
Vent.   Well, I dare.
But I'll observe him first unseen and find
Which way his humor drives: the rest I'll venture.
                              Withdraws.

*Enter Antony, walking with a disturbed motion
              before he speaks.*

Ant. They tell me 'tis my birthday, and I'll keep it
With double pomp of sadness.   230
'Tis what the day deserves which gave me breath.
Why was I raised the meteor of the world,
Hung in the skies, and blazing as I traveled
Till all my fires were spent, and then cast downward
To be trod out by Caesar?   235
Vent. (*Aside*)   On my soul,
'Tis mournful, wondrous mournful!
Ant.   Count thy gains.
Now, Antony, wouldst thou be born for this?
Glutton of fortune, thy devouring youth   240
Has starved thy wanting age.
Vent. (*Aside*)   How sorrow shakes him!
So, now the tempest tears him up by th' roots,
And on the ground extends the noble ruin.

---
262. COMMONER . . . NATURE: citizen of the wilderness.

Ant. (*Having thrown himself down*) Lie there, thou   245
    shadow of an emperor;
The place thou pressest on thy mother earth
Is all thy empire now: now it contains thee;
Some few days hence and then 'twill be too large,
When thou'rt contracted in thy narrow urn,   250
Shrunk to a few cold ashes; then Octavia
(For Cleopatra will not live to see it),
Octavia then will have thee all her own,
And bear thee in her widowed hand to Caesar;
Caesar will weep, the crocodile will weep,   255
To see his rival of the universe
Lie still and peaceful there. I'll think no more on't.
Give me some music; look that it be sad:
I'll soothe my melancholy till I swell
And burst myself with sighing.   *Soft music.*   260
'Tis somewhat to my humor. Stay, I fancy
I'm now turned wild, a commoner of nature,
Of all forsaken and forsaking all;
Live in a shady forest's sylvan scene;
Stretched at my length beneath some blasted oak,   265
I lean my head upon the mossy bark,
And look just of a piece as I grew from it:
My uncombed locks, matted like mistletoe,
Hang o'er my hoary face; a murm'ring brook
Runs at my foot.   270
    Vent.   Methinks I fancy
Myself there too.
    Ant.   The herd come jumping by me,
And, fearless, quench their thirst while I look on,
And take me for their fellow-citizen.   275
More of this image, more; it lulls my thoughts.
                  Soft music again.
    Vent. I must disturb him; I can hold no longer.
                  Stands before him.
    Ant. (*Starting up*) Art thou Ventidius?

Vent.   Are you Antony?
I'm liker what I was than you to him   280
I left you last.
    Ant.   I'm angry.
    Vent.   So am I.
    Ant. I would be private; leave me.
    Vent.   Sir, I love you,   285
And therefore will not leave you.
    Ant.   Will not leave me!
Where have you learnt that answer? Who am I?
    Vent. My emperor; the man I love next Heaven:
If I said more, I think 'twere scarce a sin;   290
Y'are all that's good and good-like.
    Ant.   All that's wretched.
You will not leave me then?
    Vent.   'Twas too presuming
To say I would not; but I dare not leave you: 295
And 'tis unkind in you to chide me hence
So soon when I so far have come to see you.
    Ant. Now thou hast seen me, art thou satisfied?
For, if a friend, thou hast beheld enough;
And, if a foe, too much.   300
    Vent. (*Weeping*) Look, Emperor, this is no com-
        mon dew.
I have not wept this forty year; but now
My mother comes afresh into my eyes;
I cannot help her softness.   305
    Ant. By Heav'n, he weeps, poor, good old man, he
        weeps!
The big round drops course one another down
The furrows of his cheeks. Stop 'em, Ventidius,
Or I shall blush to death: they set my shame,   310
That caused 'em, full before me.
    Vent.   I'll do my best.
    Ant. Sure there's contagion in the tears of friends:
See, I have caught it too. Believe me, 'tis not

For my own griefs, but thine.—Nay, father.   315
   Vent.   Emperor.
   Ant. Emperor! Why, that's the style of victory;
The conqu'ring soldier, red with unfelt wounds,
Salutes his general so; but never more
Shall that sound reach my ears.   320
   Vent.   I warrant you.
   Ant. Actium, Actium! O!—
   Vent.   It sits too near you.
   Ant. Here, here it lies; a lump of lead by day,
And, in my short, distracted, nightly slumbers,   325
The hag that rides my dreams—
   Vent. Out with it; give it vent.
   Ant.   Urge not my shame.
I lost a battle.
   Vent.   So has Julius done.   330
   Ant. Thou favor'st me and speak'st not half thou
    think'st;
For Julius fought it out and lost it fairly;
But Antony—
   Vent.   Nay, stop not.   335
   Ant.   Antony,
(Well, thou wilt have it) like a coward, fled,
Fled while his soldiers fought; fled first, Ventidius.
Thou long'st to curse me, and I give thee leave.
I know thou camest prepared to rail.   340
   Vent.   I did.
   Ant. I'll help thee. I have been a man, Ventidius—
   Vent. Yes, and a brave one; but—
   Ant.   I know thy meaning.
But I have lost my reason, have disgraced   345
The name of soldier with inglorious ease.
In the full vintage of my flowing honors
Sat still and saw it pressed by other hands.
Fortune came smiling to my youth and wooed it,
And purple greatness met my ripened years.   350

When first I came to empire, I was borne
On tides of people, crowding to my triumphs,
The wish of nations; and the willing world
Received me as its pledge of future peace;
I was so great, so happy, so beloved,   355
Fate could not ruin me; till I took pains
And worked against my Fortune, chid her from me
And turned her loose; yet still she came again.
My careless days and my luxurious nights
At length have wearied her, and now she's gone,   360
Gone, gone, divorced forever. Help me, soldier,
To curse this madman, this industrious fool,
Who labored to be wretched: prithee curse me.

 Vent. No.

 Ant.   Why?   365

 Vent.   You are too sensible already
Of what y'have done, too conscious of your failings;
And, like a scorpion, whipped by others first
To fury, sting yourself in mad revenge.
I would bring balm and pour it in your wounds,   370
Cure your distempered mind and heal your fortunes.

 Ant. I know thou wouldst.

 Vent.   I will.

 Ant.   Ha, ha, ha, ha!

 Vent. You laugh.   375

 Ant.   I do, to see officious love
Give cordials to the dead.

 Vent.   You would be lost, then?

 Ant. I am.

 Vent.   I say you are not. Try your fortune.   380

 Ant. I have, to th' utmost. Dost thou think me desperate

---

377. CORDIALS: tonics.
390. TULLY: Marcus Tullius Cicero, who opposed Antony and was killed by Antony's order.
402. MARCHES: borders.
404. CHOPPED: chapped.

Without just cause? No, when I found all lost
Beyond repair, I hid me from the world
And learned to scorn it here; which now I do   385
So heartily I think it is not worth
The cost of keeping.
   Vent.   Caesar thinks not so;
He'll thank you for the gift he could not take.
You would be killed like Tully, would you? Do,   390
Hold out your throat to Caesar and die tamely.
   Ant. No, I can kill myself; and so resolve.
   Vent. I can die with you too, when time shall serve,
But fortune calls upon us now to live,
To fight, to conquer.   395
   Ant.   Sure thou dream'st, Ventidius.
   Vent. No; 'tis you dream; you sleep away your hours
In desperate sloth, miscalled philosophy.
Up, up, for honor's sake; twelve legions wait you
And long to call you chief; by painful journeys   400
I led 'em, patient both of heat and hunger,
Down from the Parthian marches to the Nile.
'Twill do you good to see their sunburnt faces,
Their scarred cheeks and chopped hands; there's vir-
    tue in 'em.   405
They'll sell those mangled limbs at dearer rates
Than yon trim bands can buy.
   Ant.   Where left you them?
   Vent. I said in Lower Syria.
   Ant.   Bring 'em hither;   410
There may be life in these.
   Vent.   They will not come.
   Ant. Why didst thou mock my hopes with promised
    aids,
To double my despair? They're mutinous.   415
   Vent. Most firm and loyal.
   Ant.   Yet they will not march
To succor me. O trifler!

Vent.   They petition
You would make haste to head 'em.   420
  Ant.   I'm besieged.
  Vent. There's but one way shut up: how came I
    hither?
  Ant. I will not stir.
  Vent.   They would perhaps desire   425
A better reason.
  Ant.   I have never used
My soldiers to demand a reason of
My actions. Why did they refuse to march?
  Vent. They said they would not fight for Cleopatra. 430
  Ant. What was't they said?
  Vent. They said they would not fight for Cleopatra.
Why should they fight, indeed, to make her conquer
And make you more a slave? to gain you kingdoms,
Which, for a kiss, at your next midnight feast,   435
You'll sell to her? Then she new-names her jewels,
And calls this diamond such or such a tax;
Each pendant in her ear shall be a province.
  Ant. Ventidius, I allow your tongue free license
On all my other faults; but, on your life,   440
No word of Cleopatra: she deserves
More worlds than I can lose.
  Vent.   Behold, you pow'rs,
To whom you have entrusted humankind;
See Europe, Afric, Asia, put in balance,   445
And all weighed down by one light, worthless woman!
I think the gods are Antonys and give,
Like prodigals, this nether world away
To none but wasteful hands.
  Ant.   You grow presumptuous.   450
  Vent. I take the privilege of plain love to speak.
  Ant. Plain love! Plain arrogance, plain insolence!

---

427. USED: accustomed.

Thy men are cowards; thou an envious traitor,
Who under seeming honesty hast vented
The burden of thy rank, o'erflowing gall.   455
O that thou wert my equal, great in arms
As the first Caesar was, that I might kill thee
Without a stain to honor!
 Vent.   You may kill me;
You have done more already—called me traitor.   460
 Ant. Art thou not one?
 Vent.   For showing you yourself,
Which none else durst have done? But had I been
That name, which I disdain to speak again,
I needed not have sought your abject fortunes,   465
Come to partake your fate, to die with you.
What hindered me t' have led my conqu'ring eagles
To fill Octavius's bands? I could have been
A traitor then, a glorious, happy traitor,
And not have been so called.   470
 Ant.   Forgive me, soldier:
I've been too passionate.
 Vent.   You thought me false;
Thought my old age betrayed you. Kill me, sir;
Pray, kill me; yet you need not, your unkindness   475
Has left your sword no work.
 Ant.   I did not think so;
I said it in my rage: prithee forgive me.
Why didst thou tempt my anger by discovery
Of what I would not hear?   480
 Vent.   No prince but you
Could merit that sincerity I used,
Nor durst another man have ventured it;
But you, ere love misled your wand'ring eyes,
Were sure the chief and best of human race,   485
Framed in the very pride and boast of nature,
So perfect that the gods who formed you wondered
At their own skill and cried, "A lucky hit

Has mended our design." Their envy hindered,
Else you had been immortal and a pattern,   490
When Heav'n would work for ostentation sake,
To copy out again.
    Ant.   But Cleopatra—
Go on; for I can bear it now.
    Vent.   No more.   495
    Ant. Thou dar'st not trust my passion, but thou
        may'st;
Thou only lov'st, the rest have flattered me.
    Vent. Heav'n's blessing on your heart for that kind
        word!   500
May I believe you love me? Speak again.
    Ant. Indeed I do. Speak this, and this, and this.
                                        Hugging him.

Thy praises were unjust; but I'll deserve 'em
And yet mend all. Do with me what thou wilt;
Lead me to victory, thou know'st the way.   505
    Vent. And will you leave this—
    Ant.   Prithee, do not curse her,
And I will leave her; though, Heav'n knows, I love
Beyond life, conquest, empire, all but honor;
But I will leave her.   510
    Vent.   That's my royal master;
And shall we fight?
    Ant.   I warrant thee, old soldier,
Thou shalt behold me once again in iron
And, at the head of our old troops that beat   515
The Parthians, cry aloud, "Come, follow me!"
    Vent. O, now I hear my Emperor! In that word
        Octavius fell.
Gods, let me see that day,
And, if I have ten years behind, take all;   520
I'll thank you for th' exchange.
    Ant.   O Cleopatra!
    Vent. Again?

Ant.   I've done: in that last sigh, she went.
Caesar shall know what 'tis to force a lover   525
From all he holds most dear.
     Vent.   Methinks you breathe
Another soul: your looks are more divine;
You speak a hero, and you move a god.
     Ant. O, thou hast fired me; my soul's up in arms   530
And mans each part about me. Once again
That noble eagerness of fight has seized me;
That eagerness with which I darted upward
To Cassius' camp; in vain the steepy hill
Opposed my way; in vain a war of spears   535
Sung round my head and planted all my shield;
I won the trenches while my foremost men
Lagged on the plain below.
     Vent.   Ye gods, ye gods,
For such another hour!   540
     Ant.   Come on, my soldier!
Our hearts and arms are still the same: I long
Once more to meet our foes, that thou and I,
Like Time and Death, marching before our troops,
May taste fate to 'em; mow 'em out a passage,   545
     And, ent'ring where the foremost squadrons yield,
     Begin the noble harvest of the field.
                              Exeunt.

ACT II

[*Enter*] *Cleopatra, Iras, and Alexas.*

Cleo. What shall I do, or whither shall I turn?
Ventidius has o'ercome, and he will go.
  Alex. He goes to fight for you.
  Cleo. Then he would see me, ere he went to fight.
Flatter me not: if once he goes, he's lost   5
And all my hopes destroyed.
  Alex.   Does this weak passion
Become a mighty queen?
  Cleo.   I am no queen:
Is this to be a queen, to be besieged   10
By yon insulting Roman and to wait
Each hour the victor's chain? These ills are small:
For Antony is lost, and I can mourn
For nothing else but him. Now come, Octavius,
I have no more to lose; prepare thy bands;   15
I'm fit to be a captive: Antony
Has taught my mind the fortune of a slave.
  Iras. Call reason to assist you.
  Cleo.   I have none,
And none would have: my love's a noble madness, 20
Which shows the cause deserved it. Moderate sorrow
Fits vulgar love and for a vulgar man:
But I have loved with such transcendent passion
I soared, at first, quite out of reason's view
And now am lost above it. No, I'm proud   25
'Tis thus: would Antony could see me now!

Think you he would not sigh? Though he must leave
    me,
Sure he would sigh; for he is noble-natured
And bears a tender heart: I know him well.   30
Ah, no, I know him not; I knew him once,
But now 'tis past.
    Iras.   Let it be past with you:
Forget him, madam.
    Cleo.   Never, never, Iras.   35
He once was mine; and once, though now 'tis gone,
Leaves a faint image of possession still.
    Alex. Think him unconstant, cruel, and ungrateful.
    Cleo. I cannot: if I could, those thoughts were vain.
Faithless, ungrateful, cruel though he be,   40
I still must love him.

Enter Charmion.

                Now, what news, my Charmion?
Will he be kind? and will he not forsake me?
Am I to live or die?—nay, do I live?
Or am I dead? For when he gave his answer,   45
Fate took the word and then I lived or died.
    Char. I found him, madam—
    Cleo.   A long speech preparing?
If thou bring'st comfort, haste and give it me,
For never was more need.   50
    Iras.   I know he loves you.
    Cleo. Had he been kind, her eyes had told me so
Before her tongue could speak it: now she studies,
To soften what he said; but give me death,
Just as he sent it, Charmion, undisguised,   55
And in the words he spoke.
    Char.   I found him, then,
Encompassed round, I think, with iron statues,
So mute, so motionless his soldiers stood,

While awfully he cast his eyes about   60
And ev'ry leader's hopes or fears surveyed:
Methought he looked resolved and yet not pleased.
When he beheld me struggling in the crowd,
He blushed and bade make way.
  Alex.   There's comfort yet.   65
  Char. Ventidius fixed his eyes upon my passage
Severely, as he meant to frown me back,
And sullenly gave place: I told my message,
Just as you gave it, broken and disordered;
I numbered in it all your sighs and tears,   70
And while I moved your pitiful request
That you but only begged a last farewell,
He fetched an inward groan and, ev'ry time
I named you, sighed as if his heart were breaking,
But shunned my eyes and guiltily looked down.   75
He seemed not now that awful Antony
Who shook an armed assembly with his nod;
But, making show as he would rub his eyes,
Disguised and blotted out a falling tear.
  Cleo. Did he then weep? and was I worth a tear?   80
If what thou hast to say be not as pleasing,
Tell me no more but let me die contented.
  Char. He bid me say he knew himself so well
He could deny you nothing if he saw you;
And therefore—   85
  Cleo.   Thou wouldst say, he would not see me?
  Char. And therefore begged you not to use a power
Which he could ill resist; yet he should ever
Respect you as he ought.   90
  Cleo.   Is that a word
For Antony to use to Cleopatra?
O that faint word "respect"! How I disdain it!

Disdain myself for loving after it!
He should have kept that word for cold Octavia.   95
Respect is for a wife. Am I that thing,
That dull, insipid lump, without desires,
And without pow'r to give 'em?
   Alex.   You misjudge;
You see through love and that deludes your sight,   100
As what is straight seems crooked through the water;
But I, who bear my reason undisturbed,
Can see this Antony, this dreaded man,
A fearful slave, who fain would run away
And shuns his master's eyes: if you pursue him,   105
My life on't, he still drags a chain along
That needs must clog his flight.
   Cleo.   Could I believe thee!—
   Alex. By ev'ry circumstance I know he loves.
True, he's hard pressed by int'rest and by honor;   110
Yet he but doubts and parleys and casts out
Many a long look for succor.
   Cleo.   He sends word
He fears to see my face.
   Alex.   And would you more?   115
He shows his weakness who declines the combat,
And you must urge your fortune. Could he speak
More plainly? To my ears, the message sounds
"Come to my rescue, Cleopatra, come;
Come, free me from Ventidius, from my tyrant: 120
See me and give me a pretense to leave him!"
I hear his trumpets. This way he must pass.
Please you, retire a while; I'll work him first,
That he may bend more easy.
   Cleo.   You shall rule me;   125
But all, I fear, in vain.   *Exit with Charmion and Iras.*
   Alex.   I fear so too;
Though I concealed my thoughts to make her bold;

But 'tis our utmost means, and Fate befriend it!
                                   Withdraws.

   Enter Lictors with fasces, one bearing the eagle:
   then enter Antony with Ventidius, followed by
              other Commanders.

  Ant. Octavius is the minion of blind chance,   130
But holds from virtue nothing.
  Vent.   Has he courage?
  Ant. But just enough to season him from coward.
O, 'tis the coldest youth upon a charge,
The most deliberate fighter! If he ventures   135
(As in Illyria once they say he did
To storm a town), 'tis when he cannot choose,
When all the world have fixed their eyes upon him,
And then he lives on that for seven years after;
But at a close revenge he never fails.   140
  Vent. I heard you challenged him.
  Ant.   I did, Ventidius.
What think'st thou was his answer? 'Twas so tame!
He said he had more ways than one to die;
I had not.   145
  Vent.   Poor!
  Ant.   He has more ways than one;
But he would choose 'em all before that one.
  Vent. He first would choose an ague or a fever.
  Ant. No; it must be an ague, not a fever;   150
He has not warmth enough to die by that.
  Vent. Or old age and a bed.
  Ant.   Ay, there's his choice,
He would live, like a lamp, to the last wink,
And crawl upon the utmost verge of life.   155

---

130. MINION: favorite.
133. SEASON: modulate.
135. DELIBERATE: circumspect.
140. CLOSE: secret; private.

O Hercules! Why should a man like this,
Who dares not trust his fate for one great action,
Be all the care of Heav'n? Why should he lord it
O'er fourscore thousand men of whom each one
Is braver than himself?   160
  Vent.   You conquered for him:
Philippi knows it; there you shared with him
That empire which your sword made all your own.
  Ant. Fool that I was, upon my eagle's wings
I bore this wren till I was tired with soaring,   165
And now he mounts above me.
Good Heav'ns, is this, is this the man who braves me?
Who bids my age make way, drives me before him
To the world's ridge, and sweeps me off like rubbish?
  Vent. Sir, we lose time; the troops are mounted all. 170
  Ant. Then give the word to march:
I long to leave this prison of a town,
To join thy legions, and in open field
Once more to show my face. Lead, my deliverer.

Enter Alexas.

  Alex. Great Emperor,   175
In mighty arms renowned above mankind,
But in soft pity to th' oppressed a god,
This message sends the mournful Cleopatra
To her departing lord.
  Vent.   Smooth sycophant!   180
  Alex. A thousand wishes, and ten thousand prayers,
Millions of blessings wait you to the wars;
Millions of sighs and tears she sends you too,
And would have sent
As many dear embraces to your arms,   185
As many parting kisses to your lips;
But those, she fears, have wearied you already.
  Vent. (*Aside*) False crocodile!

  Alex. And yet she begs not now you would not leave
     her;   190
That were a wish too mighty for her hopes,
Too presuming for her low fortune and your ebbing
     love;
That were a wish for her more prosp'rous days,
Her blooming beauty and your growing kindness.   195
  Ant. (*Aside*) Well, I must man it out!—What would
     the Queen?
  Alex. First, to these noble warriors who attend
Your daring courage in the chase of fame
(Too daring, and too dang'rous for her quiet),   200
She humbly recommends all she holds dear,
All her own cares and fears—the care of you.
  Vent. Yes, witness Actium.
  Ant.   Let him speak, Ventidius.
  Alex. You, when his matchless valor bears him for-   205
     ward
With ardor too heroic on his foes,
Fall down, as she would do, before his feet;
Lie in his way and stop the paths of death.
Tell him, this god is not invulnerable;   210
That absent Cleopatra bleeds in him;
And, that you may remember her petition,
She begs you wear these trifles, as a pawn
Which, at your wished return, she will redeem
                    Gives jewels to the Commanders.
With all the wealth of Egypt: 215
This to the great Ventidius she presents,
Whom she can never count her enemy
Because he loves her lord.
  Vent.   Tell her I'll none on't;
I'm not ashamed of honest poverty: 220
Not all the diamonds of the East can bribe
Ventidius from his faith. I hope to see
These, and the rest of all her sparkling store,

Where they shall more deservingly be placed.
 Ant. And who must wear 'em then?   225
 Vent.   The wronged Octavia.
 Ant. You might have spared that word.
 Vent.   And he that bribe.
 Ant. But have I no remembrance?
 Alex.   Yes, a dear one: 230
Your slave the Queen—
 Ant.   My mistress.
 Alex.   Then your mistress;
Your mistress would, she says, have sent her soul,
But that you had long since; she humbly begs 235
This ruby bracelet, set with bleeding hearts
(The emblems of her own), may bind your arm.
        Presenting a bracelet.
 Vent. Now, my best lord, in honor's name I ask you,
For manhood's sake, and for your own dear safety,
Touch not these poisoned gifts,   240
Infected by the sender; touch 'em not;
Myriads of bluest plagues lie underneath 'em,
And more than aconite has dipped the silk.
 Ant. Nay, now you grow too cynical, Ventidius:
A lady's favors may be worn with honor. 245
What, to refuse her bracelet! On my soul,
When I lie pensive in my tent alone,
'Twill pass the wakeful hours of winter nights
To tell these pretty beads upon my arm,
To count for every one a soft embrace, 250
A melting kiss at such and such a time,
And now and then the fury of her love,
When—And what harm's in this?
 Alex.   None, none, my lord,
But what's to her that now 'tis past forever. 255
 Ant. (*Going to tie it*) We soldiers are so awkward—
  help me tie it.
 Alex. In faith, my lord, we courtiers too are awkward

In these affairs: so are all men indeed;
Ev'n I, who am not one. But shall I speak?   260
  Ant. Yes, freely.
  Alex.   Then, my lord, fair hands alone
Are fit to tie it; she who sent it can.
  Vent. Hell, death! This eunuch pander ruins you.
You will not see her?   265

        Alexas whispers an Attendant, who goes out.

  Ant.   But to take my leave.
  Vent. Then I have washed an Ethiope. Y'are undone;
Y'are in the toils; y'are taken; y'are destroyed:
Her eyes do Caesar's work.
  Ant.   You fear too soon.   270
I'm constant to myself; I know my strength;
And yet she shall not think me barbarous neither,
Born in the depths of Afric: I'm a Roman,
Bred to the rules of soft humanity.
A guest, and kindly used, should bid farewell.   275
  Vent. You do not know
How weak you are to her, how much an infant:
You are not proof against a smile or glance;
A sigh will quite disarm you.
  Ant.   See, she comes!   280
Now you shall find your error. Gods, I thank you:
I formed the danger greater than it was,
And now 'tis near, 'tis lessened.
  Vent.   Mark the end yet.

        Enter Cleopatra, Charmion, and Iras.

  Ant. Well, madam, we are met.   285
  Cleo.   Is this a meeting?
Then, we must part?

---

267. WASHED . . . ETHIOPE: attempted a hopeless task (proverbial
idea).
284. MARK THE END: wait and see the conclusion.

 Ant.   We must.

 Cleo.   Who says we must?

 Ant. Our own hard fates.   290

 Cleo.   We make those fates ourselves.

 Ant. Yes, we have made 'em; we have loved each other

Into our mutual ruin.

 Cleo. The gods have seen my joys with envious 295 eyes;

I have no friends in Heav'n; and all the world,

(As 'twere the bus'ness of mankind to part us)

Is armed against my love: ev'n you yourself

Join with the rest; you, you are armed against me. 300

 Ant. I will be justified in all I do

To late posterity, and therefore hear me.

If I mix a lie

With any truth, reproach me freely with it;

Else, favor me with silence.   305

 Cleo.   You command me

And I am dumb.

 Vent. I like this well: he shows authority.

 Ant. That I derive my ruin

From you alone—   310

 Cleo.   O Heav'ns! I ruin you!

 Ant. You promised me your silence, and you break it

Ere I have scarce begun.

 Cleo.   Well, I obey you. 315

 Ant. When I beheld you first, it was in Egypt,

Ere Caesar saw your eyes; you gave me love,

And were too young to know it; that I settled

Your father in his throne was for your sake;

I left th' acknowledgment for time to ripen. 320

Caesar stepped in and with a greedy hand

Plucked the green fruit, ere the first blush of red,

Yet cleaving to the bough. He was my lord,

And was, beside, too great for me to rival;
But I deserved you first, though he enjoyed you.   325
When, after, I beheld you in Cilicia,
An enemy to Rome, I pardoned you.
   Cleo. I cleared myself—
   Ant.   Again you break your promise.
I loved you still and took your weak excuses,   330
Took you into my bosom, stained by Caesar,
And not half mine. I went to Egypt with you,
And hid me from the bus'ness of the world,
Shut out inquiring nations from my sight,
To give whole years to you.   335
   Vent. (*Aside*) Yes, to your shame be't spoken.
   Ant.   How I loved,
Witness, ye days and nights and all your hours,
That danced away with down upon your feet,
As all your bus'ness were to count my passion!   340
One day passed by and nothing saw but love;
Another came and still 'twas only love:
The suns were wearied out with looking on
And I untired with loving.
I saw you ev'ry day and all the day;   345
And ev'ry day was still but as the first,
So eager was I still to see you more.
   Vent. 'Tis all too true.
   Ant.   Fulvia, my wife, grew jealous,
As she indeed had reason; raised a war   350
In Italy, to call me back.
   Vent.   But yet
You went not.
   Ant.   While within your arms I lay,
The world fell mold'ring from my hands each hour,   355
And left me scarce a grasp (I thank your love for't).
   Vent. Well pushed: that last was home.
   Cleo.   Yet may I speak?
   Ant. If I have urged a falsehood, yes; else, not.

Your silence says I have not. Fulvia died,   360
(Pardon, you gods; with my unkindness died);
To set the world at peace, I took Octavia,
This Caesar's sister; in her pride of youth
And flow'r of beauty did I wed that lady,
Whom blushing I must praise, because I left her.   365
You called; my love obeyed the fatal summons:
This raised the Roman arms; the cause was yours.
I would have fought by land, where I was stronger;
You hindered it: yet, when I fought at sea,
Forsook me fighting; and (O stain to honor!   370
O lasting shame!) I knew not that I fled,
But fled to follow you.

   Vent. What haste she made to hoist her purple sails!
And, to appear magnificent in flight,
Drew half our strength away.   375

   Ant.   All this you caused,
And would you multiply more ruins on me?
This honest man, my best, my only friend,
Has gathered up the shipwrack of my fortunes;
Twelve legions I have left, my last recruits,   380
And you have watched the news and bring your eyes
To seize them too. If you have aught to answer,
Now speak, you have free leave.

   Alex. (*Aside*)   She stands confounded:
Despair is in her eyes.   385

   Vent. Now lay a sigh i' th' way to stop his passage:
Prepare a tear and bid it for his legions;
'Tis like they shall be sold.

   Cleo. How shall I plead my cause, when you, my
       judge,   390
Already have condemned me? Shall I bring
The love you bore me for my advocate?
That now is turned against me, that destroys me;
For love, once past, is, at the best, forgotten;
But oft'ner sours to hate: 'twill please my lord   395

To ruin me, and therefore I'll be guilty.
But could I once have thought it would have pleased
   you
That you would pry with narrow searching eyes
Into my faults, severe to my destruction,   400
And watching all advantages with care
That serve to make me wretched? Speak, my lord,
For I end here. Though I deserve this usage,
Was it like you to give it?
   Ant.   O, you wrong me   405
To think I sought this parting or desired
To accuse you more than what will clear myself
And justify this breach.
   Cleo.   Thus low I thank you.
And since my innocence will not offend   410
I shall not blush to own it.
   Vent.   After this,
I think she'll blush at nothing.
   Cleo.   You seem grieved
(And therein you are kind) that Caesar first   415
Enjoyed my love, though you deserved it better;
I grieve for that, my lord, much more than you;
For had I first been yours it would have saved
My second choice: I never had been his,
And ne'er had been but yours. But Caesar first,   420
You say, possessed my love. Not so, my lord:
He first possessed my person, you, my love:
Caesar loved me; but I loved Antony.
If I endured him after, 'twas because
I judged it due to the first name of men;   425
And, half constrained, I gave, as to a tyrant,
What he would take by force.
   Vent.   O siren! siren!
Yet grant that all the love she boasts were true,
Has she not ruined you? I still urge that,   430
The fatal consequence.

Cleo.   The consequence indeed,
For I dare challenge him, my greatest foe,
To say it was designed: 'tis true, I loved you,
And kept you far from an uneasy wife—   435
Such Fulvia was.
Yes, but he'll say you left Octavia for me,
And can you blame me to receive that love
Which quitted such desert for worthless me?
How often have I wished some other Caesar,   440
Great as the first, and as the second young,
Would court my love, to be refused for you!

    Vent. Words, words; but Actium, sir, remember
      Actium.

    Cleo. Ev'n there, I dare his malice. True, I coun- 445
      seled
To fight at sea; but I betrayed you not.
I fled, but not to the enemy. 'Twas fear;
Would I had been a man, not to have feared!
For none would then have envied me your friendship, 450
Who envy me your love.

    Ant.   We're both unhappy:
If nothing else, yet our ill fortune parts us.
Speak; would you have me perish by my stay?

    Cleo. If as a friend you ask my judgment, go;   455
If as a lover, stay. If you must perish—
'Tis a hard word—but stay.

    Vent. See now th' effects of her so boasted love!
She strives to drag you down to ruin with her:
But could she 'scape without you, O how soon   460
Would she let go her hold and haste to shore,
And never look behind!

    Cleo. Then judge my love by this.

                           Giving Antony a writing.
                           Could I have borne
A life or death, a happiness or woe,   465
From yours divided, this had giv'n me means.

Ant. By Hercules, the writing of Octavius!
I know it well: 'tis that proscribing hand,
Young as it was, that led the way to mine
And left me but the second place in murder.— 470
See, see, Ventidius! here he offers Egypt,
And joins all Syria to it, as a present,
So, in requital, she forsake my fortunes
And join her arms with his.

    Cleo.   And yet you leave me! 475
You leave me, Antony; and yet I love you,
Indeed I do: I have refused a kingdom—
That's a trifle:
For I could part with life, with anything,
But only you. O, let me die but with you! 480
Is that a hard request?

    Ant.   Next living with you,
'Tis all that Heav'n can give.

    Alex. (*Aside*)   He melts; we conquer.

    Cleo. No, you shall go; your int'rest calls you hence; 485
Yes, your dear interest pulls too strong, for these
Weak arms to hold you here.—   *Takes his hand.*
        Go; leave me, soldier
(For you're no more a lover); leave me dying:
Push me all pale and panting from your bosom, 490
And when your march begins let one run after,
Breathless almost for joy, and cry, "She's dead."
The soldiers shout; you then, perhaps, may sigh
And muster all your Roman gravity:
Ventidius chides; and straight your brow clears up, 495
As I had never been.

    Ant.   Gods, 'tis too much,
Too much for man to bear!

    Cleo.   What is't for me, then,
A weak, forsaken woman and a lover? 500
Here let me breathe my last: envy me not
This minute in your arms: I'll die apace,

As fast as e'er I can, and end your trouble.

   Ant. Die! Rather let me perish: loosened nature
Leap from its hinges! Sink the props of Heav'n,   505
And fall the skies to crush the nether world!
My eyes, my soul, my all!—   *Embraces her.*
   Vent.   And what's this toy,
In balance with your fortune, honor, fame?
   Ant. What is't, Ventidius?—it outweighs 'em all;   510
Why, we have more than conquered Caesar now:
My queen's not only innocent but loves me.
This, this is she who drags me down to ruin!
"But could she 'scape without me with what haste
Would she let slip her hold and make to shore,   515
And never look behind!"
Down on thy knees, blasphemer as thou art,
And ask forgiveness of wronged innocence.
   Vent. I'll rather die than take it. Will you go?
   Ant. Go! whither? Go from all that's excellent?   520
Faith, honor, virtue, all good things forbid
That I should go from her who sets my love
Above the price of kingdoms. Give, you gods,
Give to your boy, your Caesar,
This rattle of a globe to play withal,   525
This gewgaw world, and put him cheaply off:
I'll not be pleased with less than Cleopatra.
   Cleo. She's wholly yours. My heart's so full of joy
That I shall do some wild extravagance
Of love in public; and the foolish world,   530
Which knows not tenderness, will think me mad.
   Vent. O women! women! women! All the gods
Have not such pow'r of doing good to man
As you of doing harm.   *Exit.*
   Ant.   Our men are armed.   535
Unbar the gate that looks to Caesar's camp;
I would revenge the treachery he meant me,
And long security makes conquest easy.

I'm eager to return before I go;
For all the pleasures I have known beat thick   540
On my remembrance. How I long for night!
     That both the sweets of mutual love may try,
     And once triumph o'er Caesar ere we die.

                                        Exeunt.

(III)
15. PHLEGRAEAN PLAINS: site of a battle between gods and giants.
17. MOUNTAINTOPS . . . BLOW: each other blow cleft the mountaintops.
19. VULCAN: reference to the net in which Vulcan snared Venus and Mars.

ACT III

At one door, enter Cleopatra, Charmion, Iras, and
Alexas, a train of Egyptians; at the other, Antony and
Romans. The entrance on both sides is prepared by
music, the trumpets first sounding on Antony's part,
then answered by timbrels, etc., on Cleopatra's.
Charmion and Iras hold a laurel wreath betwixt them.
A dance of Egyptians. After the ceremony, Cleopatra
crowns Antony.

Ant. I thought how those white arms would fold me
   in
And strain me close and melt me into love;
So pleased with that sweet image, I sprung forwards,
And added all my strength to every blow.   5

Cleo. Come to me, come, my soldier, to my arms!
You've been too long away from my embraces;
But when I have you fast and all my own,
With broken murmurs and with amorous sighs
I'll say you were unkind and punish you,   10
And mark you red with many an eager kiss.

Ant. My brighter Venus!

Cleo.   O my greater Mars!

Ant. Thou join'st us well, my love!
Suppose me come from the Phlegraean plains,   15
Where gasping giants lay, cleft by my sword,
And mountaintops pared off each other blow,
To bury those I slew. Receive me, goddess!
Let Caesar spread his subtile nets, like Vulcan;

In thy embraces I would be beheld   20
By Heav'n and earth at once,
And make their envy what they meant their sport.
Let those who took us blush; I would love on
With awful state, regardless of their frowns,
As their superior god.   25
There's no satiety of love in thee;
Enjoyed, thou still art new; perpetual spring
Is in thy arms; the ripened fruit but falls,
And blossoms rise to fill its empty place,
And I grow rich by giving.   30

       Enter Ventidius, and stands apart.

  Alex. O, now the danger's past, your general comes!
He joins not in your joys, nor minds your triumphs;
But, with contracted brows, looks frowning on,
As envying your success.
  Ant. Now, on my soul, he loves me, truly loves me;   35
He never flattered me in any vice,
But awes me with his virtue: ev'n this minute,
Methinks, he has a right of chiding me.—
Lead to the temple: I'll avoid his presence;
It checks too strong upon me.   40
     Exeunt the rest. As Antony is going, Ventidius
               pulls him by the robe.
  Vent.   Emperor!
  Ant. (*Looking back*) 'Tis the old argument; I prith-
ee, spare me.
  Vent. But this one hearing, Emperor.
  Ant.   Let go   45
My robe; or, by my father Hercules—

---

47. HERCULES HIS FATHER: old form of the possessive; Jove was the
father of Hercules.
72. HIS . . . ADVANTAGE: he prudently considers how he can best
effect his hostile intent.

Vent. By Hercules his father, that's yet greater,
I bring you somewhat you would wish to know.

Ant. Thou see'st we are observed; attend me here,
And I'll return.   *Exit.* 50

Vent. I'm waning in his favor, yet I love him;
I love this man, who runs to meet his ruin;
And sure the gods, like me, are fond of him:
His virtues lie so mingled with his crimes
As would confound their choice to punish one   55
And not reward the other.

Enter Antony.

Ant.   We can conquer,
You see, without your aid.
We have dislodged their troops;
They look on us at distance, and, like curs   60
'Scaped from the lion's paws, they bay far off,
And lick their wounds, and faintly threaten war.
Five thousand Romans, with their faces upward,
Lie breathless on the plain.

Vent.   'Tis well: and he   65
Who lost 'em could have spared ten thousand more.
Yet if by this advantage you could gain
An easier peace, while Caesar doubts the chance
Of arms!—

Ant.   O, think not on't, Ventidius!   70
The boy pursues my ruin, he'll no peace;
His malice is considerate in advantage;
O, he's the coolest murderer! so staunch,
He kills and keeps his temper.

Vent.   Have you no friend   75
In all his army who has power to move him?
Maecenas or Agrippa might do much.

Ant. They're both too deep in Caesar's interests.
We'll work it out by dint of sword or perish.

Vent. Fain I would find some other.   80
   Ant.   Thank thy love.
Some four or five such victories as this
Will save thy farther pains.
   Vent. Expect no more; Caesar is on his guard:
I know, sir, you have conquered against odds;   85
But still you draw supplies from one poor town
And of Egyptians: he has all the world,
And at his back nations come pouring in
To fill the gaps you make. Pray, think again.
   Ant. Why dost thou drive me from myself to search 90
For foreign aids? to hunt my memory
And range all o'er a waste and barren place
To find a friend? The wretched have no friends.—
Yet I had one, the bravest youth of Rome,
Whom Caesar loves beyond the love of women;   95
He could resolve his mind, as fire does wax,
From that hard rugged image melt him down,
And mold him in what softer form he pleased.
   Vent. Him would I see, that man of all the world;
Just such a one we want.   100
   Ant.   He loved me too,
I was his soul; he lived not but in me;
We were so closed within each other's breasts
The rivets were not found that joined us first.
That does not reach us yet: we were so mixed,   105
As meeting streams, both to ourselves were lost;
We were one mass; we could not give or take
But from the same; for he was I, I he!
   Vent. (*Aside*) He moves as I would wish him.
   Ant.   After this 110
I need not tell his name—'twas Dolabella.
   Vent. He's now in Caesar's camp.
   Ant.   No matter where,
Since he's no longer mine. He took unkindly
That I forbade him Cleopatra's sight,   115

Because I feared he loved her: he confessed
He had a warmth, which for my sake he stifled;
For 'twere impossible that two so one
Should not have loved the same. When he departed,
He took no leave; and that confirmed my thoughts. 120
   Vent. It argues that he loved you more than her,
Else he had stayed; but he perceived you jealous
And would not grieve his friend: I know he loves you.
   Ant. I should have seen him, then, ere now.
   Vent.   Perhaps 125
He has thus long been lab'ring for your peace.
   Ant. Would he were here!
   Vent.   Would you believe he loved you?
I read your answer in your eyes; you would.
Not to conceal it longer, he has sent   130
A messenger from Caesar's camp with letters.
   Ant. Let him appear.
   Vent.   I'll bring him instantly.
Exit Ventidius, and re-enters immediately with
                              Dolabella.
   Ant. 'Tis he himself! himself, by holy friendship!
                     Runs to embrace him.
Art thou returned at last, my better half?   135
Come, give me all myself! Let me not live
If the young bridegroom, longing for his night,
Was ever half so fond.
   Dola. I must be silent, for my soul is busy
About a nobler work: she's new come home,   140
Like a long-absent man, and wanders o'er
Each room, a stranger to her own, to look
If all be safe.
   Ant.   Thou hast what's left of me;
For I am now so sunk from what I was   145
Thou find'st me at my lowest watermark.
The rivers that ran in and raised my fortunes
Are all dried up or take another course.

What I have left is from my native spring;
I've still a heart that swells, in scorn of Fate,   150
And lifts me to my banks.

    Dola. Still you are lord of all the world to me.

    Ant. Why, then I yet am so; for thou art all.
If I had any joy when thou wert absent,
I grudged it to myself; methought I robbed   155
Thee of thy part. But, O my Dolabella!
Thou hast beheld me other than I am.
Hast thou not seen my morning chambers filled
With sceptered slaves, who waited to salute me?
With eastern monarchs, who forgot the sun   160
To worship my uprising? Menial kings
Ran coursing up and down my palace yard,
Stood silent in my presence, watched my eyes,
And at my least command all started out,
Like racers to the goal.   165

    Dola.   Slaves to your fortune.

    Ant. Fortune is Caesar's now; and what am I?

    Vent. What you have made yourself; I will not flatter.

    Ant. Is this friendly done?

    Dola. Yes, when his end is so, I must join with him;   170
Indeed I must, and yet you must not chide:
Why am I else your friend?

    Ant.   Take heed, young man,
How thou upbraid'st my love; the Queen has eyes,
And thou, too, hast a soul. Canst thou remember   175
When, swelled with hatred, thou beheld'st her first,
As accessary to thy brother's death?

    Dola. Spare my remembrance; 'twas a guilty day,
And still the blush hangs here.

    Ant.   To clear herself   180
For sending him no aid, she came from Egypt.
Her galley down the silver Cydnus rowed,

---

185. NEREIDS: sea nymphs, daughters of Nereus and Doris.

The tackling silk, the streamers waved with gold;
The gentle winds were lodged in purple sails;
Her nymphs, like Nereids, round her couch were 185
    placed,
Where she, another sea-born Venus, lay.
    Dola. No more: I would not hear it.
    Ant.   O, you must!
She lay, and leant her cheek upon her hand,   190
And cast a look so languishingly sweet,
As if, secure of all beholders' hearts,
Neglecting, she could take 'em: boys, like Cupids,
Stood fanning with their painted wings the winds
That played about her face: but if she smiled   195
A darting glory seemed to blaze abroad,
That men's desiring eyes were never wearied
But hung upon the object. To soft flutes
The silver oars kept time; and while they played
The hearing gave new pleasure to the sight,   200
And both to thought. 'Twas Heav'n, or somewhat
    more;
For she so charmed all hearts that gazing crowds
Stood panting on the shore and wanted breath
To give their welcome voice.   205
Then, Dolabella, where was then thy soul?
Was not thy fury quite disarmed with wonder?
Didst thou not shrink behind me from those eyes,
And whisper in my ear, "O, tell her not
That I accused her of my brother's death"?   210
    Dola. And should my weakness be a plea for yours?
Mine was an age when love might be excused,
When kindly warmth and when my springing youth
Made it a debt to nature. Yours—
    Vent.   Speak boldly.   215
Yours, he would say, in your declining age,
When no more heat was left but what you forced,
When all the sap was needful for the trunk,

When it went down, then you constrained the course
And robbed from nature to supply desire;   220
In you (I would not use so harsh a word)
But 'tis plain dotage.

   Ant.   Ha!

   Dola.   'Twas urged too home.
But yet the loss was private that I made;   225
'Twas but myself I lost: I lost no legions;
I had no world to lose, no people's love.

   Ant. This from a friend?

   Dola.   Yes, Antony, a true one;
A friend so tender that each word I speak   230
Stabs my own heart before it reach your ear.
O, judge me not less kind because I chide!
To Caesar I excuse you.

   Ant.   O ye gods!
Have I then lived to be excused to Caesar?   235

   Dola. As to your equal.

   Ant.   Well, he's but my equal;
While I wear this, he never shall be more.

   Dola. I bring conditions from him.

   Ant.   Are they noble? 240
Methinks thou shouldst not bring 'em else; yet he
Is full of deep dissembling; knows no honor
Divided from his int'rest. Fate mistook him;
For nature meant him for an usurer:
He's fit indeed to buy, not conquer, kingdoms.   245

   Vent. Then, granting this,
What pow'r was theirs who wrought so hard a temper
To honorable terms?

   Ant. It was my Dolabella, or some god.

   Dola. Nor I, nor yet Maecenas, nor Agrippa: 250
They were your enemies; and I, a friend,

---

224. URGED . . . HOME: expressed too bluntly.
238. THIS: presumably, he indicates his head.
281. CONFESS: i.e., profess yourself.

Too weak alone; yet 'twas a Roman's deed.
   Ant. 'Twas like a Roman done: show me that man
Who has preserved my life, my love, my honor;
Let me but see his face.   255
   Vent.   That task is mine,
And, Heav'n, thou know'st how pleasing.
                           Exit Ventidius.
   Dola.   You'll remember
To whom you stand obliged?
   Ant.   When I forget it,   260
Be thou unkind, and that's my greatest curse.
My queen shall thank him too.
   Dola.   I fear she will not.
   Ant. But she shall do't—the Queen, my Dolabella!
Hast thou not still some grudgings of thy fever?   265
   Dola. I would not see her lost.
   Ant.   When I forsake her,
Leave me, my better stars! for she has truth
Beyond her beauty. Caesar tempted her,
At no less price than kingdoms, to betray me;   270
But she resisted all: and yet thou chid'st me
For loving her too well. Could I do so?
   Dola. Yes; there's my reason.

   *Re-enter Ventidius, with Octavia, leading Antony's
             two little daughters.*

   Ant. (*Starting back*) Where?—Octavia there!
   Vent. What, is she poison to you? a disease?   275
Look on her, view her well, and those she brings:
Are they all strangers to your eyes? Has nature
No secret call, no whisper they are yours?
   Dola. For shame, my lord, if not for love, receive
   'em   280
With kinder eyes. If you confess a man,
Meet 'em, embrace 'em, bid 'em welcome to you.

Your arms should open, ev'n without your knowledge,
To clasp 'em in; your feet should turn to wings
To bear you to 'em; and your eyes dart out   285
And aim a kiss ere you could reach the lips.

    Ant. I stood amazed to think how they came hither.

    Vent. I sent for 'em; I brought 'em in, unknown
To Cleopatra's guards.

    Dola.   Yet are you cold?   290

    Octav. Thus long I have attended for my welcome,
Which, as a stranger, sure I might expect.
Who am I?

    Ant.   Caesar's sister.

    Octav.   That's unkind.   295
Had I been nothing more than Caesar's sister,
Know, I had still remained in Caesar's camp;
But your Octavia, your much injured wife,
Though banished from your bed, driv'n from your
          house,   300
In spite of Caesar's sister, still is yours.
'Tis true, I have a heart disdains your coldness
And prompts me not to seek what you should offer;
But a wife's virtue still surmounts that pride:
I come to claim you as my own; to show   305
My duty first; to ask, nay beg, your kindness:
Your hand, my lord; 'tis mine, and I will have it.
                                    Taking his hand.

    Vent. Do, take it; thou deserv'st it.

    Dola.   On my soul,
And so she does: she's neither too submissive,   310
Nor yet too haughty; but so just a mean
Shows, as it ought, a wife and Roman too.

    Ant. I fear, Octavia, you have begged my life.

    Octav. Begged it, my lord?

    Ant.   Yes, begged it, my ambassadress,   315
Poorly and basely begged it of your brother.

    Octav. Poorly and basely I could never beg;

Nor could my brother grant.

    Ant. Shall I, who to my kneeling slave could say,
"Rise up, and be a king," shall I fall down   320
And cry, "Forgive me, Caesar"? Shall I set
A man, my equal, in the place of Jove,
As he could give me being? No; that word
"Forgive" would choke me up
And die upon my tongue.   325
    Dola.   You shall not need it.
    Ant. I will not need it. Come, you've all betrayed
    me—
My friend too!—to receive some vile conditions.
My wife has bought me with her prayers and tears,   330
And now I must become her branded slave:
In every peevish mood she will upbraid
The life she gave: if I but look awry,
She cries, "I'll tell my brother."
    Octav.   My hard fortune   335
Subjects me still to your unkind mistakes.
But the conditions I have brought are such
You need not blush to take: I love your honor
Because 'tis mine; it never shall be said
Octavia's husband was her brother's slave.   340
Sir, you are free—free, ev'n from her you loathe;
For, though my brother bargains for your love,
Makes me the price and cement of your peace,
I have a soul like yours; I cannot take
Your love as alms, nor beg what I deserve.   345
I'll tell my brother we are reconciled;
He shall draw back his troops and you shall march
To rule the East: I may be dropped at Athens;
No matter where, I never will complain,
But only keep the barren name of wife   350
And rid you of the trouble.
    Vent. Was ever such a strife of sullen honor!
Both scorn to be obliged.

Dola. O, she has touched him in the tender'st part;
See how he reddens with despite and shame,   355
To be outdone in generosity!

Vent. See how he winks! How he dries up a tear
That fain would fall!

Ant. Octavia, I have heard you and must praise
The greatness of your soul,   360
But cannot yield to what you have proposed;
For I can ne'er be conquered but by love;
And you do all for duty. You would free me,
And would be dropped at Athens; was't not so?

Octav. It was, my lord.   365

Ant.   Then I must be obliged
To one who loves me not, who, to herself,
May call me thankless and ungrateful man—
I'll not endure it; no.

Vent. (*Aside*) I'm glad it pinches there.   370

Octav. Would you triumph o'er poor Octavia's vir-
    tue?
That pride was all I had to bear me up:
That you might think you owed me for your life,
And owed it to my duty, not my love.   375
I have been injured, and my haughty soul
Could brook but ill the man who slights my bed.

Ant. Therefore you love me not.

Octav.   Therefore, my lord,
I should not love you.   380

Ant.   Therefore you would leave me?

Octav. And therefore I should leave you—if I could.

Dola. Her soul's too great, after such injuries,
To say she loves; and yet she lets you see it.
Her modesty and silence plead her cause.   385

Ant. O Dolabella, which way shall I turn?
I find a secret yielding in my soul;
But Cleopatra, who would die with me,
Must she be left? Pity pleads for Octavia;

But does it not plead more for Cleopatra?   390
  Vent. Justice and pity both plead for Octavia;
For Cleopatra, neither.
One would be ruined with you, but she first
Had ruined you: the other you have ruined,
And yet she would preserve you.   395
In everything their merits are unequal.
  Ant. O my distracted soul!
  Octav.   Sweet Heav'n compose it!
Come, come, my lord, if I can pardon you,
Methinks you should accept it. Look on these;   400
Are they not yours? Or stand they thus neglected
As they are mine? Go to him, children, go;
Kneel to him, take him by the hand, speak to him;
For you may speak, and he may own you too,
Without a blush; and so he cannot all   405
His children: go, I say, and pull him to me,
And pull him to yourselves, from that bad woman.
You, Agrippina, hang upon his arms;
And you, Antonia, clasp about his waist:
If he will shake you off, if he will dash you   410
Against the pavement, you must bear it, children;
For you are mine, and I was born to suffer.
              Here the Children go to him, etc.
  Vent. Was ever sight so moving?—Emperor!
  Dola. Friend!
  Octav.   Husband!
  Both Child.   Father!
  Ant.   I am vanquished; take me,
Octavia; take me, children; share me all.
                   Embracing them.
I've been a thriftless debtor to your loves,
And run out much, in riot, from your stock;   420
But all shall be amended.
  Octav.   O blest hour!
  Dola. O happy change!

Vent.   My joy stops at my tongue;
But it has found two channels here for one,   425
And bubbles out above.
   Ant. (*To Octavia*) This is thy triumph; lead me
     where thou wilt,
Ev'n to thy brother's camp.
   Octav.   All there are yours.   430

Enter Alexas hastily.

   Alex. The Queen, my mistress, sir, and yours—
   Ant.   'Tis past.—
Octavia, you shall stay this night; tomorrow,
Caesar and we are one.   *Exit leading Octavia; Dola-
               bella and the Children follow.*
   Vent. There's news for you; run, my officious eunuch, 435
Be sure to be the first; haste forward;
Haste, my dear eunuch, haste!   *Exit.*
   Alex. This downright fighting fool, this thick-skulled
     hero,
This blunt, unthinking instrument of death,   440
With plain, dull virtue has outgone my wit.
Pleasure forsook my earliest infancy;
The luxury of others robbed my cradle
And ravished thence the promise of a man.
Cast out from Nature, disinherited   445
Of what her meanest children claim by kind,
Yet greatness kept me from contempt: that's gone.
Had Cleopatra followed my advice,
Then he had been betrayed who now forsakes.
She dies for love, but she has known its joys: 450
Gods, is this just, that I, who know no joys,
Must die because she loves?

Enter Cleopatra, Charmion, Iras, and Train.

443. LUXURY: lust.

O madam, I have seen what blasts my eyes!
Octavia's here!

   Cleo.   Peace with that raven's note.   455
I know it too and now am in
The pangs of death.

   Alex.   You are no more a queen;
Egypt is lost.

   Cleo.   What tell'st thou me of Egypt?   460
My life, my soul is lost! Octavia has him!
O fatal name to Cleopatra's love!
My kisses, my embraces now are hers;
While I—But thou hast seen my rival; speak,
Does she deserve this blessing? Is she fair?   465
Bright as a goddess? And is all perfection
Confined to her? It is. Poor I was made
Of that coarse matter which, when she was finished,
The gods threw by for rubbish.

   Alex. She's indeed a very miracle.   470

   Cleo. Death to my hopes, a miracle!

   Alex. (*Bowing*)   A miracle;
I mean of goodness; for in beauty, madam,
You make all wonders cease.

   Cleo.   I was too rash: 475
Take this in part of recompense. But, O! *Giving a ring.*
I fear thou flatter'st me.

   Char. She comes! She's here!

   Iras.   Fly, madam, Caesar's sister!

   Cleo. Were she the sister of the thund'rer Jove,   480
And bore her brother's lightning in her eyes,
Thus would I face my rival.

     *Meets Octavia with Ventidius. Octavia bears up to
         her. Their trains come up on either side.*

   Octav. I need not ask if you are Cleopatra;
Your haughty carriage—

   Cleo.   Shows I am a queen: 485

Nor need I ask you who you are.

   Octav.   A Roman:

A name that makes and can unmake a queen.

   Cleo. Your lord, the man who serves me, is a
     Roman.   490

   Octav. He was a Roman, till he lost that name

To be a slave in Egypt; but I come

To free him thence.

   Cleo.   Peace, peace, my lover's Juno.

When he grew weary of that household clog,   495

He chose my easier bonds.

   Octav.   I wonder not

Your bonds are easy; you have long been practiced

In that lascivious art: he's not the first

For whom you spread your snares: let Caesar witness. 500

   Cleo. I loved not Caesar; 'twas but gratitude

I paid his love. The worst your malice can

Is but to say the greatest of mankind

Has been my slave. The next, but far above him

In my esteem, is he whom law calls yours,   505

But whom his love made mine.

   Octav. (*Coming up close to her*) I would view
     nearer

That face which has so long usurped my right,

To find th' inevitable charms that catch   510

Mankind so sure, that ruined my dear lord.

   Cleo. O, you do well to search; for had you known

But half these charms you had not lost his heart.

   Octav. Far be their knowledge from a Roman lady,

Far from a modest wife! Shame of our sex,   515

Dost thou not blush to own those black endearments

That make sin pleasing?

   Cleo.   You may blush, who want 'em.

If bounteous nature, if indulgent Heav'n,

---

510. INEVITABLE: irresistible.

Have giv'n me charms to please the bravest man,   520
Should I not thank 'em? Should I be ashamed
And not be proud? I am, that he has loved me;
And when I love not him, Heav'n change this face
For one like that.

    Octav.   Thou lov'st him not so well.   525

    Cleo. I love him better, and deserve him more.

    Octav. You do not, cannot: you have been his ruin.
Who made him cheap at Rome but Cleopatra?
Who made him scorned abroad but Cleopatra?
At Actium who betrayed him? Cleopatra.   530
Who made his children orphans and poor me
A wretched widow? Only Cleopatra.

    Cleo. Yet she who loves him best is Cleopatra.
If you have suffered, I have suffered more.
You bear the specious title of a wife   535
To gild your cause and draw the pitying world
To favor it: the world contemns poor me,
For I have lost my honor, lost my fame,
And stained the glory of my royal house,
And all to bear the branded name of mistress.   540
There wants but life, and that too I would lose
For him I love.

    Octav.   Be't so, then; take thy wish.

                           Exit cum suis.

    Cleo. And 'tis my wish,
Now he is lost for whom alone I lived.   545
My sight grows dim, and every object dances
And swims before me in the maze of death.
My spirits, while they were opposed, kept up;
They could not sink beneath a rival's scorn:
But, now she's gone, they faint.   550

    Alex.   Mine have had leisure
To recollect their strength and furnish counsel
To ruin her who else must ruin you.

    Cleo.   Vain promiser!

Lead me, my Charmion; nay, your hand too, Iras: 555
My grief has weight enough to sink you both.
Conduct me to some solitary chamber
And draw the curtains round;
Then leave me to myself, to take alone
My fill of grief. 560
    There I till death will his unkindness weep;
    As harmless infants moan themselves asleep.

                               Exeunt.

ACT IV

[Enter] Antony, Dolabella.

Dola. Why would you shift it from yourself on me?
Can you not tell her you must part?
    Ant.   I cannot.
I could pull out an eye and bid it go,
And t'other should not weep. O Dolabella,   5
How many deaths are in this word "depart"!
I dare not trust my tongue to tell her so:
One look of hers would thaw me into tears,
And I should melt till I were lost again.
    Dola. Then let Ventidius;   10
He's rough by nature.
    Ant.   O, he'll speak too harshly;
He'll kill her with the news: thou, only thou.
    Dola. Nature has cast me in so soft a mold
That but to hear a story feigned for pleasure   15
Of some sad lover's death moistens my eyes
And robs me of my manhood. I should speak
So faintly, with such fear to grieve her heart,
She'd not believe it earnest.
    Ant.   Therefore, therefore,   20
Thou, only thou, art fit; think thyself me,
And when thou speak'st (but let it first be long),
Take off the edge from every sharper sound,
And let our parting be as gently made
As other loves begin: wilt thou do this?   25

Dola. What you have said so sinks into my soul
That, if I must speak, I shall speak just so.
  Ant. I leave you then to your sad task. Farewell!
I sent her word to meet you.   *Goes to the door,*
                                    and comes back.
                    I forgot;   30
Let her be told I'll make her peace with mine:
Her crown and dignity shall be preserved,
If I have pow'r with Caesar. O, be sure
To think on that.
  Dola.   Fear not; I will remember.   35
      Antony goes again to the door, and comes back.
  Ant. And tell her, too, how much I was constrained;
I did not this but with extremest force:
Desire her not to hate my memory,
For I still cherish hers; insist on that.
  Dola. Trust me; I'll not forget it.   40
  Ant.   Then that's all.
                Goes out, and returns again.
Wilt thou forgive my fondness this once more?
Tell her, though we shall never meet again,
If I should hear she took another love,
The news would break my heart.—Now I must go;   45
For every time I have returned I feel
My soul more tender; and my next command
Would be to bid her stay, and ruin both.   *Exit.*
  Dola. Men are but children of a larger growth;
Our appetites as apt to change as theirs,   50
And full as craving, too, and full as vain;
And yet the soul, shut up in her dark room,
Viewing so clear abroad, at home sees nothing;
But, like a mole in earth, busy and blind,
Works all her folly up and casts it outward   55
To the world's open view: thus I discovered

(IV)
79. PORCPISCE: porpoise (Latin *porcus piscis*).

And blamed the love of ruined Antony,
Yet wish that I were he, to be so ruined.

Enter Ventidius above.

Vent. Alone? And talking to himself? Concerned too?
Perhaps my guess is right; he loved her once   60
And may pursue it still.
Dola.   O friendship! friendship!
Ill canst thou answer this, and reason, worse:
Unfaithful in th' attempt, hopeless to win,
And if I win, undone: mere madness all.   65
And yet th' occasion's fair. What injury
To him, to wear the robe which he throws by?
Vent. None, none at all. This happens as I wish,
To ruin her yet more with Antony.

*Enter Cleopatra, talking with Alexas; Charmion,
Iras, on the other side.*

Dola. She comes! What charms have sorrow on that   70
    face!
Sorrow seems pleased to dwell with so much sweet-
    ness;
Yet now and then a melancholy smile
Breaks loose, like lightning in a winter's night,   75
And shows a moment's day.
Vent. If she should love him too! Her eunuch
    there!
That porcpisce bodes ill weather. Draw, draw nearer,
Sweet devil, that I may hear.   80
Alex.   Believe me; try
        *Dolabella goes over to Charmion and Iras;
              seems to talk with them.*
To make him jealous; jealousy is like

A polished glass held to the lips when life's in doubt:
If there be breath, 'twill catch the damp and show it.

Cleo. I grant you, jealousy's a proof of love,   85
But 'tis a weak and unavailing med'cine;
It puts out the disease and makes it show,
But has no pow'r to cure.

Alex. 'Tis your last remedy, and strongest too:
And then this Dolabella—who so fit   90
To practice on? He's handsome, valiant, young,
And looks as he were laid for nature's bait
To catch weak women's eyes.
He stands already more than half suspected
Of loving you: the least kind word or glance   95
You give this youth will kindle him with love:
Then, like a burning vessel set adrift,
You'll send him down amain before the wind,
To fire the heart of jealous Antony.

Cleo. Can I do this? Ah, no; my love's so true   100
That I can neither hide it where it is
Nor show it where it is not. Nature meant me
A wife, a silly, harmless, household dove,
Fond without art and kind without deceit;
But Fortune, that has made a mistress of me,   105
Has thrust me out to the wide world unfurnished
Of falsehood to be happy.

Alex.   Force yourself.
Th' event will be your lover will return
Doubly desirous to possess the good   110
Which once he feared to lose.

Cleo.   I must attempt it;
But, O, with what regret!   *Exit Alexas.*
                    She comes up to Dolabella.

---

124. GALLUS . . . TIBULLUS: contemporary Roman poets. CYTHERIS
and DELIA were the names by which they addressed their respective mistresses in verse.
128. SEEN: Dolabella interrupts himself before uttering Cleopatra's
name.

Vent. So, now the scene draws near; they're in my
　　reach.   115
　　Cleo. (*To Dolabella*) Discoursing with my wom-
　　en! Might not I
Share in your entertainment?
　　Char.　　　　　　　　You have been
The subject of it, madam.   120
　　Cleo.　　　　　　　How! and how?
　　Iras. Such praises of your beauty!
　　Cleo.　　　　　　　　Mere poetry.
Your Roman wits, your Gallus and Tibullus,
Have taught you this from Cytheris and Delia.   125
　　Dola. Those Roman wits have never been in Egypt;
Cytheris and Delia else had been unsung:
I, who have seen—had I been born a poet,
Should choose a nobler name.
　　Cleo.　　　　　　　You flatter me.   130
But, 'tis your nation's vice: all of your country
Are flatterers and all false. Your friend's like you.
I'm sure he sent you not to speak these words.
　　Dola. No, madam; yet he sent me—
　　Cleo.　　　　　　　Well, he sent you—   135
　　Dola. Of a less pleasing errand.
　　Cleo.　　　　　　　　How less pleasing?
Less to yourself or me?
　　Dola.　　　　Madam, to both;
For you must mourn, and I must grieve to cause it.   140
　　Cleo. You, Charmion, and your fellow, stand at dis-
　　tance.—
(*Aside*) Hold up, my spirits.—Well, now your mourn-
　　ful matter;
For I'm prepared; perhaps can guess it too.   145
　　Dola. I wish you would; for 'tis a thankless office
To tell ill news: and I, of all your sex,
Most fear displeasing you.
　　Cleo.　　　　　　Of all your sex,

I soonest could forgive you, if you should.   150
　　Vent. Most delicate advances! Woman! Woman!
Dear, damned, inconstant sex!
　　Cleo.　　　　　　　　　　In the first place,
I am to be forsaken; is't not so?
　　Dola. I wish I could not answer to that question.   155
　　Cleo. Then pass it o'er, because it troubles you:
I should have been more grieved another time.
Next, I'm to lose my kingdom.—Farewell, Egypt!
Yet, is there any more?
　　Dola.　　　　　　　Madam, I fear   160
Your too deep sense of grief has turned your reason.
　　Cleo. No, no, I'm not run mad; I can bear fortune:
And love may be expelled by other love,
As poisons are by poisons.
　　Dola. You o'erjoy me, madam,   165
To find your griefs so moderately borne.
You've heard the worst; all are not false like him.
　　Cleo. No; Heav'n forbid they should.
　　Dola.　　　　　　　Some men are constant.
　　Cleo. And constancy deserves reward, that's certain.   170
　　Dola. Deserves it not; but give it leave to hope.
　　Vent. I'll swear thou hast my leave. I have enough.
But how to manage this! Well, I'll consider.   *Exit.*
　　Dola. I came prepared
To tell you heavy news; news which I thought   175
Would fright the blood from your pale cheeks to
　　hear:
But you have met it with a cheerfulness
That makes my task more easy; and my tongue,
Which on another's message was employed,   180
Would gladly speak its own.
　　Cleo.　　　　　　　Hold, Dolabella.
First tell me, were you chosen by my lord?
Or sought you this employment?
　　Dola. He picked me out; and as his bosom friend   185

He charged me with his words.
    Cleo.   The message, then,
I know, was tender and each accent smooth,
To mollify that rugged word "depart."
    Dola. O, you mistake: he chose the harshest words; 190
With fiery eyes and with contracted brows
He coined his face in the severest stamp,
And fury shook his fabric like an earthquake;
He heaved for vent and burst like bellowing Etna
In sounds scarce human, "Hence, away forever: 195
Let her be gone, the blot of my renown
And bane of all my hopes!

    *All the time of this speech, Cleopatra seems more
        and more concerned, till she sinks quite down.*

Let her be driv'n as far as men can think
From man's commerce! She'll poison to the center."
    Cleo. O, I can bear no more! 200
    Dola. Help, help!—O wretch! O cursed, cursed
    wretch!
What have I done!
    Char.   Help, chafe her temples, Iras.
    Iras. Bend, bend her forward quickly. 205
    Char.   Heav'n be praised,
She comes again.
    Cleo.   O, let him not approach me.
Why have you brought me back to this loathed being,
Th' abode of falsehood, violated vows, 210
And injured love? For pity, let me go;
For if there be a place of long repose,
I'm sure I want it. My disdainful lord
Can never break that quiet, nor awake
The sleeping soul with holloing in my tomb 215
Such words as fright her hence. Unkind, unkind!
    Dola. (*Kneeling*) Believe me, 'tis against myself I
    speak,
That sure deserves belief; I injured him:

My friend ne'er spoke those words. O, had you seen 220
How often he came back, and every time
With something more obliging and more kind
To add to what he said; what dear farewells;
How almost vanquished by his love he parted
And leaned to what unwillingly he left! 225
I, traitor as I was, for love of you
(But what can you not do, who made me false!)
I forged that lie; for whose forgiveness kneels
This self-accused, self-punished criminal.

   Cleo. With how much ease believe we what we 230
     wish!
Rise, Dolabella; if you have been guilty,
I have contributed, and too much love
Has made me guilty too.
Th' advance of kindness which I made was feigned, 235
To call back fleeting love by jealousy;
But 'twould not last. O, rather let me lose
Than so ignobly trifle with his heart.

   Dola. I find your breast fenced round from human
     reach, 240
Transparent as a rock of solid crystal,
Seen through but never pierced. My friend, my friend!
What endless treasure hast thou thrown away,
And scattered, like an infant, in the ocean
Vain sums of wealth, which none can gather thence! 245

   Cleo. Could you not beg
An hour's admittance to his private ear?
Like one who wanders through long barren wilds,
And yet foreknows no hospitable inn
Is near to succor hunger, eats his fill 250
Before his painful march,
So would I feed a while my famished eyes

----

280. THESSALIAN CHARMS: Thessaly was a notorious center of witchcraft.

Before we part; for I have far to go,
If death be far, and never must return.

Ventidius with Octavia, behind.

Vent. From hence you may discover—O, sweet, 255
   sweet!
Would you indeed? the pretty hand in earnest?
  Dola. I will, for this reward.—(*Takes her hand*)
   Draw it not back,
'Tis all I e'er will beg. 260
  Vent. They turn upon us.
  Octav.   What quick eyes has guilt!
  Vent. Seem not to have observed 'em and go on.

They enter.

  Dola. Saw you the emperor, Ventidius?
  Vent.   No. 265
I sought him; but I heard that he was private,
None with him but Hipparchus, his freedman.
  Dola. Know you his bus'ness?
  Vent.   Giving him instructions,
And letters to his brother Caesar. 270
  Dola.   Well,
He must be found.   *Exeunt Dolabella and Cleopatra.*
  Octav.   Most glorious impudence!
  Vent. She looked, methought,
As she would say, "Take your old man, Octavia; 275
Thank you, I'm better here." Well, but what use
Make we of this discovery?
  Octav.   Let it die.
  Vent. I pity Dolabella; but she's dangerous:
Her eyes have pow'r beyond Thessalian charms 280
To draw the moon from heav'n; for eloquence,
The sea-green sirens taught her voice their flatt'ry,
And while she speaks night steals upon the day,
Unmarked of those that hear. Then she's so charming,

Age buds at sight of her and swells to youth: 285
The holy priests gaze on her when she smiles,
And with heaved hands, forgetting gravity,
They bless her wanton eyes: even I, who hate her,
With a malignant joy behold such beauty,
And, while I curse, desire it. Antony   290
Must needs have some remains of passion still,
Which may ferment into a worse relapse
If now not fully cured. I know, this minute,
With Caesar he's endeavoring her peace.

   Octav. You have prevailed:—but for a farther pur- 295
      pose   *Walks off.*
I'll prove how he will relish this discovery.
What, make a strumpet's peace! It swells my heart:
It must not, sha' not be.

   Vent.   His guards appear.   300
Let me begin, and you shall second me.

Enter Antony.

   Ant. Octavia, I was looking you, my love:
What, are your letters ready? I have giv'n
My last instructions.

   Octav.   Mine, my lord, are written.   305
   Ant. Ventidius!   *Drawing him aside.*
   Vent.   My lord?
   Ant.   A word in private.
When saw you Dolabella?
   Vent.   Now, my lord,   310
He parted hence; and Cleopatra with him.
   Ant. Speak softly.—'Twas by my command he went,
To bear my last farewell.
   Vent. (*Aloud*)   It looked indeed
Like your farewell.   315

---

302. LOOKING: seeking.

Ant. More softly.—My farewell?
What secret meaning have you in those words
Of "my farewell"? He did it by my order.

  Vent. (*Aloud*) Then he obeyed your order. I sup-
    pose 320
You bid him do it with all gentleness,
All kindness, and all—love.

  Ant. How she mourned,
The poor forsaken creature!

  Vent. She took it as she ought; she bore your part- 325
    ing
As she did Caesar's, as she would another's,
Were a new love to come.

  Ant. (*Aloud*) Thou dost belie her;
Most basely and maliciously belie her. 330

  Vent. I thought not to displease you; I have done.

  Octav. (*Coming up*) You seem disturbed, my lord.

  Ant. A very trifle.
Retire, my love.

  Vent. It was indeed a trifle. 335
He sent—

  Ant. (*Angrily*) No more. Look how thou disobey'st
    me;
Thy life shall answer it.

  Octav. Then 'tis no trifle. 340

  Vent. (*To Octavia*) 'Tis less, a very nothing; you,
    too, saw it
As well as I, and therefore 'tis no secret.

  Ant. She saw it!

  Vent. Yes: she saw young Dolabella— 345

  Ant. Young Dolabella!

  Vent. Young, I think him young,
And handsome too; and so do others think him.
But what of that? He went by your command,
Indeed, 'tis probable, with some kind message; 350
For she received it graciously; she smiled;

And then he grew familiar with her hand,
Squeezed it and worried it with ravenous kisses;
She blushed, and sighed, and smiled, and blushed
    again;   355
At last she took occasion to talk softly,
And brought her cheek up close and leaned on his;
At which he whispered kisses back on hers;
And then she cried aloud that constancy
Should be rewarded.   360
    Octav.   This I saw and heard.
    Ant. What woman was it whom you heard and saw
So playful with my friend? Not Cleopatra?
    Vent. Ev'n she, my lord.
    Ant.   My Cleopatra?   365
    Vent. Your Cleopatra;
Dolabella's Cleopatra;
Every man's Cleopatra.
    Ant. Thou li'st.
    Vent.   I do not lie, my lord.   370
Is this so strange? Should mistresses be left
And not provide against a time of change?
You know she's not much used to lonely nights.
    Ant. I'll think no more on't.
I know 'tis false and see the plot betwixt you.   375
You needed not have gone this way, Octavia.
What harms it you that Cleopatra's just?
She's mine no more. I see, and I forgive:
Urge it no farther, love.
    Octav.   Are you concerned   380
That she's found false?
    Ant.   I should be, were it so;
For, though 'tis past, I would not that the world
Should tax my former choice that I loved one
Of so light note; but I forgive you both.   385
    Vent. What has my age deserved that you should
    think

I would abuse your ears with perjury?
If Heav'n be true, she's false.
    Ant.   Though Heav'n and earth 390
Should witness it, I'll not believe her tainted.
    Vent. I'll bring you, then, a witness
From hell to prove her so. (*Seeing Alexas just enter-
    ing, and starting back*)—Nay, go not back;
For stay you must and shall.   395
    Alex.   What means my lord?
    Vent. To make you do what most you hate—speak
    truth.
You are of Cleopatra's private counsel,
Of her bed-counsel, her lascivious hours,   400
Are conscious of each nightly change she makes,
And watch her, as Chaldeans do the moon;
Can tell what signs she passes through, what day.
    Alex. My noble lord!
    Vent.   My most illustrious pander, 405
No fine set speech, no cadence, no turned periods,
But a plain homespun truth is what I ask:
I did, myself, o'erhear your queen make love
To Dolabella. Speak; for I will know
By your confession what more passed betwixt 'em; 410
How near the bus'ness draws to your employment;
And when the happy hour.
    Ant. Speak truth, Alexas; whether it offend
Or please Ventidius care not: justify
Thy injured queen from malice: dare his worst. 415
    Octav. (*Aside*) See how he gives him courage!
    How he fears
To find her false and shuts his eyes to truth,
Willing to be misled!
    Alex. As far as love may plead for woman's frailty, 420
Urged by desert and greatness of the lover,
So far, divine Octavia, may my queen
Stand ev'n excused to you for loving him

Who is your lord: so far, from brave Ventidius,
May her past actions hope a fair report.   425
  Ant. 'Tis well and truly spoken: mark, Ventidius.
  Alex. To you, most noble emperor, her strong pas-
    sion
Stands not excused but wholly justified.
Her beauty's charms alone, without her crown,   430
From Ind and Meroe drew the distant vows
Of sighing kings; and at her feet were laid
The scepters of the earth, exposed on heaps,
To choose where she would reign.
She thought a Roman only could deserve her,   435
And, of all Romans, only Antony,
And to be less than wife to you disdained
Their lawful passion.
  Ant.   'Tis but truth.
  Alex. And yet, though love and your unmatched 440
    desert
Have drawn her from the due regard of honor,
At last Heav'n opened her unwilling eyes
To see the wrongs she offered fair Octavia,
Whose holy bed she lawlessly usurped.   445
The sad effects of this improsperous war
Confirmed those pious thoughts.
  Vent. (*Aside*)   O, wheel you there?
Observe him now; the man begins to mend
And talk substantial reason.—Fear not, eunuch;   450
The emperor has giv'n thee leave to speak.
  Alex. Else had I never dared t'offend his ears
With what the last necessity has urged
On my forsaken mistress; yet I must not
Presume to say her heart is wholly altered.   455
  Ant. No, dare not for thy life, I charge thee dare not
Pronounce that fatal word!
  Octav. (*Aside*) Must I bear this? Good Heav'n,
    afford me patience.

Vent. On, sweet eunuch; my dear half-man, pro- 460
ceed.

Alex. Yet Dolabella
Has loved her long; he, next my godlike lord,
Deserves her best; and should she meet his passion,
Rejected as she is by him she loved— 465

Ant. Hence, from my sight! for I can bear no more:
Let Furies drag thee quick to hell; let all
The longer damned have rest; each torturing hand
Do thou employ till Cleopatra comes;
Then join thou too and help to torture her! 470

              Exit Alexas, thrust out by Antony.

Octav. 'Tis not well,
Indeed, my lord, 'tis much unkind to me,
To show this passion, this extreme concernment,
For an abandoned, faithless prostitute.

Ant. Octavia, leave me: I am much disordered. 475
Leave me, I say.

Octav.   My lord!

Ant.   I bid you leave me.

Vent. Obey him, madam: best withdraw a while,
And see how this will work. 480

Octav. Wherein have I offended you, my lord,
That I am bid to leave you? Am I false
Or infamous? Am I a Cleopatra?
Were I she,
Base as she is, you would not bid me leave you, 485
But hang upon my neck, take slight excuses,
And fawn upon my falsehood.

Ant.   'Tis too much,
Too much, Octavia; I am pressed with sorrows
Too heavy to be borne; and you add more. 490
I would retire and recollect what's left
Of man within to aid me.

Octav.   You would mourn,
In private, for your love, who has betrayed you;

You did but half return to me: your kindness   495
Lingered behind with her. I hear, my lord,
You make conditions for her
And would include her treaty. Wondrous proofs
Of love to me!

   Ant.   Are you my friend, Ventidius?   500
Or are you turned a Dolabella too,
And let this Fury loose?

   Vent.   O, be advised,
Sweet madam, and retire.

   Octav. Yes, I will go; but never to return.   505
You shall no more be haunted with this Fury.
My lord, my lord, love will not always last
When urged with long unkindness and disdain;
Take her again whom you prefer to me;
She stays but to be called. Poor cozened man!   510
Let a feigned parting give her back your heart,
Which a feigned love first got; for injured me,
Though my just sense of wrongs forbid my stay,
My duty shall be yours.

To the dear pledges of our former love   515
My tenderness and care shall be transferred,
And they shall cheer, by turns, my widowed nights:
So, take my last farewell; for I despair
To have you whole and scorn to take you half.   *Exit.*

   Vent. I combat Heav'n, which blasts my best de-   520
     signs:
My last attempt must be to win her back;
But O! I fear, in vain.   *Exit.*

   Ant. Why was I framed with this plain, honest
     heart,   525
Which knows not to disguise its griefs and weakness,
But bears its workings outward to the world?

---

510. COZENED: duped.
515. PLEDGES: i.e., their children.
532. CLEARNESS: virtuous qualities.
536. SECURE: guilt-free; SPECIOUS FORM: deceptively friendly manner.

I should have kept the mighty anguish in
And forced a smile at Cleopatra's falsehood:
Octavia had believed it and had stayed.   530
But I am made a shallow-forded stream,
Seen to the bottom, all my clearness scorned,
And all my faults exposed!—See where he comes

Enter Dolabella.

Who has profaned the sacred name of friend
And worn it into vileness!   535
With how secure a brow and specious form,
He gilds the secret villain! Sure that face
Was meant for honesty; but Heav'n mismatched it
And furnished treason out with Nature's pomp,
To make its work more easy.   540
 Dola.   O my friend!
 Ant. Well, Dolabella, you performed my message?
 Dola. I did, unwillingly.
 Ant.   Unwillingly?
Was it so hard for you to bear our parting?   545
You should have wished it.
 Dola.   Why?
 Ant.   Because you love me.
And she received my message with as true,
With as unfeigned a sorrow as you brought it?   550
 Dola. She loves you, ev'n to madness.
 Ant.   O, I know it.
You, Dolabella, do not better know
How much she loves me. And should I
Forsake this beauty, this all-perfect creature?   555
 Dola. I could not, were she mine.
 Ant.   And yet you first
Persuaded me: how come you altered since?
 Dola. I said at first I was not fit to go;
I could not hear her sighs and see her tears   560

But pity must prevail: and so, perhaps,
It may again with you; for I have promised
That she should take her last farewell: and, see,
She comes to claim my word.

Enter Cleopatra.

Ant. False Dolabella! 565
Dola. What's false, my lord?
Ant. Why, Dolabella's false,
And Cleopatra's false; both false and faithless.
Draw near, you well-joined wickedness, you serpents,
Whom I have in my kindly bosom warmed 570
Till I am stung to death.
Dola. My lord, have I
Deserved to be thus used?
Cleo. Can Heav'n prepare
A newer torment? Can it find a curse 575
Beyond our separation?
Ant. Yes, if Fate
Be just, much greater: Heav'n should be ingenious
In punishing such crimes. The rolling stone
And gnawing vulture were slight pains, invented 580
When Jove was young and no examples known
Of mighty ills; but you have ripened sin
To such a monstrous growth 'twill pose the gods
To find an equal torture. Two, two such!—
O, there's no farther name, two such!—to me, 585
To me, who locked my soul within your breasts,
Had no desires, no joys, no life, but you;
When half the globe was mine, I gave it you
In dowry with my heart; I had no use,
No fruit of all, but you: a friend and mistress 590

579–80. ROLLING STONE, GNAWING VULTURE: the tortures of Sisyphus
and Tityus respectively.
589. USE: profit.

Was what the world could give. O Cleopatra!
O Dolabella! How could you betray
This tender heart, which with an infant fondness
Lay lulled betwixt your bosoms and there slept,
Secure of injured faith?　　　　　　　　　　595
　　Dola.　　　　　　If she has wronged you,
Heav'n, hell, and you revenge it.
　　Ant.　　　　　　　　If she wronged me!
Thou wouldst evade thy part of guilt; but swear
Thou lov'st not her.　　　　　　　　　　600
　　Dola.　　　　Not so as I love you.
　　Ant. Not so! Swear, swear, I say, thou dost not love
　　her.
　　Dola. No more than friendship will allow.
　　Ant.　　　　　　　　No more?　605
Friendship allows thee nothing; thou art perjured—
And yet thou didst not swear thou lovedst her not;
But not so much, no more. O trifling hypocrite,
Who dar'st not own to her thou dost not love,
Nor own to me thou dost! Ventidius heard it;　610
Octavia saw it.
　　Cleo.　　　They are enemies.
　　Ant. Alexas is not so: he, he confessed it:
He, who, next hell, best knew it, he avowed it.
(*To Dolabella*) Why do I seek a proof beyond your-　615
　　self?
You, whom I sent to bear my last farewell,
Returned to plead her stay.
　　Dola.　　　　　　What shall I answer?
If to have loved be guilt, then I have sinned;　620
But if to have repented of that love
Can wash away my crime, I have repented.
Yet, if I have offended past forgiveness,
Let not her suffer: she is innocent.
　　Cleo. Ah, what will not a woman do who loves!　625
What means will she refuse to keep that heart

Where all her joys are placed? 'Twas I encouraged,
'Twas I blew up the fire that scorched his soul,
To make you jealous and by that regain you.
But all in vain; I could not counterfeit.   630
In spite of all the dams, my love broke o'er
And drowned my heart again. Fate took th' occasion;
And thus one minute's feigning has destroyed
My whole life's truth.

    Ant.   Thin cobweb arts of falsehood, 635
Seen and broke through at first.

    Dola.   Forgive your mistress.

    Cleo. Forgive your friend.

    Ant.   You have convinced yourselves;
You plead each other's cause. What witness have you 640
That you but meant to raise my jealousy?

    Cleo. Ourselves and Heav'n.

    Ant. Guilt witnesses for guilt. Hence, love and
        friendship!
You have no longer place in human breasts;   645
These two have driv'n you out. Avoid my sight!
I would not kill the man whom I have loved
And cannot hurt the woman; but avoid me—
I do not know how long I can be tame,
For, if I stay one minute more to think   650
How I am wronged, my justice and revenge
Will cry so loud within me that my pity
Will not be heard for either.

    Dola.   Heav'n has but
Our sorrow for our sins, and then delights   655
To pardon erring man: sweet mercy seems
Its darling attribute, which limits justice,
As if there were degrees in Infinite,
And Infinite would rather want perfection
Than punish to extent.   660

654–55. Heav'n . . . sins: Heaven is content to let sorrow be our
sole punishment.

 Ant.   I can forgive
A foe, but not a mistress and a friend.
Treason is there in its most horrid shape
Where trust is greatest and the soul resigned
Is stabbed by its own guards. I'll hear no more; 665
Hence from my sight forever!
 Cleo.   How? forever!
I cannot go one moment from your sight,
And must I go forever?
My joys, my only joys, are centered here. 670
What place have I to go to? My own kingdom?
That I have lost for you. Or to the Romans?
They hate me for your sake. Or must I wander
The wide world o'er, a helpless, banished woman,
Banished for love of you, banished from you? 675
Ay, there's the banishment! O, hear me! hear me,
With strictest justice, for I beg no favor;
And if I have offended you, then kill me,
But do not banish me.
 Ant.   I must not hear you. 680
I have a fool within me takes your part;
But honor stops my ears.
 Cleo.   For pity hear me!
Would you cast off a slave who followed you?
Who crouched beneath your spurn?—He has no pity! 685
See if he gives one tear to my departure,
One look, one kind farewell: O iron heart!
Let all the gods look down and judge betwixt us
If he did ever love!
 Ant.   No more.—Alexas! 690
 Dola. A perjured villain!
 Ant. (To Cleopatra) Your Alexas, yours!
 Cleo. O, 'twas his plot, his ruinous design,
T' engage you in my love by jealousy.
Hear him; comfort him with me; let him speak. 695
 Ant. I have; I have.

Cleo.   And if he clear me not—
  Ant. Your creature! One who hangs upon your
    smiles!
Watches your eye, to say or to unsay   700
Whate'er you please! I am not to be moved.
  Cleo. Then must we part? Farewell, my cruel lord!
Th' appearance is against me; and I go,
Unjustified, forever from your sight.
How I have loved, you know; how yet I love,   705
My only comfort is, I know myself:
I love you more, ev'n now you are unkind,
Than when you loved me most: so well, so truly,
I'll never strive against it but die pleased
To think you once were mine.   710
  Ant. Good Heav'n, they weep at parting!
Must I weep too? That calls 'em innocent.
I must not weep; and yet I must, to think
That I must not forgive.—
Live, but live wretched; 'tis but just you should   715
Who made me so. Live from each other's sight;
Let me not hear you meet; set all the earth
And all the seas betwixt your sundered loves;
View nothing common but the sun and skies.
Now, all take several ways;   720
  And each your own sad fate with mine deplore;
  That you were false, and I could trust no more.
                              Exeunt severally.

---

704. UNJUSTIFIED: without exoneration.
720. SEVERAL: separate.

ACT V

[Enter] Cleopatra, Charmion, Iras.

Char. Be juster, Heav'n: such virtue punished thus
Will make us think that Chance rules all above
And shuffles, with a random hand, the lots
Which man is forced to draw.
    Cleo. I could tear out these eyes that gained his heart   5
And had not pow'r to keep it. O the curse
Of doting on, ev'n when I find it dotage!
Bear witness, gods, you heard him bid me go;
You, whom he mocked with imprecating vows
Of promised faith!—I'll die; I will not bear it.   10
       She pulls out her dagger, and they hold her.
You may hold me—
But I can keep my breath; I can die inward
And choke this love.

Enter Alexas.

    Iras.   Help, O Alexas, help!
The Queen grows desperate; her soul struggles in her   15
With all the agonies of love and rage,
And strives to force its passage.
    Cleo.   Let me go.
Art thou there, traitor!—O!
O for a little breath, to vent my rage!   20
Give, give me way, and let me loose upon him.
    Alex. Yes, I deserve it for my ill-timed truth.
Was it for me to prop
The ruins of a falling majesty?
To place myself beneath the mighty flaw,   25

Thus to be crushed and pounded into atoms
By its o'erwhelming weight? 'Tis too presuming
For subjects to preserve that willful pow'r
Which courts its own destruction.

   Cleo.   I would reason   30
More calmly with you. Did not you o'errule
And force my plain, direct, and open love
Into these crooked paths of jealousy?
Now, what's th' event? Octavia is removed,
But Cleopatra's banished. Thou, thou, villain,   35
Hast pushed my boat to open sea, to prove,
At my sad cost, if thou canst steer it back.
It cannot be; I'm lost too far; I'm ruined!
Hence, thou impostor, traitor, monster, devil!
I can no more: thou and my griefs have sunk   40
Me down so low that I want voice to curse thee.

   Alex. Suppose some shipwrecked seaman near the
      shore,
Dropping and faint with climbing up the cliff:
If, from above, some charitable hand   45
Pull him to safety, hazarding himself
To draw the other's weight, would he look back
And curse him for his pains? The case is yours;
But one step more and you have gained the height.

   Cleo. Sunk, nevermore to rise.   50

   Alex. Octavia's gone and Dolabella banished.
Believe me, madam, Antony is yours.
His heart was never lost but started off
To jealousy, love's last retreat and covert,
Where it lies hid in shades, watchful in silence,   55
And list'ning for the sound that calls it back.
Some other, any man ('tis so advanced),
May perfect this unfinished work, which I
(Unhappy only to myself) have left

(V)
34. EVENT: outcome.

So easy to his hand.   60
  Cleo.   Look well thou do't; else—
  Alex. Else, what your silence threatens.—Antony
Is mounted up the Pharos, from whose turret
He stands surveying our Egyptian galleys,
Engaged with Caesar's fleet. Now death or conquest! 65
If the first happen, Fate acquits my promise;
If we o'ercome, the conqueror is yours.
                    A distant shout within.
  Char. Have comfort, madam; did you mark that
    shout?   *Second shout nearer.*
  Iras. Hark! they redouble it.   70
  Alex.   'Tis from the port.
The loudness shows it near. Good news, kind Heavens!
  Cleo. Osiris make it so!

            Enter Serapion.

  Serap.   Where, where's the Queen?
  Alex. How frightfully the holy coward stares!   75
As if not yet recovered of th' assault,
When all his gods and, what's more dear to him,
His offerings, were at stake.
  Serap.   O horror, horror!
Egypt has been; our latest hour is come: 80
The queen of nations, from her ancient seat,
Is sunk forever in the dark abyss:
Time has unrolled her glories to the last
And now closed up the volume.
  Cleo.   Be more plain: 85
Say whence thou com'st (though Fate is in thy face,
Which from thy haggard eyes looks wildly out,
And threatens ere thou speak'st).
  Serap.   I came from Pharos;
From viewing (spare me and imagine it)   90
Our land's last hope, your navy—

Cleo.   Vanquished?
 Serap.   No.
They fought not.
 Cleo.   Then they fled?   95
  Serap.   Nor that. I saw,
With Antony, your well-appointed fleet
Row out; and thrice he waved his hand on high,
And thrice with cheerful cries they shouted back.
'Twas then false Fortune, like a fawning strumpet,   100
About to leave the bankrupt prodigal,
With a dissembled smile would kiss at parting
And flatter to the last; the well-timed oars
Now dipped from every bank, now smoothly run
To meet the foe; and soon indeed they met,   105
But not as foes. In few, we saw their caps
On either side thrown up; th' Egyptian galleys
(Received like friends) passed through and fell be-
 hind
The Roman rear; and now they all come forward   110
And ride within the port.
 Cleo.   Enough, Serapion:
I've heard my doom.—This needed not, you gods:
When I lost Antony your work was done;
'Tis but superfluous malice.—Where's my lord?   115
How bears he this last blow?
 Serap. His fury cannot be expressed by words:
Thrice he attempted headlong to have fall'n
Full on his foes, and aimed at Caesar's galley:
Withheld, he raves on you; cries he's betrayed.   120
Should he now find you—
 Alex.   Shun him; seek your safety,
Till you can clear your innocence.
 Cleo.   I'll stay.

---

106. IN FEW: in short.

Alex. You must not; haste you to your monument,   125
While I make speed to Caesar.
  Cleo.   Caesar! No,
I have no business with him.
  Alex.   I can work him
To spare your life and let this madman perish.   130
  Cleo. Base fawning wretch! Wouldst thou betray
    him too?
Hence from my sight! I will not hear a traitor;
'Twas thy design brought all this ruin on us.
Serapion, thou art honest; counsel me: 135
But haste, each moment's precious.
  Serap. Retire; you must not yet see Antony.
He who began this mischief,
'Tis just he tempt the danger: let him clear you;
And, since he offered you his servile tongue   140
To gain a poor precarious life from Caesar,
Let him expose that fawning eloquence
And speak to Antony.
  Alex.   O Heavens! I dare not;
I meet my certain death.   145
  Cleo.   Slave, thou deserv'st it.—
Not that I fear my lord will I avoid him;
I know him noble: when he banished me
And thought me false, he scorned to take my life;
But I'll be justified and then die with him.   150
  Alex. O, pity me, and let me follow you!
  Cleo. To death, if thou stir hence. Speak, if thou
    canst,
Now for thy life, which basely thou wouldst save;
While mine I prize at—this! [*Snaps fingers.*] Come,   155
    good Serapion.
      Exeunt Cleopatra, Serapion, Charmion, Iras.
  Alex. O that I less could fear to lose this being,
Which, like a snowball in my coward hand,
The more 'tis grasped, the faster melts away.

Poor reason! What a wretched aid art thou!   160
For still, in spite of thee,
These two long lovers, soul and body, dread
Their final separation. Let me think:
What can I say to save myself from death?
No matter what becomes of Cleopatra.   165

   Ant. (*Within*) Which way? Where?
   Vent. (*Within*)   This leads to the monument.
   Alex. Ah me! I hear him; yet I'm unprepared:
My gift of lying's gone;
And this court-devil, which I so oft have raised,   170
Forsakes me at my need. I dare not stay,
Yet cannot far go hence.   *Exit.*

Enter Antony and Ventidius.

   Ant. O happy Caesar! thou hast men to lead:
Think not 'tis thou hast conquered Antony,
But Rome has conquered Egypt. I'm betrayed.   175
   Vent. Curse on this treach'rous train!
Their soil and Heav'n infect 'em all with baseness;
And their young souls come tainted to the world
With the first breath they draw.
   Ant. Th' original villain sure no god created;   180
He was a bastard of the sun, by Nile,
Aped into man, with all his mother's mud
Crusted about his soul.
   Vent.   The nation is
One universal traitor, and their queen   185
The very spirit and extract of 'em all.
   Ant. Is there yet left
A possibility of aid from valor?
Is there one god unsworn to my destruction?

---

170. COURT-DEVIL: his plausible tongue.
182. APED INTO MAN: manlike only by imitation.
191. FATE: doom.
203. STARS: fortunes.

The least unmortgaged hope? For, if there be,   190
Methinks I cannot fall beneath the fate
Of such a boy as Caesar.
The world's one half is yet in Antony;
And from each limb of it that's hewed away
The soul comes back to me.   195

  Vent.   There yet remain
Three legions in the town: the last assault
Lopped off the rest. If death be your design
(As I must wish it now), these are sufficient
To make a heap about us of dead foes,   200
An honest pile for burial.

  Ant.   They're enough.
We'll not divide our stars but side by side
Fight emulous and with malicious eyes
Survey each other's acts: so every death   205
Thou giv'st I'll take on me, as a just debt,
And pay thee back a soul.

  Vent. Now you shall see I love you. Not a word
Of chiding more. By my few hours of life,
I am so pleased with this brave Roman fate   210
That I would not be Caesar, to outlive you.
When we put off this flesh and mount together,
I shall be shown to all th' ethereal crowd,
"Lo, this is he who died with Antony!"

  Ant. Who knows but we may pierce through all 215
   their troops
And reach my veterans yet? 'Tis worth the 'tempting,
T' o'erleap this gulf of fate,
And leave our wond'ring destinies behind.

Enter Alexas, trembling.

  Vent. See, see, that villain!   220
See Cleopatra stamped upon that face,
With all her cunning, all her arts of falsehood!

How she looks out through those dissembling eyes!
How he has set his count'nance for deceit
And promises a lie before he speaks!   225
Let me dispatch him first.   *Drawing.*

   Alex.   O, spare me, spare me!
   Ant. Hold; he's not worth your killing.—On thy
    life
(Which thou may'st keep, because I scorn to take it),   230
No syllable to justify thy queen;
Save thy base tongue its office.

   Alex.   Sir, she's gone,
Where she shall never be molested more
By love or you.   235

   Ant.   Fled to her Dolabella!
Die, traitor! I revoke my promise! die!
                    Going to kill him.

   Alex. O, hold! She is not fled.
   Ant.   She is: my eyes
Are open to her falsehood; my whole life   240
Has been a golden dream of love and friendship.
But, now I wake, I'm like a merchant roused
From soft repose, to see his vessel sinking
And all his wealth cast o'er. Ingrateful woman!
Who followed me but as the swallow summer,   245
Hatching her young ones in my kindly beams,
Singing her flatt'ries to my morning wake;
But, now my winter comes, she spreads her wings
And seeks the spring of Caesar.

   Alex.   Think not so: 250
Her fortunes have in all things mixed with yours.
Had she betrayed her naval force to Rome,
How easily might she have gone to Caesar,
Secure by such a bribe!

   Vent.   She sent it first,   255

---
283. THIS . . . ABOVE: i.e., this injustice must displease Heaven.

To be more welcome after.

    Ant.   'Tis too plain;
Else would she have appeared, to clear herself.

    Alex. Too fatally she has; she could not bear
To be accused by you but shut herself   260
Within her monument, looked down and sighed,
While from her unchanged face the silent tears
Dropped, as they had not leave but stole their parting.
Some undistinguished words she inly murmured;
At last she raised her eyes and, with such looks   265
As dying Lucrece cast—

    Ant.   My heart forbodes—

    Vent. All for the best; go on.

    Alex.   She snatched her poniard,
And, ere we could prevent the fatal blow,   270
Plunged it within her breast, then turned to me:
"Go, bear my lord," said she, "my last farewell,
And ask him if he yet suspect my faith."
More she was saying, but death rushed betwixt.
She half pronounced your name with her last breath, 275
And buried half within her.

    Vent.   Heav'n be praised!

    Ant. Then art thou innocent, my poor dear love,
And art thou dead?
O those two words! their sound should be divided: 280
Hadst thou been false and died, or hadst thou lived
And hadst been true.—But innocence and death!
This shows not well above. Then what am I,
The murderer of this truth, this innocence!
Thoughts cannot form themselves in words so horrid 285
As can express my guilt!

    Vent. Is't come to this? The gods have been too
         gracious:
And thus you thank 'em for't!

    Ant. (*To Alexas*)   Why stay'st thou here? 290
Is it for thee to spy upon my soul

And see its inward mourning? Get thee hence!
Thou art not worthy to behold what now
Becomes a Roman emperor to perform.

    Alex. (*Aside*) He loves her still: 295
His grief betrays it. Good! The joy to find
She's yet alive completes the reconcilement.
I've saved myself and her. But, O! the Romans!
Fate comes too fast upon my wit,
Hunts me too hard and meets me at each double.   300
                                    Exit.

    Vent. Would she had died a little sooner, though,
Before Octavia went; you might have treated:
Now 'twill look tame and would not be received.
Come, rouse yourself, and let's die warm together.

    Ant. I will not fight: there's no more work for war. 305
The bus'ness of my angry hours is done.

    Vent. Caesar is at your gates.

    Ant.   Why, let him enter;
He's welcome now.

    Vent. What lethargy has crept into your soul?   310

    Ant. 'Tis but a scorn of life and just desire
To free myself from bondage.

    Vent.   Do it bravely.

    Ant. I will; but not by fighting. O Ventidius!
What should I fight for now? My queen is dead.   315
I was but great for her; my pow'r, my empire,
Were but my merchandise to buy her love,
And conquered kings my factors. Now she's dead,
Let Caesar take the world—
An empty circle, since the jewel's gone   320
Which made it worth my strife: my being's nauseous,
For all the bribes of life are gone away.

---

   300. DOUBLE: evasive action.
   302. TREATED: parleyed with Caesar.
   303. TAME: cowardly.
   318. FACTORS: agents.

Vent. Would you be taken?

Ant.   Yes, I would be taken;
But as a Roman ought—dead, my Ventidius: 325
For I'll convey my soul from Caesar's reach
And lay down life myself. 'Tis time the world
Should have a lord and know whom to obey.
We two have kept its homage in suspense
And bent the globe, on whose each side we trod,   330
Till it was dinted inwards. Let him walk
Alone upon't; I'm weary of my part.
My torch is out; and the world stands before me
Like a black desert at th' approach of night:
I'll lay me down and stray no farther on.   335

    Vent. I could be grieved,
But that I'll not outlive you: choose your death;
For I have seen him in such various shapes,
I care not which I take: I'm only troubled
The life I bear is worn to such a rag   340
'Tis scarce worth giving. I could wish, indeed,
We threw it from us with a better grace,
That, like two lions taken in the toils,
We might at least thrust out our paws and wound
The hunters that enclose us.   345

    Ant.   I have thought on't.
Ventidius, you must live.

    Vent.   I must not, sir.

    Ant. Wilt thou not live, to speak some good of me?
To stand by my fair fame and guard th' approaches   350
From the ill tongues of men?

    Vent.   Who shall guard mine,
For living after you?

    Ant.   Say, I command it.

    Vent. If we die well, our deaths will speak them-   355
    selves
And need no living witness.

    Ant.   Thou hast loved me,

And fain I would reward thee. I must die;
Kill me and take the merit of my death　　　　　　　360
To make thee friends with Caesar.

 Vent.　　　　　　　　　　　Thank your kindness.
You said I loved you, and, in recompense,
You bid me turn a traitor. Did I think
You would have used me thus?—that I should die　　365
With a hard thought of you?

 Ant.　　　　　　　　　Forgive me, Roman.
Since I have heard of Cleopatra's death,
My reason bears no rule upon my tongue,
But lets my thoughts break all at random out.　　　370
I've thought better; do not deny me twice.

 Vent. By Heav'n, I will not.
Let it not be t' outlive you.

 Ant.　　　　　　　　Kill me first,
And then die thou; for 'tis but just thou serve　　375
Thy friend before thyself.

 Vent.　　　　　　　Give me your hand.
We soon shall meet again. Now, farewell, Emperor!—
　　　　　　　　　　　　　　　　Embrace.

Methinks that word's too cold to be my last:
Since death sweeps all distinctions, farewell, friend!　380
That's all.—
I will not make a bus'ness of a trifle;
And yet I cannot look on you and kill you;
Pray turn your face.

 Ant.　　　　　　I do: strike home, be sure.　　385
 Vent. Home as my sword will reach.　*Kills himself.*
 Ant.　　　　　　　　　O, thou mistak'st!
That wound was none of thine; give it me back;
Thou robb'st me of my death!

 Vent.　　　　　　　I do indeed;　　　　390

---

402. HAD: i.e., would have, had he been bookish.
409. JADES: cheats.
414. PLAYED . . . LIFE: i.e., only feigned suicide.

But think 'tis the first time I e'er deceived you,
If that may plead my pardon. And you, gods,
Forgive me, if you will; for I die perjured
Rather than kill my friend.   _Dies._

   Ant. Farewell! Ever my leader, ev'n in death!   395
My queen and thou have got the start of me,
And I'm the lag of honor.—Gone so soon?
Is Death no more? He used him carelessly,
With a familiar kindness; ere he knocked,
Ran to the door and took him in his arms,   400
As who should say, "Y'are welcome at all hours;
A friend need give no warning." Books had spoiled him;
For all the learn'd are cowards by profession.
'Tis not worth
My farther thought; for death, for aught I know,   405
Is but to think no more. Here's to be satisfied.
                      Falls on his sword.
I've missed my heart. O unperforming hand!
Thou never couldst have erred in a worse time.
My fortune jades me to the last; and Death,
Like a great man, takes state and makes me wait   410
For my admittance.—   _Trampling within._
        Some, perhaps, from Caesar:
If he should find me living and suspect
That I played booty with my life! I'll mend
My work ere they can reach me. _Rises upon his knees._ 415

     Enter Cleopatra, Charmion, Iras.

   Cleo. Where is my lord! where is he?
   Char.   There he lies,
And dead Ventidius by him.
   Cleo. My fears were prophets; I am come too late.
O that accurst Alexas!   _Runs to him._   420
   Ant.   Art thou living?
Or am I dead before I knew and thou

The first kind ghost that meets me?
  Cleo.   Help me seat him.
Send quickly, send for help!   425
                 They place him in a chair.
  Ant.   I am answered.
We live both. Sit thee down, my Cleopatra:
I'll make the most I can of life, to stay
A moment more with thee.
  Cleo. How is it with you?   430
  Ant.   'Tis as with a man
Removing in a hurry; all packed up
But one dear jewel that his haste forgot;
And he, for that, returns upon the spur:
So I come back for thee.   435
  Cleo. Too long, you Heav'ns, you have been cruel to
     me;
Now show your mended faith and give me back
His fleeting life!
  Ant.   It will not be, my love.   440
I keep my soul by force.
Say but thou art not false.
  Cleo.   'Tis now too late
To say I'm true: I'll prove it and die with you.
Unknown to me, Alexas feigned my death;   445
Which, when I knew, I hasted to prevent
This fatal consequence. My fleet betrayed
Both you and me.
  Ant.   And Dolabella—
  Cleo.   Scarce   450
Esteemed before he loved; but hated now.
  Ant. Enough: my life's not long enough for more.
Thou say'st thou wilt come after: I believe thee;
For I can now believe whate'er thou say'st,
That we may part more kindly.   455
  Cleo.   I will come.
Doubt not, my life, I'll come, and quickly too;

Caesar shall triumph o'er no part of thee.

  Ant. But grieve not, while thou stay'st,
My last disastrous times: 460
Think we have had a clear and glorious day,
And Heav'n did kindly to delay the storm
Just till our close of ev'ning. Ten years' love,
And not a moment lost, but all improved
To th' utmost joys. What ages have we lived!   465
And now to die each other's; and, so dying,
While hand in hand we walk in groves below,
Whole troops of lovers' ghosts shall flock about us
And all the train be ours.

  Cleo. Your words are like the notes of dying swans, 470
Too sweet to last. Were there so many hours
For your unkindness and not one for love?

  Ant. No, not a minute.—This one kiss—more worth
Than all I leave to Caesar.   *Dies.*

  Cleo. O, tell me so again,   475
And take ten thousand kisses for that word.
My lord, my lord! speak, if you yet have being;
Sigh to me, if you cannot speak; or cast
One look! Do anything that shows you live.

  Iras. He's gone too far to hear you;   480
And this you see, a lump of senseless clay,
The leavings of a soul.

  Char.   Remember, madam,
He charged you not to grieve.

  Cleo.   And I'll obey him.   485
I have not loved a Roman not to know
What should become his wife; his wife, my Charmion,
For 'tis to that high title I aspire,
And now I'll not die less! Let dull Octavia
Survive, to mourn him dead: my nobler fate   490
Shall knit our spousals with a tie too strong
For Roman laws to break.

  Iras.   Will you, then, die?

Cleo. Why shouldst thou make that question?

Iras. Caesar is merciful.   495

Cleo.   Let him be so

To those that want his mercy: my poor lord
Made no such cov'nant with him, to spare me
When he was dead. Yield me to Caesar's pride?
What! to be led in triumph through the streets,   500
A spectacle to base plebeian eyes,
While some dejected friend of Antony's,
Close in a corner, shakes his head and mutters
A secret curse on her who ruined him?
I'll none of that.   505

Char.   Whatever you resolve,
I'll follow, ev'n to death.

Iras.   I only feared
For you, but more should fear to live without you.

Cleo. Why, now 'tis as it should be. Quick, my   510
    friends,
Dispatch; ere this, the town's in Caesar's hands.
My lord looks down concerned and fears my stay,
Lest I should be surprised;
Keep him not waiting for his love too long.   515
You, Charmion, bring my crown and richest jewels,
With 'em, the wreath of victory I made
(Vain augury!) for him who now lies dead.
You, Iras, bring the cure of all our ills.

Iras. The aspics, madam?   520

Cleo.   Must I bid you twice?
                    Exeunt Charmion and Iras.

'Tis sweet to die when they would force life on me,
To rush into the dark abode of Death
And seize him first; if he be like my love,
He is not frightful, sure.   525
We're now alone, in secrecy and silence;

514. SURPRISED: captured.

And is not this like lovers? I may kiss
These pale, cold lips; Octavia does not see me;
And, O! 'tis better far to have him thus
Than see him in her arms.—O, welcome, welcome!   530

Enter Charmion and Iras.

  Char. What must be done?
  Cleo.   Short ceremony, friends;
But yet it must be decent. First, this laurel
Shall crown my hero's head: he fell not basely,
Nor left his shield behind him. Only thou   535
Couldst triumph o'er thyself, and thou alone
Wert worthy so to triumph.
  Char.   To what end
These ensigns of your pomp and royalty?
  Cleo. Dull that thou art! Why, 'tis to meet my love, 540
As when I saw him first on Cydnus' bank,
All sparkling, like a goddess: so adorned,
I'll find him once again; my second spousals
Shall match my first in glory. Haste, haste, both,
And dress the bride of Antony.   545
  Char.   'Tis done.
  Cleo. Now seat me by my lord. I claim this place;
For I must conquer Caesar too, like him,
And win my share o' th' world.—Hail, you dear relics
Of my immortal love!   550
O, let no impious hand remove you hence,
But rest forever here! Let Egypt give
His death that peace which it denied his life.—
Reach me the casket.
  Iras.   Underneath the fruit   555
The aspic lies.
  Cleo. (*Putting aside the leaves*) Welcome, thou
     kind deceiver!
Thou best of thieves, who, with an easy key,

Dost open life and, unperceived by us,   560
Ev'n steal us from ourselves; discharging so
Death's dreadful office better than himself,
Touching our limbs so gently into slumber
That Death stands by, deceived by his own image,
And thinks himself but Sleep.   565

   Serap. (*Within*)   The Queen, where is she?
The town is yielded; Caesar's at the gates.

   Cleo. He comes too late t' invade the rites of death.
Haste, bare my arm, and rouse the serpent's fury.

         Holds out her arm, and draws it back.

Coward flesh,   570
Wouldst thou conspire with Caesar to betray me,
As thou wert none of mine? I'll force thee to't,
And not be sent by him,
But bring, myself, my soul to Antony.

       Turns aside, and then shows her arm bloody.

Take hence; the work is done.   575

   Serap. (*Within*)   Break ope the door,
And guard the traitor well.

   Char.   The next is ours.

   Iras. Now, Charmion, to be worthy
Of our great queen and mistress.   580

         They apply the aspics.

   Cleo. Already, Death, I feel thee in my veins;
I go with such a will to find my lord
That we shall quickly meet.
A heavy numbness creeps through every limb,
And now 'tis at my head: my eyelids fall,   585
And my dear love is vanished in a mist.
Where shall I find him, where? O turn me to him,
And lay me on his breast!—Caesar, thy worst;
Now part us, if thou canst.   *Dies.*

---

  572. As: as if.
  586. MY . . . MIST: she can no longer see Antony with her failing
vision.

*Iras sinks down at her feet and dies; Charmion stands
                behind her chair, as dressing her head.*

Enter Serapion, two Priests, Alexas bound, Egyptians.

2 *Priests.*   Behold, Serapion,   590
What havoc death has made!
    Serap.   'Twas what I feared.—
Charmion, is this well done?
    Char. Yes, 'tis well done, and like a queen, the last
Of her great race: I follow her.   *Sinks down; dies.* 595
    Alex.   'Tis true,
She has done well: much better thus to die
Than live to make a holiday in Rome.
    Serap. See,
See how the lovers sit in state together,   600
As they were giving laws to half mankind!
Th' impression of a smile, left in her face,
Shows she died pleased with him for whom she lived,
And went to charm him in another world.
Caesar's just ent'ring: grief has now no leisure.   605
Secure that villain, as our pledge of safety,
To grace th' imperial triumph.—Sleep, blest pair,
Secure from human chance, long ages out,
While all the storms of fate fly o'er your tomb,
    And fame to late posterity shall tell,   610
    No lovers lived so great or died so well.

EPILOGUE

Poets, like disputants, when reasons fail,
Have one sure refuge left—and that's to rail.
"Fop," "coxcomb," "fool," are thundered through the
    pit;
And this is all their equipage of wit.   5
We wonder how the Devil this diff'rence grows,
Betwixt our fools in verse and yours in prose:
For, 'faith, the quarrel rightly understood,
'Tis civil war with their own flesh and blood.
The threadbare author hates the gaudy coat,   10
And swears at the gilt coach, but swears afoot:
For 'tis observed of every scribbling man,
He grows a fop as fast as e'er he can;
Prunes up and asks his oracle, the glass,
If pink or purple best become his face.   15
For our poor wretch, he neither rails nor prays;
Nor likes your wit just as you like his plays;
He has not yet so much of Mr. Bayes.
He does his best; and if he cannot please,
Would quietly sue out his writ of ease.   20
Yet, if he might his own grand jury call,
By the fair sex he begs to stand or fall.
Let Caesar's pow'r the men's ambition move,
But grace you him who lost the world for love!

(Epilogue)
18. MR. BAYES: character in Buckingham's *The Rehearsal*, presumed
a satire on Dryden himself.
20. SUE OUT: apply for; WRIT OF EASE: certificate of release from
employment.

Yet if some antiquated lady say 25
The last age is not copied in his play,
Heav'n help the man who for that face must drudge,
Which only has the wrinkles of a judge.
Let not the young and beauteous join with those;
For should you raise such numerous hosts of foes, 30
Young wits and sparks he to his aid must call;
'Tis more than one man's work to please you all.

THE WAY OF THE WORLD

A Comedy by William Congreve

Audire est operae pretium, procedere recte
Qui moechis non vultis.   Horace, *Satires.*

Metuat doti deprensa.   *Ibid.*

[DEDICATION]

To the Right Honorable Ralph, Earl of Montague, etc.

My Lord,

Whether the world will arraign me of vanity or not that I have presumed to dedicate this comedy to your Lordship, I am yet in doubt; though it may be it is some degree of vanity even to doubt of it. One who has at any time had the honor of your Lordship's conversation cannot be supposed to think very meanly of that which he would prefer to your perusal; yet it were to incur the imputation of too much sufficiency to pretend to such a merit as might abide the test of your Lordship's censure.

Whatever value may be wanting to this play while it is yet mine will be sufficiently made up to it when it is once become your Lordship's; and it is my security that I cannot have overrated it more by my dedication than your Lordship will dignify it by your patronage.

That it succeeded on the stage was almost beyond my expectation, for but little of it was prepared for that general taste which seems now to be predominant in the palates of our audience.

(Dedication)
9. SUFFICIENCY: conceit.

Those characters which are meant to be ridiculous in most of our comedies are of fools so gross that, in my humble opinion, they should rather disturb than divert the well-natured and reflecting part of an audience; they are rather objects of charity than contempt, and instead of moving our mirth they ought very often to excite our compassion. 25

This reflection moved me to design some characters which should appear ridiculous not so much through a natural folly (which is incorrigible and therefore not proper for the stage) as through an affected wit, a wit which at the same time that it is affected is also false. As there is some difficulty in the formation of a character of this nature, so there is some hazard which attends the progress of its success upon the stage; for many come to a play so overcharged with criticism that they very often let fly their censure when through their rashness they have mistaken their aim. This I had occasion lately to observe; for this play had been acted two or three days before some of these hasty judges could find the leisure to distinguish betwixt the character of a Witwoud and a Truewit. 30 35 40

I must beg your Lordship's pardon for this digression from the true course of this epistle; but that it may not seem altogether impertinent, I beg that I may plead the occasion of it, in part of that excuse of which I stand in need for recommending this comedy to your protection. It is only by the countenance of your Lordship and the few so qualified that such who write with care and pains can hope to be distinguished; for the prostituted name of "poet" promiscuously levels all that bear it. 45 50

44. TRUEWIT: character in Ben Jonson's *Epicoene* (1609).
47. IMPERTINENT: irrelevant.
58-59. COUNTENANCE: approval.
60. TURNS: i.e., intricacies of plot.

Terence, the most correct writer in the world, had 55
a Scipio and a Laelius, if not to assist him at least
to support him in his reputation; and notwithstand-
ing his extraordinary merit, it may be their countenance was not more than necessary.

The purity of his style, the delicacy of his turns, 60
and the justness of his characters were all of them
beauties which the greater part of his audience
were incapable of tasting; some of the coarsest
strokes of Plautus, so severely censured by Horace,
were more likely to affect the multitude—such who 65
come with expectation to laugh out the last act of a
play and are better entertained with two or three
unseasonable jests than with the artful solution of
the fable.

As Terence excelled in his performance, so had 70
he great advantages to encourage his undertakings;
for he built most on the foundations of Menander:
his plots were generally modeled and his characters
ready drawn to his hand. He copied Menander;
and Menander had no less light in the formation of 75
his characters from the observations of Theophrastus, of whom he was a disciple; and Theophrastus,
it is known, was not only the disciple but the im-
mediate successor of Aristotle, the first and greatest
judge of poetry. These were great models to de- 80
sign by; and the further advantage which Terence
possessed towards giving his plays the due ornaments of purity of style and justness of manners was
not less considerable from the freedom of conversation which was permitted him with Laelius and 85
Scipio, two of the greatest and most polite men of
his age. And, indeed, the privilege of such a conversation is the only certain means of attaining to
the perfection of dialogue.

If it has happened in any part of this comedy 90

that I have gained a turn of style or expression more correct, or at least more corrigible, than in those which I have formerly written, I must, with equal pride and gratitude, ascribe it to the honor of your Lordship's admitting me into your conversation and 95 that of a society where everybody else was so well worthy of you, in your retirement last summer from the town; for it was immediately after that this comedy was written. If I have failed in my performance, it is only to be regretted, where there 100 were so many not inferior either to a Scipio or a Laelius, that there should be one wanting equal to the capacity of a Terence.

If I am not mistaken, poetry is almost the only art which has not yet laid claim to your Lordship's 105 patronage. Architecture and Painting, to the great honor of our country, have flourished under your influence and protection. In the meantime, Poetry, the eldest sister of all arts and parent of most, seems to have resigned her birthright, by having neglected 110 to pay her duty to your Lordship and by permitting others of a later extraction to prepossess that place in your esteem to which none can pretend a better title. Poetry, in its nature, is sacred to the good and great; the relation between them is reciprocal, 115 and they are ever propitious to it. It is the privilege of Poetry to address to them, and it is their prerogative alone to give it protection.

This received maxim is a general apology for all writers who consecrate their labors to great men; 120 but I could wish at this time that this address were exempted from the common pretense of all dedications, and that, as I can distinguish your Lordship even among the most deserving, so this offering might become remarkable by some particular in- 125 stance of respect which should assure your Lordship that I am, with all due sense of your extreme worthiness and humanity, my Lord, your Lordship's most obedient and most obliged humble servant,

130

WILL. CONGREVE.

PROLOGUE

Spoken by Mr. Betterton [*Fainall*]

Of those few fools who with ill stars are cursed,
Sure scribbling fools called poets fare the worst;
For they're a sort of fools which Fortune makes,
And, after she has made 'em fools, forsakes.
With Nature's oafs 'tis quite a diff'rent case,   5
For Fortune favors all her idiot race;
In her own nest the cuckoo-eggs we find,
O'er which she broods to hatch the changeling kind.
No portion for her own she has to spare,
So much she dotes on her adopted care.   10

Poets are bubbles, by the town drawn in,
Suffered at first some trifling stakes to win;
But what unequal hazards do they run!
Each time they write, they venture all they've won;
The squire that's buttered still is sure to be undone.   15
This author heretofore has found your favor,
But pleads no merit from his past behavior.
To build on that might prove a vain presumption,
Should grants to poets made admit resumption;
And in Parnassus he must lose his seat   20
If that be found a forfeited estate.

He owns, with toil he wrought the following scenes,
But if they're naught, ne'er spare him for his pains.

(Prologue)
11. BUBBLES: dupes.
15. BUTTERED: flattered.
19. RESUMPTION: reclamation by the giver.

Damn him the more; have no commiseration
For dullness on mature deliberation.   25
He swears he'll not resent one hissed-off scene,
Nor, like those peevish wits, his play maintain,
Who, to assert their sense, your taste arraign.
Some plot we think he has, and some new thought,
Some humor, too, no farce—but that's a fault.   30
Satire, he thinks, you ought not to expect;
For, so reformed a town who dares correct?
To please, this time, has been his sole pretense;
He'll not instruct, lest it should give offense.
Should he by chance a knave or fool expose,   35
That hurts none here; sure here are none of those.
In short, our play shall (with your leave to show it)
Give you one instance of a passive poet,
Who to your judgments yields all resignation:
So save or damn, after your own discretion.   40

Personae Dramatis

MEN: **By**

Fainall, in love with Mrs.* Marwood.   Mr. Betterton.

Mirabell, in love with Mrs. Millamant.   Mr. Verbruggen.

Witwoud,   Mr. Bowen.

             } followers of Mrs. Millamant.

Petulant,   Mr. Bowman.

Sir Willful Witwoud, half-brother to Witwoud, and nephew to Lady Wishfort.   Mr. Underhill.

Waitwell, servant to Mirabell.   Mr. Bright.

WOMEN:

Lady Wishfort, enemy to Mirabell, for having falsely pretended love to her.   Mrs. Leigh.

Mrs. Millamant, a fine lady, niece to Lady Wishfort, and loves Mirabell.   Mrs. Bracegirdle.

Mrs. Marwood, friend to Mr. Fainall, and likes Mirabell.   Mrs. Barry.

Mrs. Fainall, daughter to Lady Wishfort, and wife to Fainall, formerly friend to Mirabell.   Mrs. Bowman.

Foible, woman to Lady Wishfort.   Mrs. Willis.

Mincing, woman to Mrs. Millamant.   Mrs. Prince.

[*Peg,* maid to Lady Wishfort.]

       Dancers, Footmen, and Attendants.

---

*Mistress, used indifferently for both married and unmarried women.

SCENE: *London.*

The time equal to that of the presentation.

ACT I

Scene I. A chocolate house.

[Enter] Mirabell and Fainall, rising from cards;
Betty waiting.

Mira. You are a fortunate man, Mr. Fainall.

Fain. Have we done?

Mira. What you please. I'll play on to entertain you.

Fain. No, I'll give you your revenge another time, when you are not so indifferent; you are thinking of something else now and play too negligently; the coldness of a losing gamester lessens the pleasure of the winner: I'd no more play with a man that slighted his ill fortune than I'd make love to a woman who undervalued the loss of her reputation.

Mira. You have a taste extremely delicate and are for refining on your pleasures.

Fain. Prithee, why so reserved? Something has put you out of humor.

Mira. Not at all: I happen to be grave today, and you are gay; that's all.

Fain. Confess, Millamant and you quarreled last night after I left you; my fair cousin has some humors that would tempt the patience of a Stoic. What? some coxcomb came in and was well received by her while you were by?

Mira. Witwoud and Petulant; and what was worse, her aunt, your wife's mother, my evil genius—or to sum up all in her own name—my old Lady Wishfort, came in.

Fain. O, there it is then! She has a lasting passion
for you, and with reason. What? then my wife was
there?

Mira. Yes, and Mrs. Marwood, and three or four
more whom I never saw before; seeing me, they all   30
put on their grave faces, whispered one another, then
complained aloud of the vapors, and after fell into a
profound silence.

Fain. They had a mind to be rid of you.

Mira. For which reason I resolved not to stir. At   35
last the good old lady broke through her painful taci-
turnity with an invective against long visits. I would
not have understood her, but Millamant joining in
the argument, I rose and with a constrained smile
told her I thought nothing was so easy as to know   40
when a visit began to be troublesome; she reddened
and I withdrew, without expecting her reply.

Fain. You were to blame to resent what she spoke
only in compliance with her aunt.

Mira. She is more mistress of herself than to be   45
under the necessity of such a resignation.

Fain. What? Though half her fortune depends
upon her marrying with My Lady's approbation?

Mira. I was then in such a humor that I should
have been better pleased if she had been less dis-   50
creet.

Fain. Now I remember, I wonder not they were
weary of you; last night was one of their cabal nights.
They have 'em three times a week and meet by turns
at one another's apartments, where they come to-   55
gether like the coroner's inquest to sit upon the murdered reputations of the week. You and I are excluded; and it was once proposed that all the male

(I.i.)
32. VAPORS: melancholia.
42. EXPECTING: waiting for.
66. RATAFIA: fruit cordial.

sex should be excepted; but somebody moved that
to avoid scandal there might be one man of the com-   60
munity; upon which motion Witwould and Petulant
were enrolled members.

Mira. And who may have been the foundress of this
sect? My Lady Wishfort, I warrant, who publishes
her detestation of mankind; and, full of the vigor of   65
fifty-five, declares for a friend and ratafia, and, let
posterity shift for itself, she'll breed no more.

Fain. The discovery of your sham addresses to her,
to conceal your love to her niece, has provoked this
separation. Had you dissembled better, things might   70
have continued in the state of nature.

Mira. I did as much as man could with any reasonable conscience; I proceeded to the very last act of
flattery with her and was guilty of a song in her commendation. Nay, I got a friend to put her into a lam-   75
poon and compliment her with the imputation of an
affair with a young fellow, which I carried so far that
I told her the malicious town took notice that she was
grown fat of a sudden and, when she lay in of a
dropsy, persuaded her she was reported to be in   80
labor. The Devil's in't if an old woman is to be flattered further, unless a man should endeavor downright personally to debauch her; and that my virtue
forbade me. But, for the discovery of that amour, I
am indebted to your friend, or your wife's friend,   85
Mrs. Marwood.

Fain. What should provoke her to be your enemy,
without she has made you advances which you have
slighted? Women do not easily forgive omissions of
that nature.   90

Mira. She was always civil to me, till of late. I confess I am not one of those coxcombs who are apt to
interpret a woman's good manners to her prejudice

and think that she who does not refuse 'em everything can refuse 'em nothing.   95

Fain. You are a gallant man, Mirabell; and though
you may have cruelty enough not to satisfy a lady's
longing, you have too much generosity not to be
tender of her honor. Yet you speak with an indifference which seems to be affected and confesses you   100
are conscious of a negligence.

Mira. You pursue the argument with a distrust that
seems to be unaffected and confesses you are conscious of a concern for which the lady is more indebted to you than your wife.   105

Fain. Fie, fie, friend, if you grow censorious I must
leave you. I'll look upon the gamesters in the next
room.

Mira. Who are they?

Fain. Petulant and Witwoud. (*To Betty*) Bring   110
me some chocolate.   *Exit.*

Mira. Betty, what says your clock?

Bet. Turned of the last canonical hour, sir.   *Exit.*

Mira. How pertinently the jade answers me! Ha!
Almost one o'clock! (*Looking on his watch.*) O, y'are   115
come—

Enter a Servant.

Well, is the grand affair over? You have been something tedious.

Serv. Sir, there's such coupling at Pancras that
they stand behind one another, as 'twere in a coun-   120

---

113. CANONICAL HOUR: period when church marriages could be legal-
ly performed.
119. PANCRAS: the church of St. Pancras, where marriages could
be performed at any time without licenses.
125. DUKE'S PLACE: to St. James's Church, another place where
irregular marriages could be performed.
136. DAME PARTLET: name of the hen in Chaucer's "Nun's Priest's
Tale."
138. ROSAMOND'S POND: body of water in St. James's Park.
139. TENDER: care for.

try dance. Ours was the last couple to lead up; and
no hopes appearing of dispatch; besides, the parson
growing hoarse, we were afraid his lungs would have
failed before it came to our turn; so we drove round
to Duke's Place and there they were riveted in a   125
trice.

Mira. So, so; you are sure they are married?

Serv. Married and bedded, sir: I am witness.

Mira. Have you the certificate?

Serv. Here it is, sir.   130

Mira. Has the tailor brought Waitwell's clothes
home and the new liveries?

Serv. Yes, sir.

Mira. That's well. Do you go home again, d'ee
hear, and adjourn the consummation till farther   135
order. Bid Waitwell shake his ears and Dame Partlet
rustle up her feathers and meet me at one o'clock by
Rosamond's Pond, that I may see her before she returns to her lady; and, as you tender your ears, be
secret.   *Exit Servant.* 140

Re-enter Fainall [and Betty].

Fain. Joy of your success, Mirabell; you look
pleased.

Mira. Ay; I have been engaged in a matter of some
sort of mirth, which is not yet ripe for discovery. I
am glad this is not a cabal night. I wonder, Fainall, 145
that you, who are married and of consequence should
be discreet, will suffer your wife to be of such a
party.

Fain. Faith, I am not jealous. Besides, most who are
engaged are women and relations; and for the men,   150
they are of a kind too contemptible to give scandal.

Mira. I am of another opinion. The greater the
coxcomb, always the more the scandal; for a woman

who is not a fool can have but one reason for asso- 155
ciating with a man that is.

Fain. Are you jealous as often as you see Witwoud
entertained by Millamant?

Mira. Of her understanding I am, if not of her
person.

Fain. You do her wrong, for, to give her due, she 160
has wit.

Mira. She has beauty enough to make any man
think so, and complaisance enough not to contradict
him who shall tell her so.

Fain. For a passionate lover, methinks you are a 165
man somewhat too discerning in the failings of your
mistress.

Mira. And for a discerning man somewhat too passionate a lover; for I like her with all her faults; nay,
like her for her faults. Her follies are so natural, or 170
so artful, that they become her; and those affecta-
tions which in another woman would be odious serve
but to make her more agreeable. I'll tell thee, Fainall,
she once used me with that insolence that in revenge
I took her to pieces, sifted her, and separated her fail- 175
ings; I studied 'em and got 'em by rote. The catalogue
was so large that I was not without hopes one day
or other to hate her heartily: to which end I so used
myself to think of 'em that at length, contrary to my
design and expectation, they gave me every hour less 180
and less disturbance; till in a few days it became
habitual to me to remember 'em without being displeased. They are now grown as familiar to me as my
own frailties; and in all probability in a little time
longer I shall like 'em as well. 185

Fain. Marry her, marry her; be half as well acquainted with her charms as you are with her defects
and, my life on't, you are your own man again.

Mira. Say you so?

Fain. Ay, ay; I have experience: I have a wife, and 190 so forth.

Enter Messenger.

Mess. Is one Squire Witwoud here?

Bet. Yes; what's your business?

Mess. I have a letter for him from his brother, Sir Willful, which I am charged to deliver into his own 195 hands.

Bet. He's in the next room, friend—that way.

Exit Messenger.

Mira. What, is the chief of that noble family in town, Sir Willful Witwoud?

Fain. He is expected today. Do you know him?   200

Mira. I have seen him; he promises to be an extraordinary person; I think you have the honor to be related to him.

Fain. Yes; he is half-brother to this Witwoud by a former wife, who was sister to My Lady Wishfort, 205 my wife's mother. If you marry Millamant, you must call cousins too.

Mira. I had rather be his relation than his acquaintance.

Fain. He comes to town in order to equip himself 210 for travel.

Mira. For travel! Why the man that I mean is above forty.

Fain. No matter for that; 'tis for the honor of England that all Europe should know we have block- 215 heads of all ages.

Mira. I wonder there is not an act of Parliament to save the credit of the nation and prohibit the exportation of fools.

Fain. By no means, 'tis better as 'tis; 'tis better to 220

trade with a little loss than to be quite eaten up with
being overstocked.

Mira. Pray, are the follies of this knight-errant and
those of the squire his brother anything related?

Fain. Not at all; Witwoud grows by the knight 225
like a medlar grafted on a crab. One will melt in
your mouth and t'other set your teeth on edge; one
is all pulp and the other all core.

Mira. So one will be rotten before he be ripe, and
the other will be rotten without ever being ripe at 230
all.

Fain. Sir Willful is an odd mixture of bashfulness
and obstinacy. But when he's drunk, he's as loving as
the monster in *The Tempest*, and much after the
same manner. To give the t'other his due, he has 235
something of good nature and does not always want
wit.

Mira. Not always, but as often as his memory fails
him and his commonplace of comparisons. He is a
fool with a good memory and some few scraps of 240
other folks' wit. He is one whose conversation can
never be approved, yet it is now and then to be endured. He has, indeed, one good quality, he is not
exceptious; for he so passionately affects the reputation of understanding raillery that he will construe 245
an affront into a jest and call downright rudeness and
ill language satire and fire.

Fain. If you have a mind to finish his picture, you
have an opportunity to do it at full length. Behold
the original. 250

Enter Witwoud.

Wit. Afford me your compassion, my dears; pity
me, Fainall; Mirabell, pity me.

239. COMMONPLACE: a notebook recording memorable sayings.
271. LE DRÔLE: funny man.

Mira. I do from my soul.

Fain. Why, what's the matter?

Wit. No letters for me, Betty? 255

Bet. Did not the messenger bring you one but now, sir?

Wit. Ay, but no other?

Bet. No, sir.

Wit. That's hard, that's very hard. A messenger, 260 a mule, a beast of burden: he has brought me a letter from the fool my brother, as heavy as a panegyric in a funeral sermon or a copy of commendatory verses from one poet to another. And what's worse, 'tis as sure a forerunner of the author as an epistle 265 dedicatory.

Mira. A fool, and your brother, Witwoud!

Wit. Ay, ay, my half-brother. My half-brother he is, no nearer, upon honor.

Mira. Then 'tis possible he may be but half a fool. 270

Wit. Good, good, Mirabell, *le drôle!* Good, good!— hang him, don't let's talk of him.—Fainall, how does your lady? Gad, I say anything in the world to get this fellow out of my head. I beg pardon that I should ask a man of pleasure and the town a question at 275 once so foreign and domestic. But I talk like an old maid at a marriage: I don't know what I say. But she's the best woman in the world.

Fain. 'Tis well you don't know what you say, or else your commendation would go near to make me either 280 vain or jealous.

Wit. No man in town lives well with a wife but Fainall. Your judgment, Mirabell.

Mira. You had better step and ask his wife, if you would be credibly informed. 285

Wit. Mirabell.

Mira. Ay.

Wit. My dear, I ask ten thousand pardons.—Gad, I
have forgot what I was going to say to you.

Mira. I thank you heartily, heartily.   290

Wit. No, but prithee excuse me; my memory is
such a memory.

Mira. Have a care of such apologies, Witwoud; for
I never knew a fool but he affected to complain either
of the spleen or his memory.   295

Fain. What have you done with Petulant?

Wit. He's reckoning his money—my money it was;
I have no luck today.

Fain. You may allow him to win of you at play, for
you are sure to be too hard for him at repartee: since 300
you monopolize the wit that is between you, the fortune must be his, of course.

Mira. I don't find that Petulant confesses the superiority of wit to be your talent, Witwoud.

Wit. Come, come, you are malicious now and 305
would breed debates. Petulant's my friend and a very
honest fellow, and a very pretty fellow, and has a
smattering—faith and troth, a pretty deal of an odd
sort of a small wit. Nay, I'll do him justice. I'm his
friend, I won't wrong him, neither. And if he had but 310
any judgment in the world, he would not be altogether contemptible. Come, come, don't detract from
the merits of my friend.

Fain. You don't take your friend to be over-nicely
bred.   315

Wit. No, no, hang him; the rogue has no manners
at all, that I must own—no more breeding than a
bum-baily, that I grant you. 'Tis pity, faith; the fellow has fire and life.

Mira. What, courage?   320

Wit. Hum, faith I don't know as to that; I can't say

---

318. BUM-BAILY: contemptuous term for "bailiff."

as to that. Yes, faith, in a controversy he'll contradict anybody.

Mira. Though 'twere a man whom he feared or a woman whom he loved.   325

Wit. Well, well, he does not always think before he speaks. We have all our failings; you're too hard upon him, you are, faith. Let me excuse him. I can defend most of his faults, except one or two; one he has, that's the truth on't, if he were my brother I 330 could not acquit him. That, indeed, I could wish were otherwise.

Mira. Ay, marry, what's that, Witwoud?

Wit. O, pardon me! Expose the infirmities of my friend? No, my dear, excuse me there.   335

Fain. What! I warrant he's unsincere, or 'tis some such trifle.

Wit. No, no, what if he be? 'Tis no matter for that, his wit will excuse that: a wit should no more be sincere than a woman constant; one argues a decay of 340 parts, as t'other of beauty.

Mira. Maybe you think him too positive?

Wit. No, no, his being positive is an incentive to argument and keeps up conversation.

Fain. Too illiterate.   345

Wit. That! That's his happiness. His want of learning gives him the more opportunities to show his natural parts.

Mira. He wants words.

Wit. Ay, but I like him for that now; for his want 350 of words gives me the pleasure very often to explain his meaning.

Fain. He's impudent.

Wit. No, that's not it.

Mira. Vain.   355

Wit. No.

Mira. What, he speaks unseasonable truths sometimes, because he has not wit enough to invent an evasion?

Wit. Truths! Ha, ha, ha! No, no, since you will have 360 it. I mean, he never speaks truth at all—that's all. He will lie like a chambermaid or a woman of quality's porter. Now that is a fault.

Enter Coachman.

Coach. Is Master Petulant here, Mistress?
Bet. Yes.   365
Coach. Three gentlewomen in the coach would speak with him.
Fain. O brave Petulant, three!
Bet. I'll tell him.
Coach. You must bring two dishes of chocolate and 370 a glass of cinnamon water.

　　　　　　　　[*Exeunt Betty and Coachman.*]
Wit. That should be for two fasting strumpets and a bawd troubled with wind. Now you may know what the three are.

Mira. You are very free with your friend's acquaint- 375 ance.

Wit. Ay, ay, friendship without freedom is as dull as love without enjoyment or wine without toasting; but, to tell you a secret, these are trulls that he allows coach-hire and something more by the week to call 380 on him once a day at public places.

Mira. How!

Wit. You shall see he won't go to 'em, because there's no more company here to take notice of him. Why, this is nothing to what he used to do; before 385 he found out this way I have known him call for himself—

---

402. 'Sbud: God's body!
420. sultana queens: whores.

Fain. Call for himself? What dost thou mean?

Wit. Mean? Why, he would slip you out of this chocolate house, just when you had been talking to 390 him. As soon as your back was turned—whip he was gone; then trip to his lodging, clap on a hood and scarf and mask, slap into a hackney coach, and drive hither to the door again in a trice; where he would send in for himself—that I mean—call for himself, 395 wait for himself, nay and what's more, not finding himself, sometimes leave a letter for himself.

Mira. I confess this is something extraordinary! I believe he waits for himself now, he is so long a-coming. O, I ask his pardon! 400

Enter Petulant and Betty.

Bet. Sir, the coach stays.   *Exit.*

Pet. Well, well; I come.—'Sbud, a man had as good be a professed midwife as a professed whoremaster, at this rate; to be knocked up and raised at all hours and in all places! Pox on 'em, I won't come. D'ee hear; 405 tell 'em I won't come. Let 'em snivel and cry their hearts out.

Fain. You are very cruel, Petulant.

Pet. All's one, let it pass—I have a humor to be cruel. 410

Mira. I hope they are not persons of condition that you use at this rate.

Pet. Condition! Condition's a dried fig, if I am not in humor. By this hand, if they were your—a—a—your what-d'ee-call-'ems themselves, they must wait or rub 415 off, if I want appetite.

Mira. What-d'ee-call-'ems! What are they, Witwoud?

Wit. Empresses, my dear; by your what-d'ee-call-'ems he means sultana queens. 420

Pet. Ay, Roxolanas.

Mira. Cry you mercy.

Fain. Witwoud says they are—

Pet. What does he say th'are?

Wit. I?—fine ladies, I say. 425

Pet. Pass on, Witwoud.—Harkee, by this light, his relations—two co-heiresses his cousins, and an old aunt, that loves caterwauling better than a conventicle.

Wit. Ha, ha, ha! I had a mind to see how the rogue would come off. Ha, ha, ha! Gad I can't be angry with 430 him if he said they were my mother and my sisters.

Mira. No!

Wit. No; the rogue's wit and readiness of invention charm me. Dear Petulant!

Re-enter Betty.

Bet. They are gone, sir, in great anger. 435

Pet. Enough, let 'em trundle. Anger helps complexion, saves paint.

Fain. This continence is all dissembled; this is in order to have something to brag of the next time he makes court to Millamant and swear he has aban- 440 doned the whole sex for her sake.

Mira. Have you not left off your impudent pretensions there yet? I shall cut your throat, sometime or other, Petulant, about that business.

Pet. Ay, ay, let that pass; there are other throats to 445 be cut—

Mira. Meaning mine, sir?

Pet. Not I—I mean nobody—I know nothing. But there are uncles and nephews in the world, and they may be rivals. What then? All's one for that— 450

---

421. Roxolana: favorite concubine of Solyman the Magnificent in Davenant's *Siege of Rhodes* (1656).
428. CONVENTICLE: church service.

Mira. How! Harkee, Petulant, come hither. Explain, or I shall call your interpreter.

Pet. Explain! I know nothing. Why, you have an uncle, have you not, lately come to town, and lodges by My Lady Wishfort's?   455

Mira. True.

Pet. Why, that's enough. You and he are not friends; and if he should marry and have a child, you may be disinherited, ha?

Mira. Where hast thou stumbled upon all this   460 truth?

Pet. All's one for that; why, then, say I know something.

Mira. Come, thou art an honest fellow, Petulant, and shalt make love to my mistress, thou shalt, faith.   465 What hast thou heard of my uncle?

Pet. I? Nothing I. If throats are to be cut, let swords clash; snug's the word; I shrug and am silent.

Mira. O raillery, raillery. Come, I know thou art in the women's secrets. What, you're a cabalist; I know   470 you stayed at Millamant's last night after I went. Was there any mention made of my uncle or me? Tell me; if thou hadst but good nature equal to thy wit, Petulant, Tony Witwoud, who is now thy competitor in fame, would show as dim by thee as a dead whiting's   475 eye by a pearl of Orient; he would no more be seen by thee than Mercury is by the sun. Come, I'm sure thou wo't tell me.

Pet. If I do, will you grant me common sense then, for the future?   480

Mira. Faith, I'll do what I can for thee; and I'll pray that Heaven may grant it thee in the meantime.

Pet. Well, harkee.

Fain. Petulant and you both will find Mirabell as warm a rival as a lover.   485

Wit. Pshaw, pshaw, that she laughs at Petulant is

plain. And for my part—but that it is almost a fashion
to admire her, I should, harkee, to tell you a secret,
but let it go no further—between friends, I shall never
break my heart for her.   490

Fain. How!

Wit. She's handsome; but she's a sort of an uncer-
tain woman.

Fain. I thought you had died for her.

Wit. Umh—no—   495

Fain. She has wit.

Wit. 'Tis what she will hardly allow anybody else.
Now, demme, I should hate that if she were as handsome as Cleopatra. Mirabell is not so sure of her as he
thinks for.   500

Fain. Why do you think so?

Wit. We stayed pretty late there last night and
heard something of an uncle to Mirabell, who is lately
come to town and is between him and the best part of
his estate. Mirabell and he are at some distance, as   505
My Lady Wishfort has been told; and you know she
hates Mirabell worse than a Quaker hates a parrot or
than a fishmonger hates a hard frost. Whether this
uncle has seen Mrs. Millamant or not, I cannot say,
but there were items of such a treaty being in em-   510
bryo; and if it should come to life, poor Mirabell
would be in some sort unfortunately fobbed, i'faith.

Fain. 'Tis impossible Millamant should hearken to
it.

Wit. Faith, my dear, I can't tell; she's a woman and   515
a kind of a humorist.

Mira. And this is the sum of what you could collect
last night?

Pet. The quintessence. Maybe Witwoud knows

---

505. AT . . . DISTANCE: on unfriendly terms.
516. HUMORIST: capricious person.
540. BEG . . . ESTATE: i.e., make application to the Court of Wards
for his guardianship on the grounds that he is *non compos mentis.*

more; he stayed longer. Besides, they never mind him; 520
they say anything before him.

Mira. I thought you had been the greatest favorite.

Pet. Ay, *tête-à-tête;* but not in public, because I
make remarks.

Mira. Do you?   525

Pet. Ay, ay; pox, I'm malicious, man. Now, he's soft,
you know; they are not in awe of him. The fellow's
well bred, he's what you call a—what-d'ee-call-'em—
a fine gentleman; but he's silly withal.

Mira. I thank you, I know as much as my curiosity 530
requires.—Fainall, are you for the Mall?

Fain. Ay, I'll take a turn before dinner.

Wit. Ay, we'll all walk in the Park; the ladies talked
of being there.

Mira. I thought you were obliged to watch for your 535
brother Sir Willful's arrival.

Wit. No, no, he comes to his aunt's, My Lady Wishfort; pox on him, I shall be troubled with him too;
what shall I do with the fool?

Pet. Beg him for his estate, that I may beg you 540
afterwards and so have but one trouble with you both.

Wit. O rare Petulant! thou art as quick as a fire in a
frosty morning; thou shalt to the Mall with us, and
we'll be very severe.

Pet. Enough! I'm in a humor to be severe.   545

Mira. Are you? Pray, then, walk by yourselves—let
not us be accessary to your putting the ladies out of
countenance with your senseless ribaldry, which you
roar out aloud as often as they pass by you; and when
you have made a handsome woman blush, then you 550
think you have been severe.

Pet. What, what? Then let 'em either show their innocence by not understanding what they hear, or else
show their discretion by not hearing what they would
not be thought to understand.   555

Mira. But hast not thou, then, sense enough to know that thou ought'st to be most ashamed thyself when thou hast put another out of countenance?

Pet. Not I, by this hand. I always take blushing either for a sign of guilt or ill breeding.   560

Mira. I confess you ought to think so. You are in the right, that you may plead the error of your judgment in defense of your practice.

> Where modesty's ill manners, 'tis but fit
> That impudence and malice pass for wit.   563

Exeunt.

ACT II

|||||||||||||||||||||||||||||||||||||||||||||||||||||||||||||||||||||||||||||||||||||||||||||||||||||||||

Scene I. St. James's Park.

Enter Mrs. Fainall and Mrs. Marwood.

Mrs. Fain. Ay, ay, dear Marwood, if we will be happy, we must find the means in ourselves and among ourselves. Men are ever in extremes; either doting or averse. While they are lovers, if they have fire and sense, their jealousies are insupportable: and 5 when they cease to love (we ought to think at least), they loathe; they look upon us with horror and distaste; they meet us like the ghosts of what we were and, as such, fly from us.

Mrs. Mar. True, 'tis an unhappy circumstance of life 10 that love should ever die before us; and that the man so often should outlive the lover. But, say what you will, 'tis better to be left than never to have been loved. To pass our youth in dull indifference, to refuse the sweets of life because they once must leave us, is 15 as preposterous as to wish to have been born old because we one day must be old. For my part, my youth may wear and waste, but it shall never rust in my possession.

Mrs. Fain. Then it seems you dissemble an aversion 20 to mankind only in compliance with my mother's humor.

Mrs. Mar. Certainly. To be free, I have no taste of those insipid dry discourses with which our sex of force must entertain themselves apart from men. We 25 may affect endearments to each other, profess eternal friendships, and seem to dote like lovers; but 'tis not in our natures long to persevere. Love will resume his empire in our breasts and every heart, or soon or late, receive and readmit him as its lawful tyrant.   30

Mrs. Fain. Bless me, how have I been deceived! Why, you profess a libertine.

Mrs. Mar. You see my friendship by my freedom. Come, be as sincere, acknowledge that your sentiments agree with mine.   35

Mrs. Fain. Never.

Mrs. Mar. You hate mankind.

Mrs. Fain. Heartily, inveterately.

Mrs. Mar. Your husband.

Mrs. Fain. Most transcendently; ay, though I say   40
it, meritoriously.

Mrs. Mar. Give me your hand upon it.

Mrs. Fain. There.

Mrs. Mar. I join with you; what I have said has been to try you.   45

Mrs. Fain. Is it possible? Dost thou hate those vipers, men?

Mrs. Mar. I have done hating 'em and am now come to despise 'em; the next thing I have to do is eternally to forget 'em.   50

Mrs. Fain. There spoke the spirit of an Amazon, a Penthesilea.

Mrs. Mar. And yet I am thinking sometimes to carry my aversion further.

Mrs. Fain. How?   55

Mrs. Mar. Faith, by marrying; if I could but find one that loved me very well and would be thoroughly sensible of ill usage, I think I should do myself the violence of undergoing the ceremony.

Mrs. Fain. You would not make him a cuckold?   60

(II.i.)
32. PROFESS: confess yourself.
60. CUCKOLD: i.e., by betraying him with another man.

Mrs. Mar. No; but I'd make him believe I did, and that's as bad.

Mrs. Fain. Why, had not you as good do it?

Mrs. Mar. O, if he should ever discover it, he would then know the worst and be out of his pain; but I would have him ever to continue upon the rack of fear and jealousy. 65

Mrs. Fain. Ingenious mischief! Would thou wert married to Mirabell.

Mrs. Mar. Would I were. 70

Mrs. Fain. You change color.

Mrs. Mar. Because I hate him.

Mrs. Fain. So do I; but I can hear him named. But what reason have you to hate him in particular?

Mrs. Mar. I never loved him; he is, and always was, insufferably proud. 75

Mrs. Fain. By the reason you give for your aversion, one would think it dissembled; for you have laid a fault to his charge of which his enemies must acquit him. 80

Mrs. Mar. O, then it seems you are one of his favorable enemies. Methinks you look a little pale, and now you flush again.

Mrs. Fain. Do I? I think I am a little sick o' the sudden. 85

Mrs. Mar. What ails you?

Mrs. Fain. My husband. Don't you see him? He turned short upon me unawares and has almost overcome me.

Enter Fainall and Mirabell.

Mrs. Mar. Ha, ha, ha! he comes opportunely for you. 90

Mrs. Fain. For you, for he has brought Mirabell with him.

Fain. My dear.

Mrs. Fain. My soul.   95

Fain. You don't look well today, child.

Mrs. Fain. D'ee think so?

Mira. He is the only man that does, madam.

Mrs. Fain. The only man that would tell me so, at least; and the only man from whom I could hear it 100 without mortification.

Fain. O my dear, I am satisfied of your tenderness; I know you cannot resent anything from me, especially what is an effect of my concern.

Mrs. Fain. Mr. Mirabell, my mother interrupted 105 you in a pleasant relation last night: I would fain hear it out.

Mira. The persons concerned in that affair have yet a tolerable reputation. I am afraid Mr. Fainall will be censorious.   110

Mrs. Fain. He has a humor more prevailing than his curiosity and will willingly dispense with the hearing of one scandalous story, to avoid giving an occasion to make another by being seen to walk with his wife. This way, Mr. Mirabell, and I dare promise you 115 will oblige us both.

              Exeunt Mrs. Fainall and Mirabell.

Fain. Excellent creature! Well, sure, if I should live to be rid of my wife, I should be a miserable man.

Mrs. Mar. Ay!

Fain. For having only that one hope, the accom- 120 plishment of it of consequence must put an end to all my hopes; and what a wretch is he who must survive his hopes! Nothing remains when that day comes but to sit down and weep like Alexander when he wanted other worlds to conquer.   125

Mrs. Mar. Will you not follow 'em?

Fain. Faith, I think not.

Mrs. Mar. Pray let us; I have a reason.

Fain. You are not jealous?

Mrs. Mar. Of whom?   130

Fain. Of Mirabell.

Mrs. Mar. If I am, is it inconsistent with my love
to you that I am tender of your honor?

Fain. You would intimate, then, as if there were a
fellow-feeling between my wife and him.   135

Mrs. Mar. I think she does not hate him to that degree she would be thought.

Fain. But he, I fear, is too insensible.

Mrs. Mar. It may be you are deceived.

Fain. It may be so. I do now begin to apprehend it.   140

Mrs. Mar. What?

Fain. That I have been deceived, madam, and you
are false.

Mrs. Mar. That I am false! What mean you?

Fain. To let you know I see through all your little   145
arts. Come, you both love him; and both have equally
dissembled your aversion. Your mutual jealousies of
one another have made you clash till you have both
struck fire. I have seen the warm confession redden-
ing on your cheeks and sparkling from your eyes.   150

Mrs. Mar. You do me wrong.

Fain. I do not. 'Twas for my ease to oversee and
willfully neglect the gross advances made him by my
wife, that by permitting her to be engaged, I might
continue unsuspected in my pleasures and take you   155
oftener to my arms in full security. But could you
think, because the nodding husband would not wake,
that e'er the watchful lover slept?

Mrs. Mar. And wherewithal can you reproach me?

Fain. With infidelity, with loving of another, with   160
love of Mirabell.

Mrs. Mar. 'Tis false. I challenge you to show an instance that can confirm your groundless accusation. I
hate him.

Fain. And wherefore do you hate him? He is insensi- 165
ble, and your resentment follows his neglect. An instance? The injuries you have done him are a proof:
your interposing in his love. What cause had you to
make discoveries of his pretended passion? To undeceive the credulous aunt and be the officious obstacle 170
of his match with Millamant?

Mrs. Mar. My obligations to my lady urged me: I
had professed a friendship to her and could not see
her easy nature so abused by that dissembler.

Fain. What, was it conscience then? Professed a 175
friendship! O, the pious friendships of the female sex!

Mrs. Mar. More tender, more sincere, and more en-
during than all the vain and empty vows of men,
whether professing love to us or mutual faith to one
another. 180

Fain. Ha, ha, ha! you are my wife's friend too.

Mrs. Mar. Shame and ingratitude! Do you reproach
me? You, you upbraid me! Have I been false to her,
through strict fidelity to you, and sacrificed my friendship to keep my love inviolate? And have you the 185
baseness to charge me with the guilt, unmindful of
the merit! To you it should be meritorious that I have
been vicious: and do you reflect that guilt upon me
which should lie buried in your bosom?

Fain. You misinterpret my reproof. I meant but to 190
remind you of the slight account you once could make
of strictest ties, when set in competition with your
love to me.

Mrs. Mar. 'Tis false; you urged it with deliberate
malice—'twas spoke in scorn, and I never will forgive 195
it.

Fain. Your guilt, not your resentment, begets your

---

202. PREVENT: forestall.
227. HEART . . . PROOF: sturdy heart.

rage. If yet you loved, you could forgive a jealousy,
but you are stung to find you are discovered.

Mrs. Mar. It shall be all discovered. You too shall 200
be discovered; be sure you shall. I can but be exposed.
If I do it myself, I shall prevent your baseness.

Fain. Why, what will you do?

Mrs. Mar. Disclose it to your wife; own what has
passed between us.   205

Fain. Frenzy!

Mrs. Mar. By all my wrongs, I'll do't!—I'll publish
to the world the injuries you have done me, both in
my fame and fortune. With both I trusted you, you
bankrupt in honor as indigent of wealth!   210

Fain. Your fame I have preserved. Your fortune has
been bestowed as the prodigality of your love would
have it, in pleasures which we both have shared. Yet,
had not you been false, I had ere this repaid it. 'Tis
true. Had you permitted Mirabell with Millamant 215
to have stolen their marriage, My Lady had been incensed beyond all means of reconcilement: Millamant
had forfeited the moiety of her fortune, which then
would have descended to my wife; and wherefore did
I marry but to make lawful prize of a rich widow's 220
wealth and squander it on love and you?

Mrs. Mar. Deceit and frivolous pretense!

Fain. Death, am I not married? What's pretense?
Am I not imprisoned, fettered? Have I not a wife?
Nay, a wife that was a widow, a young widow, a 225
handsome widow; and would be again a widow but
that I have a heart of proof and something of a constitution to bustle through the ways of wedlock and this
world. Will you yet be reconciled to truth and me?

Mrs. Mar. Impossible. Truth and you are inconsist- 230
ent—I hate you, and shall forever.

Fain. For loving you?

Mrs. Mar. I loathe the name of love after such

usage; and next to the guilt with which you would
asperse me, I scorn you most. Farewell.   235

Fain. Nay, we must not part thus.

Mrs. Mar. Let me go.

Fain. Come, I'm sorry.

Mrs. Mar. I care not—let me go—break my hands,
do—I'd leave 'em to get loose.   240

Fain. I would not hurt you for the world. Have I no
other hold to keep you here?

Mrs. Mar. Well, I have deserved it all.

Fain. You know I love you.

Mrs. Mar. Poor dissembling!—O, that—well, it is not   245
yet—

Fain. What? What is it not? What is it not yet? It is
not yet too late—

Mrs. Mar. No, it is not yet too late. I have that comfort.   250

Fain. It is, to love another.

Mrs. Mar. But not to loathe, detest, abhor mankind,
myself, and the whole treacherous world.

Fain. Nay, this is extravagance. Come, I ask your
pardon—no tears—I was to blame; I could not love   255
you and be easy in my doubts. Pray forbear—I believe
you; I'm convinced I've done you wrong; and any
way, every way will make amends; I'll hate my wife
yet more, damn her; I'll part with her, rob her of all
she's worth, and will retire somewhere, anywhere, to   260
another world. I'll marry thee—be pacified.—'Sdeath,
they come; hide your face, your tears. You have a
mask, wear it a moment. This way, this way, be persuaded.   *Exeunt.*

Enter Mirabell and Mrs. Fainall.

Mrs. Fain. They are here yet.   265

Mira. They are turning into the other walk.

Mrs. Fain. While I only hated my husband, I could bear to see him; but since I have despised him, he's too offensive.

Mira. O, you should hate with prudence. 270

Mrs. Fain. Yes, for I have loved with indiscretion.

Mira. You should have just so much disgust for your husband as may be sufficient to make you relish your lover.

Mrs. Fain. You have been the cause that I have 275 loved without bounds, and would you set limits to that aversion of which you have been the occasion? Why did you make me marry this man?

Mira. Why do we daily commit disagreeable and dangerous actions? To save that idol, Reputation. If 280 the familiarities of our loves had produced that consequence of which you were apprehensive, where could you have fixed a father's name with credit but on a husband? I knew Fainall to be a man lavish of his morals, an interested and professing friend, a false 285 and a designing lover; yet one whose wit and outward fair behavior have gained a reputation with the town, enough to make that woman stand excused who has suffered herself to be won by his addresses. A better man ought not to have been sacrificed to the occa- 290 sion; a worse had not answered to the purpose. When you are weary of him, you know your remedy.

Mrs. Fain. I ought to stand in some degree of credit with you, Mirabell.

Mira. In justice to you, I have made you privy to 295 my whole design, and put it in your power to ruin or advance my fortune.

Mrs. Fain. Whom have you instructed to represent your pretended uncle?

Mira. Waitwell, my servant. 300

Mrs. Fain. He is an humble servant to Foible, my mother's woman, and may win her to your interest.

Mira. Care is taken for that. She is won and worn
by this time. They were married this morning.

Mrs. Fain. Who?   305

Mira. Waitwell and Foible. I would not tempt my
servant to betray me by trusting him too far. If your
mother, in hopes to ruin me, should consent to marry
my pretended uncle, he might, like Mosca in *The Fox*,
stand upon terms; so I made him sure beforehand.   310

Mrs. Fain. So, if my poor mother is caught in a contract, you will discover the imposture betimes and
release her by producing a certificate of her gallant's
former marriage.

Mira. Yes, upon condition she consent to my mar-   315
riage with her niece and surrender the moiety of her
fortune in her possession.

Mrs. Fain. She talked last night of endeavoring at a
match between Millamant and your uncle.

Mira. That was by Foible's direction and my in-   320
struction, that she might seem to carry it more privately.

Mrs. Fain. Well, I have an opinion of your success,
for I believe my lady will do anything to get a husband; and when she has this, which you have provid- 325
ed for her, I suppose she will submit to anything to
get rid of him.

Mira. Yes, I think the good lady would marry anything that resembled a man, though 'twere no more
than what a butler could pinch out of a napkin.   330

Mrs. Fain. Female frailty! We must all come to it,
if we live to be old, and feel the craving of a false
appetite when the true is decayed.

Mira. An old woman's appetite is depraved like that
of a girl. 'Tis the greensickness of a second childhood;   335
and, like the faint offer of a latter spring, serves but

---

309. THE FOX: Ben Jonson's *Volpone*.
310. STAND . . . TERMS: make demands.

to usher in the fall and withers in an affected bloom.

Mrs. Fain. Here's your mistress.

Enter Mrs. Millamant, Witwoud, and Mincing.

Mira. Here she comes, i'faith, full sail, with her fan spread and her streamers out and a shoal of fools for 340 tenders. Ha, no, I cry her mercy!

Mrs. Fain. I see but one poor empty sculler; and he tows her woman after him.

Mira. You seem to be unattended, madam. You used to have the *beau monde* throng after you and a 345 flock of gay, fine perukes hovering round you.

Wit. Like moths about a candle.—I had like to have lost my comparison for want of breath.

Milla. O, I have denied myself airs today. I have walked as fast through the crowd— 350

Wit. As a favorite in disgrace; and with as few followers.

Milla. Dear Mr. Witwoud, truce with your similitudes: for I am as sick of 'em—

Wit. As a physician of a good air.—I cannot help it, 355 madam, though 'tis against myself.

Milla. Yet again! Mincing, stand between me and his wit.

Wit. Do, Mrs. Mincing, like a screen before a great fire. I confess I do blaze today, I am too bright. 360

Mrs. Fain. But, dear Millamant, why were you so long?

Milla. Long! Lord, have I not made violent haste? I have asked every living thing I met for you; I have inquired after you as after a new fashion. 365

Wit. Madam, truce with your similitudes. No, you met her husband and did not ask him for her.

Mira. By your leave, Witwoud, that were like in-

quiring after an old fashion, to ask a husband for his
wife. 370

Wit. Hum, a hit, a hit, a palpable hit, I confess it.

Mrs. Fain. You were dressed before I came abroad.

Milla. Ay, that's true—O, but then I had—Mincing,
what had I? Why was I so long?

Minc. O mem, your La'ship stayed to peruse a pec- 375
quet of letters.

Milla. O, ay, letters—I had letters—I am persecuted
with letters—I hate letters. Nobody knows how to
write letters; and yet one has 'em, one does not know
why. They serve one to pin up one's hair. 380

Wit. Is that the way? Pray, madam, do you pin up
you hair with all your letters? I find I must keep
copies.

Milla. Only with those in verse, Mr. Witwoud. I
never pin up my hair with prose. I fancy one's hair 385
would not curl if it were pinned up with prose. I think
I tried once, Mincing.

Minc. O mem, I shall never forget it.

Milla. Ay, poor Mincing tift and tift all the morning. 390

Minc. Till I had the cremp in my fingers, I'll vow,
mem. And all to no purpose. But when your La'ship
pins it up with poetry, it sits so pleasant the next
day as anything, and is so pure and so crips.

Wit. Indeed, so "crips"? 395

Minc. You're such a critic, Mr. Witwoud.

Milla. Mirabell, did not you take exceptions last
night? O, ay, and went away. Now I think on't, I'm
angry.—No, now I think on't, I'm pleased; for I believe
I gave you some pain. 400

Mira. Does that please you?

Milla. Infinitely; I love to give pain.

389. TIFT: dressed (Millamant's hair).

Mira. You would affect a cruelty which is not in your nature; your true vanity is in the power of pleasing. 405

Milla. O, I ask your pardon for that. One's cruelty is one's power, and when one parts with one's cruelty, one parts with one's power; and when one has parted with that, I fancy one's old and ugly.

Mira. Ay, ay, suffer your cruelty to ruin the object 410 of your power, to destroy your lover, and then how vain, how lost a thing you'll be! Nay, 'tis true: you are no longer handsome when you've lost your lover; your beauty dies upon the instant: for beauty is the lover's gift; 'tis he bestows your charms—your glass 415 is all a cheat. The ugly and the old, whom the looking glass mortifies, yet after commendation can be flattered by it and discover beauties in it; for that reflects our praises, rather than your face.

Milla. O, the vanity of these men! Fainall, d'ee hear 420 him? If they did not commend us, we were not handsome! Now you must know, they could not commend one if one was not handsome. Beauty the lover's gift! Lord, what is a lover, that it can give? Why, one makes lovers as fast as one pleases, and they live as 425 long as one pleases, and they die as soon as one pleases; and then if one pleases, one makes more.

Wit. Very pretty. Why you make no more of making of lovers, madam, than of making so many cardmatches. 430

Milla. One no more owes one's beauty to a lover than one's wit to an echo; they can but reflect what we look and say—vain empty things if we are silent or unseen, and want a being.

Mira. Yet, to those two vain empty things you owe 435 two the greatest pleasures of your life.

Milla. How so?

Mira. To your lover you owe the pleasure of hearing yourselves praised, and to an echo the pleasure of hearing yourselves talk. 440

Wit. But I know a lady that loves talking so incessantly she won't give an echo fair play; she has that everlasting rotation of tongue that an echo must wait till she dies before it can catch her last words.

Milla. O, fiction! Fainall, let us leave these men. 445

Mira. (*Aside to Mrs. Fainall*) Draw off Witwoud.

Mrs. Fain. Immediately.—I have a word or two for Mr. Witwoud.

Mira. I would beg a little private audience too.

> *Exeunt Witwoud and Mrs. Fainall.*

You had the tyranny to deny me last night, though 450 you knew I came to impart a secret to you that concerned my love.

Milla. You saw I was engaged.

Mira. Unkind. You had the leisure to entertain a herd of fools; things who visit you from their exces- 455 sive idleness, bestowing on your easiness that time which is the encumbrance of their lives. How can you find delight in such society? It is impossible they should admire you, they are not capable; or if they were, it should be to you as a mortification, for, sure, 460 to please a fool is some degree of folly.

Milla. I please myself. Besides, sometimes to converse with fools is for my health.

Mira. Your health! Is there a worse disease than the conversation of fools? 465

Milla. Yes, the vapors; fools are physic for it, next to asafoetida.

Mira. You are not in a course of fools?

Milla. Mirabell, if you persist in this offensive free-

---

468. IN . . . FOOLS: i.e., taking fools as physic.
498. WATCH LIGHT: a slow-burning taper in a sick room.

dom, you'll displease me. I think I must resolve, after 470
all, not to have you. We shan't agree.

Mira. Not in our physic, it may be.

Milla. And yet our distemper in all likelihood will
be the same; for we shall be sick of one another. I
shan't endure to be reprimanded nor instructed; 'tis 475
so dull to act always by advice, and so tedious to be
told of one's faults—I can't bear it. Well, I won't have
you, Mirabell—I'm resolved—I think—you may go—ha,
ha, ha! What would you give, that you could help
loving me? 480

Mira. I would give something that you did not know
I could not help it.

Milla. Come, don't look grave then. Well, what do
you say to me?

Mira. I say that a man may as soon make a friend 485
by his wit or a fortune by his honesty as win a woman
with plain dealing and sincerity.

Milla. Sententious Mirabell! Prithee, don't look with
that violent and inflexible wise face, like Solomon at
the dividing of the child in an old tapestry hanging. 490

Mira. You are merry, madam, but I would persuade
you for one moment to be serious.

Milla. What, with that face? No, if you keep your
countenance, 'tis impossible I should hold mine. Well,
after all, there is something very moving in a lovesick 495
face. Ha, ha, ha! Well, I won't laugh, don't be peevish
—heigho! Now I'll be melancholy, as melancholy as
a watch light. Well, Mirabell, if ever you will win me,
woo me now.—Nay, if you are so tedious, fare you
well; I see they are walking away. 500

Mira. Can you not find in the variety of your dispo-
sition one moment—

Milla. To hear you tell me that Foible's married
and your plot like to speed? No.

Mira. But how you came to know it— 505

Milla. Unless by the help of the Devil, you can't imagine; unless she should tell me herself. Which of the two it may have been, I will leave you to consider; and when you have done thinking of that, think of me.   *Exit.* 510

Mira. I have something more—Gone!—Think of you! To think of a whirlwind, though 'twere in a whirlwind, were a case of more steady contemplation, a very tranquillity of mind and mansion. A fellow that lives in a windmill has not a more whimsical dwelling 515 than the heart of a man that is lodged in a woman. There is no point of the compass to which they cannot turn and by which they are not turned, and by one as well as another; for motion, not method, is their occupation. To know this, and yet continue to be in 520 love, is to be made wise from the dictates of reason and yet persevere to play the fool by the force of instinct. O, here come my pair of turtles!—What, billing so sweetly! Is not Valentine's Day over with you yet?

Enter Waitwell and Foible.

Sirrah Waitwell, why sure you think you were mar- 525 ried for your own recreation and not for my conveniency.

Wait. Your pardon, sir. With submission, we have indeed been solacing in lawful delights; but still with an eye to business, sir. I have instructed her as well as 530 I could. If she can take your directions as readily as my instructions, sir, your affairs are in a prosperous way.

Mira. Give you joy, Mrs. Foible.

Foib. O 'las, sir, I'm so ashamed—I'm afraid My 535

---

570. B'w'y: God be with you.

Lady has been in a thousand inquietudes for me. But
I protest, sir, I made as much haste as I could.

Wait. That she did indeed, sir. It was my fault that
she did not make more.

Mira. That I believe.   540

Foib. But I told My Lady as you instructed me, sir:
that I had a prospect of seeing Sir Rowland, your
uncle; and that I would put Her Ladyship's picture
in my pocket to show him; which I'll be sure to say
has made him so enamored of her beauty that he   545
burns with impatience to lie at Her Ladyship's feet
and worship the original.

Mira. Excellent Foible! Matrimony has made you
eloquent in love.

Wait. I think she has profited, sir. I think so.   550

Foib. You have seen Madam Millamant, sir?

Mira. Yes.

Foib. I told her, sir, because I did not know that
you might find an opportunity; she had so much company last night.   555

Mira. Your diligence will merit more. In the meantime—   *Gives money.*

Foib. O dear sir, your humble servant.

Wait. Spouse!

Mira. Stand off, sir, not a penny.—Go on and pros-   560
per, Foible. The lease shall be made good and the
farm stocked, if we succeed.

Foib. I don't question your generosity, sir; and you
need not doubt of success. If you have no more commands, sir, I'll be gone; I'm sure My Lady is at her   565
toilet and can't dress 'till I come.—O, dear! I'm sure
that (*Looking out*) was Mrs. Marwood that went by
in a mask; if she has seen me with you, I'm sure she'll
tell My Lady. I'll make haste home and prevent her.
Your servant, sir. B'w'y, Waitwell.   *Exit Foible.*   570

Wait. Sir Rowland, if you please. The jade's so pert upon her preferment she forgets herself.

Mira. Come, sir, will you endeavor to forget yourself and transform into Sir Rowland?

Wait. Why, sir, it will be impossible I should re- 575 member myself—married, knighted, and attended all in one day! 'Tis enough to make any man forget himself. The difficulty will be how to recover my acquaintance and familiarity with my former self, and fall from my transformation to a reformation into 580 Waitwell. Nay, I shan't be quite the same Waitwell neither; for, now I remember me, I am married and can't be my own man again.

Ay, there's the grief; that's the sad change of life;
To lose my title and yet keep my wife. 585

Exeunt.

ACT III

Scene I. A room in Lady Wishfort's house.

[*Enter*] *Lady Wishfort at her toilet, Peg waiting.*

Lady Wish. Merciful! no news of Foible yet?
Peg. No, madam.
Lady Wish. I have no more patience. If I have not fretted myself till I am pale again, there's no veracity in me. Fetch me the red—the red, do you hear, sweet- 5
heart? An arrant ash color, as I'm a person. Look you how this wench stirs! Why dost thou not fetch me a little red? Didst thou not hear me, mopus?
Peg. The red ratafia does your Ladyship mean, or the cherry brandy? 10
Lady Wish. Ratafia, fool! No, fool. Not the ratafia, fool—grant me patience! I mean the Spanish paper, idiot—complexion, darling. Paint, paint, paint, dost thou understand that, changeling, dangling thy hands like bobbins before thee? Why dost thou not stir, 15
puppet? Thou wooden thing upon wires!
Peg. Lord, madam, your Ladyship is so impatient. I cannot come at the paint, madam; Mrs. Foible has locked it up and carried the key with her.
Lady Wish. A pox take you both! Fetch me the 20
cherry brandy then. (*Exit Peg.*) I'm as pale and as faint, I look like Mrs. Qualmsick the curate's wife, that's always breeding.—Wench, come, come, wench, what art thou doing, sipping? tasting? Save thee, dost thou not know the bottle? 25

Enter Peg with a bottle and china cup.

Peg. Madam, I was looking for a cup.

Lady Wish. A cup, save thee, and what a cup hast thou brought? Dost thou take me for a fairy, to drink out of an acorn? Why didst thou not bring thy thimble? Hast thou ne'er a brass thimble clinking in thy   30
pocket with a bit of nutmeg? I warrant thee. Come, fill, fill.—So—again. (*One knocks.*) See who that is. Set down the bottle first. Here, here, under the table. What, wouldst thou go with the bottle in thy hand like a tapster? As I'm a person, this wench has lived   35
in an inn upon the road, before she came to me, like Maritornes the Asturian in *Don Quixote.* No Foible yet?

Peg. No, madam, Mrs. Marwood.

Lady Wish. O, Marwood! Let her come in. Come   40
in, good Marwood.

Enter Mrs. Marwood.

Mrs. Mar. I'm surprised to find your Ladyship in dishabille at this time of day.

Lady Wish. Foible's a lost thing; has been abroad since morning and never heard of since.   45

Mrs. Mar. I saw her but now, as I came masked through the Park, in conference with Mirabell.

Lady Wish. With Mirabell! You call my blood into my face with mentioning that traitor. She durst not

---

63. CLOSET: boudoir.
65. QUARLES: Francis Quarles (1592-1644), prolific writer on moral themes.
66. PRYNNE: William Prynne (1600-1669), Puritan writer of numerous tracts, books, and pamphlets. His *Histriomastix* (1633) censured the stage. SHORT VIEW: Jeremy Collier's *A Short View of the Immorality and Profaneness of the English Stage* (1698), to which Congreve replied in his *Amendments of Mr. Collier's False and Imperfect Citations,* published later in 1698.

have the confidence. I sent her to negotiate an affair,   50
in which if I'm detected I'm undone. If that wheedling
villain has wrought upon Foible to detect me, I'm
ruined. O, my dear friend, I'm a wretch of wretches if
I'm detected!

Mrs. Mar. O madam, you cannot suspect Mrs.   55
Foible's integrity.

Lady Wish. O, he carries poison in his tongue that
would corrupt integrity itself. If she has given him
an opportunity, she has as good as put her integrity
into his hands. Ah, dear Marwood, what's integrity to   60
an opportunity?—Hark! I hear her.—Go, you thing,
and send her in! (*Exit Peg.*) Dear friend, retire into
my closet, that I may examine her with more freedom.
—You'll pardon me, dear friend, I can make bold with
you.—There are books over the chimney: Quarles and   65
Prynne, and *The Short View of the Stage*, with Bunyan's works, to entertain you.   *Exit Marwood.*

Enter Foible.

O Foible, where hast thou been? What hast thou been
doing?

Foib. Madam, I have seen the party.   70

Lady Wish. But what hast thou done?

Foib. Nay, 'tis your Ladyship has done, and are to
do; I have only promised. But a man so enamored—so
transported! Well, here it is, all that is left; all that is
not kissed away. Well, if worshipping of pictures be a   75
sin—poor Sir Rowland, I say.

Lady Wish. The miniature has been counted like—
But hast thou not betrayed me, Foible? Hast thou not
detected me to that faithless Mirabell? What hadst
thou to do with him in the Park? Answer me, has he   80
got nothing out of thee?

Foib. So, the Devil has been beforehand with me:

what shall I say?—Alas, madam, could I help it if I
met that confident thing? Was I in fault? If you had
heard how he used me, and all upon your Ladyship's 85
account, I'm sure you would not suspect my fidelity.
Nay, if that had been the worst, I could have borne;
but he had a fling at your Ladyship too, and then I
could not hold, but, i'faith, I gave him his own.

Lady Wish. Me? What did the filthy fellow say? 90

Foib. O madam, 'tis a shame to say what he said—
with his taunts and his fleers, tossing up his nose.
"Humh!" says he, "what, you are a-hatching some
plot," says he, "you are so early abroad, or catering,"
says he, "ferreting for some disbanded officer, I war- 95
rant—half pay is but thin subsistence," says he. "Well,
what pension does your lady propose? Let me see,"
says he; "what, she must come down pretty deep now:
she's superannuated," says he, "and—"

Lady Wish. Ods my life, I'll have him—I'll have him 100
murdered. I'll have him poisoned. Where does he eat?
I'll marry a drawer to have him poisoned in his wine.
I'll send for Robin from Locket's immediately.

Foib. Poison him? Poisoning's too good for him.
Starve him, madam, starve him; marry Sir Rowland 105
and get him disinherited. O, you would bless yourself,
to hear what he said.

Lady Wish. A villain! "superannuated!"

Foib. "Humh!" says he, "I hear you are laying designs against me, too," says he, "and Mrs. Millamant 110
is to marry my uncle" (he does not suspect a word of
your Ladyship) "but," says he, "I'll fit you for that, I

---

102. DRAWER: tapster.
103. LOCKET'S: a London tavern.
114. FRIPPERY: bundle of old clothes.
131. LONG LANE PENTHOUSE: a stall selling rags and secondhand
clothes; such stalls were numerous in Long Lane, Aldersgate.
134. BIRTHDAY: i.e., of the sovereign.
137. LUDGATE: the prison where debtors were confined.
188. ANGLE: i.e., beg of passers-by by means of a mitten lowered into
the street.

warrant you," says he. "I'll hamper you for that," says
he, "you and your old frippery, too," says he, "I'll
handle you—"   115

Lady Wish. Audacious villain! handle me! Would
he durst!—"Frippery"? "old frippery"! Was there ever
such a foul-mouthed fellow? I'll be married tomorrow;
I'll be contracted tonight.

Foib. The sooner the better, madam.   120

Lady Wish. Will Sir Rowland be here, say'st thou?
When, Foible?

Foib. Incontinently, madam. No new sheriff's wife
expects the return of her husband after knighthood
with that impatience in which Sir Rowland burns for   125
the dear hour of kissing your Ladyship's hands after
dinner.

Lady Wish. "Frippery"? "superannuated frippery"!
I'll frippery the villain; I'll reduce him to frippery and
rags. A tatterdemalion!—I hope to see him hung with   130
tatters, like a Long Lane penthouse or a gibbet thief.
A slander-mouthed railer. I warrant the spendthrift
prodigal's in debt as much as the million lottery or the
whole court upon a birthday. I'll spoil his credit with
his tailor. Yes, he shall have my niece with her for-   135
tune, he shall.

Foib. He! I hope to see him lodge in Ludgate first
and angle into Blackfriars for brass farthings with an
old mitten.

Lady Wish. Ay, dear Foible; thank thee for that,   140
dear Foible. He has put me out of all patience. I shall
never recompose my features to receive Sir Rowland
with any economy of face. This wretch has fretted
me that I am absolutely decayed. Look, Foible.

Foib. Your Ladyship has frowned a little too rashly,   145
indeed, madam. There are some cracks discernible in
the white varnish.

Lady Wish. Let me see the glass.—Cracks, say'st

thou? Why, I am arrantly flayed. I look like an old
peeled wall. Thou must repair me, Foible, before Sir 150
Rowland comes, or I shall never keep up to my picture.

Foib. I warrant you, madam; a little art once made
your picture like you, and now a little of the same
art must make you like your picture. Your picture 155
must sit for you, madam.

Lady Wish. But art thou sure Sir Rowland will not
fail to come? Or will 'a not fail when he does come?
Will he be importunate, Foible, and push? For if he
should not be importunate—I shall never break de- 160
corums—I shall die with confusion, if I am forced to
advance—O, no, I can never advance—I shall swoon if
he should expect advances. No, I hope Sir Rowland is
better bred than to put a lady to the necessity of
breaking her forms. I won't be too coy neither. I won't 165
give him despair—but a little disdain is not amiss; a
little scorn is alluring.

Foib. A little scorn becomes your Ladyship.

Lady Wish. Yes, but tenderness becomes me best—a
sort of a dyingness. You see that picture has a sort of 170
a—ha, Foible?—a swimminess in the eyes. Yes, I'll look
so. My niece affects it; but she wants features. Is Sir
Rowland handsome? Let my toilet be removed—I'll
dress above. I'll receive Sir Rowland here. Is he handsome? Don't answer me. I won't know; I'll be sur- 175
prised. I'll be taken by surprise.

Foib. By storm, madam. Sir Rowland's a brisk man.

Lady Wish. Is he! O, then he'll importune, if he's a
brisk man. I shall save decorums if Sir Rowland im-
portunes. I have a mortal terror at the apprehension 180
of offending against decorums. Nothing but importunity can surmount decorums. O, I'm glad he's a

158. 'A: he.

brisk man! Let my things be removed, good Foible.

Exit.

Enter Mrs. Fainall.

Mrs. Fain. O Foible, I have been in a fright lest I should come too late. That devil Marwood saw you in 185 the Park with Mirabell and I'm afraid will discover it to My Lady.

Foib. Discover what, madam?

Mrs. Fain. Nay, nay, put not on that strange face. I am privy to the whole design and know that Waitwell, 190 to whom thou wert this morning married, is to personate Mirabell's uncle, and as such, winning My Lady, to involve her in those difficulties from which Mirabell only must release her, by his making his conditions to have my cousin and her fortune left to her 195 own disposal.

Foib. O dear madam, I beg your pardon. It was not my confidence in your Ladyship that was deficient; but I thought the former good correspondence between your Ladyship and Mr. Mirabell might have 200 hindered his communicating this secret.

Mrs. Fain. Dear Foible, forget that.

Foib. O dear madam, Mr. Mirabell is such a sweet winning gentleman—but your Ladyship is the pattern of generosity. Sweet lady, to be so good! Mr. Mirabell 205 cannot choose but be grateful. I find your Ladyship has his heart still. Now, madam, I can safely tell your Ladyship our success. Mrs. Marwood had told My Lady, but I warrant I managed myself. I turned it all for the better. I told My Lady that Mr. Mirabell railed 210 at her. I laid horrid things to his charge, I'll vow; and My Lady is so incensed that she'll be contracted to Sir Rowland tonight, she says. I warrant I worked her up

that he may have her for asking for, as they say of a
Welsh maidenhead.   215

Mrs. Fain. O rare Foible!

Foib. Madam, I beg your Ladyship to acquaint Mr.
Mirabell of his success. I would be seen as little as
possible to speak to him; besides, I believe Madam
Marwood watches me. She has a month's mind, but I 220
know Mr. Mirabell can't abide her.

Enter Footman.

John, remove My Lady's toilet. Madam, your servant.
My Lady is so impatient, I fear she'll come for me if I
stay.

Mrs. Fain. I'll go with you up the back stairs, lest I 225
should meet her.   *Exeunt.*

Enter Mrs. Marwood.

Mrs. Mar. Indeed, Mrs. Engine, is it thus with you?
Are you become a go-between of this importance?
Yes, I shall watch you. Why, this wench is the *passe-
partout*, a very master key to everybody's strongbox. 230
My friend Fainall, have you carried it so swimmingly?
I thought there was something in it; but it seems it's
over with you. Your loathing is not from a want of
appetite, then, but from a surfeit. Else you could
never be so cool to fall from a principal to be an 235
assistant, to procure for him! A pattern of generosity,
that I confess. Well, Mr. Fainall, you have met with
your match.—O man, man! Woman, woman! The
Devil's an ass: if I were a painter, I would draw him

220. MONTH'S MIND: passionate yearning.
227. MRS. ENGINE: Mrs. Ingenuity, or Artful Contrivance.
241. HORNS: sign of cuckoldom.
251–52. DAY . . . PROJECTION: projected day for attempting the trans-
mutation of base metals into gold.
260. OLIO: mixture.

like an idiot, a driveler, with a bib and bells. Man 240
should have his head and horns and woman the rest
of him. Poor simple fiend! "Madam Marwood has a
month's mind, but he can't abide her."—'Twere better
for him you had not been his confessor in that affair,
without you could have kept his counsel closer. I shall 245
not prove another pattern of generosity and stalk for
him till he takes his stand to aim at a fortune; he has
not obliged me to that with those excesses of himself;
and now I'll have none of him. Here comes the good
lady, panting ripe; with a heart full of hope and a 250
head full of care, like any chemist upon the day of
projection.

Enter Lady Wishfort.

Lady Wish. O dear Marwood, what shall I say for
this rude forgetfulness? But my dear friend is all
goodness.   255

Mrs. Mar. No apologies, dear madam. I have been
very well entertained.

Lady Wish. As I'm a person, I am in a very chaos to
think I should so forget myself—but I have such an
olio of affairs, really I know not what to do.— (*Calls*) 260
Foible!—I expect my nephew Sir Willful every moment too.—Why, Foible!—He means to travel for im-
provement.

Mrs. Mar. Methinks Sir Willful should rather think
of marrying than traveling at his years. I hear he is 265
turned of forty.

Lady Wish. O, he's in less danger of being spoiled
by his travels. I am against my nephew's marrying too
young. It will be time enough when he comes back
and has acquired discretion to choose for himself.   270

Mrs. Mar. Methinks Mrs. Millamant and he would

make a very fit match. He may travel afterwards. 'Tis
a thing very usual with young gentlemen.

Lady Wish. I promise you I have thought on't; and
since 'tis your judgment, I'll think on't again. I assure   275
you I will; I value your judgment extremely. On my
word, I'll propose it.

Enter Foible.

Come, come, Foible—I had forgot my nephew will be
here before dinner. I must make haste.

Foib. Mr. Witwoud and Mr. Petulant are come to   280
dine with your Ladyship.

Lady Wish. O dear, I can't appear till I'm dressed.
Dear Marwood, shall I be free with you again and
beg you to entertain 'em? I'll make all imaginable
haste. Dear friend, excuse me.   285

                    Exeunt Lady Wishfort and Foible.

Enter Mrs. Millamant and Mincing.

Milla. Sure never anything was so unbred as that
odious man.—Marwood, your servant.

Mrs. Mar. You have a color; what's the matter?

Milla. That horrid fellow, Petulant, has provoked
me into a flame. I have broke my fan.—Mincing, lend   290
me yours. Is not all the powder out of my hair?

Mrs. Mar. No. What has he done?

Milla. Nay, he has done nothing; he has only talked.
Nay, he has said nothing neither; but he has contra-
dicted everything that has been said. For my part, I   295
thought Witwoud and he would have quarreled.

Minc. I vow, mem, I thought once they would have
fit.

---

309. DRAP-DE-BERRY: woolen fabric from Berry in France.
326. RHENISH-WINE TEA: a remedy for obesity.

Milla. Well, 'tis a lamentable thing, I'll swear, that one has not the liberty of choosing one's acquaintance as one does one's clothes.

Mrs. Mar. If we had the liberty, we should be as weary of one set of acquaintance, though never so good, as we are of one suit, though never so fine. A fool and a doily stuff would now and then find days of grace and be worn for variety.

Milla. I could consent to wear 'em, if they would wear alike; but fools never wear out—they are such *drap-de-Berry* things!—without one could give 'em to one's chambermaid after a day or two.

Mrs. Mar. 'Twere better so indeed. Or what think you of the playhouse? A fine, gay, glossy fool should be given there, like a new masking habit, after the masquerade is over and we have done with the disguise. For a fool's visit is always a disguise and never admitted by a woman of wit but to blind her affair with a lover of sense. If you would but appear barefaced now and own Mirabell, you might as easily put off Petulant and Witwoud as your hood and scarf. And indeed 'tis time, for the town has found it: the secret is grown too big for the pretense. 'Tis like Mrs. Primly's great belly; she may lace it down before, but it burnishes on her hips. Indeed, Millamant, you can no more conceal it than my Lady Strammel can her face, that goodly face, which in defiance of her Rhenish-wine tea will not be comprehended in a mask.

Milla. I'll take my death, Marwood, you are more censorious than a decayed beauty or a discarded toast.—Mincing, tell the men they may come up. My aunt is not dressing.—Their folly is less provoking than your malice. The town has found it! (*Exit Mincing.*) What has it found? That Mirabell loves me is no more a secret than it is a secret that you discov-

ered it to my aunt, or than the reason why you dis- 335
covered it is a secret.

Mrs. Mar. You are nettled.

Milla. You're mistaken. Ridiculous!

Mrs. Mar. Indeed, my dear, you'll tear another fan
if you don't mitigate those violent airs. 340

Milla. O silly! Ha, ha, ha! I could laugh immoder-
ately. Poor Mirabell! His constancy to me has quite
destroyed his complaisance for all the world beside.
I swear, I never enjoined it him to be so coy. If I had
the vanity to think he would obey me, I would com- 345
mand him to show more gallantry. 'Tis hardly well
bred to be so particular on one hand and so insensible on the other. But I despair to prevail and so let
him follow his own way. Ha, ha, ha! Pardon me, dear
creature, I must laugh, ha, ha, ha!—though I grant 350
you 'tis a little barbarous, ha, ha, ha!

Mrs. Mar. What pity 'tis so much fine raillery, and
delivered with so significant gesture, should be so
unhappily directed to miscarry.

Milla. Heh? Dear creature, I ask your pardon—I 355
swear I did not mind you.

Mrs. Mar. Mr. Mirabell and you both may think it
a thing impossible when I shall tell him by telling
you—

Milla. O dear, what? for it is the same thing, if I 360
hear it—ha, ha, ha!

Mrs. Mar. That I detest him, hate him, madam.

Milla. O madam, why so do I; and yet the creature
loves me, ha, ha, ha! How can one forbear laughing
to think of it? I am a sibyl if I am not amazed to 365
think what he can see in me. I'll take my death, I
think you are handsomer—and within a year or two

---

380. Song. John Eccles: contemporary composer and Master of the
King's Band; Mrs. Hodgson: popular singer of the Lincoln's Inn Fields
company.

as young. If you could but stay for me, I should over-
take you—but that cannot be. Well, that thought
makes me melancholy. Now I'll be sad.   370

Mrs. Mar. Your merry note may be changed sooner
than you think.

Milla. D'ee say so? Then I'm resolved I'll have a
song to keep up my spirits.

Enter Mincing.

Minc. The gentlemen stay but to comb, madam,   375
and will wait on you.

Milla. Desire Mrs.—— that is in the next room to
sing the song I would have learnt yesterday. You shall
hear it, madam—not that there's any great matter in
it—but 'tis agreeable to my humor.   380

Song

Set by Mr. John Eccles, and sung by Mrs. Hodgson

I

Love's but the frailty of the mind,
     When 'tis not with ambition joined;
A sickly flame which, if not fed, expires;
And, feeding, wastes in self-consuming fires.

II

'Tis not to wound a wanton boy   385
     Or am'rous youth that gives the joy;
But 'tis the glory to have pierced a swain,
For whom inferior beauties sighed in vain.

III

Then I alone the conquest prize,
     When I insult a rival's eyes: 390
If there's delight in love, 'tis when I see
That heart which others bleed for bleed for me.

Enter Petulant and Witwoud.

Milla. Is your animosity composed, gentlemen?

Wit. Raillery, raillery, madam; we have no animosity; we hit off a little wit now and then, but no   395
animosity. The falling out of wits is like the falling
out of lovers. We agree in the main, like treble and
bass. Ha, Petulant?

Pet. Ay, in the main. But when I have a humor to
contradict—   400

Wit. Ay, when he has a humor to contradict, then
I contradict too. What, I know my cue. Then we
contradict one another like two battledores, for contradictions beget one another like Jews.

Pet. If he says black's black—if I have a humor to   405
say 'tis blue—let that pass—all's one for that. If I have
a humor to prove it, it must be granted.

Wit. Not positively must—but it may—it may.

Pet. Yes, it positively must, upon proof positive.

Wit. Ay, upon proof positive it must; but upon   410
proof presumptive it only may. That's a logical distinction now, madam.

Mrs. Mar. I perceive your debates are of importance and very learnedly handled.

Pet. Importance is one thing and learning's an-   415
other; but a debate's a debate, that I assert.

Wit. Petulant's an enemy to learning; he relies altogether on his parts.

Pet. No, I'm no enemy to learning; it hurts not me.

Mrs. Mar. That's a sign, indeed, it's no enemy to   420
you.

Pet. No, no, it's no enemy to anybody but them
that have it.

---

432. ORDINARY: a clergyman, specifically the chaplain of Newgate
Prison, whose duty it was to prepare a criminal for death.
439. BARTLEMEW . . . FAIR: the annual fair of St. Bartholomew in
London, at which many curiosities were displayed.

Milla. Well, an illiterate man's my aversion. I wonder at the impudence of any illiterate man to offer 425 to make love.

Wit. That, I confess, I wonder at too.

Milla. Ah! to marry an ignorant that can hardly read or write!

Pet. Why should a man be ever the further from 430 being married though he can't read, any more than he is from being hanged? The ordinary's paid for setting the psalm and the parish priest for reading the ceremony. And for the rest which is to follow in both cases, a man may do it without book—so all's one for 435 that.

Milla. D'ee hear the creature? Lord, here's company; I'll be gone.   *Exeunt Millamant and Mincing.*

Wit. In the name of Bartlemew and his fair, what have we here?   440

Mrs. Mar. 'Tis your brother, I fancy. Don't you know him?

Wit. Not I—yes, I think it is he—I've almost forgot him; I have not seen him since the Revolution.

Enter Sir Willful Witwoud, in a country riding habit, and Servant to Lady Wishfort.

Serv. Sir, My Lady's dressing. Here's company, if 445 you please to walk in, in the meantime.

Sir Will. Dressing! What, it's but morning here, I warrant, with you in London; we should count it towards afternoon in our parts, down in Shropshire. Why then belike my aunt han't dined yet—ha, friend? 450

Serv. Your aunt, sir?

Sir Will. My aunt, sir, yes, my aunt, sir, and your lady, sir; your lady is my aunt, sir. Why, what, dost thou not know me, friend? Why, then send somebody

here that does. How long hast thou lived with thy 455
lady, fellow, ha?

Serv. A week, sir; longer than anybody in the
house, except my lady's woman.

Sir Will. Why then belike thou dost not know thy
lady, if thou seest her, ha, friend? 460

Serv. Why truly, sir, I cannot safely swear to her
face in a morning, before she is dressed. 'Tis like I
may give a shrewd guess at her by this time.

Sir Will. Well, prithee try what thou canst do; if
thou canst not guess, inquire her out, dost hear, fel- 465
low? And tell her, her nephew, Sir Willful Witwoud,
is in the house.

Serv. I shall, sir.

Sir Will. Hold ye, hear me, friend; a word with you
in your ear; prithee who are these gallants? 470

Serv. Really, sir, I can't tell; there come so many
here, 'tis hard to know 'em all.   *Exit Servant.*

Sir Will. Oons! this fellow knows less than a star-
ling; I don't think 'a knows his own name.

Mrs. Mar. Mr. Witwoud, your brother is not be- 475
hindhand in forgetfulness—I fancy he has forgot you
too.

Wit. I hope so—the Devil take him that remembers first, I say.

Sir Will. Save you, gentlemen and lady. 480

Mrs. Mar. For shame, Mr. Witwoud; why won't you
speak to him?—And you, sir.

Wit. Petulant, speak.

Pet. And you, sir.

Sir Will. No offense, I hope.   *Salutes Marwood.* 485

Mrs. Mar. No, sure, sir.

Wit. This is a vile dog, I see that already. No of-

---

473. Oons: God's wounds!
485. S.D. Salutes: i.e., kisses.
488. Smoke: inspect.
519. Wrekin: a hill in Shropshire, formerly an active volcano.

fense! Ha, ha, ha! To him; to him, Petulant, smoke
him.

Pet. It seems as if you had come a journey, sir; 490
hem, hem.   *Surveying him round.*

Sir Will. Very likely, sir, that it may seem so.

Pet. No offense, I hope, sir.

Wit. Smoke the boots, the boots, Petulant, the
boots; ha, ha, ha!   495

Sir Will. Maybe not, sir; thereafter as 'tis meant,
sir.

Pet. Sir, I presume upon the information of your
boots.

Sir Will. Why, 'tis like you may, sir: if you are not 500
satisfied with the information of my boots, sir, if you
will step to the stable, you may inquire further of my
horse, sir.

Pet. Your horse, sir! Your horse is an ass, sir!

Sir Will. Do you speak by way of offense, sir?   505

Mrs. Mar. The gentleman's merry, that's all, sir.—
'Slife, we shall have a quarrel betwixt an horse and an
ass before they find one another out.—You must not
take anything amiss from your friends, sir. You are
among your friends here, though it may be you don't 510
know it. If I am not mistaken, you are Sir Willful
Witwoud.

Sir Will. Right, lady; I am Sir Willful Witwoud, so
I write myself; no offense to anybody, I hope; and
nephew to the Lady Wishfort of this mansion.   515

Mrs. Mar. Don't you know this gentleman, sir?

Sir Will. Hum! What, sure 'tis not.—Yea, by'r Lady,
but 'tis.—'Sheart, I know not whether 'tis or no.—Yea,
but 'tis, by the Wrekin. Brother Anthony! What, Tony,
i'faith! What, dost thou not know me? By'r Lady, nor 520
I thee, thou art so becravatted and beperiwigged.—
'Sheart, why dost not speak? Art thou o'erjoyed?

Wit. Odso, brother, is it you? Your servant, brother.

Sir Will. Your servant! Why yours, sir. Your servant again.—'Sheart, and your friend and servant to that— 525 and a—(*Puff*) and a flapdragon for your service, sir, and a hare's foot, and a hare's scut for your service, sir, an you be so cold and so courtly!

Wit. No offense, I hope, brother.

Sir Will. 'Sheart, sir, but there is, and much offense. 530 A pox, is this your Inns o' Court breeding, not to know your friends and your relations, your elders and your betters?

Wit. Why, Brother Willful of Salop, you may be as short as a Shrewsbury cake, if you please. But I 535 tell you 'tis not modish to know relations in town. You think you're in the country, where great lubberly brothers slabber and kiss one another when they meet like a call of sergeants. 'Tis not the fashion here; 'tis not indeed, dear brother. 540

Sir Will. The fashion's a fool; and you're a fop, dear brother. 'Sheart, I've suspected this. By'r Lady, I conjectured you were a fop since you began to change the style of your letters and write in a scrap of paper, gilt round the edges, no broader than a *subpoena*. I 545 might expect this when you left off "Honored Brother," and "hoping you are in good health," and so forth, to begin with a "Rat me, knight, I'm so sick of a last night's debauch"—Od's heart, and then tell a familiar tale of a cock and a bull, and a whore and a bottle, 550

523. ODSO: God's soul!
526. FLAPDRAGON: tidbit featured in a party game, used here to mean something of little value.
534. SALOP: Shropshire.
535. SHREWSBURY CAKE: a biscuit-like cake.
539. CALL . . . SERGEANTS: i.e., sergeants-at-law, when they receive their appointments.
548. RAT ME: God rot me.
552. TIME: term of apprenticeship in law.
556. DAWKS'S LETTER: newsletter begun in 1696 by Ichabod Dawks and issued three times weekly. A unique feature was its type face, designed to resemble script; WEEKLY BILL: the mortality bill for the London area, issued weekly.
582. AT . . . ADVENTURES: no matter what.

and so conclude. You could write news before you
were out of your time, when you lived with honest
Pumple Nose, the attorney of Furnival's Inn. You
could entreat to be remembered then to your friends
round the Wrekin. We could have gazettes then, and 555
Dawks's Letter, and the weekly bill, till of late days.

Pet. 'Slife, Witwoud, were you ever an attorney's
clerk? Of the family of the Furnivals. Ha, ha, ha!

Wit. Ay, ay, but that was for a while. Not long, not
long. Pshaw! I was not in my own power then. An 560
orphan, and this fellow was my guardian; ay, ay, I
was glad to consent to that man to come to London.
He had the disposal of me then. If I had not agreed
to that, I might have been bound prentice to a felt-
maker in Shrewsbury; this fellow would have bound 565
me to a maker of felts.

Sir Will. 'Sheart, and better than to be bound to a
maker of fops; where, I suppose, you have served
your time and now you may set up for yourself.

Mrs. Mar. You intend to travel, sir, as I'm informed. 570

Sir Will. Belike I may, madam. I may chance to sail
upon the salt seas, if my mind hold.

Pet. And the wind serve.

Sir Will. Serve or not serve, I shan't ask license of
you, sir; nor the weathercock your companion. I di- 575
rect my discourse to the lady, sir. 'Tis like my aunt
may have told you, madam—yes, I have settled my
concerns, I may say now, and am minded to see foreign parts. If an how that the peace holds whereby,
that is, taxes abate.   580

Mrs. Mar. I thought you had designed for France
at all adventures.

Sir Will. I can't tell that; 'tis like I may, and 'tis
like I may not. I am somewhat dainty in making a
resolution, because when I make it I keep it. I don't 585
stand shill I, shall I, then; if I say't, I'll do't: but I

have thoughts to tarry a small matter in town, to
learn somewhat of your lingo first, before I cross the
seas. I'd gladly have a spice of your French, as they
say, whereby to hold discourse in foreign countries. 590

Mrs. Mar. Here is an academy in town for that use.

Sir Will. There is? 'Tis like there may.

Mrs. Mar. No doubt you will return very much
improved.

Wit. Yes, refined, like a Dutch skipper from a 595
whale-fishing.

Enter Lady Wishfort and Fainall.

Lady Wish. Nephew, you are welcome.

Sir Will. Aunt, your servant.

Fain. Sir Willful, your most faithful servant.

Sir Will. Cousin Fainall, give me your hand. 600

Lady Wish. Cousin Witwoud, your servant; Mr.
Petulant, your servant.—Nephew, you are welcome
again. Will you drink anything after your journey,
nephew, before you eat? Dinner's almost ready.

Sir Will. I'm very well, I thank you, aunt—how- 605
ever, I thank you for your courteous offer. 'Sheart, I
was afraid you would have been in the fashion too
and have remembered to have forgot your relations.
Here's your Cousin Tony; belike, I mayn't call him
brother for fear of offense. 610

Lady Wish. O, he's a rallier, nephew—my cousin's
a wit; and your great wits always rally their best
friends to choose. When you have been abroad,
nephew, you'll understand raillery better.

Fainall and Mrs. Marwood talk apart.

613. TO CHOOSE: at will.
635–36. CITIZEN'S CHILD: i.e., a bastard, the horns symbolizing his
cuckold father.
647. FOND: foolish.

Sir Will. Why, then, let him hold his tongue in the 615
meantime and rail when that day comes.

Enter Mincing.

Minc. Mem, I come to acquaint your La'ship that
dinner is impatient.

Sir Will. Impatient? Why then belike it won't stay
till I pull off my boots. Sweetheart, can you help me 620
to a pair of slippers? My man's with his horses, I
warrant.

Lady Wish. Fie, fie, nephew, you would not pull
off your boots here. Go down into the hall—dinner
shall stay for you.—My nephew's a little unbred, 625
you'll pardon him, madam.—Gentlemen, will you
walk? Marwood—

Mrs. Mar. I'll follow you, madam, before Sir Willful
is ready.   *Manent Mrs. Marwood and Fainall.*

Fain. Why then Foible's a bawd, an arrant, rank, 630
matchmaking bawd. And I, it seems, am a husband,
a rank husband; and my wife a very arrant, rank wife
—all in the way of the world. 'Sdeath, to be an antici-
pated cuckold, a cuckold in embryo! Sure I was born
with budding antlers like a young satyr or a citizen's 635
child. 'Sdeath, to be out-witted, to be out-jilted—out-
matrimonied! If I had kept my speed like a stag,
'twere somewhat, but to crawl after with my horns
like a snail and outstripped by my wife—'tis scurvy
wedlock.   640

Mrs. Mar. Then shake it off: you have often wished
for an opportunity to part, and now you have it. But
first prevent their plot—the half of Millamant's fortune is too considerable to be parted with to a foe,
to Mirabell.   645

Fain. Damn him, that had been mine, had you not
made that fond discovery; that had been forfeited,

had they been married. My wife had added luster to
my horns by that increase of fortune; I could have
worn 'em tipt with gold, though my forehead had 650
been furnished like a deputy lieutenant's hall.

Mrs. Mar. They may prove a cap of maintenance
to you still, if you can away with your wife. And she's
no worse than when you had her. I dare swear she
had given up her game before she was married. 655

Fain. Hum! That may be. She might throw up her
cards; but I'll be hanged if she did not put Pam in
her pocket.

Mrs. Mar. You married her to keep you; and if you
can contrive to have her keep you better than you 660
expected, why should you not keep her longer than
you intended?

Fain. The means, the means!

Mrs. Mar. Discover to My Lady your wife's conduct; threaten to part with her. My Lady loves her 665
and will come to any composition to save her reputation. Take the opportunity of breaking it, just upon
the discovery of this imposture. My Lady will be en-
raged beyond bounds and sacrifice niece and fortune and all at that conjuncture. And let me alone to 670
keep her warm; if she should flag in her part, I will
not fail to prompt her.

Fain. Faith, this has an appearance.

Mrs. Mar. I'm sorry I hinted to My Lady to endeavor a match between Millamant and Sir Willful; 675
that may be an obstacle.

Fain. O, for that matter leave me to manage him;

651. DEPUTY LIEUTENANT'S HALL: the great hall of a county officer,
decorated with the heads of horned deer.
652. CAP . . . MAINTENANCE: heraldic term for a cap with horn-like
projections at the back, a device sometimes used in the crests of royal
bastards instead of a crowning wreath. There is a pun on MAINTENANCE
in the sense "financial support."
653. AWAY WITH: put up with.
657. PAM: highest trump card in the game of Loo.
679. SET . . . IN: get him started.

I'll disable him for that; he will drink like a Dane: after dinner, I'll set his hand in.

Mrs. Mar. Well, how do you stand affected to- 680 wards your lady?

Fain. Why, faith, I'm thinking of it.—Let me see— I am married already, so that's over; my wife has played the jade with me—well, that's over too; I never loved her, or if I had, why that would have been over 685 too by this time.—Jealous of her I cannot be, for I am certain—so there's an end of jealousy. Weary of her I am and shall be—no, there's no end of that; no, no, that were too much to hope. Thus far concerning my repose. Now for my reputation. As to my own, I mar- 690 ried not for it; so that's out of the question. And as to my part in my wife's—why, she had parted with hers before; so, bringing none to me, she can take none from me; 'tis against all rule of play that I should lose to one who has not wherewithal to stake. 695

Mrs. Mar. Besides, you forget, marriage is honorable.

Fain. Hum! Faith, and that's well thought on; marriage is honorable, as you say; and if so, wherefore should cuckoldom be a discredit, being derived from 700 so honorable a root?

Mrs. Mar. Nay, I know not; if the root be honorable, why not the branches?

Fain. So, so, why this point's clear. Well, how do we proceed? 705

Mrs. Mar. I will contrive a letter which shall be delivered to My Lady at the time when that rascal who is to act Sir Rowland is with her. It shall come as from an unknown hand—for the less I appear to know of the truth, the better I can play the incen- 710 diary. Besides, I would not have Foible provoked if I could help it, because you know she knows some passages. Nay, I expect all will come out—but let the

mine be sprung first, and then I care not if I'm discovered.   715

Fain. If the worst come to the worst, I'll turn my
wife to grass. I have already a deed of settlement of
the best part of her estate, which I wheedled out of
her, and that you shall partake at least.

Mrs. Mar. I hope you are convinced that I hate   720
Mirabell; now you'll be no more jealous.

Fain. Jealous, no!—by this kiss—let husbands be
jealous, but let the lover still believe; or if he doubt,
let it be only to endear his pleasure and prepare the
joy that follows when he proves his mistress true; 725
but let husbands' doubts convert to endless jealousy;
or if they have belief, let it corrupt to superstition
and blind credulity. I am single and will herd no
more with 'em. True, I wear the badge, but I'll disown the order. And since I take my leave of 'em, I 730
care not if I leave 'em a common motto to their common crest:

All husbands must or pain or shame endure;
The wise too jealous are, fools too secure.

                                            Exeunt.

---

734. SECURE: trusting.

(IV.i.)
7. PULVILLED: sprinkled with sachet powder known as "pulvillio."

ACT IV

Scene I. Scene continues.

Enter Lady Wishfort and Foible.

Lady Wish. Is Sir Rowland coming, say'st thou, Foible? And are things in order?

Foib. Yes, madam. I have put waxlights in the sconces and placed the footmen in a row in the hall, in their best liveries, with the coachman and postilion to fill up the equipage.

Lady Wish. Have you pulvilled the coachman and postilion, that they may not stink of the stable when Sir Rowland comes by?

Foib. Yes, madam.

Lady Wish. And are the dancers and the music ready, that he may be entertained in all points with correspondence to his passion?

Foib. All is ready, madam.

Lady Wish. And—well—and how do I look, Foible?

Foib. Most killing well, madam.

Lady Wish. Well, and how shall I receive him? In what figure shall I give his heart the first impression? There is a great deal in the first impression. Shall I sit?—No, I won't sit—I'll walk—ay, I'll walk from the door upon his entrance and then turn full upon him. —No, that will be too sudden. I'll lie—ay, I'll lie down —I'll receive him in my little dressing room; there's a couch—yes, yes, I'll give the first impression on a couch.—I won't lie neither but loll and lean upon one elbow, with one foot a little dangling off, jogging in

a thoughtful way—yes—and then, as soon as he appears, start, ay, start and be surprised, and rise to
meet him in a pretty disorder—yes—O, nothing is
more alluring than a levee from a couch in some con-   30
fusion. It shows the foot to advantage and furnishes
with blushes and recomposing airs beyond comparison. Hark! There's a coach.

Foib. 'Tis he, madam.

Lady Wish. O, dear, has my nephew made his   35
addresses to Millamant? I ordered him.

Foib. Sir Willful is set in to drinking, madam, in the
parlor.

Lady Wish. Ods my life! I'll send him to her. Call
her down, Foible; bring her hither. I'll send him as I   40
go. When they are together, then come to me, Foible,
that I may not be too long alone with Sir Rowland.

Exit.

Enter Mrs. Millamant and Mrs. Fainall.

Foib. Madam, I stayed here to tell your Ladyship
that Mr. Mirabell has waited this half-hour for an
opportunity to talk with you, though My Lady's or-   45
ders were to leave you and Sir Willful together. Shall
I tell Mr. Mirabell that you are at leisure?

Milla. No; what would the dear man have? I am
thoughtful and would amuse myself—bid him come
another time.   50

Repeating and walking about.

"There never yet was woman made,
    Nor shall, but to be cursed."

---

39. ODS MY LIFE: God save me!
51–52. THERE . . . CURSED: quote from an untitled poem by Sir
John Suckling (cf. his *Poems, Plays, etc.*, edited by W. Carew Hazlitt,
London, 1892, I, 19).
62. THYRSIS . . . TRAIN: from Edmund Waller's "The Story of
Phoebus and Daphne Applied."

That's hard!

Mrs. Fain. You are very fond of Sir John Suckling today, Millamant, and the poets. 55

Milla. Heh? Ay, and filthy verses—so I am.

Foib. Sir Willful is coming, madam. Shall I send Mr. Mirabell away?

Milla. Ay, if you please, Foible, send him away—or send him hither—just as you will, dear Foible.—I think 60 I'll see him.— Shall I? Ay, let the wretch come.

Repeating.

"Thyrsis, a youth of the inspired train."

Dear Fainall, entertain Willful—thou hast philosophy to undergo a fool; thou art married and hast patience. —I would confer with my own thoughts. 65

Mrs. Fain. I am obliged to you, that you would make me your proxy in this affair; but I have business of my own.

Enter Sir Willful.

O Sir Willful, you are come at the critical instant. There's your mistress up to the ears in love and con- 70 templation; pursue your point, now or never.

Sir Will. Yes; my aunt would have it so. I would gladly have been encouraged with a bottle or two, because I'm somewhat wary at first, before I am ac- quainted.—(*This while Millamant walks about re-* 75 *peating to herself*) But I hope, after a time, I shall break my mind—that is, upon further acquaintance. So for the present, cousin, I'll take my leave. If so be you'll be so kind to make my excuse, I'll return to my company— 80

Mrs. Fain. O, fie, Sir Willful! What, you must not be daunted.

Sir Will. Daunted! no, that's not it, it is not so much for that—for if so be that I set on't, I'll do't. But only for the present, 'tis sufficient till further acquaintance,   85
that's all—your servant.

Mrs. Fain. Nay, I'll swear you shall never lose so favorable an opportunity if I can help it. I'll leave you together and lock the door.   *Exit.*

Sir Will. Nay, nay, cousin—I have forgot my gloves.   90
What d'ee do? 'Sheart, 'a has locked the door indeed, I think. Nay, Cousin Fainall, open the door.—
Pshaw, what a vixen trick is this?—Nay, now 'a has seen me too.—Cousin, I made bold to pass through, as it were—I think this door's enchanted—   95

Milla. (*Repeating*)

> "I prithee spare me, gentle boy,
>   Press me no more for that slight toy—"

Sir Will. Anan? Cousin, your servant.
Milla. (*Repeating*)

> "That foolish trifle of a heart—"

Sir Willful!   100
Sir Will. Yes—your servant. No offense, I hope, cousin.

Milla. (*Repeating*)

> "I swear it will not do its part,
>   Though thou dost thine, employ'st thy power
>   and art."   105

Natural, easy Suckling!

96–97, 99, 103–5. I . . . TOY; THAT . . . HEART; I . . . ART: excerpts from another of Suckling's poems (p. 22 in Hazlitt edition cited above).
98. ANAN: how's that again?
128. L'ÉTOURDIE: the giddy (town).

Sir Will. Anan? Suckling? No such suckling neither,
cousin, nor stripling: I thank heaven, I'm no minor.

Milla. Ah, rustic, ruder than Gothic!

Sir Will. Well, well, I shall understand your lingo 110
one of these days, cousin; in the meanwhile I must
answer in plain English.

Milla. Have you any business with me, Sir Willful?

Sir Will. Not at present, cousin.—Yes, I made bold
to see, to come and know if that how you were dis- 115
posed to fetch a walk this evening, if so be that I
might not be troublesome, I would have sought a
walk with you.

Milla. A walk? What then?

Sir Will. Nay, nothing—only for the walk's sake, 120
that's all—

Milla. I nauseate walking; 'tis a country diversion;
I loathe the country and everything that relates to it.

Sir Will. Indeed! Hah! Look ye, look ye, you do?
Nay, 'tis like you may. Here are choice of pastimes 125
here in town, as plays and the like; that must be confessed indeed.

Milla. Ah, *l'étourdie!* I hate the town too.

Sir Will. Dear heart, that's much. Hah! that you
should hate 'em both! Hah! 'tis like you may; there 130
are some can't relish the town, and others can't away
with the country—'tis like you may be one of those,
cousin.

Milla. Ha, ha, ha! Yes, 'tis like I may. You have
nothing further to say to me?   135

Sir Will. Not at present, cousin. 'Tis like when I
have an opportunity to be more private, I may break
my mind in some measure—I conjecture you partly
guess. However, that's as time shall try—but spare to
speak and spare to speed, as they say.   140

Milla. If it is of no great importance, Sir Willful,

you will oblige me to leave me: I have just now a
little business—

Sir Will. Enough, enough, cousin: yes, yes, all a
case. When you're disposed, when you're disposed. 145
Now's as well as another time; and another time as
well as now. All's one for that—yes, yes, if your concerns call you, there's no haste; it will keep cold as
they say. Cousin, your servant.—I think this door's
locked.   150

Milla. You may go this way, sir.

Sir Will. Your servant! Then with your leave I'll
return to my company.   *Exit.*

Milla. Ay, ay; ha, ha, ha!

"Like Phoebus sung the no less am'rous boy."   155

Enter Mirabell.

Mira.

"Like Daphne she, as lovely and as coy."

Do you lock yourself up from me, to make my search
more curious? Or is this pretty artifice contrived to
signify that here the chase must end and my pursuit
be crowned, for you can fly no further?   160

Milla. Vanity! No—I'll fly and be followed to the
last moment. Though I am upon the very verge of
matrimony, I expect you should solicit me as much
as if I were wavering at the grate of a monastery,
with one foot over the threshold. I'll be solicited to 165
the very last, nay, and afterwards.

155–56. LIKE . . . BOY; LIKE . . . COY: further quotes from Waller's
poem.
158. CURIOUS: difficult.
172. INSTANT: pressing.
181. PRAGMATICAL: dogmatic.
191–92. DOUCEURS: comforts; SOMMEILS . . . MATIN: morning slumbers.

Mira. What, after the last?

Milla. O, I should think I was poor and had nothing
to bestow if I were reduced to an inglorious ease
and freed from the agreeable fatigues of solicitation. 170

Mira. But do not you know that when favors are
conferred upon instant and tedious solicitation, that
they diminish in their value, and that both the giver
loses the grace and the receiver lessens his pleasure?

Milla. It may be in things of common application, 175
but never, sure, in love. O, I hate a lover that can
dare to think he draws a moment's air independent
on the bounty of his mistress. There is not so impudent a thing in nature as the saucy look of an assured
man, confident of success. The pedantic arrogance 180
of a very husband has not so pragmatical an air. Ah!
I'll never marry unless I am first made sure of my
will and pleasure.

Mira. Would you have 'em both before marriage?
Or will you be contented with the first now and stay 185
for the other till after grace?

Milla. Ah, don't be impertinent.—My dear liberty,
shall I leave thee? My faithful solitude, my darling
contemplation, must I bid you then adieu? Ay-h,
adieu—my morning thoughts, agreeable wakings, in- 190
dolent slumbers, all ye *douceurs,* ye *sommeils du
matin,* adieu?—I can't do't, 'tis more than impossible.
Positively, Mirabell, I'll lie abed in a morning as long
as I please.

Mira. Then I'll get up in a morning as early as I 195
please.

Milla. Ah! Idle creature, get up when you will. And
d'ee hear, I won't be called names after I'm married;
positively I won't be called names.

Mira. Names!   200

Milla. Ay, as "wife," "spouse," "my dear," "joy,"
"jewel," "love," "sweetheart," and the rest of that

nauseous cant in which men and their wives are so
fulsomely familiar—I shall never bear that. Good
Mirabell, don't let us be familiar or fond, nor kiss be- 205
fore folks, like my Lady Fadler and Sir Francis: nor
go to Hyde Park together the first Sunday in a new
chariot, to provoke eyes and whispers, and then never
to be seen there together again, as if we were proud
of one another the first week and ashamed of one 210
another forever after. Let us never visit together,
nor go to a play together, but let us be very strange
and well bred: let us be as strange as if we had been
married a great while, and as well bred as if we were
not married at all.   215

  Mira. Have you any more conditions to offer?
Hitherto your demands are pretty reasonable.

  Milla. Trifles—as, liberty to pay and receive visits
to and from whom I please; to write and receive letters, without interrogatories or wry faces on your 220
part. To wear what I please; and choose conversation
with regard only to my own taste; to have no obligation upon me to converse with wits that I don't like,
because they are your acquaintance; or to be intimate
with fools, because they may be your relations. Come 225
to dinner when I please, dine in my dressing room
when I'm out of humor, without giving a reason. To
have my closet inviolate; to be sole empress of my
tea table, which you must never presume to approach
without first asking leave. And lastly, wherever I am, 230
you shall always knock at the door before you come
in. These articles subscribed, if I continue to endure
you a little longer, I may by degrees dwindle into
a wife.

---

  241. IMPRIMIS: first.
  246. WHEEDLE . . . A-FOP-SCRAMBLING: coax you into the pursuit of
fops.
  255. PASSES CURRENT: is acceptable.
  264. ATLASES: lengths of satin.

Mira. Your bill of fare is something advanced in this 235
latter account. Well, have I liberty to offer conditions
—that when you are dwindled into a wife, I may not
be beyond measure enlarged into a husband?

Milla. You have free leave; propose your utmost;
speak and spare not. 240

Mira. I thank you. *Imprimis* then, I covenant that
your acquaintance be general; that you admit no
sworn confidante or intimate of your own sex; no she-
friend to screen her affairs under your countenance
and tempt you to make trial of a mutual secrecy. No 245
decoy-duck, to wheedle you a-fop-scrambling to the
play in a mask; then bring you home in a pretended fright, when you think you shall be found out,
and rail at me for missing the play and disappointing
the frolic which you had, to pick me up and prove my 250
constancy.

Milla. Detestable *imprimis!* I go to the play in a
mask!

Mira. Item, I article that you continue to like your
own face as long as I shall; and while it passes current 255
with me that you endeavor not to new-coin it. To
which end, together with all vizards for the day, I
prohibit all masks for the night, made of oiled-skins
and I know not what—hog's bones, hare's gall, pig
water, and the marrow of a roasted cat. In short, I 260
forbid all commerce with the gentlewoman in What-
d'ye-call-it Court. *Item,* I shut my doors against all
bawds with baskets and pennyworths of muslin, china,
fans, atlases, etc.—*Item,* when you shall be breeding—

Milla. Ah! name it not. 265

Mira. Which may be presumed, with a blessing on
our endeavors—

Milla. Odious endeavors!

Mira. I denounce against all strait lacing, squeezing
for a shape, till you mold my boy's head like a sugar 270

loaf and, instead of a man-child, make me the father
to a crooked billet. Lastly, to the dominion of the tea
table I submit, but with *proviso* that you exceed not
in your province but restrain yourself to native and
simple tea-table drinks, as tea, chocolate, and coffee, 275
as likewise to genuine and authorized tea-table talk,
such as mending of fashions, spoiling reputations, railing at absent friends, and so forth; but that on no account you encroach upon the men's prerogative and
presume to drink healths or toast fellows; for preven- 280
tion of which I banish all foreign forces, all auxiliaries
to the tea table, as orange brandy, all aniseed, cinnamon, citron, and Barbados waters, together with ratafia and the most noble spirit of clary, but for cowslip
wine, poppy water, and all dormitives, those I allow. 285
These *provisos* admitted, in other things I may prove a
tractable and complying husband.

Milla. O, horrid *provisos!* Filthy strong waters! I
toast fellows, odious men! I hate your odious *provisos.*

Mira. Then we're agreed. Shall I kiss your hand 290
upon the contract? And here comes one to be a witness to the sealing of the deed.

Enter Mrs. Fainall.

Milla. Fainall, what shall I do? Shall I have him?
I think I must have him.

Mrs. Fain. Ay, ay, take him, take him, what should 295
you do?

Milla. Well then—I'll take my death, I'm in a horrid
fright—Fainall, I shall never say it—well—I think—I'll
endure you.

Mrs. Fain. Fie, fie! have him, have him, and tell him 300

---

284. CLARY: cordial flavored with flowers of the herb CLARY.
285. DORMITIVES: soporifics.

so in plain terms: for I am sure you have a mind to
him.

Milla. Are you? I think I have—and the horrid man
looks as if he thought so too.—Well, you ridiculous
thing you, I'll have you—I won't be kissed, nor I won't 305
be thanked—here, kiss my hand though. So, hold your
tongue now and don't say a word.

Mrs. Fain. Mirabell, there's a necessity for your
obedience; you have neither time to talk nor stay. My
mother is coming; and, in my conscience, if she should 310
see you, would fall into fits and maybe not recover
time enough to return to Sir Rowland, who, as Foible
tells me, is in a fair way to succeed. Therefore spare
your ecstasies for another occasion and slip down the
back stairs, where Foible waits to consult you. 315

Milla. Ay, go, go. In the meantime, I suppose you
have said something to please me.

Mira. I am all obedience.   *Exit Mirabell.*

Mrs. Fain. Yonder Sir Willful's drunk and so noisy
that my mother has been forced to leave Sir Rowland 320
to appease him; but he answers her only with singing
and drinking. What they have done by this time I
know not; but Petulant and he were upon quarreling
as I came by.

Milla. Well, if Mirabell should not make a good 325
husband, I am a lost thing, for I find I love him violently.

Mrs. Fain. So it seems, when you mind not what's
said to you. If you doubt him, you had best take up
with Sir Willful. 330

Milla. How can you name that superannuated lub-
ber? foh!

Enter Witwoud from drinking.

Mrs. Fain. So, is the fray made up, that you have
left 'em?

Wit. Left 'em? I could stay no longer—I have 335
laughed like ten christenings—I am tipsy with laughing. If I had stayed any longer I should have burst;
I must have been let out and pieced in the sides like
an unsized camlet. Yes, yes, the fray is composed; my
lady came in like a *nolle prosequi* and stopped their 340
proceedings.

Milla. What was the dispute?

Wit. That's the jest: there was no dispute. They
could neither of 'em speak for rage, and so fell a-sput-
tering at one another like two roasting apples. 345

Enter Petulant, drunk.

Now, Petulant, all's over, all's well. Gad, my head
begins to whim it about. Why dost thou not speak?
Thou art both as drunk and as mute as a fish.

Pet. Look you, Mrs. Millamant—if you can love me,
dear nymph, say it—and that's the conclusion. Pass 350
on, or pass off—that's all.

Wit. Thou hast uttered volumes, folios, in less than
decimo sexto, my dear Lacedemonian. Sirrah Petulant, thou art an epitomizer of words.

Pet. Witwoud—you are an annihilator of sense. 355

Wit. Thou art a retailer of phrases, and dost deal in
remnants of remnants like a maker of pincushions;
thou art in truth (metaphorically speaking) a speak-
er of shorthand.

Pet. Thou art (without a figure) just one half of an 360
ass; and Baldwin yonder, thy half-brother, is the rest.

---

339. CAMLET: i.e., a cheap imitation of a fine imported fabric.
340. NOLLE PROSEQUI: the legal term signifying unwillingness to
prosecute.
353. DECIMO SEXTO: sixteenmo (a very small book); LACEDEMONIAN:
Spartan (sparing of speech).
360. FIGURE: metaphor.
361. BALDWIN: name of the ass in the epic of Reynard the Fox.
362. GEMINI: pair of twins.
377. CONCLUDE PREMISES: constitute sufficient reason.

A gemini of asses split would make just four of you.

Wit. Thou dost bite, my dear mustard seed; kiss me
for that.

Pet. Stand off—I'll kiss no more males—I have kissed 365
your twin yonder in a humor of reconciliation, till he
(*Hiccup*) rises upon my stomach like a radish.

Milla. Eh! filthy creature!—What was the quarrel?

Pet. There was no quarrel—there might have been a
quarrel.   370

Wit. If there had been words enow between 'em to
have expressed provocation, they had gone together
by the ears like a pair of castanets.

Pet. You were the quarrel.

Milla. Me!   375

Pet. If I have a humor to quarrel, I can make less
matters conclude premises. If you are not handsome,
what then, if I have a humor to prove it? If I shall
have my reward, say so; if not, fight for your face the
next time yourself.—I'll go sleep.   380

Wit. Do; wrap thyself up like a woodlouse and
dream revenge; and, hear me, if thou canst learn to
write by tomorrow morning, pen me a challenge—I'll
carry it for thee.

Pet. Carry your mistress' monkey a spider—go flea 385
dogs and read romances!—I'll go to bed to my maid.

Exit.

Mrs. Fain. He's horridly drunk. How came you all
in this pickle?

Wit. A plot, a plot, to get rid of the knight—your
husband's advice; but he sneaked off.   390

Enter Lady Wishfort, and Sir Willful, drunk.

Lady Wish. Out upon't, out upon't, at years of discretion and comport yourself at this rantipole rate!

Sir. Will. No offense, aunt.

Lady Wish. Offense? As I'm a person, I'm ashamed of you. Foh! how you stink of wine! D'ee think my 395 niece will ever endure such a borachio! You're an absolute borachio.

Sir Will. Borachio!

Lady Wish. At a time when you should commence an amour and put your best foot foremost— 400

Sir Will. 'Sheart, an you grutch me your liquor, make a bill. Give me more drink, and take my purse.

Sings.

> Prithee fill me the glass
> Till it laugh in my face,
> With ale that is potent and mellow; 405
> He that whines for a lass,
> Is an ignorant ass,
> For a bumper has not its fellow.

But if you would have me marry my cousin, say the word, and I'll do't—Willful will do't, that's the word— 410 Willful will do't, that's my crest—my motto I have forgot.

Lady Wish. My nephew's a little overtaken, cousin, but 'tis with drinking your health. O' my word you are obliged to him— 415

Sir Will. *In vino veritas,* aunt.—If I drunk your health today, cousin—I am a borachio. But if you have a mind to be married, say the word and send for the piper; Willful will do't. If not, dust it away, and let's have t'other round.—Tony—Odsheart! where's Tony? 420 Tony's an honest fellow, but he spits after a bumper, and that's a fault. *Sings.*

> We'll drink and we'll never ha' done, boys,
> Put the glass then around with the sun, boys,

396. BORACHIO: drunkard.
419. DUST . . . AWAY: drink it off.
429. PIMPLE: boon companion.

Let Apollo's example invite us;   425
   For he's drunk every night,
   And that makes him so bright,
That he's able next morning to light us.

The sun's a good pimple, an honest soaker, he has a
cellar at your Antipodes. If I travel, aunt, I touch at   430
your Antipodes. Your Antipodes are a good rascally
sort of topsy-turvy fellows. If I had a bumper, I'd
stand upon my head and drink a health to 'em.—A
match or no match, cousin with the hard name?—
Aunt, Willful will do't. If she has her maidenhead,   435
let her look to't; if she has not, let her keep her own
counsel in the meantime and cry out at the nine
months' end.

  Milla. Your pardon, madam, I can stay no longer—
Sir Willful grows very powerful. Eh! how he smells!   440
I shall be overcome if I stay. Come, cousin.

        Exeunt Millamant and Mrs. Fainall.

  Lady Wish. Smells! He would poison a tallow-
chandler and his family. Beastly creature, I know not
what to do with him.—Travel, quotha; ay, travel,
travel, get thee gone, get thee but far enough, to the   445
Saracens, or the Tartars, or the Turks; for thou art not
fit to live in a Christian commonwealth, thou beastly
pagan.

  Sir Will. Turks, no; no Turks, aunt: your Turks are
infidels and believe not in the grape. Your Mahome-   450
tan, your Mussulman, is a dry stinkard—no offense,
aunt. My map says that your Turk is not so honest a
man as your Christian. I cannot find by the map that
your Mufti is orthodox—whereby it is a plain case
that orthodox is a hard word, aunt, and (*Hiccup*)   455
Greek for claret.   *Sings.*

   To drink is a Christian diversion,
   Unknown to the Turk and the Persian:

> Let Mahometan fools
> Live by heathenish rules,   460
> And be damned over teacups and coffee.
> But let British lads sing,
> Crown a health to the king,
> And a fig for your Sultan and Sophy.

Ah, Tony!   465

Enter Foible and whispers Lady Wishfort.

Lady Wish. Sir Rowland impatient? Good lack!
what shall I do with this beastly tumbril?—Go lie
down and sleep, you sot—or as I'm a person, I'll have
you bastinadoed with broomsticks!—Call up the
wenches.   *Exit Foible.* 470

Sir Will. Ahey! Wenches, where are the wenches?

Lady Wish. Dear Cousin Witwoud, get him away
and you will bind me to you inviolably. I have an
affair of moment that invades me with some precipi-
tation. You will oblige me to all futurity.   475

Wit. Come, knight.—Pox on him, I don't know what
to say to him.—Will you go to a cock-match?

Sir Will. With a wench, Tony? Is she a shake-bag,
sirrah? Let me bite your cheek for that.

Wit. Horrible! He has a breath like a bagpipe.—Ay, 480
ay; come, will you march, my Salopian?

Sir Will. Lead on, little Tony—I'll follow thee, my
Anthony, my Tantony. Sirrah, thou shalt be my Tantony, and I'll be thy pig.

> —And a fig for your Sultan and Sophy.   485
>   *Exit singing with Witwoud.*

---

467. TUMBRIL: literally a dung-cart (or one of several types of dumpcarts).
478. SHAKE-BAG: large fighting cock, and slang for "whore."
483-84. TANTONY: i.e., St. Antony, in whose legend a pig is featured.

Lady Wish. This will never do. It will never make a
match—at least before he has been abroad.

Enter Waitwell, disguised as for Sir Rowland.

Dear Sir Rowland, I am confounded with confusion
at the retrospection of my own rudeness—I have more
pardons to ask than the Pope distributes in the year   490
of jubilee. But I hope, where there is likely to be so
near an alliance, we may unbend the severity of
decorum and dispense with a little ceremony.

Wait. My impatience, madam, is the effect of my
transport, and till I have the possession of your adora-   495
able person, I am tantalized on a rack and do but
hang, madam, on the tenter of expectation.

Lady Wish. You have excess of gallantry, Sir Rowland, and press things to a conclusion with a most
prevailing vehemence. But a day or two for decency   500
of marriage—

Wait. For decency of funeral, madam. The delay
will break my heart—or if that should fail, I shall be
poisoned. My nephew will get an inkling of my designs and poison me—and I would willingly starve   505
him before I die—I would gladly go out of the world
with that satisfaction. That would be some comfort
to me, if I could but live so long as to be revenged on
that unnatural viper.

Lady Wish. Is he so unnatural, say you? Truly I   510
would contribute much both to the saving of your life
and the accomplishment of your revenge. Not that I
respect myself, though he has been a perfidious
wretch to me.

Wait. Perfidious to you!   515

Lady Wish. O Sir Rowland, the hours that he has
died away at my feet, the tears that he has shed, the

oaths that he has sworn, the palpitations that he has
felt, the trances and the tremblings, the ardors and
the ecstasies, the kneelings and the risings, the heart-   520
heavings and the hand-gripings, the pangs and the
pathetic regards of his protesting eyes! O, no memory
can register!

Wait. What, my rival! Is the rebel my rival? 'A dies.

Lady Wish. No, don't kill him at once, Sir Rowland;   525
starve him gradually, inch by inch.

Wait. I'll do't. In three weeks he shall be barefoot;
in a month out at knees with begging an alms; he
shall starve upward and upward till he has nothing
living but his head and then go out in a stink, like a   530
candle's end upon a save-all.

Lady Wish. Well, Sir Rowland, you have the way—
you are no novice in the labyrinth of love—you have
the clew. But as I am a person, Sir Rowland, you must
not attribute my yielding to any sinister appetite or   535
indigestion of widowhood, nor impute my complacen-
cy to any lethargy of continence. I hope you do not
think me prone to any iteration of nuptials.

Wait. Far be it from me—

Lady Wish. If you do, I protest I must recede—or   540
think that I have made a prostitution of decorums
but in the vehemence of compassion, and to save the
life of a person of so much importance—

Wait. I esteem it so—

Lady Wish. Or else you wrong my condescension—   545

Wait. I do not, I do not—

Lady Wish. Indeed you do.

Wait. I do not, fair shrine of virtue.

Lady Wish. If you think the least scruple of car-
nality was an ingredient—   550

---

531. SAVE-ALL: a candleholder so contrived that the candle will
burn down to the very end.
570. CHAIRMAN: bearer of a sedan chair.

Wait. Dear madam, no. You are all camphire and frankincense, all chastity and odor.

Lady Wish. Or that—

Enter Foible.

Foib. Madam, the dancers are ready, and there's one with a letter who must deliver it into your own 555 hands.

Lady Wish. Sir Rowland, will you give me leave? Think favorably, judge candidly, and conclude you have found a person who would suffer racks in honor's cause, dear Sir Rowland, and will wait on you 560 incessantly.   *Exit.*

Wait. Fie, fie! What a slavery have I undergone! Spouse, hast thou any cordial?—I want spirits.

Foib. What a washy rogue art thou, to pant thus for a quarter of an hour's lying and swearing to a fine 565 lady!

Wait. O, she is the antidote to desire. Spouse, thou wilt fare the worse for't. I shall have no appetite to iteration of nuptials this eight-and-forty hours. By this hand I'd rather be a chairman in the dog days 570 than act Sir Rowland till this time tomorrow.

Enter Lady Wishfort with a letter.

Lady Wish. Call in the dancers.—Sir Rowland, we'll sit, if you please, and see the entertainment.   *Dance.* Now with your permission, Sir Rowland, I will peruse my letter—I would open it in your presence, because 575 I would not make you uneasy. If it should make you uneasy I would burn it—speak if it does—but you may see by the superscription it is like a woman's hand.

Foib. (*To him*) By Heaven! Mrs. Marwood's, I know it—my heart aches—get it from her—   580

Wait. A woman's hand? No, madam, that's no woman's hand, I see that already. That's somebody whose throat must be cut.

Lady Wish. Nay, Sir Rowland, since you give me a proof of your passion by your jealousy, I promise you 585 I'll make you a return by a frank communication. You shall see it—we'll open it together—look you here.

Reads. "Madam, though unknown to you,"—Look you there, 'tis from nobody that I know—"I have that honor for your character that I think myself obliged 590 to let you know you are abused. He who pretends to be Sir Rowland is a cheat and a rascal—" O Heavens! what's this?

Foib. Unfortunate, all's ruined.

Wait. How, how, let me see, let me see! (*Reading*) 595 "A rascal, and disguised and suborned for that imposture,"—O villainy! O villainy!—"by the contrivance of—"

Lady Wish. I shall faint, I shall die, I shall die, O!

Foib. (*To him*) Say 'tis your nephew's hand. Quick- 600 ly, his plot, swear, swear it.

Wait. Here's a villain! Madam, don't you perceive it, don't you see it?

Lady Wish. Too well, too well. I have seen too much. 605

Wait. I told you at first I knew the hand. A woman's hand? The rascal writes a sort of a large hand, your Roman hand. I saw there was a throat to be cut presently. If he were my son, as he is my nephew, I'd pistol him— 610

Foib. O treachery! But you are sure, Sir Rowland, it is his writing?

Wait. Sure? Am I here? Do I live? Do I love this pearl of India? I have twenty letters in my pocket from him, in the same character. 615

608. ROMAN HAND: bold, cursive script.

Lady Wish. How!

Foib. O, what luck it is, Sir Rowland, that you were
present at this juncture! This was the business that
brought Mr. Mirabell disguised to Madam Millamant
this afternoon. I thought something was contriving 620
when he stole by me and would have hid his face.

Lady Wish. How, how! I heard the villain was in
the house indeed, and now I remember, my niece
went away abruptly when Sir Willful was to have
made his addresses.   625

Foib. Then, then, madam, Mr. Mirabell waited for
her in her chamber, but I would not tell your Ladyship to discompose you when you were to receive Sir
Rowland.

Wait. Enough, his date is short.   630

Foib. No, good Sir Rowland, don't incur the law.

Wait. Law! I care not for law. I can but die, and 'tis
in a good cause—my lady shall be satisfied of my truth
and innocence, though it cost me my life.

Lady Wish. No, dear Sir Rowland, don't fight; if 635
you should be killed, I must never show my face; or
hanged—O, consider my reputation, Sir Rowland! No,
you shan't fight. I'll go in and examine my niece; I'll
make her confess. I conjure you, Sir Rowland, by all
your love, not to fight.   640

Wait. I am charmed, madam, I obey. But some
proof you must let me give you; I'll go for a black box,
which contains the writings of my whole estate, and
deliver that into your hands.

Lady Wish. Ay, dear Sir Rowland, that will be some 645
comfort; bring the black box.

Wait. And may I presume to bring a contract to be
signed this night? May I hope so far?

Lady Wish. Bring what you will; but come alive,
pray come alive. O, this is a happy discovery!   650

Wait. Dead or alive I'll come—and married we will

be in spite of treachery; ay, and get an heir that shall
defeat the last remaining glimpse of hope in my
abandoned nephew. Come, my buxom widow:

Ere long you shall substantial proof receive 655
That I'm an errant knight—

Foib.   Or arrant knave.

Exeunt.

---

13. BULK: stall.
14. FRISONEER GORGET: coarse woolen neckerchief.
15. COLBERTEEN: cheap lace.

ACT V

Scene I. Scene continues.

[*Enter*] *Lady Wishfort and Foible*.

Lady Wish. Out of my house, out of my house, thou viper, thou serpent, that I have fostered! Thou bosom traitress, that I raised from nothing!—begone, begone, begone, go, go!—that I took from washing of old gauze and weaving of dead hair, with a bleak blue 5 nose, over a chafing-dish of starved embers, and dining behind a traverse rag, in a shop no bigger than a bird cage,—go, go, starve again, do, do!

Foib. Dear madam, I'll beg pardon on my knees.

Lady Wish. Away, out, out, go set up for yourself 10 again! Do, drive a trade, do, with your threepenny-worth of small ware, flaunting upon a pack-thread, under a brandy-seller's bulk, or against a dead wall by a ballad-monger! Go hang out an old Frisoneer gorget, with a yard of yellow colberteen again! do! an old 15 gnawed mask, two rows of pins, and a child's fiddle; a glass necklace with the beads broken, and a quilted nightcap with one ear! Go, go, drive a trade! These were your commodities, you treacherous trull, this was your merchandise you dealt in, when I took you 20 into my house, placed you next myself, and made you governante of my whole family! You have forgot this, have you, now you have feathered your nest?

Foib. No, no, dear madam. Do but hear me; have but a moment's patience—I'll confess all. Mr. Mirabell 25

347

seduced me; I am not the first that he has wheedled with his dissembling tongue; your Ladyship's own wisdom has been deluded by him—then how should I, a poor ignorant, defend myself? O madam, if you knew but what he promised me, and how he assured me your Ladyship should come to no damage!—Or else the wealth of the Indies should not have bribed me to conspire against so good, so sweet, so kind a lady as you have been to me.

Lady Wish. No damage? What, to betray me, to marry me to a cast servingman; to make me a receptacle, an hospital for a decayed pimp? No damage? O thou frontless impudence, more than a big-bellied actress!

Foib. Pray, do but hear me, madam; he could not marry your Ladyship, madam.—No indeed, his marriage was to have been void in law; for he was married to me first, to secure your Ladyship. He could not have bedded your Ladyship; for if he had consummated with your Ladyship, he must have run the risk of the law and been put upon his clergy.—Yes indeed, I inquired of the law in that case before I would meddle or make.

Lady Wish. What? Then I have been your property, have I? I have been convenient to you, it seems; while you were catering for Mirabell, I have been broker for you? What? have you made a passive bawd of me? This exceeds all precedent; I am brought to fine uses,

---

36. CAST: dismissed.
38. FRONTLESS: shameless.
46. PUT . . . CLERGY: forced to plead benefit of clergy; i.e., prove himself literate and therefore not subject to capital punishment.
49. PROPERTY: tool.
54. BOTCHER: patcher-up.
55. ABIGAILS . . . ANDREWS: servantmaids and servingmen.
56. PHILANDER: lover.
57. DUKE'S PLACE: the church where her secret marriage was performed.
61. BRIDEWELL: a London prison.
64-65. BEAT HEMP: a labor performed by female inmates of Bridewell.

to become a botcher of secondhand marriages between Abigails and Andrews! I'll couple you! Yes, I'll 55
baste you together, you and your Philander! I'll
Duke's Place you, as I'm a person. Your turtle is in
custody already; you shall coo in the same cage, if
there be constable or warrant in the parish. *Exit.*

Foib. O that ever I was born! O that I was ever 60
married!—A bride, ay, I shall be a Bridewell-bride. O!

Enter Mrs. Fainall.

Mrs. Fain. Poor Foible, what's the matter?

Foib. O madam, My Lady's gone for a constable; I
shall be had to a justice and put to Bridewell to beat
hemp! Poor Waitwell's gone to prison already. 65

Mrs. Fain. Have a good heart, Foible; Mirabell's
gone to give security for him. This is all Marwood's
and my husband's doing.

Foib. Yes, yes; I know it, madam; she was in My
Lady's closet and overheard all that you said to me 70
before dinner. She sent the letter to My Lady; and,
that missing effect, Mr. Fainall laid this plot to arrest
Waitwell when he pretended to go for the papers; and
in the meantime Mrs. Marwood declared all to My
Lady. 75

Mrs. Fain. Was there no mention made of me in the
letter? My mother does not suspect my being in the
confederacy? I fancy Marwood has not told her,
though she has told my husband.

Foib. Yes, madam; but My Lady did not see that 80
part; we stifled the letter before she read so far. Has
that mischievous devil told Mr. Fainall of your Ladyship then?

Mrs. Fain. Ay, all's out—my affair with Mirabell,
everything, discovered. This is the last day of our liv- 85
ing together, that's my comfort.

Foib. Indeed, madam, and so 'tis a comfort if you knew all; he has been even with your Ladyship, which I could have told you long enough since, but I love to keep peace and quietness, by my good will: I had 90 rather bring friends together than set 'em at distance. But Mrs. Marwood and he are nearer related than ever their parents thought for.

Mrs. Fain. Say'st thou so, Foible? Canst thou prove this? 95

Foib. I can take my oath of it, madam, so can Mrs. Mincing; we have had many a fair word from Madam Marwood to conceal something that passed in our chamber one evening when you were at Hyde Park and we were thought to have gone a-walking, but we 100 went up unawares—though we were sworn to secrecy too. Madam Marwood took a book and swore us upon it; but it was but a book of verses and poems. So as long as it was not a Bible oath, we may break it with a safe conscience. 105

Mrs. Fain. This discovery is the most opportune thing I could wish.—Now, Mincing?

Enter Mincing.

Minc. My Lady would speak with Mrs. Foible, mem. Mr. Mirabell is with her; he has set your spouse at liberty, Mrs. Foible, and would have you hide your- 110 self in My Lady's closet till my old lady's anger is abated. O, my old lady is in a perilous passion at something Mr. Fainall has said; he swears, and my old lady cries. There's a fearful hurricane, I vow. He says, mem, how that he'll have My Lady's fortune made 115 over to him or he'll be divorced.

Mrs. Fain. Does your lady and Mirabell know that?

Minc. Yes, mem, they have sent me to see if Sir Willful be sober and to bring him to them. My Lady

is resolved to have him, I think, rather than lose such 120
a vast sum as six thousand pound. O, come, Mrs.
Foible, I hear my old lady.

Mrs. Fain. Foible, you must tell Mincing that she
must prepare to vouch when I call her.

Foib. Yes, yes, madam.   125

Minc. O, yes, mem, I'll vouch anything for your
Ladyship's service, be what it will.

Exeunt Mincing and Foible.

Enter Lady Wishfort and Mrs. Marwood.

Lady Wish. O, my dear friend, how can I enumerate
the benefits that I have received from your goodness?
To you I owe the timely discovery of the false vows 130
of Mirabell; to you the detection of the impostor Sir
Rowland. And now you are become an intercessor
with my son-in-law to save the honor of my house and
compound for the frailties of my daughter. Well,
friend, you are enough to reconcile me to the bad 135
world, or else I would retire to deserts and solitudes
and feed harmless sheep by groves and purling
streams. Dear Marwood, let us leave the world and
retire by ourselves and be shepherdesses.

Mrs. Mar. Let us first dispatch the affair in hand, 140
madam. We shall have leisure to think of retirement
afterwards.—Here is one who is concerned in the
treaty.

Lady Wish. O daughter, daughter, is it possible
thou shouldst be my child, bone of my bone and flesh 145
of my flesh, and as I may say, another me, and yet
transgress the most minute particle of severe virtue?
Is it possible you should lean aside to iniquity, who
have been cast in the direct mold of virtue? I have not
only been a mold but a pattern for you and a model 150
for you, after you were brought into the world.

Mrs. Fain. I don't understand your Ladyship.

Lady Wish. Not understand? Why, have you not been naught? Have you not been sophisticated? Not understand? Here I am ruined to compound for your 155 caprices and your cuckoldoms. I must pawn my plate and my jewels and ruin my niece, and all little enough—

Mrs. Fain. I am wronged and abused, and so are you. 'Tis a false accusation, as false as hell, as false as 160 your friend there, ay, or your friend's friend, my false husband.

Mrs. Mar. My friend, Mrs. Fainall? Your husband my friend! what do you mean?

Mrs. Fain. I know what I mean, madam, and so do 165 you; and so shall the world at a time convenient.

Mrs. Mar. I am sorry to see you so passionate, madam. More temper would look more like innocence. But I have done. I am sorry my zeal to serve your Ladyship and family should admit of misconstruction 170 or make me liable to affronts. You will pardon me, madam, if I meddle no more with an affair in which I am not personally concerned.

Lady Wish. O dear friend, I am so ashamed that you should meet with such returns!—You ought to 175 ask pardon on your knees, ungrateful creature! She deserves more from you than all your life can accomplish.—O, don't leave me destitute in this perplexity! No, stick to me, my good genius.

Mrs. Fain. I tell you, madam, you're abused.—Stick 180 to you? ay, like a leech, to suck your best blood—she'll drop off when she's full. Madam, you sha' not pawn a bodkin nor part with a brass counter in composition for me. I defy 'em all. Let 'em prove their aspersions:

---

154. NAUGHT: wicked; SOPHISTICATED: corrupted.
168. TEMPER: moderation.
196. BABIES: dolls.
199. MADE . . . FOR: passed off as.

I know my own innocence and dare stand by a trial. 185
Exit.

Lady Wish. Why, if she should be innocent, if she
should be wronged after all, ha? I don't know what to
think—and I promise you, her education has been un-
exceptionable—I may say it, for I chiefly made it my
own care to initiate her very infancy in the rudiments 190
of virtue and to impress upon her tender years a
young odium and aversion to the very sight of men;
ay, friend, she would ha' shrieked if she had but seen
a man, till she was in her teens. As I'm a person, 'tis
true. She was never suffered to play with a male-child, 195
though but in coats; nay, her very babies were of the
feminine gender. O, she never looked a man in the
face but her own father, or the chaplain, and him we
made a shift to put upon her for a woman, by the help
of his long garments and his sleek face, till she was 200
going in her fifteen.

Mrs. Mar. 'Twas much she should be deceived so
long.

Lady Wish. I warrant you, or she would never have
borne to have been catechized by him; and have 205
heard his long lectures against singing and dancing
and such debaucheries, and going to filthy plays and
profane music-meetings, where the lewd trebles
squeak nothing but bawdy and the basses roar blas-
phemy. O, she would have swooned at the sight or 210
name of an obscene playbook—and can I think, after
all this, that my daughter can be naught? What, a
whore? And thought it excommunication to set her
foot within the door of a playhouse! O my dear friend,
I can't believe it, no, no! As she says, let him prove it, 215
let him prove it!

Mrs. Mar. Prove it, madam? What, and have your
name prostituted in a public court! yours and your
daughter's reputation worried at the bar by a pack of

bawling lawyers? To be ushered in with an "Oyez" 220
of scandal; and have your case opened by an old
fumbling lecher in a quoif like a man midwife, to
bring your daughter's infamy to light; to be a theme
for legal punsters and quibblers by the statute; and
become a jest, against a rule of court, where there is 225
no precedent for a jest in any record, not even in
Doomsday Book; to discompose the gravity of the
bench and provoke naughty interrogatories in more
naughty law Latin; while the good judge, tickled with
the proceeding, simpers under a grey beard and fidges 230
off and on his cushion as if he had swallowed
cantharides or sat upon cowitch!

Lady Wish. O, 'tis very hard!

Mrs. Mar. And then to have my young revelers of
the Temple take notes, like prentices at a conventicle, 235
and after, talk it all over again in commons or before
drawers in an eating house.

Lady Wish. Worse and worse!

Mrs. Mar. Nay, this is nothing; if it would end here,
'twere well. But it must after this be consigned by the 240
shorthand writers to the public press; and from thence
be transferred to the hands, nay, into the throats and
lungs of hawkers, with voices more licentious than the
loud flounder-man's or the woman that cries grey
pease; and this you must hear till you are stunned; 245
nay, you must hear nothing else for some days.

Lady Wish. O, 'tis insupportable. No, no, dear
friend, make it up, make it up; ay, ay, I'll compound.
I'll give up all, myself and my all, my niece and her
all—anything, everything, for composition. 250

Mrs. Mar. Nay, madam, I advise nothing; I only lay

232. CANTHARIDES: an aphrodisiac; COWITCH: cowhage, the hairy
pods of which cause severe itching.
235. CONVENTICLE: church meeting (where the apprentices were to
make notes on the sermon for their masters).
236. COMMONS: communal dining hall.
253. OVERSEEN: overlooked.

before you, as a friend, the inconveniencies which perhaps you have overseen. Here comes Mr. Fainall. If he will be satisfied to huddle up all in silence, I shall be glad. You must think I would rather congratu- 255 late than condole with you.

Enter Fainall.

Lady Wish. Ay, ay, I do not doubt it, dear Marwood; no, no, I do not doubt it.

Fain. Well, madam; I have suffered myself to be overcome by the importunity of this lady your friend 260 and am content you shall enjoy your own proper estate during life, on condition you oblige yourself never to marry, under such penalty as I think convenient.

Lady Wish. Never to marry? 265

Fain. No more Sir Rowlands; the next imposture may not be so timely detected.

Mrs. Mar. That condition, I dare answer, My Lady will consent to without difficulty; she has already but too much experienced the perfidiousness of men. Be- 270 sides, madam, when we retire to our pastoral solitude we shall bid adieu to all other thoughts.

Lady Wish. Ay, that's true; but in case of necessity, as of health, or some such emergency—

Fain. O, if you are prescribed marriage, you shall be 275 considered; I will only reserve to myself the power to choose for you. If your physic be wholesome, it matters not who is your apothecary. Next, my wife shall settle on me the remainder of her fortune not made over already, and for her maintenance depend entirely 280 on my discretion.

Lady Wish. This is most inhumanly savage, exceeding the barbarity of a Muscovite husband.

Fain. I learned it from His Czarish Majesty's retinue, in a winter evening's conference over brandy and pepper, amongst other secrets of matrimony and policy as they are at present practiced in the Northern Hemisphere. But this must be agreed unto, and that positively. Lastly, I will be endowed, in right of my wife, with that six thousand pound which is the moiety of Mrs. Millamant's fortune in your possession, and which she has forfeited (as will appear by the last will and testament of your deceased husband, Sir Jonathan Wishfort) by her disobedience in contracting herself against your consent or knowledge, and by refusing the offered match with Sir Willful Witwoud, which you, like a careful aunt, had provided for her.

Lady Wish. My nephew was *non compos* and could not make his addresses.

Fain. I come to make demands—I'll hear no objections.

Lady Wish. You will grant me time to consider?

Fain. Yes, while the instrument is drawing to which you must set your hand till more sufficient deeds can be perfected, which I will take care shall be done with all possible speed. In the meanwhile, I will go for the said instrument, and till my return you may balance this matter in your own discretion.

Exit Fainall.

Lady Wish. This insolence is beyond all precedent, all parallel; must I be subject to this merciless villain?

Mrs. Mar. 'Tis severe indeed, madam, that you should smart for your daughter's wantonness.

Lady Wish. 'Twas against my consent that she mar-

---

284. CZARISH MAJESTY: Peter the Great, who visited England in 1697.
315. YEAR: i.e., customary year of mourning for her husband.
317-18. WITH . . . WITNESS: with a vengeance.
319. CONFISCATED . . . RATE: as the property of rebels was confiscated.
325. IN DISGUISE: intoxicated.

285

290

295

300

305

310

ried this barbarian, but she would have him, though
her year was not out. Ah! her first husband, my son   315
Languish, would not have carried it thus. Well, that
was my choice, this is hers; she is matched now with a
witness. I shall be mad, dear friend—is there no comfort for me? Must I live to be confiscated at this rebel
rate?—Here come two more of my Egyptian plagues   320
too.

Enter Millamant and Sir Willful.

Sir Will. Aunt, your servant.
Lady Wish. Out, caterpillar, call not me aunt! I
know thee not!
Sir Will. I confess I have been a little in disguise, as   325
they say—'sheart! and I'm sorry for't. What would you
have? I hope I committed no offense, aunt—and if I
did I am willing to make satisfaction; and what can
a man say fairer? If I have broke anything, I'll pay
for't, an it cost a pound. And so let that content for   330
what's past, and make no more words. For what's to
come, to pleasure you I'm willing to marry my cousin.
So pray let's all be friends; she and I are agreed upon
the matter before a witness.
Lady Wish. How's this, dear niece? Have I any   335
comfort? Can this be true?
Milla. I am content to be a sacrifice to your repose,
madam; and to convince you that I had no hand in the
plot, as you were misinformed, I have laid my commands on Mirabell to come in person and be a witness   340
that I give my hand to this flower of knighthood; and
for the contract that passed between Mirabell and me,
I have obliged him to make a resignation of it in your
Ladyship's presence; he is without and waits your
leave for admittance.   345
Lady Wish. Well, I'll swear I am something revived

at this testimony of your obedience; but I cannot
admit that traitor; I fear I cannot fortify myself to
support his appearance. He is as terrible to me as a
Gorgon; if I see him, I fear I shall turn to stone, 350
petrify incessantly.

Milla. If you disoblige him, he may resent your
refusal and insist upon the contract still. Then, 'tis
the last time he will be offensive to you.

Lady Wish. Are you sure it will be the last time? If 355
I were sure of that—shall I never see him again?

Milla. Sir Willful, you and he are to travel together,
are you not?

Sir Will. 'Sheart, the gentleman's a civil gentleman,
aunt, let him come in; why, we are sworn brothers and 360
fellow travelers. We are to be Pylades and Orestes,
he and I. He is to be my interpreter in foreign parts.
He has been overseas once already; and, with *proviso*
that I marry my cousin, will cross 'em once again, only
to bear me company. 'Sheart, I'll call him in; an I set 365
on't once, he shall come in; and see who'll hinder him.
Exit.

Mrs. Mar. This is precious fooling, if it would pass;
but I'll know the bottom of it.

Lady Wish. O dear Marwood, you are not going?

Mrs. Mar. Not far, madam; I'll return immediately. 370
Exit.

Re-enter Sir Willful and Mirabell.

Sir Will. Look up, man, I'll stand by you. 'Sbud, an
she do frown, she can't kill you; besides, harkee, she
dare not frown desperately, because her face is none
of her own. 'Sheart, an she should, her forehead would

---

405. o' . . . QUORUM: one of the justices of the peace whose presence was necessary for the determination of certain sorts of cases.

wrinkle like the coat of a cream cheese; but mum for 375
that, fellow traveler.

Mira. If a deep sense of the many injuries I have
offered to so good a lady, with a sincere remorse and
a hearty contrition, can but obtain the least glance of
compassion, I am too happy. Ah, madam, there was a 380
time—but let it be forgotten—I confess I have de-
servedly forfeited the high place I once held, of sighing at your feet; nay, kill me not by turning from me
in disdain—I come not to plead for favor—nay, not for
pardon; I am a suppliant only for your pity—I am 385
going where I never shall behold you more—

Sir Will. How, fellow traveler! You shall go by yourself then.

Mira. Let me be pitied first and afterwards forgotten; I ask no more. 390

Sir Will. By'r Lady, a very reasonable request and
will cost you nothing, aunt. Come, come, forgive and
forget, aunt; why you must, an you are a Christian.

Mira. Consider, madam, in reality you could not
receive much prejudice; it was an innocent device; 395
though I confess it had a face of guiltiness, it was at
most an artifice which love contrived—and errors
which love produces have ever been accounted venial.
At least think it is punishment enough that I have lost
what in my heart I hold most dear, that to your cruel 400
indignation I have offered up this beauty, and with
her my peace and quiet, nay, all my hopes of future
comfort.

Sir Will. An he does not move me, would I might
never be o' the quorum! An it were not as good a deed 405
as to drink, to give her to him again, I would I might
never take shipping!—Aunt, if you don't forgive
quickly, I shall melt, I can tell you that. My contract
went no further than a little mouth glue, and that's

hardly dry—one doleful sigh more from my fellow 410
traveler and 'tis dissolved.

Lady Wish. Well, nephew, upon your account.—Ah,
he has a false insinuating tongue!—Well, sir, I will
stifle my just resentment at my nephew's request. I
will endeavor what I can to forget—but on *proviso* 415
that you resign the contract with my niece immediately.

Mira. It is in writing and with papers of concern;
but I have sent my servant for it and will deliver it to
you, with all acknowledgments for your transcendent 420
goodness.

Lady Wish. (*Apart*) O, he has witchcraft in his eyes
and tongue! When I did not see him, I could have
bribed a villain to his assassination; but his appearance rakes the embers which have so long lain 425
smothered in my breast.

Enter Fainall and Mrs. Marwood.

Fain. Your date of deliberation, madam, is expired.
Here is the instrument; are you prepared to sign?

Lady Wish. If I were prepared, I am not em-
powered. My niece exerts a lawful claim, having 430
matched herself by my direction to Sir Willful.

Fain. That sham is too gross to pass on me, though
'tis imposed on you, madam.

Milla. Sir, I have given my consent.

Mira. And, sir, I have resigned my pretensions. 435

Sir Will. And, sir, I assert my right; and will maintain it in defiance of you, sir, and of your instrument.
'Sheart, an you talk of an instrument, sir, I have an
old fox by my thigh shall hack your instrument of ram

439. FOX: sword.
439–40. RAM VELLUM: sheepskin.
441. MITTIMUS: warrant for commitment to prison.
446. BEEFEATER: guard of the Tower of London.

vellum to shreds, sir! It shall not be sufficient for a 440
mittimus or a tailor's measure; therefore, withdraw
your instrument, sir, or by'r Lady I shall draw mine.

Lady Wish. Hold, nephew, hold!

Milla. Good Sir Willful, respite your valor!

Fain. Indeed? Are you provided of a guard, with 445
your single beefeater there? But I'm prepared for you
and insist upon my first proposal. You shall submit
your own estate to my management and absolutely
make over my wife's to my sole use, as pursuant to
the purport and tenor of this other covenant. I sup- 450
pose, madam, your consent is not requisite in this
case; nor, Mr. Mirabell, your resignation; nor, Sir
Willful, your right. You may draw your fox if you
please, sir, and make a bear-garden flourish somewhere else, for here it will not avail. This, My Lady 455
Wishfort, must be subscribed, or your darling daughter's turned adrift like a leaky hulk, to sink or swim
as she and the current of this lewd town can agree.

Lady Wish. Is there no means, no remedy, to stop
my ruin? Ungrateful wretch! Dost thou not owe thy 460
being, thy subsistence, to my daughter's fortune?

Fain. I'll answer you when I have the rest of it in
my possession.

Mira. But that you would not accept of a remedy
from my hands—I own I have not deserved you should 465
owe any obligation to me, or else perhaps I could
advise—

Lady Wish. O, what? what? To save me and my
child from ruin, from want, I'll forgive all that's past;
nay, I'll consent to anything to come, to be delivered 470
from this tyranny.

Mira. Ay, madam; but that is too late, my reward is
intercepted. You have disposed of her who only could
have made me a compensation for all my services. But

be it as it may, I am resolved I'll serve you; you shall 475
not be wronged in this savage manner!

Lady Wish. How! Dear Mr. Mirabell, can you be so
generous at last! But it is not possible. Harkee, I'll
break my nephew's match, you shall have my niece
yet and all her fortune, if you can but save me from 480
this imminent danger.

Mira. Will you? I take you at your word. I ask no
more. I must have leave for two criminals to appear.

Lady Wish. Ay, ay, anybody, anybody!

Mira. Foible is one, and a penitent.   485

Enter Mrs. Fainall, Foible, and Mincing.

Mrs. Mar. (*To Fainall*) O, my shame! These corrupt things are bought and brought hither to expose
me.   *Mirabell and Lady Wishfort go to*
                              Mrs. Fainall and Foible.

Fain. If it must all come out, why let 'em know it;
'tis but the way of the world. That shall not urge me 490
to relinquish or abate one tittle of my terms; no, I will
insist the more.

Foib. Yes, indeed, madam, I'll take my Bible oath
of it.

Minc. And so will I, mem.   495

Lady Wish. O Marwood, Marwood, art thou false?
My friend deceive me? Hast thou been a wicked ac-
complice with that profligate man?

Mrs. Mar. Have you so much ingratitude and injustice to give credit, against your friend, to the as- 500
persions of two such mercenary trulls?

Minc. Mercenary, mem? I scorn your words. 'Tis
true we found you and Mr. Fainall in the blue garret;
by the same token, you swore us to secrecy upon

---

505. MESSALINA'S POEMS: possibly a comic error for "miscellaneous."

Messalina's poems. Mercenary! No, if we would have 505
been mercenary, we should have held our tongues;
you would have bribed us sufficiently.

Fain. Go, you are an insignificant thing!—Well,
what are you the better for this! Is this Mr. Mirabell's
expedient? I'll be put off no longer.—You thing that 510
was a wife shall smart for this! I will not leave thee
wherewithal to hide thy shame; your body shall be
naked as your reputation.

Mrs. Fain. I despise you and defy your malice! You
have aspersed me wrongfully—I have proved your 515
falsehood. Go you and your treacherous—I will not
name it—but starve together—perish!

Fain. Not while you are worth a groat, indeed, my
dear. Madam, I'll be fooled no longer.

Lady Wish. Ah, Mr. Mirabell, this is small comfort, 520
the detection of this affair.

Mira. O, in good time. Your leave for the other offender and penitent to appear, madam.

Enter Waitwell with a box of writings.

Lady Wish. O Sir Rowland!—Well, rascal!

Wait. What your Ladyship pleases. I have brought 525
the black box at last, madam.

Mira. Give it me. Madam, you remember your
promise.

Lady Wish. Ay, dear sir.

Mira. Where are the gentlemen? 530

Wait. At hand, sir, rubbing their eyes—just risen
from sleep.

Fain. 'Sdeath, what's this to me? I'll not wait your
private concerns.

Enter Petulant and Witwoud.

Pet. How now? What's the matter? Whose hand's 535 out?

Wit. Heyday! What, are you all got together, like players at the end of the last act?

Mira. You may remember, gentlemen, I once requested your hands as witnesses to a certain parch- 540 ment.

Wit. Ay, I do, my hand I remember—Petulant set his mark.

Mira. You wrong him, his name is fairly written, as shall appear. You do not remember, gentlemen, any- 545 thing of what that parchment contained?

> *Undoing the box.*

Wit. No.

Pet. Not I. I writ; I read nothing.

Mira. Very well, now you shall know.—Madam, your promise. 550

Lady Wish. Ay, ay, sir, upon my honor.

Mira. Mr. Fainall, it is now time that you should know that your lady, while she was at her own disposal, and before you had by your insinuations wheedled her out of a pretended settlement of the greatest 555 part of her fortune—

Fain. Sir! pretended!

Mira. Yes, sir. I say that this lady while a widow, having, it seems, received some cautions respecting your inconstancy and tyranny of temper, which from 560 her own partial opinion and fondness of you she could never have suspected—she did, I say, by the wholesome advice of friends and of sages learned in the laws of this land, deliver this same as her act and deed to me in trust, and to the uses within mentioned. 565 You may read if you please (*Holding out the parchment*)—though perhaps what is inscribed on the back may serve your occasions.

Fain. Very likely, sir. What's here? Damnation!

(*Reads*) "A deed of conveyance of the whole estate 570
real of Arabella Languish, widow, in trust to Edward
Mirabell."

Confusion!

Mira. Even so, sir; 'tis the way of the world, sir—
of the widows of the world. I suppose this deed may 575
bear an elder date than what you have obtained from
your lady.

Fain. Perfidious fiend! Then thus I'll be revenged—
                    Offers to run at Mrs. Fainall.

Sir Will. Hold, sir! now you may make your bear-
garden flourish somewhere else, sir. 580

Fain. Mirabell, you shall hear of this, sir, be sure
you shall.—Let me pass, oaf. *Exit.*

Mrs. Fain. Madam, you seem to stifle your resentment. You had better give it vent.

Mrs. Mar. Yes, it shall have vent, and to your con- 585
fusion, or I'll perish in the attempt. *Exit.*

Lady Wish. O daughter, daughter! 'tis plain thou
hast inherited thy mother's prudence.

Mrs. Fain. Thank Mr. Mirabell, a cautious friend,
to whose advice all is owing. 590

Lady Wish. Well, Mr. Mirabell, you have kept your
promise—and I must perform mine. First, I pardon for
your sake Sir Rowland there and Foible. The next
thing is to break the matter to my nephew—and how
to do that— 595

Mira. For that, madam, give yourself no trouble; let
me have your consent. Sir Willful is my friend; he has
had compassion upon lovers and generously engaged
a volunteer in this action for our service, and now designs to prosecute his travels. 600

Sir Will. 'Sheart, aunt, I have no mind to marry.
My cousin's a fine lady, and the gentleman loves her
and she loves him, and they deserve one another; my
resolution is to see foreign parts. I have set on't, and

when I'm set on't, I must do't. And if these two gentle- 605
men would travel too, I think they may be spared.

Pet. For my part, I say little. I think things are best
off or on.

Wit. Egad, I understand nothing of the matter; I'm
in a maze yet, like a dog in a dancing school. 610

Lady Wish. Well, sir, take her, and with her all the
joy I can give you.

Milla. Why does not the man take me? Would you
have me give myself to you over again?

Mira. Ay, and over and over again; for I would 615
have you as often as possibly I can. (*Kisses her hand.*)
Well, Heaven grant I love you not too well, that's all
my fear.

Sir Will. 'Sheart, you'll have him time enough to
toy after you're married; or if you will toy now, let us 620
have a dance in the meantime, that we who are not
lovers may have some other employment besides looking on.

Mira. With all my heart, dear Sir Willful. What
shall we do for music? 625

Foib. O sir, some that were provided for Sir Rowland's entertainment are yet within call.   *A dance.*

Lady Wish. As I am a person, I can hold out no
longer; I have wasted my spirits so today already that
I am ready to sink under the fatigue; and I cannot but 630
have some fears upon me yet that my son Fainall
will pursue some desperate course.

Mira. Madam, disquiet not yourself on that account; to my knowledge his circumstances are such
he must of force comply. For my part, I will con- 635
tribute all that in me lies to a reunion; in the meantime, madam (*To Mrs. Fainall*), let me before these
witnesses restore to you this deed of trust. It may be

---

608. OFF . . . ON: one way or the other.

a means, well managed, to make you live easily together.   640

    From hence let those be warned who mean to wed
    Lest mutual falsehood stain the bridal-bed;
    For each deceiver to his cost may find
    That marriage frauds too oft are paid in kind.

Exeunt omnes.

EPILOGUE

Spoken by Mrs. Bracegirdle [*Millamant*]

After our epilogue this crowd dismisses,
In thinking how this play'll be pulled to pieces.
But pray consider, ere you doom its fall,
How hard a thing 'twould be to please you all.
There are some critics so with spleen diseased,   5
They scarcely come inclining to be pleased:
And sure he must have more than mortal skill
Who pleases anyone against his will.
Then, all bad poets, we are sure, are foes;
And how their number's swelled the town well knows.   10
In shoals I've marked 'em judging in the pit;
Though they're on no pretense for judgment fit,
But that they have been damned for want of wit.
Since when they, by their own offenses taught,
Set up for spies on plays and finding fault.   15
Others there are whose malice we'd prevent;
Such who watch plays with scurrilous intent
To mark out who by characters are meant.
And though no perfect likeness they can trace,
Yet each pretends to know the copied face.   20
These with false glosses feed their own ill nature,
And turn to libel what was meant a satire.
May such malicious fops this fortune find,
To think themselves alone the fools designed!
If any are so arrogantly vain   25
To think they singly can support a scene
And furnish fool enough to entertain.
For well the learned and the judicious know

(Epilogue)
21. GLOSSES: explanations.

That satire scorns to stoop so meanly low
As any one abstracted fop to show. 30
For, as when painters form a matchless face,
They from each fair one catch some different grace,
And shining features in one portrait blend,
To which no single beauty must pretend;
So poets oft do in one piece expose 35
Whole *belles assemblées* of coquettes and beaux.

FINIS

THE BEAUX' STRATAGEM

A Comedy by George Farquhar

PROLOGUE

Spoken by Mr. Wilks [Archer]

When strife disturbs or sloth corrupts an age,
Keen satire is the business of the stage.
When the Plain Dealer writ he lashed those crimes
Which then infested most the modish times:
But now, when faction sleeps and sloth is fed,   5
And all our youth in active fields are bred;
When through Great Britain's fair extensive round
The trumps of Fame the notes of Union sound;
When Anna's scepter points the laws their course,
And her example gives her precepts force,   10
There scarce is room for satire: all our lays
Must be or songs of triumph or of praise.
But as in grounds best cultivated tares
And poppies rise among the golden ears,
Our products so, fit for the field or school,   15
Must mix with Nature's favorite plant—a fool:
A weed that has to twenty summers ran,
Shoots up in stalk and vegetates to man.
Simpling, our author goes from field to field
And culls such fools as may diversion yield;   20
And, thanks to Nature, there's no want of those,
For, rain or shine, the thriving coxcomb grows.
Follies tonight we show ne'er lashed before,
Yet such as Nature shows you every hour;
Nor can the pictures give a just offense,   25
For fools are made for jests to men of sense.

(Prologue)

3. THE PLAIN DEALER: William Wycherley, author of the play of
that name (1676).

8. NOTES . . . UNION: the Act of Union, forming England and Scotland into the United Kingdom, was signed on March 6, 1707, two days before the first performance of this play.

19. SIMPLING: collecting "simples" (medicinal herbs).

Dramatis Personae

MEN	[By]
Aimwell, ⎫ two gentlemen of broken fortunes, the first as master	Mr. Mills.
Archer, ⎭ and the second as servant.	Mr. Wilks.
Count Bellair, a French officer, prisoner at Lichfield.	Mr. Bowman.
Sullen, a country blockhead, brutal to his wife.	Mr. Verbruggen.
Freeman, a gentleman from London.	Mr. Keen.
Foigard, a priest, chaplain to the French officers.	Mr. Bowen.
Gibbet, a highwayman.	Mr. Cibber.
Hounslow, ⎫ his *Bagshot,* ⎭ companions.	
Bonniface, landlord of the inn.	Mr. Bullock.
Scrub, servant to Mr. Sullen.	Mr. Norris.

WOMEN	
Lady Bountiful, an old, civil country gentlewoman that cures all her neighbors of all distempers and foolishly fond of her son, Sullen.	Mrs. Powell.
Dorinda, Lady Bountiful's daughter.	Mrs. Bradshaw.
Mrs. Sullen, her daughter-in-law.	Mrs. Oldfield.
Gypsy, maid to the ladies.	Mrs. Mills.
Cherry, the landlord's daughter in the inn.	Mrs. Bicknell.

[Tapster, Coach Passenger, Countryman, Countrywoman, and Servants.]

SCENE: *Lichfield.*

ACT I

Scene I. An inn.

Enter Bonniface, running.

Bon. Chamberlain! maid! Cherry! daughter Cherry! all asleep? all dead?

Enter Cherry, running.

Cher. Here, here! Why d'ye bawl so, father? d'ye think we have no ears?

Bon. You deserve to have none, you young minx! 5
The company of the Warrington coach has stood in the hall this hour, and nobody to show them to their chambers.

Cher. And let 'em wait farther; there's neither red coat in the coach nor footman behind it. 10

Bon. But they threaten to go to another inn tonight.

Cher. That they dare not, for fear the coachman should overturn them tomorrow.—Coming! coming!—Here's the London coach arrived.

Enter several people with trunks, bandboxes,
and other luggage, and cross the stage.

Bon. Welcome, ladies! 15
Cher. Very welcome, gentlemen!—Chamberlain, show the Lion and the Rose. *Exit with the company.*

(I.i.)
17. LION . . . ROSE: two chambers in the inn.

*Enter Aimwell in riding-habit, Archer as
footman carrying a portmanteau.*

Bon. This way, this way, gentlemen!

Aim. Set down the things; go to the stable and see
my horses well rubbed. 20

Arch. I shall, sir. *Exit.*

Aim. You're my landlord, I suppose?

Bon. Yes, sir, I'm old Will Bonniface, pretty well
known upon this road, as the saying is.

Aim. O Mr. Bonniface, your servant! 25

Bon. O sir! What will your Honor please to drink,
as the saying is?

Aim. I have heard your town of Lichfield much
famed for ale; I think I'll taste that.

Bon. Sir, I have now in my cellar ten tun of the best 30
ale in Staffordshire; 'tis smooth as oil, sweet as milk,
clear as amber, and strong as brandy, and will be just
fourteen year old the fifth day of next March, old
style.

Aim. You're very exact, I find, in the age of your 35
ale.

Bon. As punctual, sir, as I am in the age of my children. I'll show you such ale!—Here, tapster, broach
number 1706, as the saying is.—Sir, you shall taste my
Anno Domini. I have lived in Lichfield, man and boy, 40
above eight-and-fifty years, and, I believe, have not
consumed eight-and-fifty ounces of meat.

Aim. At a meal, you mean, if one may guess your
sense by your bulk.

Bon. Not in my life, sir. I have fed purely upon ale; 45

---

s.d. GLASS: i.e., glassware; glasses.
s.d. FILLING . . . OUT: filling the glasses.
70. TYMPANIES: tympanites (abdominal distentions from gas).
73. ODS . . . LIFE: God save me!
79. GREENSICKNESS: anemia.
80. MOTHER: hysteria.
80–81. KING'S EVIL: scrofula; CHINCOUGH: whooping cough.

I have eat my ale, drank my ale, and I always sleep upon ale.

Enter Tapster with a bottle and glass and exit.

Now, sir, you shall see!—(*Filling it out*) Your Worship's health.—Ha! delicious, delicious!—fancy it burgundy, only fancy it, and 'tis worth ten shillings a 50
quart.

Aim. (*Drinks*) 'Tis confounded strong!

Bon. Strong! It must be so, or how should we be strong that drink it?

Aim. And have you lived so long upon this ale, 55
landlord?

Bon. Eight-and-fifty years, upon my credit, sir; but it killed my wife, poor woman, as the saying is.

Aim. How came that to pass?

Bon. I don't know how, sir; she would not let the ale 60
take its natural course, sir; she was for qualifying it every now and then with a dram, as the saying is; and an honest gentleman that came this way from Ireland made her a present of a dozen bottles of usquebaugh —but the poor woman was never well after. But, 65
howe'er, I was obliged to the gentleman, you know.

Aim. Why, was it the usquebaugh that killed her?

Bon. My Lady Bountiful said so. She, good lady, did what could be done; she cured her of three tympanies, but the fourth carried her off. But she's 70
happy, and I'm contented, as the saying is.

Aim. Who's that Lady Bountiful you mentioned?

Bon. Ods my life, sir! We'll drink her health. (*Drinks*) My Lady Bountiful is one of the best of women. Her last husband, Sir Charles Bountiful, left 75
her worth a thousand pound a year; and, I believe, she lays out one-half on't in charitable uses for the good of her neighbors; she cures rheumatisms, rup-

tures, and broken shins in men; greensickness, ob- 80
structions, and fits of the mother in women; the king's
evil, chincough, and chilblains in children: in short,
she has cured more people in and about Lichfield
within ten years than the doctors have killed in
twenty; and that's a bold word.

Aim. Has the lady been any other way useful in her 85
generation?

Bon. Yes, sir; she has a daughter by Sir Charles, the
finest woman in all our country and the greatest fortune. She has a son too, by her first husband, Squire
Sullen, who married a fine lady from London t'other 90
day; if you please, sir, we'll drink his health.

Aim. What sort of a man is he?

Bon. Why, sir, the man's well enough; says little,
thinks less, and does—nothing at all, faith. But he's a
man of a great estate, and values nobody. 95

Aim. A sportsman, I suppose?

Bon. Yes, sir, he's a man of pleasure; he plays at
whisk and smokes his pipe eight-and-forty hours together sometimes.

Aim. And married, you say? 100

Bon. Ay, and to a curious woman, sir. But he's a—he
wants it here, sir.   *Pointing to his forehead.*

Aim. He has it there, you mean.

Bon. That's none of my business; he's my landlord,
and so a man, you know, would not—But, ecod, he's 105
no better than—Sir, my humble service to you.
(*Drinks*) Though I value not a farthing what he can
do to me; I pay him his rent at quarter day; I have a
good running trade; I have but one daughter, and I
can give her—but no matter for that. 110

---

98. WHISK: whist.
101. CURIOUS: fastidious.
103. IT: Aimwell refers to horns, symbol of a wife's betrayal.
105. ECOD: egad.
114. FRENCH OFFICERS: prisoners taken in Marlborough's campaigns.

Aim. You're very happy, Mr. Bonniface; pray, what other company have you in town?

Bon. A power of fine ladies; and then we have the French officers.

Aim. O, that's right, you have a good many of those 115 gentlemen. Pray, how do you like their company?

Bon. So well, as the saying is, that I could wish we had as many more of 'em; they're full of money and pay double for everything they have: they know, sir, that we paid good round taxes for the taking of 'em, 120 and so they are willing to reimburse us a little. One of 'em lodges in my house.

Enter Archer.

Arch. Landlord, there are some French gentlemen below that ask for you.

Bon. I'll wait on 'em. (*To Archer*) Does your master 125 stay long in town, as the saying is?

Arch. I can't tell, as the saying is.

Bon. Come from London?

Arch. No.

Bon. Going to London, mayhap?   130

Arch. No.

Bon. An odd fellow this.—I beg your Worship's pardon, I'll wait on you in half a minute.   *Exit.*

Aim. The coast's clear, I see. Now, my dear Archer, welcome to Lichfield!   135

Arch. I thank thee, my dear brother in iniquity.

Aim. Iniquity! Prithee, leave canting; you need not change your style with your dress.

Arch. Don't mistake me, Aimwell, for 'tis still my maxim that there is no scandal like rags nor any crime 140 so shameful as poverty.

Aim. The world confesses it every day in its practice, though men won't own it for their opinion. Who did that worthy lord, my brother, single out of the side box to sup with him t'other night? 145

Arch. Jack Handicraft, a handsome, well-dressed, mannerly, sharping rogue, who keeps the best company in town.

Aim. Right! And, pray, who married My Lady Manslaughter t'other day, the great fortune? 150

Arch. Why, Nick Marrabone, a professed pickpocket and a good bowler; but he makes a handsome figure and rides in his coach, that he formerly used to ride behind.

Aim. But did you observe poor Jack Generous in the 155 Park last week?

Arch. Yes, with his autumnal periwig shading his melancholy face, his coat older than anything but its fashion, with one hand idle in his pocket, and with the other picking his useless teeth; and though the Mall 160 was crowded with company, yet was poor Jack as single and solitary as a lion in a desert.

Aim. And as much avoided, for no crime upon earth but the want of money.

Arch. And that's enough. Men must not be poor; 165 idleness is the root of all evil; the world's wide enough, let 'em bustle. Fortune has taken the weak under her protection, but men of sense are left to their industry.

Aim. Upon which topic we proceed, and, I think, 170 luckily hitherto. Would not any man swear now that I am a man of quality, and you my servant, when if our intrinsic value were known—

Arch. Come, come, we are the men of intrinsic value who can strike our fortunes out of ourselves, 175 whose worth is independent of accidents in life or

---

175. STRIKE: i.e., coin, as though they were made of precious metal.

revolutions in government; we have heads to get
money and hearts to spend it.

Aim. As to our hearts, I grant ye, they are as willing
tits as any within twenty degrees; but I can have no 180
great opinion of our heads from the service they have
done us hitherto, unless it be that they have brought
us from London hither to Lichfield; made me a lord
and you my servant.

Arch. That's more than you could expect already. 185
But what money have we left?

Aim. But two hundred pound.

Arch. And our horses, clothes, rings, etc. Why, we
have very good fortunes now for moderate people;
and let me tell you, besides, that this two hundred 190
pound, with the experience that we are now masters
of, is a better estate than the ten thousand we have
spent. Our friends, indeed, began to suspect that our
pockets were low; but we came off with flying colors,
showed no signs of want either in word or deed.   195

Aim. Ay, and our going to Brussels was a good
pretense enough for our sudden disappearing; and, I
warrant you, our friends imagine that we are gone
a-volunteering.

Arch. Why, faith, if this prospect fails, it must e'en 200
come to that. I am for venturing one of the hundreds,
if you will, upon this knight-errantry; but, in case it
should fail, we'll reserve the t'other to carry us to
some counterscarp, where we may die, as we lived,
in a blaze.   205

Aim. With all my heart; and we have lived justly,
Archer; we can't say that we have spent our fortunes
but that we have enjoyed 'em.

Arch. Right! So much pleasure for so much money;
we have had our pennyworths, and, had I millions, I 210
would go to the same market again. O London! London! Well, we have had our share, and let us be

thankful; past pleasures, for aught I know, are best, such as we are sure of: those to come may disappoint us. 215

Aim. It has often grieved the heart of me to see how some inhuman wretches murder their kind fortunes; those that, by sacrificing all to one appetite, shall starve all the rest. You shall have some that live only in their palates, and in their sense of tasting shall 220 drown the other four. Others are only epicures in appearances, such who shall starve their nights to make a figure a-days and famish their own to feed the eyes of others: a contrary sort confine their pleasures to the dark and contract their spacious acres to the circuit 225 of a muff-string.

Arch. Right! But they find the Indies in that spot where they consume 'em, and I think your kind keepers have much the best on't; for they indulge the most senses by one expense: there's the seeing, hear- 230 ing, and feeling, amply gratified; and some philoso- phers will tell you that from such a commerce there arises a sixth sense that gives infinitely more pleasure than the other five put together.

Aim. And to pass to the other extremity, of all 235 keepers I think those the worst that keep their money.

Arch. Those are the most miserable wights in being; they destroy the rights of Nature and disappoint the blessings of Providence. Give me a man that keeps his five senses keen and bright as his sword, that has 240 'em always drawn out in their just order and strength, with his reason as commander at the head of 'em, that detaches 'em by turns upon whatever party of pleasure agreeably offers and commands 'em to retreat

228–29. YOUR . . . KEEPERS: men who allow women to make fools of them.
250. ACTAEON: youth in Greek mythology who displeased Diana and was punished by transformation to a stag.
258. OUT . . . DOORS: unfashionable.
270. A MATCH: agreed!

upon the least appearance of disadvantage or danger. 245
For my part, I can stick to my bottle while my wine,
my company, and my reason holds good; I can be
charmed with Sappho's singing without falling in love
with her face; I love hunting, but would not, like
Actaeon, be eaten up by my own dogs; I love a fine 250
house but let another keep it; and just so I love a fine
woman.

Aim. In that last particular you have the better of
me.

Arch. Ay, you're such an amorous puppy that I'm 255
afraid you'll spoil our sport; you can't counterfeit the
passion without feeling it.

Aim. Though the whining part be out of doors in
town, 'tis still in force with the country ladies; and let
me tell you, Frank, the fool in that passion shall outdo 260
the knave at any time.

Arch. Well, I won't dispute it now; you command
for the day, and so I submit. At Nottingham, you
know, I am to be master.

Aim. And at Lincoln, I again. 265

Arch. Then, at Norwich I mount, which, I think,
shall be our last stage; for, if we fail there, we'll em-
bark for Holland, bid adieu to Venus and welcome
Mars.

Aim. A match! 270

Enter Bonniface.

Mum!

Bon. What will your Worship please to have for
supper?

Aim. What have you got?

Bon. Sir, we have a delicate piece of beef in the pot 275
and a pig at the fire.

Aim. Good supper meat, I must confess. I can't eat beef, landlord.

Arch. And I hate pig.

Aim. Hold your prating, sirrah! Do you know who 280 you are?

Bon. Please to bespeak something else: I have everything in the house.

Aim. Have you any veal?

Bon. Veal! Sir, we had a delicate loin of veal on 285 Wednesday last.

Aim. Have you got any fish or wild fowl?

Bon. As for fish, truly, sir, we are an inland town and indifferently provided with fish, that's the truth on't; and then for wild fowl—we have a delicate 290 couple of rabbits.

Aim. Get me the rabbits fricasseed.

Bon. Fricasseed! Lard, sir, they'll eat much better smothered with onions.

Arch. Pshaw! Damn your onions! 295

Aim. Again, sirrah!—Well, landlord, what you please. But hold, I have a small charge of money, and your house is so full of strangers that I believe it may be safer in your custody than mine; for when this fellow of mine gets drunk, he minds nothing.—Here, 300 sirrah, reach me the strongbox.

Arch. Yes, sir. (*Aside*) This will give us a reputation. *Brings the box.*

Aim. Here, landlord; the locks are sealed down both for your security and mine; it holds somewhat above 305 two hundred pound. If you doubt it, I'll count it to you after supper; but be sure you lay it where I may have it at a minute's warning; for my affairs are a little dubious at present; perhaps I may be gone in half an hour, perhaps I may be your guest till the best part 310 of that be spent; and pray order your ostler to keep my horses always saddled. But one thing above the

rest I must beg, that you would let this fellow have
none of your *Anno Domini*, as you call it, for he's the
most insufferable sot.—Here, sirrah, light me to my 315
chamber. *Exit, lighted by Archer.*

Bon. Cherry! Daughter Cherry!

Enter Cherry.

Cher. D'ye call, father?

Bon. Ay, child, you must lay by this box for the
gentleman; 'tis full of money. 320

Cher. Money! all that money! Why sure, father, the
gentleman comes to be chosen parliament-man. Who
is he?

Bon. I don't know what to make of him; he talks of
keeping his horses ready saddled, and of going per- 325
haps at a minute's warning, or of staying, perhaps, till
the best part of this be spent.

Cher. Ay, ten to one, father, he's a highwayman.

Bon. A highwayman! Upon my life, girl, you have
hit it, and this box is some new-purchased booty. 330
Now, could we find him out, the money were ours.

Cher. He don't belong to our gang?

Bon. What horses have they?

Cher. The master rides upon a black.

Bon. A black! Ten to one the man upon the black 335
mare; and since he don't belong to our fraternity, we
may betray him with a safe conscience. I don't think
it lawful to harbor any rogues but my own. Look ye,
child, as the saying is, we must go cunningly to work;
proofs we must have. The gentleman's servant loves 340
drink—I'll ply him that way; and ten to one loves a
wench—you must work him t'other way.

Cher. Father, would you have me give my secret
for his?

Bon. Consider, child, there's two hundred pound to 345
boot.　　　　　　　　　　*Ringing without.*
Coming! coming!—Child, mind your business.　　*Exit.*

Cher. What a rogue is my father! My father! I deny
it. My mother was a good, generous, free-hearted
woman, and I can't tell how far her good nature might 350
have extended for the good of her children. This landlord of mine, for I think I can call him no more, would
betray his guest and debauch his daughter into the
bargain—by a footman, too!

Enter Archer.

Arch. What footman, pray, mistress, is so happy as 355
to be the subject of your contemplation?

Cher. Whoever he is, friend, he'll be but little the
better for't.

Arch. I hope so, for I'm sure you did not think of
me.　　　　　　　　　　　　　　　　　　360

Cher. Suppose I had?

Arch. Why, then you're but even with me; for the
minute I came in I was a-considering in what manner
I should make love to you.

Cher. Love to me, friend!　　　　　　　　365

Arch. Yes, child.

Cher. Child! manners! If you kept a little more distance, friend, it would become you much better.

Arch. Distance! Good night, saucebox.　　*Going.*

Cher. A pretty fellow! I like his pride.—Sir, pray, 370
sir, you see, sir, (*Archer returns*) I have the credit to
be entrusted with your master's fortune here, which
sets me a degree above his footman; I hope, sir, you
an't affronted?

Arch. Let me look you full in the face and I'll tell 375
you whether you can affront me or no.—'Sdeath, child,

you have a pair of delicate eyes, and you don't know
what to do with 'em!

Cher. Why, sir, don't I see everybody?

Arch. Ay, but if some women had 'em, they would 380
kill everybody. Prithee, instruct me; I would fain
make love to you, but I don't know what to say.

Cher. Why, did you never make love to anybody
before?

Arch. Never to a person of your figure, I can assure 385
you, madam; my addresses have been always confined
to people within my own sphere; I never aspired so
high before.   *A song.*

> But you look so bright,
> And are dressed so tight, etc.   390

Cher. (*Aside*) What can I think of this man?—Will
you give me that song, sir?

Arch. Ay, my dear, take it while 'tis warm.—

                                        Kisses her.

Death and fire! Her lips are honeycombs.

Cher. And I wish there had been bees too, to have 395
stung you for your impudence.

Arch. There's a swarm of Cupids, my little Venus,
that has done the business much better.

Cher. (*Aside*) This fellow is misbegotten as well as
I.—What's your name, sir?   400

Arch. (*Aside*) Name! egad, I have forgot it.—O!
Martin.

Cher. Where were you born?

Arch. In St. Martin's parish.

Cher. What was your father?   405

Arch. St. Martin's parish.

Cher. Then, friend, good night.

Arch. I hope not.

Cher. You may depend upon't.

Arch. Upon what?   410
Cher. That you're very impudent.
Arch. That you're very handsome.
Cher. That you're a footman.
Arch. That you're an angel.
Cher. I shall be rude.   415
Arch. So shall I.
Cher. Let go my hand.
Arch. Give me a kiss.   *Kisses her.*
                  Call without. "Cherry! Cherry!"
Cher. Im—m—my father calls; you plaguy devil, 420
how durst you stop my breath so? Offer to follow me
one step, if you dare.   *Exit.*
Arch. A fair challenge, by this light! This is a pretty
fair opening of an adventure; but we are knight-
errants, and so Fortune be our guide.   425
                                                   Exit.

(II.i.)
6–7. DOCTORS' COMMONS: the court that handled divorce proceedings.

ACT II

Scene I. A gallery in Lady Bountiful's house.

[Enter] Mrs. Sullen and Dorinda, meeting.

Dor. Morrow, my dear sister; are you for church this morning?

Mrs. Sul. Anywhere to pray; for Heaven alone can help me. But I think, Dorinda, there's no form of prayer in the liturgy against bad husbands.   5

Dor. But there's a form of law in Doctors' Commons; and I swear, Sister Sullen, rather than see you thus continually discontented, I would advise you to apply to that: for besides the part that I bear in your vexatious broils, as being sister to the husband and   10 friend to the wife, your example gives me such an impression of matrimony that I shall be apt to condemn my person to a long vacation all its life. But supposing, madam, that you brought it to a case of separation, what can you urge against your husband? My   15 brother is, first, the most constant man alive.

Mrs. Sul. The most constant husband, I grant ye.

Dor. He never sleeps from you.

Mrs. Sul. No, he always sleeps with me.

Dor. He allows you a maintenance suitable to your   20 quality.

Mrs. Sul. A maintenance! Do you take me, madam, for an hospital child, that I must sit down and bless my benefactors for meat, drink, and clothes? As I take it, madam, I brought your brother ten thousand   25 pounds, out of which I might expect some pretty things called pleasures.

Dor. You share in all the pleasures that the country affords.

Mrs. Sul. Country pleasures! Racks and torments! 30
Dost think, child, that my limbs were made for leaping of ditches and clambering over stiles? or that my parents, wisely foreseeing my future happiness in country pleasures, had early instructed me in the rural accomplishments of drinking fat ale, playing at 35
whisk, and smoking tobacco with my husband? or of spreading of plasters, brewing of diet-drinks, and stilling rosemary water with the good old gentlewoman, my mother-in-law?

Dor. I'm sorry, madam, that it is not more in our 40
power to divert you; I could wish, indeed, that our entertainments were a little more polite, or your taste a little less refined. But, pray, madam, how came the poets and philosophers, that labored so much in hunting after pleasure, to place it at last in a country life? 45

Mrs. Sul. Because they wanted money, child, to find out the pleasures of the town. Did you ever see a poet or philosopher worth ten thousand pound? If you can show me such a man, I'll lay you fifty pound you'll find him somewhere within the weekly bills. Not that 50
I disapprove rural pleasures, as the poets have painted them; in their landscape, every Phyllis has her Corydon, every murmuring stream and every flow'ry mead gives fresh alarms to love. Besides, you'll find that their couples were never married.—But yonder I see 55
my Corydon, and a sweet swain it is, Heaven knows! Come, Dorinda, don't be angry, he's my husband and your brother; and, between both, is he not a sad brute?

---

35. FAT ALE: draft ale.
50. WEEKLY BILLS: i.e., the limits of the city of London, which issued weekly bills reporting births and deaths.

Dor. I have nothing to say to your part of him— 60
you're the best judge.

Mrs. Sul. O sister, sister! if ever you marry, beware
of a sullen, silent sot, one that's always musing but
never thinks. There's some diversion in a talking
blockhead; and since a woman must wear chains, I 65
would have the pleasure of hearing 'em rattle a little.
Now you shall see, but take this by the way. He came
home this morning at his usual hour of four, wakened
me out of a sweet dream of something else by tum-
bling over the tea table, which he broke all to pieces. 70
After his man and he had rolled about the room, like
sick passengers in a storm, he comes flounce into bed,
dead as a salmon into a fishmonger's basket; his feet
cold as ice, his breath hot as a furnace, and his hands
and his face as greasy as his flannel nightcap. O matri- 75
mony! He tosses up the clothes with a barbarous
swing over his shoulders, disorders the whole
economy of my bed, leaves me half naked, and my
whole night's comfort is the tuneable serenade of that
wakeful nightingale, his nose! O, the pleasure of 80
counting the melancholy clock by a snoring husband!
—But now, sister, you shall see how handsomely,
being a well-bred man, he will beg my pardon.

Enter Sullen.

Sul. My head aches consumedly.

Mrs. Sul. Will you be pleased, my dear, to drink tea 85
with us this morning? It may do your head good.

Sul. No.

Dor. Coffee, brother?

Sul. Pshaw!

Mrs. Sul. Will you please to dress and go to church 90
with me? The air may help you.

Sul. Scrub!

Enter Scrub.

Scrub. Sir.

Sul. What day o' the week is this?

Scrub. Sunday, an't please your Worship.   95

Sul. Sunday! Bring me a dram; and d'ye hear, set out the venison pasty and a tankard of strong beer upon the hall table; I'll go to breakfast.   *Going.*

Dor. Stay, stay, brother, you shan't get off so; you were very naughty last night, and must make your 100 wife reparation. Come, come, brother, won't you ask pardon?

Sul. For what?

Dor. For being drunk last night.

Sul. I can afford it, can't I?   105

Mrs. Sul. But I can't, sir.

Sul. Then you may let it alone.

Mrs. Sul. But I must tell you, sir, that this is not to be borne.

Sul. I'm glad on't.   110

Mrs. Sul. What is the reason, sir, that you use me thus inhumanely?

Sul. Scrub!

Scrub. Sir.

Sul. Get things ready to shave my head.   *Exit.* 115

Mrs. Sul. Have a care of coming near his temples, Scrub, for fear you meet something there that may turn the edge of your razor. (*Exit Scrub.*) Inveterate stupidity! Did you ever know so hard, so obstinate a spleen as his? O sister, sister! I shall never ha' good of 120 the beast till I get him to town: London, dear London, is the place for managing and breaking a husband.

Dor. And has not a husband the same opportunities there for humbling a wife?

Mrs. Sul. No, no, child, 'tis a standing maxim in con- 125

jugal discipline that when a man would enslave his
wife he hurries her into the country; and when a lady
would be arbitrary with her husband she wheedles
her booby up to town. A man dare not play the tyrant
in London, because there are so many examples to 130
encourage the subject to rebel. O Dorinda, Dorinda! a
fine woman may do anything in London: o' my conscience, she may raise an army of forty thousand men.

Dor. I fancy, sister, you have a mind to be trying
your power that way here in Lichfield; you have 135
drawn the French count to your colors already.

Mrs. Sul. The French are a people that can't live
without their gallantries.

Dor. And some English that I know, sister, are not
averse to such amusements.   140

Mrs. Sul. Well, sister, since the truth must out, it
may do as well now as hereafter: I think one way to
rouse my lethargic, sottish husband is to give him a
rival. Security begets negligence in all people, and
men must be alarmed to make 'em alert in their duty: 145
women are like pictures, of no value in the hands of
a fool till he hears men of sense bid high for the purchase.

Dor. This might do, sister, if my brother's understanding were to be convinced into a passion for you; 150
but I fancy there's a natural aversion of his side; and
I fancy, sister, that you don't come much behind him,
if you dealt fairly.

Mrs. Sul. I own it; we are united contradictions, fire
and water. But I could be contented, with a great 155
many other wives, to humor the censorious mob and
give the world an appearance of living well with my
husband, could I bring him but to dissemble a little
kindness to keep me in countenance.

Dor. But how do you know, sister, but that, instead 160

of rousing your husband by this artifice to a counterfeit kindness, he should awake in a real fury?

Mrs. Sul. Let him: if I can't entice him to the one,
I would provoke him to the other.

Dor. But how must I behave myself between ye?   165

Mrs. Sul. You must assist me.

Dor. What, against my own brother!

Mrs. Sul. He's but half a brother, and I'm your
entire friend. If I go a step beyond the bounds of
honor, leave me; till then, I expect you should go   170
along with me in everything. While I trust my honor
in your hands, you may trust your brother's in mine.
The count is to dine here today.

Dor. 'Tis a strange thing, sister, that I can't like that
man.   175

Mrs. Sul. You like nothing; your time is not come:
love and death have their fatalities and strike home
one time or other. You'll pay for all one day, I warrant
ye. But come, my lady's tea is ready, and 'tis almost
church time.   180

Exeunt.

Scene II. *The inn.*

Enter Aimwell, dressed, and Archer.

Aim. And was she the daughter of the house?

Arch. The landlord is so blind as to think so; but I
dare swear she has better blood in her veins.

Aim. Why dost think so?

Arch. Because the baggage has a pert *je ne sais*   5
quoi; she reads plays, keeps a monkey, and is troubled
with vapors.

(II.ii.)
7. VAPORS: blue moods.

Aim. By which discoveries I guess that you know
nore of her.

Arch. Not yet, faith; the lady gives herself airs; 10
orsooth, nothing under a gentleman!

Aim. Let me take her in hand.

Arch. Say one word more o' that and I'll declare
nyself, spoil your sport there and everywhere else.
Look ye, Aimwell, every man in his own sphere. 15

Aim. Right; and therefore you must pimp for your
naster.

Arch. In the usual forms, good sir, after I have
erved myself. But to our business. You are so well
dressed, Tom, and make so handsome a figure, that I 20
ancy you may do execution in a country church; the
exterior part strikes first, and you're in the right to
nake that impression favorable.

Aim. There's something in that which may turn to
advantage. The appearance of a stranger in a country 25
church draws as many gazers as a blazing star; no
sooner he comes into the cathedral, but a train of
vhispers runs buzzing round the congregation in a
moment: "Who is he?" "Whence comes he?" "Do you
know him?" Then I, sir, tips me the verger with half 30
a crown; he pockets the simony and inducts me into
the best pew in the church. I pull out my snuffbox,
urn myself round, bow to the bishop, or the dean, if
he be the commanding officer; single out a beauty,
ivet both my eyes to hers, set my nose a-bleeding by 35
the strength of imagination, and show the whole
church my concern by my endeavoring to hide it.
After the sermon, the whole town gives me to her for
a lover, and by persuading the lady that I am a-dying
or her the tables are turned, and she in good earnest 40
alls in love with me.

Arch. There's nothing in this, Tom, without a precedent; but instead of riveting your eyes to a beauty,

try to fix 'em upon a fortune; that's our business at
present.　　　　　　　　　　　　　　　　　　　　　　45

Aim. Pshaw! No woman can be a beauty without a
fortune. Let me alone, for I am a marksman.

Arch. Tom!

Aim. Ay.

Arch. When were you at church before, pray?　　50

Aim. Um—I was there at the coronation.

Arch. And how can you expect a blessing by going
to church now?

Aim. Blessing! nay, Frank, I ask but for a wife. *Exit.*

Arch. Truly, the man is not very unreasonable in his　55
demands.　　　　　　　　　*Exit at the opposite door.*

Enter Bonniface and Cherry.

Bon. Well, daughter, as the saying is, have you
brought Martin to confess?

Cher. Pray, father, don't put me upon getting anything out of a man. I'm but young, you know, father,　60
and I don't understand wheedling.

Bon. Young! why, you jade, as the saying is, can
any woman wheedle that is not young? Your mother
was useless at five-and-twenty. Not wheedle! Would
you make your mother a whore and me a cuckold, as　65
the saying is? I tell you his silence confesses it, and
his master spends his money so freely and is so much
a gentleman every manner of way that he must be a
highwayman.

Enter Gibbet, in a cloak.

Gib. Landlord, landlord, is the coast clear?　　70

---

92. CERUSE: rouge.
97–98. PREMISES: the articles already mentioned.
102. GENTLEMEN . . . PAD: highwaymen.

Bon. O Mr. Gibbet, what's the news?

Gib. No matter, ask no questions, all fair and honorable.—Here, my dear Cherry. (*Gives her a bag.*) Two
hundred sterling pounds, as good as any that ever
hanged or saved a rogue; lay 'em by with the rest;   75
and here—three wedding or mourning rings, 'tis much
the same, you know.—Here, two silver-hilted swords;
I took those from fellows that never show any part of
their swords but the hilts. Here is a diamond necklace, which the lady hid in the privatest place in the   80
coach, but I found it out. This gold watch I took from
a pawnbroker's wife; it was left in her hands by a person of quality—there's the arms upon the case.

Cher. But who had you the money from?

Gib. Ah! poor woman! I pitied her; from a poor   85
lady just eloped from her husband. She had made up
her cargo and was bound for Ireland as hard as she
could drive. She told me of her husband's barbarous
usage, and so I left her half a crown. But I had almost
forgot, my dear Cherry, I have a present for you.   90

Cher. What is't?

Gib. A pot of ceruse, my child, that I took out of a
lady's underpocket.

Cher. What! Mr. Gibbet, do you think that I paint?

Gib. Why, you jade, your betters do; I'm sure the   95
lady that I took it from had a coronet upon her hand-
kerchief. Here, take my cloak and go secure the premises.

Cher. I will secure 'em.   *Exit.*

Bon. But, hark ye, where's Hounslow and Bagshot?   100

Gib. They'll be here tonight.

Bon. D'ye know of any other gentlemen o' the pad
on this road?

Gib. No.

Bon. I fancy that I have two that lodge in the house   105
just now.

Gib. The Devil! How d'ye smoke 'em?

Bon. Why, the one is gone to church.

Gib. That's suspicious, I must confess.

Bon. And the other is now in his master's chamber. 110
He pretends to be servant to the other. We'll call him
out and pump him a little.

Gib. With all my heart.

Bon. Mr. Martin! Mr. Martin!

Enter Archer, combing a periwig and singing.

Gib. The roads are consumed deep; I'm as dirty as 115
old Brentford at Christmas.—A good pretty fellow
that.—Whose servant are you, friend?

Arch. My master's.

Gib. Really?

Arch. Really.   120

Gib. That's much.—The fellow has been at the bar,
by his evasions.—But pray, sir, what is your master's
name?

Arch. Tall, all, dall! (*Sings and combs the periwig.*)
This is the most obstinate curl—   125

Gib. I ask you his name.

Arch. Name, sir—tall, all, dall!—I never asked him
his name in my life. Tall, all, dall!

Bon. What think you now?

Gib. Plain, plain; he talks now as if he were before 130
a judge.—But pray, friend, which way does your master travel?

Arch. A-horseback.

Gib. Very well again, an old offender, right.—But I
mean, does he go upwards or downwards?   135

Arch. Downwards, I fear, sir.—Tall, all!

107. SMOKE: detect.
116. BRENTFORD: a Middlesex town notorious for its mire in winter.
137. CONTRARY WAY: i.e., aloft on the gallows.

Gib. I'm afraid my fate will be a contrary way.

Bon. Ha, ha, ha! Mr. Martin, you're very arch. This gentleman is only traveling towards Chester and would be glad of your company, that's all.—Come, 140 Captain, you'll stay tonight, I suppose? I'll show you a chamber. Come, Captain.

Gib. Farewell, friend!

Arch. Captain, your servant.

                    Exeunt Bonniface and Gibbet.

Captain! a pretty fellow! 'Sdeath, I wonder that the 145 officers of the army don't conspire to beat all scoundrels in red but their own.

Enter Cherry.

Cher. (*Aside*) Gone! and Martin here! I hope he did not listen; I would have the merit of the discovery all my own, because I would oblige him to love me.— 150 Mr. Martin, who was that man with my father?

Arch. Some recruiting sergeant or whipped-out trooper, I suppose.

Cher. (*Aside*) All's safe, I find.

Arch. Come, my dear, have you conned over the 155 catechise I taught you last night?

Cher. Come, question me.

Arch. What is love?

Cher. Love is I know not what, it comes I know not how, and goes I know not when.   160

Arch. Very well, an apt scholar. *Chucks her under*
                              the chin.

Where does love enter?

Cher. Into the eyes.

Arch. And where go out?

Cher. I won't tell ye.   165

Arch. What are the objects of that passion?

Cher. Youth, beauty, and clean linen.

Arch. The reason?

Cher. The two first are fashionable in nature and
the third at court.   170

Arch. That's my dear. What are the signs and tokens
of that passion?

Cher. A stealing look, a stammering tongue, words
improbable, designs impossible, and actions imprac-
ticable.   175

Arch. That's my good child, kiss me.—What must a
lover do to obtain his mistress?

Cher. He must adore the person that disdains him,
he must bribe the chambermaid that betrays him, and
court the footman that laughs at him.—He must, he   180
must—

Arch. Nay, child, I must whip you if you don't mind
your lesson; he must treat his—

Cher. O, ay! he must treat his enemies with respect,
his friends with indifference, and all the world with   185
contempt; he must suffer much and fear more; he
must desire much and hope little: in short, he must
embrace his ruin and throw himself away.

Arch. Had ever man so hopeful a pupil as mine?
Come, my dear, why is Love called a riddle?   190

Cher. Because, being blind, he leads those that see,
and, though a child, he governs a man.

Arch. Mighty well!—And why is Love pictured
blind?

Cher. Because the painters out of the weakness or   195
privilege of their art chose to hide those eyes that they
could not draw.

Arch. That's my dear little scholar, kiss me again.—
And why should Love, that's a child, govern a man?

Cher. Because that a child is the end of love.   200

---

210. OONS: God's wounds!

Arch. And so ends love's catechism.—And now, my dear, we'll go in and make my master's bed.

Cher. Hold, hold, Mr. Martin! You have taken a great deal of pains to instruct me, and what d'ye think I have learnt by it?   205

Arch. What?

Cher. That your discourse and your habit are contradictions, and it would be nonsense in me to believe you a footman any longer.

Arch. Oons, what a witch it is!   210

Cher. Depend upon this, sir: nothing in this garb shall ever tempt me, for though I was born to servitude I hate it. Own your condition, swear you love me, and then—

Arch. And then we shall go make the bed?   215

Cher. Yes.

Arch. You must know, then, that I am born a gentleman, my education was liberal; but I went to London a younger brother, fell into the hands of sharpers, who stripped me of my money; my friends disowned   220 me, and now my necessity brings me to what you see.

Cher. Then take my hand; promise to marry me before you sleep, and I'll make you master of two thousand pound.

Arch. How!   225

Cher. Two thousand pound that I have this minute in my own custody; so, throw off your livery this instant, and I'll go find a parson.

Arch. What said you? A parson!

Cher. What! do you scruple?   230

Arch. Scruple! no, no, but—two thousand pound, you say?

Cher. And better.

Arch. 'Sdeath, what shall I do?—But harkee child: what need you make me master of yourself and   235

money, when you may have the same pleasure out of
me and still keep your fortune in your hands?

Cher. Then you won't marry me?

Arch. I would marry you, but—

Cher. O sweet sir, I'm your humble servant! You're 240
fairly caught: would you persuade me that any gentleman who could bear the scandal of wearing a livery
would refuse two thousand pound, let the condition
be what it would? No, no, sir. But I hope you'll pardon the freedom I have taken, since it was only to 245
inform myself of the respect that I ought to pay you.
                                                                    Going.

Arch. Fairly bit, by Jupiter!—Hold! hold! And have
you actually two thousand pound?

Cher. Sir, I have my secrets as well as you. When
you please to be more open, I shall be more free, and 250
be assured that I have discoveries that will match
yours, be what they will. In the meanwhile, be satisfied that no discovery I make shall ever hurt you; but
beware of my father!   *Exit.*

Arch. So! we're like to have as many adventures in 255
our inn as Don Quixote had in his. Let me see—two
thousand pound! If the wench would promise to die
when the money were spent, egad, one would marry
her; but the fortune may go off in a year or two, and
the wife may live—Lord knows how long. Then an 260
innkeeper's daughter! Ay, that's the Devil—there my
pride brings me off.

> For whatsoe'er the sages charge on pride,
> The angels' fall and twenty faults beside,
> On earth, I'm sure, 'mong us of mortal calling, 265
> Pride saves man oft, and woman too, from falling.
>   *Exit.*

ACT III

Scene I. [Lady Bountiful's house.]

Enter Mrs. Sullen, Dorinda.

Mrs. Sul. Ha, ha, ha! my dear sister, let me embrace thee. Now we are friends indeed; for I shall have a secret of yours as a pledge for mine. Now you'll be good for something; I shall have you conversable in the subjects of the sex. 5

Dor. But do you think that I am so weak as to fall in love with a fellow at first sight?

Mrs. Sul. Pshaw! now you spoil all; why should not we be as free in our friendships as the men? I warrant you the gentleman has got to his confidant already, 10 has avowed his passion, toasted your health, called you ten thousand angels; has run over your lips, eyes, neck, shape, air, and everything, in a description that warms their mirth to a second enjoyment.

Dor. Your hand, sister, I an't well. 15

Mrs. Sul. So, she's breeding already! Come, child, up with it—hem a little—so. Now tell me, don't you like the gentleman that we saw at church just now?

Dor. The man's well enough.

Mrs. Sul. Well enough! Is he not a demigod, a Nar- 20 cissus, a star, the man i' the moon?

Dor. O sister, I'm extremely ill!

Mrs. Sul. Shall I send to your mother, child, for a little of her cephalic plaster to put to the soles of your feet; or shall I send to the gentleman for something 25 for you? Come, unlace your stays, unbosom yourself—

the man is perfectly a pretty fellow; I saw him when
he first came into church.

Dor. I saw him too, sister, and with an air that
shone, methought, like rays about his person.　　30

Mrs. Sul. Well said, up with it!

Dor. No forward coquette behavior, no airs to set
him off, no studied looks nor artful posture; but Nature did it all—

Mrs. Sul. Better and better! One touch more—come!　　35

Dor. But then his looks. Did you observe his eyes?

Mrs. Sul. Yes, yes, I did. His eyes, well, what of his
eyes?

Dor. Sprightly, but not wandering; they seemed to
view but never gazed on anything but me. And then　　40
his looks so humble were, and yet so noble, that they
aimed to tell me that he could with pride die at my
feet, though he scorned slavery anywhere else.

Mrs. Sul. The physic works purely!—How d'ye find
yourself now, my dear?　　45

Dor. Hem! much better, my dear.—O, here comes
our Mercury!

Enter Scrub.

Well, Scrub, what news of the gentleman?

Scrub. Madam, I have brought you a packet of
news.　　50

Dor. Open it quickly, come.

Scrub. In the first place I inquired who the gentleman was: they told me he was a stranger. Secondly,
I asked what the gentleman was: they answered and
said that they never saw him before. Thirdly, I in-　　55
quired what countryman he was: they replied 'twas

(III.i.)
47. MERCURY: messenger.
66. JESUIT: the Jesuits were believed to be plotting to restore the
house of Stuart to the throne.

more than they knew. Fourthly, I demanded whence he came: their answer was they could not tell. And, fifthly, I asked whither he went: and they replied they knew nothing of the matter—and this is all I could learn. 60

Mrs. Sul. But what do the people say? Can't they guess?

Scrub. Why, some think he's a spy, some guess he's a mountebank, some say one thing, some another; but for my own part, I believe he's a Jesuit. 65

Dor. A Jesuit. Why a Jesuit?

Scrub. Because he keeps his horses always ready saddled, and his footman talks French.

Mrs. Sul. His footman! 70

Scrub. Ay, he and the count's footman were jabbering French like two intriguing ducks in a millpond; and I believe they talked of me, for they laughed consumedly.

Dor. What sort of livery has the footman? 75

Scrub. Livery! Lord, madam, I took him for a captain, he's so bedizened with lace! And then he has tops to his shoes, up to his mid-leg, a silver-headed cane dangling at his knuckles; he carries his hands in his pockets just so—(*Walks in the French air*)—and 80 has a fine long periwig tied up in a bag. Lord, madam, he's clear another sort of man than I!

Mrs. Sul. That may easily be.—But what shall we do now, sister?

Dor. I have it. This fellow has a world of simplicity 85 and some cunning; the first hides the latter by abundance.—Scrub!

Scrub. Madam!

Dor. We have a great mind to know who this gentleman is, only for our satisfaction. 90

Scrub. Yes, madam, it would be a satisfaction, no doubt.

Dor. You must go and get acquainted with his footman and invite him hither to drink a bottle of your ale, because you're butler today.   95

Scrub. Yes, madam, I am butler every Sunday.

Mrs. Sul. O brave, sister! O' my conscience, you understand the mathematics already. 'Tis the best plot in the world: your mother, you know, will be gone to church, my spouse will be got to the alehouse with 100 his scoundrels, and the house will be our own; so we drop in by accident and ask the fellow some questions ourselves. In the country, you know, any stranger is company, and we're glad to take up with the butler in a country dance and happy if he'll do us the favor. 105

Scrub. O madam, you wrong me! I never refused your Ladyship the favor in my life.

Enter Gypsy.

Gyp. Ladies, dinner's upon table.

Dor. Scrub, we'll excuse your waiting. Go where we ordered you.   110

Scrub. I shall.

                              Exeunt.

(III.ii.)
5–6. OROONDATES, CESARIO: characters in two romances by La Calprenède, the former in *Cassandre*, the latter in *Cléopâtre*; AMADIS: the hero, Amadis de Gaul, of the old Spanish romance.

[Scene II.] Scene changes to the inn.

Enter Aimwell and Archer.

Arch. Well, Tom, I find you're a marksman.

Aim. A marksman! Who so blind could be as not discern a swan among the ravens?

Arch. Well, but harkee, Aimwell—

Aim. Aimwell! Call me Oroondates, Cesario, Ama-   5
dis, all that romance can in a lover paint, and then I'll
answer. O Archer! I read her thousands in her looks.
She looked like Ceres in her harvest: corn, wine and
oil, milk and honey, gardens, groves, and purling
streams played on her plenteous face.   10

Arch. Her face! Her pocket, you mean; the corn,
wine, and oil lies there. In short, she has ten thousand
pound, that's the English on't.

Aim. Her eyes—

Arch. Are demicannons, to be sure; so I won't stand   15
their battery.   *Going.*

Aim. Pray excuse me; my passion must have vent.

Arch. Passion! What! a plague! d'ee think these
romantic airs will do our business? Were my temper
as extravagant as yours, my adventures have some-   20
thing more romantic by half.

Aim. Your adventures!

Arch. Yes,

> The nymph that with her twice ten hundred
>   pounds,   25
> With brazen engine hot and quoif clear starched,
> Can fire the guest in warming of the bed—

There's a touch of sublime Milton for you, and the

subject but an innkeeper's daughter! I can play with
a girl as an angler does with his fish; he keeps it at 30
the end of his line, runs it up the stream and down
the stream, till at last he brings it to hand, tickles the
trout, and so whips it into his basket.

Enter Boniface.

Bon. Mr. Martin, as the saying is, yonder's an honest
fellow below, my Lady Bountiful's butler, who begs 35
the honor that you would go home with him and see
his cellar.

Arch. Do my *baise-mains* to the gentleman and tell
him I will do myself the honor to wait on him immediately.   *Exit Boniface.* 40

Aim. What do I hear?

Soft Orpheus play, and fair Toftida sing!

Arch. Pshaw! Damn your raptures! I tell you, here's
a pump going to be put into the vessel, and the ship
will get into harbor, my life on't. You say there's an- 45
other lady very handsome there?

Aim. Yes, faith.

Arch. I am in love with her already.

Aim. Can't you give me a bill upon Cherry in the
meantime?   50

Arch. No, no, friend, all her corn, wine, and oil is
engrossed to my market. And once more I warn you
to keep your anchorage clear of mine; for if you fall
foul of me, by this light, you shall go to the bottom!
What! make prize of my little frigate, while I am upon 55
the cruise for you!

Aim. Well, well, I won't.   *Exit Archer.*

---

38. BAISE-MAINS: "kiss-hands," i.e., courtesies.
42. TOFTIDA: a noted soprano of the day, Katherine Tofts.

Enter Bonniface.

Landlord, have you any tolerable company in the
house? I don't care for dining alone.

Bon. Yes, sir, there's a captain below, as the saying   60
is, that arrived about an hour ago.

Aim. Gentlemen of his coat are welcome everywhere; will you make him a compliment from me and
tell him I should be glad of his company?

Bon. Who shall I tell him, sir, would—   65

Aim. Ha! that stroke was well thrown in!—I'm only
a traveler like himself and would be glad of his company, that's all.

Bon. I obey your commands, as the saying is. *Exit.*

Enter Archer.

Arch. 'Sdeath! I had forgot; what title will you give   70
yourself?

Aim. My brother's, to be sure; he would never give
me anything else, so I'll make bold with his honor
this bout. You know the rest of your cue.

Arch. Ay, ay.   *Exit.*   75

Enter Gibbet.

Gib. Sir, I'm yours.

Aim. 'Tis more than I deserve, sir, for I don't know
you.

Gib. I don't wonder at that, sir, for you never saw
me before—(*Aside*) I hope.   80

Aim. And pray, sir, how came I by the honor of
seeing you now?

Gib. Sir, I scorn to intrude upon any gentleman, but
my landlord—

Aim. O sir, I ask your pardon! You're the captain he   85
told me of.

Gib. At your service, sir.

Aim. What regiment, may I be so bold?

Gib. A marching regiment, sir, an old corps.

Aim. (*Aside*) Very old, if your coat be regimental.—   90
You have served abroad, sir?

Gib. Yes, sir, in the plantations; 'twas my lot to be
sent into the worst service. I would have quitted it,
indeed, but a man of honor, you know—Besides, 'twas
for the good of my country that I should be abroad.   95
Anything for the good of one's country—I'm a Roman
for that.

Aim. (*Aside*) One of the first, I'll lay my life.—You
found the West Indies very hot, sir?

Gib. Ay, sir, too hot for me.   100

Aim. Pray, sir, han't I seen your face at Will's Coffee
House?

Gib. Yes, sir, and at White's too.

Aim. And where is your company now, Captain?

Gib. They an't come yet.   105

Aim. Why, d'ye expect 'em here?

Gib. They'll be here tonight, sir.

Aim. Which way do they march?

Gib. Across the country.—The Devil's in't, if I han't
said enough to encourage him to declare; but I'm   110
afraid he's not right; I must tack about.

Aim. Is your company to quarter in Lichfield?

Gib. In this house, sir.

Aim. What! all?

Gib. My company's but thin, ha, ha, ha! we are but   115
three, ha, ha, ha!

Aim. You're merry, sir.

---

98. ONE . . . FIRST: Aimwell puns on "Roman" as a cant term for
"thief."
121. CHARGE: (1) large sum of money; (2) company (of thieves
under his command).

Gib. Ay, sir, you must excuse me, sir; I understand
the world, especially the art of traveling. I don't care,
sir, for answering questions directly upon the road,   120
for I generally ride with a charge about me.

Aim. (*Aside*) Three or four, I believe.

Gib. I am credibly informed that there are highwaymen upon this quarter; not, sir, that I could suspect a gentleman of your figure. But truly, sir, I have   125
got such a way of evasion upon the road, that I don't
care for speaking truth to any man.

Aim. Your caution may be necessary. Then I presume you're no captain?

Gib. Not I, sir; captain is a good traveling name,   130
and so I take it; it stops a great many foolish inquiries
that are generally made about gentlemen that travel.
It gives a man an air of something and makes the
drawers obedient; and thus far I am a captain, and
no farther.   135

Aim. And pray, sir, what is your true profession?

Gib. O sir, you must excuse me! Upon my word, sir,
I don't think it safe to tell you.

Aim. Ha, ha, ha! upon my word, I commend you.

Enter Bonniface.

Well, Mr. Bonniface, what's the news?   140

Bon. There's another gentleman below, as the saying is, that hearing you were but two, would be glad
to make the third man, if you would give him leave.

Aim. What is he?

Bon. A clergyman, as the saying is.   145

Aim. A clergyman! Is he really a clergyman? or is
it only his traveling name, as my friend the captain
has it?

Bon. O sir, he's a priest and chaplain to the French
officers in town.   150

Aim. Is he a Frenchman?

Bon. Yes, sir, born at Brussels.

Gib. A Frenchman, and a priest! I won't be seen in his company, sir; I have a value for my reputation, sir.

Aim. Nay, but, Captain, since we are by ourselves— 155
Can he speak English, landlord?

Bon. Very well, sir; you may know him, as the saying is, to be a foreigner by his accent, and that's all.

Aim. Then he has been in England before?

Bon. Never, sir; but he's a master of languages, as 160
the saying is—he talks Latin—it does me good to hear him talk Latin.

Aim. Then you understand Latin, Mr. Bonniface?

Bon. Not I, sir, as the saying is; but he talks it so very fast that I'm sure it must be good. 165

Aim. Pray, desire him to walk up.

Bon. Here he is, as the saying is.

Enter Foigard.

Foi. Save you, gentlemens, both.

Aim. A Frenchman!—Sir, your most humble servant.

Foi. Och, dear joy, I am your most faithful shervant, 170
and yours alsho.

Gib. Doctor, you talk very good English, but you have a mighty twang of the foreigner.

Foi. My English is very vel for the vords, but we foreigners, you know, cannot bring our tongues about 175
the pronunciation so soon.

Aim. (*Aside*) A foreigner! a downright Teague, by this light!—Were you born in France, Doctor?

Foi. I was educated in France, but I was borned at Brussels; I am a subject of the King of Spain, joy. 180

Gib. What King of Spain, sir? speak!

177. TEAGUE: Irishman.
191. FAIT: faith.

Foi. Upon my shoul, joy, I cannot tell you as yet.

Aim. Nay, Captain, that was too hard upon the doctor; he's a stranger.

Foi. O, let him alone, dear joy; I am of a nation that 185
is not easily put out of countenance.

Aim. Come, gentlemen, I'll end the dispute.—Here, landlord, is dinner ready?

Bon. Upon the table, as the saying is.

Aim. Gentlemen—pray—that door—   190

Foi. No, no, fait, the captain must lead.

Aim. No, Doctor, the church is our guide.

Gib. Ay, ay, so it is.

Exit foremost; they follow.

[Scene III.] Scene changes to a gallery in Lady
Bountiful's house.

*Enter Archer and Scrub, singing and hugging one
another, Scrub with a tankard in his hand; Gypsy
listening at a distance.*

Scrub. Tall, all, dall!—Come, my dear boy, let's
have that song once more.

Arch. No, no, we shall disturb the family. But will
you be sure to keep the secret?

Scrub. Pho! upon my honor, as I'm a gentleman.   5

Arch. 'Tis enough.—You must know, then, that my
master is the Lord Viscount Aimwell. He fought a
duel t'other day in London, wounded his man so
dangerously that he thinks fit to withdraw till he hears
whether the gentleman's wounds be mortal or not. He 10
never was in this part of England before, so he chose
to retire to this place, that's all.

Gyp. And that's enough for me.   *Exit.*

Scrub. And where were you when your master fought? 15

Arch. We never know of our masters' quarrels.

Scrub. No? If our masters in the country here receive a challenge, the first thing they do is to tell their wives; the wife tells the servants, the servants alarm the tenants, and in half an hour you shall have the 20 whole county in arms.

Arch. To hinder two men from doing what they have no mind for.—But if you should chance to talk now of my business?

Scrub. Talk! ay, sir, had I not learnt the knack of 25 holding my tongue, I had never lived so long in a great family.

Arch. Ay, ay, to be sure there are secrets in all families.

Scrub. Secrets! ay—but I'll say no more. Come, sit 30 down; we'll make an end of our tankard: here—

Arch. With all my heart; who knows but you and I may come to be better acquainted, eh?—Here's your ladies' healths; you have three, I think, and to be sure there must be secrets among 'em. 35

Scrub. Secrets! ay, friend. I wish I had a friend—

Arch. Am not I your friend? Come, you and I will be sworn brothers.

Scrub. Shall we?

Arch. From this minute.—Give me a kiss. And now, 40 Brother Scrub—

Scrub. And now, Brother Martin, I will tell you a secret that will make your hair stand on end. You must know that I am consumedly in love.

Arch. That's a terrible secret, that's the truth on't. 45

Scrub. That jade, Gypsy, that was with us just now in the cellar, is the arrantest whore that ever wore a petticoat; and I'm dying for love of her.

Arch. Ha, ha, ha! Are you in love with her person r her virtue, Brother Scrub?   50

Scrub. I should like virtue best, because it is more lurable than beauty; for virtue holds good with some vomen long and many a day after they have lost it.

Arch. In the country, I grant ye, where no woman's irtue is lost till a bastard be found.   55

Scrub. Ay, could I bring her to a bastard, I should lave her all to myself; but I dare not put it upon that ay, for fear of being sent for a soldier.—Pray, brother, low do you gentlemen in London like that same 'ressing Act?   60

Arch. Very ill, Brother Scrub; 'tis the worst that ever vas made for us. Formerly I remember the good days, when we could dun our masters for our wages, and if hey refused to pay us, we could have a warrant to carry 'em before a justice; but now, if we talk of eat-   65 ing, they have a warrant for us and carry us before three justices.

Scrub. And, to be sure, we go, if we talk of eating; for the justices won't give their own servants a bad example. Now this is my misfortune—I dare not speak   70 in the house, while that jade Gypsy dings about like a fury. Once I had the better end of the staff.

Arch. And how comes the change now?

Scrub. Why, the mother of all this mischief is a priest.   75

Arch. A priest!

Scrub. Ay, a damned son of a whore of Babylon that came over hither to say grace to the French officers and eat up our provisions. There's not a day goes over his head without dinner or supper in this house.   80

Arch. How came he so familiar in the family?

Scrub. Because he speaks English as if he had lived here all his life and tells lies as if he had been a traveler from his cradle.

Arch. And this priest, I'm afraid, has converted the 85
affections of your Gypsy.

Scrub. Converted! ay, and perverted, my dear
friend: for I'm afraid he has made her a whore and
a papist! But this is not all: there's the French count
and Mrs. Sullen, they're in the confederacy, and for 90
some private ends of their own, to be sure.

Arch. A very hopeful family yours, Brother Scrub! I
suppose the maiden lady has her lover too.

Scrub. Not that I know. She's the best on 'em, that's
the truth on't. But they take care to prevent my 95
curiosity, by giving me so much business that I'm a
perfect slave. What d'ye think is my place in this
family?

Arch. Butler, I suppose.

Scrub. Ah, Lord help you!—I'll tell you. Of a Mon- 100
day I drive the coach; of a Tuesday I drive the plow;
on Wednesday I follow the hounds; a-Thursday I dun
the tenants; on Friday I go to market; on Saturday I
draw warrants; and a-Sunday I draw beer.

Arch. Ha, ha, ha! If variety be a pleasure in life, 105
you have enough on't, my dear brother.—But what
ladies are those?

Scrub. Ours, ours; that upon the right hand is Mrs.
Sullen, and the other is Mrs. Dorinda. Don't mind
'em; sit still, man. 110

Enter Mrs. Sullen and Dorinda.

Mrs. Sul. I have heard my brother talk of my Lord
Aimwell; but they say that his brother is the finer
gentleman.

Dor. That's impossible, sister.

Mrs. Sul. He's vastly rich, but very close, they say. 115

(III.iii.)
95. PREVENT: interfere with.

Dor. No matter for that; if I can creep into his heart,
I'll open his breast, I warrant him. I have heard say
that people may be guessed at by the behavior of their
servants; I could wish we might talk to that fellow.

Mrs. Sul. So do I; for I think he's a very pretty fel- 120
low. Come this way, I'll throw out a lure for him
presently.

> *They walk a turn towards the opposite side of the*
> *stage. Mrs. Sullen drops her glove; Archer runs,*
> *takes it up and gives it to her.*

Arch. Corn, wine, and oil, indeed! But, I think, the
wife has the greatest plenty of flesh and blood; she
should be my choice.—Ah, a, say you so!—Madam, 125
your Ladyship's glove.

Mrs. Sul. O sir, I thank you!—What a handsome
bow the fellow has!

Dor. Bow! Why, I have known several footmen
come down from London set up here for dancing 130
masters and carry off the best fortunes in the country.

Arch. (*Aside*) That project, for aught I know, had
been better than ours.— Brother Scrub, why don't you
introduce me?

Scrub. Ladies, this is the strange gentleman's serv- 135
ant that you see at church today. I understood he
came from London, and so I invited him to the cellar,
that he might show me the newest flourish in whetting
my knives.

Dor. And I hope you have made much of him? 140

Arch. O, yes, madam, but the strength of your Ladyship's liquor is a little too potent for the constitution
of your humble servant.

Mrs. Sul. What, then you don't usually drink ale?

Arch. No, madam; my constant drink is tea, or a 145
little wine and water. 'Tis prescribed me by the physician for a remedy against the spleen.

Scrub. O la! O la! a footman have the spleen!

Mrs. Sul. I thought that distemper had been only proper to people of quality. 150

Arch. Madam, like all other fashions it wears out and so descends to their servants; though in a great many of us I believe it proceeds from some melancholy particles in the blood, occasioned by the stagnation of wages. 155

Dor. How affectedly the fellow talks!—How long, pray, have you served your present master?

Arch. Not long; my life has been mostly spent in the service of the ladies.

Mrs. Sul. And pray, which service do you like best? 160

Arch. Madam, the ladies pay best; the honor of serving them is sufficient wages. There is a charm in their looks that delivers a pleasure with their commands and gives our duty the wings of inclination.

Mrs. Sul. That flight was above the pitch of a livery. 165 —And, sir, would not you be satisfied to serve a lady again?

Arch. As a groom of the chamber, madam, but not as a footman.

Mrs. Sul. I suppose you served as footman before. 170

Arch. For that reason I would not serve in that post again; for my memory is too weak for the load of messages that the ladies lay upon their servants in London. My Lady Howd'ye, the last mistress I served, called me up one morning and told me, "Martin, go 17 to my Lady Allnight with my humble service; tell her I was to wait on Her Ladyship yesterday and left word with Mrs. Rebecca that the preliminaries of the affair she knows of are stopped till we know the concurrence of the person that I know of, for which there 18 are circumstances wanting which we shall accommodate at the old place; but that in the meantime there is a person about Her Ladyship that, from several hints and surmises, was accessary at a certain time to

the disappointments that naturally attend things that 185
to her knowledge are of more importance—"

Mrs. Sul., Dor. Ha, ha, ha! Where are you going,
sir?

Arch. Why, I han't half done!—The whole howd'ye
was about half an hour long; so I happened to mis- 190
place two syllables, and was turned off and rendered
incapable.

Dor. The pleasantest fellow, sister, I ever saw!—
But, friend, if your master be married, I presume you
still serve a lady. 195

Arch. No, madam, I take care never to come into a
married family. The commands of the master and
mistress are always so contrary that 'tis impossible to
please both.

Dor. (*Aside*) There's a main point gained.—My 200
Lord is not married, I find.

Mrs. Sul. But I wonder, friend, that in so many good
services you had not a better provision made for you.

Arch. I don't know how, madam. I had a lieu-
tenancy offered me three or four times; but that is 205
not bread, madam—I live much better as I do.

Scrub. Madam, he sings rarely.—I was thought to do
pretty well here in the country till he came; but
alackaday, I'm nothing to my brother Martin!

Dor. Does he?—Pray, sir, will you oblige us with a 210
song?

Arch. Are you for passion or humor?

Scrub. Oh la! he has the purest ballad about a
trifle—

Mrs. Sul. A trifle! Pray, sir, let's have it. 215

Arch. I'm ashamed to offer you a trifle, madam; but
since you command me—

Sings to the tune of "Sir Simon the King."

A trifling song you shall hear,
Begun with a trifle and ended, etc.

Mrs. Sul. Very well, sir, we're obliged to you.—   220
Something for a pair of gloves.   *Offering him money.*

Arch. I humbly beg leave to be excused: my master,
madam, pays me; nor dare I take money from any
other hand without injuring his honor and disobeying
his commands.   *Exit Archer and Scrub.*   225

Dor. This is surprising! Did you ever see so pretty
a well-bred fellow?

Mrs. Sul. The Devil take him for wearing that
livery!

Dor. I fancy, sister, he may be some gentleman, a   230
friend of My Lord's, that His Lordship has pitched
upon for his courage, fidelity, and discretion, to bear
him company in this dress, and who, ten to one, was
his second too.

Mrs. Sul. It is so, it must be so, and it shall be so—   235
for I like him.

Dor. What! better than the count?

Mrs. Sul. The count happened to be the most agreeable man upon the place; and so I chose him to serve
me in my design upon my husband. But I should like   240
this fellow better in a design upon myself.

Dor. But now, sister, for an interview with this lord
and this gentleman; how shall we bring that about?

Mrs. Sul. Patience! You country ladies give no quarter if once you be entered.—Would you prevent their   245
desires and give the fellows no wishing-time?—Look
ye, Dorinda, if My Lord Aimwell loves you or deserves you, he'll find a way to see you, and there we
must leave it. My business comes now upon the tapis.
Have you prepared your brother?   250

---

249. TAPIS: carpet.

Dor. Yes, yes.

Mrs. Sul. And how did he relish it?

Dor. He said little, mumbled something to himself, promised to be guided by me—but here he comes.

Enter Sullen.

Sul. What singing was that I heard just now?   255

Mrs. Sul. The singing in your head, my dear; you complained of it all day.

Sul. You're impertinent.

Mrs. Sul. I was ever so, since I became one flesh with you.   260

Sul. One flesh! Rather two carcasses joined unnaturally together.

Mrs. Sul. Or rather a living soul coupled to a dead body.

Dor. So, this is fine encouragement for me!   265

Sul. Yes, my wife shows you what you must do.

Mrs. Sul. And my husband shows you what you must suffer.

Sul. 'Sdeath, why can't you be silent?

Mrs. Sul. 'Sdeath, why can't you talk?   270

Sul. Do you talk to any purpose?

Mrs. Sul. Do you think to any purpose?

Sul. Sister, harkee! (*Whispers*)—I shan't be home till it be late.   *Exit.*

Mrs. Sul. What did he whisper to ye?   275

Dor. That he would go round the back way, come into the closet, and listen as I directed him. But let me beg you once more, dear sister, to drop this project; for as I told you before, instead of awakening him to kindness, you may provoke him to a rage, and   280 then who knows how far his brutality may carry him?

Mrs. Sul. I'm provided to receive him, I warrant you. But here comes the count—vanish!   *Exit Dorinda.*

Enter Count Bellair.

Don't you wonder, Monsieur le Count, that I was not
at church this afternoon?   285

Count Bel. I more wonder, madam, that you go
dere at all, or how you dare to lift those eyes to
Heaven that are guilty of so much killing.

Mrs. Sul. If Heaven, sir, has given to my eyes, with
the power of killing, the virtue of making a cure, I   290
hope the one may atone for the other.

Count Bel. O, largely, madam. Would your Ladyship be as ready to apply the remedy as to give the
wound? Consider, madam, I am doubly a prisoner:
first, to the arms of your general, then, to your more   295
conquering eyes. My first chains are easy: there a
ransom may redeem me; but from your fetters I never
shall get free.

Mrs. Sul. Alas, sir! why should you complain to me
of your captivity who am in chains myself? You know,   300
sir, that I am bound, nay, most be-tied up in that
particular that might give you ease: I am, like you, a
prisoner of war—of war, indeed! I have given my
parole of honor; would you break yours to gain your
liberty?   305

Count Bel. Most certainly I would, were I a prisoner among the Turks. Dis is your case: you're a slave,
madam, slave to the worst of Turks, a husband.

Mrs. Sul. There lies my foible, I confess; no fortifi-
cations, no courage, conduct, nor vigilancy can pre-   310
tend to defend a place where the cruelty of the
governor forces the garrison to mutiny.

Count Bel. And where de besieger is resolved to
die before de place. Here will I fix (*Kneels*)—with
tears, vows, and prayers assault your heart, and never   315

rise till you surrender; or if I must storm—Love and
St. Michael! And so I begin the attack.

Mrs. Sul. Stand off!—(*Aside*) Sure he hears me not!
And I could almost wish he—did not! The fellow
makes love very prettily.—But, sir, why should you 320
put such a value upon my person, when you see it
despised by one that knows it so much better?

Count Bel. He knows it not, though he possesses it.
If he but knew the value of the jewel he is master of,
he would always wear it next his heart and sleep with 325
it in his arms.

Mrs. Sul. But since he throws me unregarded from
him—

Count Bel. And one that knows your value well
comes by and takes you up, is it not justice? 330

Goes to lay hold on her.

Enter Sullen, with his sword drawn.

Sul. Hold, villain, hold!

Mrs. Sul. (*Presenting a pistol*) Do you hold!

Sul. What! murder your husband to defend your
bully!

Mrs. Sul. Bully! for shame, Mr. Sullen. Bullies wear 335
long swords, the gentleman has none; he's a prisoner,
you know. I was aware of your outrage and prepared
this to receive your violence, and, if occasion were, to
preserve myself against the force of this other gentleman. 340

Count Bel. O madam, your eyes be bettre firearms
than your pistol; they nevre miss.

Sul. What! court my wife to my face!

Mrs. Sul. Pray, Mr. Sullen, put up; suspend your
fury for a minute. 345

Sul. To give you time to invent an excuse!

Mrs. Sul. I need none.

Sul. No, for I heard every syllable of your discourse.

Count Bel. Ay! and begar, I tink de dialogue was
vera pretty.   350

Mrs. Sul. Then I suppose, sir, you heard something
of your own barbarity?

Sul. Barbarity! Oons, what does the woman call
barbarity? do I ever meddle with you?

Mrs. Sul. No.   355

Sul. As for you, sir, I shall take another time.

Count Bel. Ah, begar, and so must I.

Sul. Look'ee, madam, don't think that my anger proceeds from any concern I have for your honor, but for
my own, and if you can contrive any way of being a   360
whore without making me a cuckold, do it and welcome.

Mrs. Sul. Sir, I thank you kindly; you would allow
me the sin but rob me of the pleasure. No, no, I'm
resolved never to venture upon the crime without the 365
satisfaction of seeing you punished for't.

Sul. Then will you grant me this, my dear? Let
anybody else do you the favor but that Frenchman,
for I mortally hate his whole generation.   *Exit.*

Count Bel. Ah, sir, that be ungrateful, for begar, I 370
love some of yours.—Madam—   *Approaching her.*

Mrs. Sul. No, sir.—

Count Bel. No, sir!—Garzoon, madam, I am not your
husband!

Mrs. Sul. 'Tis time to undeceive you, sir. I believed   375
your addresses to me were no more than an amuse-
ment, and I hope you will think the same of my complaisance; and to convince you that you ought, you
must know that I brought you hither only to make you
instrumental in setting me right with my husband, for 380
he was planted to listen by my appointment.

---

373. GARZOON: "God's wounds," with a French accent.

Count Bel. By your appointment?

Mrs. Sul. Certainly.

Count Bel. And so, madam, while I was telling twenty stories to part you from your husband, begar, I 385 was bringing you together all the while?

Mrs. Sul. I ask your pardon, sir, but I hope this will give you a taste of the virtue of the English ladies.

Count Bel. Begar, madam, your virtue be vera great, but garzoon, your honeste be vera little. 390

Enter Dorinda.

Mrs. Sul. Nay, now, you're angry, sir.

Count Bel. Angry!—"Fair Dorinda."

Sings "Dorinda," the opera tune, and addresses to Dorinda.

Madam, when your Ladyship want a fool, send for me. "Fair Dorinda, Revenge, etc." *Exit.*

Mrs. Sul. There goes the true humor of his nation: 395 resentment with good manners, and the height of anger in a song!—Well, sister, you must be judge, for you have heard the trial.

Dor. And I bring in my brother guilty.

Mrs. Sul. But I must bear the punishment. 'Tis hard, 400 sister.

Dor. I own it; but you must have patience.

Mrs. Sul. Patience! the cant of custom. Providence sends no evil without a remedy. Should I lie groaning under a yoke I can shake off, I were accessary to my 405 ruin and my patience were no better than self-murder.

Dor. But how can you shake off the yoke? Your divisions don't come within the reach of the law for a divorce.

Mrs. Sul. Law! What law can search into the remote 410 abyss of nature? What evidence can prove the unac-

countable disaffections of wedlock? Can a jury sum up
the endless aversions that are rooted in our souls, or
can a bench give judgment upon antipathies?

Dor. They never pretended, sister; they never med- 415
dle but in case of uncleanness.

Mrs. Sul. Uncleanness! O sister! Casual violation is
a transient injury and may possibly be repaired, but
can radical hatreds be ever reconciled?—No, no, sister,
Nature is the first lawgiver, and when she has set 420
tempers opposite, not all the golden links of wedlock
nor iron manacles of law can keep 'um fast.

 Wedlock we own ordained by Heaven's decree,
 But such as Heaven ordained it first to be:
 Concurring tempers in the man and wife,   425
 As mutual helps to draw the load of life.
 View all the works of Providence above,
 The stars with harmony and concord move;
 View all the works of Providence below,
 The fire, the water, earth, and air, we know, 430
 All in one plant agree to make it grow.
 Must man, the chiefest work of art divine,
 Be doomed in endless discord to repine?
 No, we should injure Heaven by that surmise;
 Omnipotence is just, were man but wise.   435
          Exeunt.

ACT IV

Scene I. Scene continues.

Enter Mrs. Sullen.

Mrs. Sul. Were I born an humble Turk, where
women have no soul nor property, there I must sit
contented. But in England, a country whose women
are its glory, must women be abused? Where women
rule, must women be enslaved? nay, cheated into   5
slavery, mocked by a promise of comfortable society
into a wilderness of solitude? I dare not keep the
thought about me.—O, here comes something to
divert me.

Enter a Country Woman.

Wom. I come, an't please your Ladyships—you're   10
My Lady Bountiful, an't ye?
Mrs. Sul. Well, good woman, go on.
Wom. I have come seventeen long mail to have a
cure for my husband's sore leg.
Mrs. Sul. Your husband! What, woman, cure your   15
husband!
Wom. Ay, poor man, for his sore leg won't let him
stir from home.
Mrs. Sul. There, I confess, you have given me a
reason. Well, good woman, I'll tell you what you must   20
do. You must lay your husband's leg upon a table, and
with a chopping-knife you must lay it open as broad
as you can; then you must take out the bone and beat

the flesh soundly with a rolling-pin; then take salt,
pepper, cloves, mace, and ginger, some sweet herbs, 25
and season it very well; then roll it up like brawn and
put it into the oven for two hours.

Wom. Heavens reward your Ladyship! I have two
little babies too that are piteous bad with the graips,
an't please ye. 30

Mrs. Sul. Put a little pepper and salt in their bellies,
good woman.

Enter Lady Bountiful.

I beg your Ladyship's pardon for taking your business
out of your hands; I have been a-tampering here a
little with one of your patients. 35

Lady Boun. Come, good woman, don't mind this
mad creature; I am the person that you want, I suppose. What would you have, woman?

Mrs. Sul. She wants something for her husband's
sore leg. 40

Lady Boun. What's the matter with his leg, goody?

Wom. It come first, as one might say, with a sort of
dizziness in his foot, then he had a kind of a laziness
in his joints, and then his leg broke out, and then it
swelled, and then it closed again, and then it broke 45
out again, and then it festered, and then it grew better, and then it grew worse again.

Mrs. Sul. Ha, ha, ha!

Lady Boun. How can you be merry with the misfortunes of other people? 50

Mrs. Sul. Because my own make me sad, madam.

Lady Boun. The worst reason in the world, daughter; your own misfortunes should teach you to pity
others.

Mrs. Sul. But the woman's misfortunes and mine are 55
nothing alike: her husband is sick, and mine, alas! is
in health.

Lady Boun. What! Would you wish your husband
sick?

Mrs. Sul. Not of a sore leg, of all things. 60

Lady Boun. Well, good woman, go to the pantry,
get your bellyful of victuals, then I'll give you a
receipt of diet-drink for your husband. But d'ye hear,
goody, you must not let your husband move too much.

Wom. No, no, madam, the poor man's inclinable 65
enough to lie still.   *Exit.*

Lady Boun. Well, Daughter Sullen, though you
laugh, I have done miracles about the country here
with my receipts.

Mrs. Sul. Miracles indeed, if they have cured any- 70
body; but I believe, madam, the patient's faith goes
farther toward the miracle than your prescription.

Lady Boun. Fancy helps in some cases; but there's
your husband, who has as little fancy as anybody; I
brought him from death's door. 75

Mrs. Sul. I suppose, madam, you made him drink
plentifully of ass's milk.

Enter Dorinda, runs to Mrs. Sullen.

Dor. News, dear sister! news! news!

Enter Archer, running.

Arch. Where, where is My Lady Bountiful? Pray,
which is the old lady of you three? 80

Lady Boun. I am.

Arch. O madam, the fame of your Ladyship's
charity, goodness, benevolence, skill, and ability, have
drawn me hither to implore your Ladyship's help in

behalf of my unfortunate master, who is this moment   85
breathing his last.

Lady Boun. Your master! Where is he?

Arch. At your gate, madam. Drawn by the appearance of your handsome house to view it nearer, and
walking up the avenue within five paces of the court-   90
yard, he was taken ill of a sudden with a sort of I
know not what, but down he fell, and there he lies.

Lady Boun. Here, Scrub! Gypsy! all run, get my
easy chair downstairs, put the gentleman in it, and
bring him in quickly, quickly!   95

Arch. Heaven will reward your Ladyship for this
charitable act.

Lady Boun. Is your master used to these fits?

Arch. O, yes, madam, frequently—I have known him
have five or six of a night.   100

Lady Boun. What's his name?

Arch. Lord, madam, he's a-dying! A minute's care or
neglect may save or destroy his life!

Lady Boun. Ah, poor gentleman! Come, friend,
show me the way; I'll see him brought in myself.   105

                              Exit with Archer.

Dor. O sister, my heart flutters about strangely! I
can hardly forbear running to his assistance.

Mrs. Sul. And I'll lay my life he deserves your assistance more than he wants it; did not I tell you that
My Lord would find a way to come at you? Love's his   110
distemper, and you must be the physician; put on all
your charms, summon all your fire into your eyes,
plant the whole artillery of your looks against his
breast, and down with him.

Dor. O sister! I'm but a young gunner; I shall be   115
afraid to shoot, for fear the piece should recoil and
hurt myself.

---

109. WANTS: needs.

Mrs. Sul. Never fear, you shall see me shoot before you, if you will.

Dor. No, no, dear sister; you have missed your mark 120 so unfortunately that I shan't care for being instructed by you.

Enter Aimwell, in a chair carried by Archer and Scrub; Lady Bountiful, Gypsy; Aimwell counterfeiting a swoon.

Lady Boun. Here, here, let's see the hartshorn drops.—Gypsy, a glass of fair water! His fit's very strong. Bless me, how his hands are clinched!   125

Arch. For shame, ladies, what d'ye do? why don't you help us?—(*To Dorinda*) Pray, madam, take his hand and open it, if you can, whilst I hold his head.
                    Dorinda takes his hand.

Dor. Poor gentleman! O! he has got my hand within his and squeezes it unmercifully—   130

Lady Boun. 'Tis the violence of his convulsion, child.

Arch. O madam, he's perfectly possessed in these cases—he'll bite if you don't have a care.

Dor. O, my hand! my hand!   135

Lady Boun. What's the matter with the foolish girl? I have got this hand open, you see, with a great deal of ease.

Arch. Ay, but, madam, your daughter's hand is somewhat warmer than your Ladyship's, and the heat 140 of it draws the force of the spirits that way.

Mrs. Sul. I find, friend, you're very learned in these sorts of fits.

Arch. 'Tis no wonder, madam, for I'm often troubled with them myself; I find myself extremely ill at 145 this minute.   *Looking hard at Mrs. Sullen.*

Mrs. Sul. (*Aside*) I fancy I could find a way to cure you.

Lady Boun. His fit holds him very long.

Arch. Longer than usual, madam.—Pray, young 150 lady, open his breast, and give him air.

Lady Boun. Where did his illness take him first, pray?

Arch. Today at church, madam.

Lady Boun. In what manner was he taken? 155

Arch. Very strangely, My Lady. He was of a sudden touched with something in his eyes, which at the first he only felt, but could not tell whether 'twas pain or pleasure.

Lady Boun. Wind, nothing but wind! 160

Arch. By soft degrees it grew and mounted to his brain; there his fancy caught it, there formed it so beautiful, and dressed it up in such gay, pleasing colors that his transported appetite seized the fair idea and straight conveyed it to his heart. That hospitable 165 seat of life sent all its sanguine spirits forth to meet, and opened all its sluicy gates to take the stranger in.

Lady Boun. Your master should never go without a bottle to smell to.—O!—He recovers! The lavender water—some feathers to burn under his nose—Hun- 170 gary-water to rub his temples.—O, he comes to himself!—Hem, a little, sir, hem.—Gypsy! bring the cordial water. *Aimwell seems to awake in amaze.*

Dor. How d'ye, sir?

Aim. Where am I? *Rising.* 175
Sure I have passed the gulf of silent death,
And now I land on the Elysian shore!
Behold the goddess of those happy plains,
Fair Proserpine. Let me adore thy bright divinity.
Kneels to Dorinda, and kisses her hand.

Mrs. Sul. So, so, so! I knew where the fit would end! 180

Aim. Eurydice perhaps—

How could thy Orpheus keep his word,
And not look back upon thee?
No treasure but thyself could sure have bribed him
To look one minute off thee. 185

Lady Boun. Delirious, poor gentleman!

Arch. Very delirious, madam, very delirious.

Aim. Martin's voice, I think.

Arch. Yes, My Lord. How does your Lordship?

Lady Boun. Lord! Did you mind that, girls? 190

Aim. Where am I?

Arch. In very good hands, sir. You were taken just
now with one of your old fits, under the trees, just by
this good lady's house; Her Ladyship had you taken
in, and has miraculously brought you to yourself, as 195
you see.

Aim. I am so confounded with shame, madam, that
I can now only beg pardon and refer my acknowledgments for your Ladyship's care till an opportunity
offers of making some amends. I dare be no longer 200
troublesome.—Martin! give two guineas to the servants.   *Going.*

Dor. Sir, you may catch cold by going so soon into
the air; you don't look, sir, as if you were perfectly
recovered. 205

Here Archer talks to Lady Bountiful in dumb show.

Aim. That I shall never be, madam; my present illness is so rooted that I must expect to carry it to my
grave.

Mrs. Sul. Don't despair, sir; I have known several in
your distemper shake it off with a fortnight's physic. 210

Lady Boun. Come, sir, your servant has been telling
me that you're apt to relapse if you go into the air.
Your good manners shan't get the better of ours. You
shall sit down again, sir. Come, sir, we don't mind
ceremonies in the country. Here, sir, my service t'ye. 215
You shall taste my water; 'tis a cordial, I can assure

you, and of my own making—drink it off, sir.—(*Aimwell drinks.*) And how d'ye find yourself now, sir?

Aim. Somewhat better—though very faint still.

Lady Boun. Ay, ay, people are always faint after 220
these fits.—Come, girls, you shall show the gentleman
the house.—'Tis but an old family building, sir; but
you had better walk about and cool by degrees than
venture immediately into the air. You'll find some
tolerable pictures.—Dorinda, show the gentleman the 225
way. I must go to the poor woman below.   *Exit.*

Dor. This way, sir.

Aim. Ladies, shall I beg leave for my servant to wait
on you? for he understands pictures very well.

Mrs. Sul. Sir, we understand originals as well as he 230
does pictures, so he may come along.

> *Exeunt Dorinda, Mrs. Sullen, Aimwell, Archer.*
> *Aimwell leads Dorinda.*

Enter Foigard and Scrub, meeting.

Foi. Save you, Master Scrub!

Scrub. Sir, I won't be saved your way. I hate a
priest, I abhor the French, and I defy the Devil. Sir,
I'm a bold Briton and will spill the last drop of my 235
blood to keep out popery and slavery.

Foi. Master Scrub, you would put me down in
politics, and so I would be speaking with Mrs. Shipsy.

Scrub. Good Mr. Priest, you can't speak with her;
she's sick, sir; she's gone abroad, sir; she's—dead two 240
months ago, sir.

Enter Gypsy.

Gyp. How now, impudence! how dare you talk so

258. CEDANT . . . TOGAE: arms give place to the gown (Cicero *De
officiis* i.22).

252. GRA: a corrupted form of the Irish for "my dear."

saucily to the doctor?—Pray, sir, don't take it ill; for
the common people of England are not so civil to
strangers as—   245

Scrub. You lie! you lie! 'Tis the common people that
are civilest to strangers.

Gyp. Sirrah, I have a good mind to—Get you out, I
say!

Scrub. I won't.   250

Gyp. You won't, saucebox!—Pray, Doctor, what is
the captain's name that came to your inn last night?

Scrub. The captain! Ah, the Devil, there she ham-
pers me again. The captain has me on one side and
the priest on t'other; so between the gown and the   255
sword, I have a fine time on't. But *cedant arma togæ.*

Going.

Gyp. What, sirrah, won't you march?

Scrub. No, my dear, I won't march—but I'll walk.—
And I'll make bold to listen a little too.

Goes behind the side-scene and listens.

Gyp. Indeed, Doctor, the count has been bar-   260
barously treated, that's the truth on't.

Foi. Ah, Mrs. Gypsy, upon my shoul, now, gra, his
complainings would mollify the marrow in your bones
and move the bowels of your commiseration! He
veeps, and he dances, and he fistles, and he swears,   265
and he laughs, and he stamps, and he sings: in conclusion, joy, he's afflicted *à la française*, and a stranger
would not know whider to cry or to laugh with him.

Gyp. What would you have me do, Doctor?

Foi. Noting joy, but only hide the count in Mrs.   270
Sullen's closet when it is dark.

Gyp. Nothing! is that nothing? It would be both a
sin and a shame, Doctor.

Foi. Here is twenty louis d'ors, joy, for your shame;
and I will give you an absolution for the shin.   275

Gyp. But won't that money look like a bribe?

Foi. Dat is according as you shall tauk it. If you
receive the money beforehand, 'twill be *logice* a bribe;
but if you stay till afterwards, 'twill be only a
gratification. 280

Gyp. Well, Doctor, I'll take it *logice.* But what must
I do with my conscience, sir?

Foi. Leave dat wid me, joy; I am your priest, gra;
and your conscience is under my hands.

Gyp. But should I put the count into the closet— 285

Foi. Vel, is dere any shin for a man's being in a
closhet? One may go to prayers in a closhet.

Gyp. But if the lady should come into her chamber
and go to bed?

Foi. Vel, and is dere any shin in going to bed, joy? 290

Gyp. Ay, but if the parties should meet, Doctor?

Foi. Vel den, the parties must be responsible. Do
you be after putting the count in the closet; and leave
the shins wid themselves. I will come with the count
to instruct you in your chamber. 295

Gyp. Well, Doctor, your religion is so pure! Methinks I'm so easy after an absolution, and can sin
afresh with so much security, that I'm resolved to die
a martyr to't. Here's the key of the garden door; come
in the back way when 'tis late. I'll be ready to receive 300
you, but don't so much as whisper, only take hold of
my hand; I'll lead you, and do you lead the count and
follow me. *Exeunt.*

Enter Scrub.

Scrub. What witchcraft now have these two imps of
the Devil been a-hatching here? There's twenty louis 305

---

280. GRATIFICATION: reward.
314. LE BRUN: Charles le Brun, French artist, first director of the
Gobelin tapestry works.
317. GRANICUS: river in Asia Minor, near the mouth of which Alexander defeated the Persians in the battle known as the Battle of Arbela;
RAMILLIES: site of Marlborough's victory over the French in 1706.

d'ors; I heard that and saw the purse. But I must give
room to my betters.   *Exit.*

*Enter Aimwell, leading Dorinda and making love
     in dumb show; Mrs. Sullen and Archer.*

Mrs. Sul. (*To Archer*) Pray, sir, how d'ye like that
piece?

Arch. O, 'tis Leda! You find, madam, how Jupiter 310
comes disguised to make love—

Mrs. Sul. But what think you there of Alexander's
battles?

Arch. We only want a Le Brun, madam, to draw
greater battles, and a greater general of our own. The 315
Danube, madam, would make a greater figure in a
picture than the Granicus; and we have our Ramillies
to match their Arbela.

Mrs. Sul. Pray, sir, what head is that in the corner
there?   320

Arch. O madam, 'tis poor Ovid in his exile.

Mrs. Sul. What was he banished for?

Arch. His ambitious love, madam. (*Bowing*) His
misfortune touches me.

Mrs. Sul. Was he successful in his amours?   325

Arch. There he has left us in the dark. He was too
much a gentleman to tell.

Mrs. Sul. If he were secret, I pity him.

Arch. And if he were successful, I envy him.

Mrs. Sul. How d'ye like that Venus over the chim- 330
ney?

Arch. Venus! I protest, madam, I took it for your
picture; but now I look again, 'tis not handsome
enough.

Mrs. Sul. O, what a charm is flattery! If you would 335
see my picture, there it is, over that cabinet.—How
d'ye like it?

Arch. I must admire anything, madam, that has the least resemblance of you. But, methinks, madam—(*He looks at the picture and Mrs. Sullen three or four times, by turns.*) Pray, madam, who drew it? 340

Mrs. Sul. A famous hand, sir.

Here Aimwell and Dorinda go off.

Arch. A famous hand, madam!—Your eyes, indeed, are featured there; but where's the sparkling moisture, shining fluid, in which they swim? The picture, in- 345 deed, has your dimples; but where's the swarm of killing Cupids that should ambush there? The lips too are figured out; but where's the carnation dew, the pouting ripeness, that tempts the taste in the original?

Mrs. Sul. (*Aside*) Had it been my lot to have 350 matched with such a man!

Arch. Your breasts too—presumptuous man!—what, paint heaven! Apropos, madam, in the very next pic- ture is Salmoneus, that was struck dead with lightning for offering to imitate Jove's thunder. I hope you 355 served the painter so, madam?

Mrs. Sul. Had my eyes the power of thunder, they should employ their lightning better.

Arch. There's the finest bed in that room, madam! I suppose 'tis your Ladyship's bedchamber. 360

Mrs. Sul. And what then, sir?

Arch. I think the quilt is the richest that ever I saw. I can't at this distance, madam, distinguish the figures of the embroidery; will you give me leave, madam—?

Mrs. Sul. The Devil take his impudence! Sure, if I 365 gave him an opportunity, he durst not offer it? I have a great mind to try.—(*Going*) 'Sdeath, what am I doing? And alone, too! (*Returns*) Sister! Sister!

Runs out.

Arch. I'll follow her close—

For where a Frenchman durst attempt to storm, 370
A Briton sure may well the work perform. *Going.*

Enter Scrub.

Scrub. Martin! Brother Martin!

Arch. O Brother Scrub, I beg your pardon, I was not a-going; here's a guinea my master ordered you.

Scrub. A guinea! hi, hi, hi! a guinea! Eh, by this 375 light it is a guinea! But I suppose you expect one-and-twenty shillings in change.

Arch. Not at all; I have another for Gypsy.

Scrub. A guinea for her! Faggot and fire for the witch! Sir, give me that guinea, and I'll discover a 380 plot.

Arch. A plot!

Scrub. Ay, sir, a plot, and a horrid plot! First, it must be a plot because there's a woman in't; second-ly, it must be a plot because there's a priest in't; 385 thirdly, it must be a plot because there's French gold in't; and fourthly, it must be a plot because I don't know what to make on't.

Arch. Nor anybody else, I'm afraid, Brother Scrub.

Scrub. Truly, I'm afraid so too; for where there's a 390 priest and a woman there's always a mystery and a riddle. This I know, that here has been the doctor with a temptation in one hand and an absolution in the other; and Gypsy has sold herself to the Devil; I saw the price paid down, my eyes shall take their 395 oath on't.

Arch. And is all this bustle about Gypsy?

Scrub. That's not all; I could hear but a word here and there; but I remember they mentioned a count, a closet, a back door, and a key.   400

Arch. The count!—Did you hear nothing of Mrs. Sullen?

Scrub. I did hear some word that sounded that way; but whether it was Sullen or Dorinda, I could not distinguish.   405

Arch. You have told this matter to nobody, brother?

Scrub. Told! No, sir, I thank you for that; I'm resolved never to speak one word *pro* nor *con,* till we
have a peace.

Arch. You're i' the right, Brother Scrub; here's a 410
treaty afoot between the count and the lady: the
priest and the chambermaid are the plenipotentiaries.
—It shall go hard but I find a way to be included in
the treaty.—Where's the doctor now?

Scrub. He and Gypsy are this moment devouring 415
My Lady's marmalade in the closet.

Aim. (*From without*) Martin! Martin!

Arch. I come, sir, I come.

Scrub. But you forget the other guinea, Brother
Martin. 420

Arch. Here, I give it with all my heart.

Scrub. And I take it with all my soul.—Ecod, I'll
spoil your plotting, Mrs. Gypsy! And if you should set
the captain upon me, these two guineas will buy me
off. *Exeunt severally.* 425

Enter Mrs. Sullen and Dorinda, meeting.

Mrs. Sul. Well, sister!

Dor. And well, sister!

Mrs. Sul. What's become of My Lord?

Dor. What's become of his servant?

Mrs. Sul. Servant! He's a prettier fellow, and a finer 430
gentleman by fifty degrees, than his master.

Dor. O' my conscience, I fancy you could beg that
fellow at the gallows foot!

Mrs. Sul. O' my conscience I could, provided I
could put a friend of yours in his room. 435

Dor. You desired me, sister, to leave you, when you
transgressed the bounds of honor.

Mrs. Sul. Thou dear censorious country girl! What

dost mean? You can't think of the man without the
bedfellow, I find.   440

Dor. I don't find anything unnatural in that thought;
while the mind is conversant with flesh and blood, it
must conform to the humors of the company.

Mrs. Sul. How a little love and good company im-
proves a woman! Why, child, you begin to live—you   445
never spoke before.

Dor. Because I was never spoke to. My Lord has
told me that I have more wit and beauty than any of
my sex; and truly I begin to think the man is sincere.

Mrs. Sul. You're in the right, Dorinda; pride is the   450
life of a woman, and flattery is our daily bread; and
she's a fool that won't believe a man there, as much
as she that believes him in anything else. But I'll lay
you a guinea that I had finer things said to me than
you had.   455

Dor. Done! What did your fellow say to ye?

Mrs. Sul. My fellow took the picture of Venus for
mine.

Dor. But my lover took me for Venus herself.

Mrs. Sul. Common cant! Had my spark called me a   460
Venus directly, I should have believed him a footman
in good earnest.

Dor. But my lover was upon his knees to me.

Mrs. Sul. And mine was upon his tiptoes to me.

Dor. Mine vowed to die for me.   465

Mrs. Sul. Mine swore to die with me.

Dor. Mine spoke the softest moving things.

Mrs. Sul. Mine had his moving things too.

Dor. Mine kissed my hand ten thousand times.

Mrs. Sul. Mine has all that pleasure to come.   470

Dor. Mine offered marriage.

Mrs. Sul. O Lard! D'ye call that a moving thing?

Dor. The sharpest arrow in his quiver, my dear sister! Why, my ten thousand pounds may lie brooding

here this seven years and hatch nothing at last but   475
some ill-natured clown like yours. Whereas, if I marry
My Lord Aimwell, there will be title, place, and pre-
cedence, the Park, the play, and the drawing room,
splendor, equipage, noise, and flambeaux.—"Hey, My
Lady Aimwell's servants there!"—"Lights, lights to the   480
stairs!"—"My Lady Aimwell's coach put forward!"—
"Stand by, make room for Her Ladyship!"—Are not
these things moving?—What! melancholy of a sudden?

Mrs. Sul. Happy, happy sister! Your angel has been
watchful for your happiness, whilst mine has slept   485
regardless of his charge. Long smiling years of circling
joys for you, but not one hour for me!   *Weeps.*

Dor. Come, my dear, we'll talk of something else.

Mrs. Sul. O Dorinda! I own myself a woman, full of
my sex, a gentle, generous soul, easy and yielding to   490
soft desires; a spacious heart, where Love and all his
train might lodge. And must the fair apartment of my
breast be made a stable for a brute to lie in?

Dor. Meaning your husband, I suppose?

Mrs. Sul. Husband! No, even husband is too soft a   495
name for him.—But, come, I expect my brother here
tonight or tomorrow. He was abroad when my father
married me; perhaps he'll find a way to make me easy.

Dor. Will you promise not to make yourself easy in
the meantime with My Lord's friend?   500

Mrs. Sul. You mistake me, sister. It happens with us
as among the men: the greatest talkers are the greatest
cowards. And there's a reason for it: those spirits
evaporate in prattle which might do more mischief if
they took another course. Though, to confess the   505
truth, I do love that fellow; and if I met him dressed
as he should be, and I undressed as I should be—
look ye, sister, I have no supernatural gifts—I can't

(IV.ii.)
19–20. SCORED . . . DOOR: on credit.

swear I could resist the temptation; though I can
safely promise to avoid it, and that's as much as the 510
best of us can do.

Exeunt Mrs. Sullen and Dorinda.

[Scene II. The inn.]

Enter Aimwell and Archer, laughing.

Arch. And the awkward kindness of the good
motherly old gentlewoman—

Aim. And the coming easiness of the young one—
'Sdeath, 'tis pity to deceive her!

Arch. Nay, if you adhere to those principles, stop   5
where you are.

Aim. I can't stop; for I love her to distraction.

Arch. 'Sdeath, if you love her a hair's breadth beyond discretion, you must go no farther.

Aim. Well, well, anything to deliver us from saun- 10
tering away our idle evenings at White's, Tom's, or
Will's, and be stinted to bear looking at our old acquaintance, the cards, because our impotent pockets
can't afford us a guinea for the mercenary drabs.

Arch. Or be obliged to some purse-proud coxcomb 15
for a scandalous bottle, where we must not pretend to
our share of the discourse, because we can't pay our
club o' the reckoning. Damn it, I had rather sponge
upon Morris and sup upon a dish of bohea scored behind the door!   20

Aim. And there expose our want of sense by talking
criticisms, as we should our want of money by railing
at the government.

Arch. Or be obliged to sneak into the side box, and

between both houses steal two acts of a play, and   25
because we han't money to see the other three, we
come away discontented and damn the whole five.

Aim. And ten thousand such rascally tricks—had we
outlived our fortunes among our acquaintance. But
now—   30

Arch. Ay, now is the time to prevent all this. Strike
while the iron is hot. This priest is the luckiest part of
our adventure; he shall marry you and pimp for me.

Aim. But I should not like a woman that can be so
fond of a Frenchman.   35

Arch. Alas, sir! necessity has no law. The lady may
be in distress; perhaps she has a confounded husband,
and her revenge may carry her farther than her love.
Egad, I have so good an opinion of her, and of myself,
that I begin to fancy strange things; and we must say   40
this for the honor of our women, and indeed of ourselves, that they do stick to their men as they do to
their *Magna Charta*. If the plot lies as I suspect, I
must put on the gentleman.—But here comes the doctor. I shall be ready.   *Exit.*   45

Enter Foigard.

Foi. Sauve you, noble friend.

Aim. O sir, your servant! Pray, Doctor, may I crave
your name?

Foi. Fat naam is upon me? My naam is Foigard,
joy.   50

Aim. Foigard! a very good name for a clergyman.
Pray, Doctor Foigard, were you ever in Ireland?

Foi. Ireland! No, joy. Fat sort of plaace is dat saam

---

25. BETWEEN . . . PLAY: the Queen's Theatre in the Haymarket and
the Drury Lane were the two playhouses operating at this time. It was
possible to enter the theatre and sample one act without paying an
admission charge.
79–81. MYNHEER . . . SACRAMANT: Sir, I know not what he says. I
understand you not, truly.

Ireland? Dey say de people are catched dere when
dey are young.   55

Aim. And some of 'em when they're old—as for
example. (*Takes Foigard by the shoulder.*) Sir, I arrest you as a traitor against the government; you're a
subject of England and this morning showed me a
commission by which you served as chaplain in the   60
French army. This is death by our law, and your Rev-
erence must hang for't.

Foi. Upon my shoul, noble friend, dis is strange
news you tell me! Fader Foigard a subject of England! De son of a burgomaster of Brussels a subject of 65
England! Ubooboo—

Aim. The son of a bog-trotter in Ireland! Sir, your
tongue will condemn you before any bench in the
kingdom.

Foi. And is my tongue all your evidensh, joy?   70

Aim. That's enough.

Foi. No, no, joy, for I vil never spake English no
more.

Aim. Sir, I have other evidence.— Here, Martin!

Enter Archer.

You know this fellow?   75

Arch. (*In a brogue*) Saave you, my dear cussen,
how does your health?

Foi. (*Aside*) Ah! upon my shoul dere is my countryman, and his brogue will hang mine.— *Mynheer, Ick
wet neat watt hey zacht. Ick universton ewe neat,*   80
sacramant!

Aim. Altering your language won't do, sir; this fellow knows your person and will swear to your face.

Foi. Faace! Fey, is dere a brogue upon my faash
too?   85

Arch. Upon my soulvation dere ish, joy! But Cussen Mackshane, vil you not put a remembrance upon me?

Foi. (*Aside*) Mackshane! By St. Paatrick, dat ish my naame, shure enough!

Aim. I fancy, Archer, you have it.   90

Foi. The Devil hang you, joy! By fat acquaintance are you my cussen?

Arch. O, de Devil hang yourshelf, joy! You know we were little boys togeder upon de school, and your foster-moder's son was married upon my nurse's 95 chister, joy, and so we are Irish cussens.

Foi. De Devil taak the relation! Vel, joy, and fat school was it?

Arch. I tinks it vas—aay—'twas Tipperary.

Foi. No, no, joy; it vas Kilkenny.   100

Aim. That's enough for us—self-confession. Come, sir, we must deliver you into the hands of the next magistrate.

Arch. He sends you to jail, you're tried next assizes, and away you go swing into purgatory.   105

Foi. And is it so wid you, cussen?

Arch. It vil be sho wid you, cussen, if you don't immediately confess the secret between you and Mrs. Gypsy. Look'ee, sir, the gallows or the secret, take your choice.   110

Foi. The gallows! Upon my shoul, I hate that saam gallow, for it is a diseash dat is fatal to our family.— Vel, den, dere is nothing, shentlemens, but Mrs. Shullen would spaak wid the count in her chamber at midnight, and dere is no haarm, joy, for I am to conduct 115 the count to the plash, myshelf.

Arch. As I guessed.— Have you communicated the matter to the count?

Foi. I have not sheen him since.

---

150. FAIRLY . . . HIM: set him to drinking.

Arch. Right again! Why then, Doctor, you shall con- 120
duct me to the lady instead of the count.

Foi. Fat, my cussen to the lady! Upon my shoul,
gra, dat is too much upon the brogue.

Arch. Come, come, Doctor; consider we have got a
rope about your neck, and if you offer to squeak, we'll 125
stop your windpipe, most certainly. We shall have
another job for you in a day or two, I hope.

Aim. Here's company coming this way; let's into my
chamber and there concert our affair farther.

Arch. Come, my dear cussen, come along.   *Exeunt.* 130

Enter Bonniface, Hounslow, and Bagshot at one door,
Gibbet at the opposite.

Gib. Well, gentlemen, 'tis a fine night for our enter-
prise.

Houn. Dark as hell.

Bag. And blows like the Devil. Our landlord here
has showed us the window where we must break in, 135
and tells us the plate stands in the wainscot cupboard
in the parlor.

Bon. Ay, ay, Mr. Bagshot, as the saying is, knives
and forks, and cups and cans, and tumblers and
tankards. There's one tankard, as the saying is, that's 140
near upon as big as me; it was a present to the squire
from his godmother and smells of nutmeg and toast
like an East India ship.

Houn. Then you say we must divide at the stair-
head? 145

Bon. Yes, Mr. Hounslow, as the saying is. At one
end of that gallery lies My Lady Bountiful and her
daughter, and at the other Mrs. Sullen. As for the
squire—

Gib. He's safe enough. I have fairly entered him, 150
and he's more than half-seas over already. But such a

parcel of scoundrels are got about him now, that,
egad, I was ashamed to be seen in their company.

Bon. 'Tis now twelve, as the saying is. Gentlemen,
you must set out at one.   155

Gib. Hounslow, do you and Bagshot see our arms
fixed, and I'll come to you presently.

Houn., Bag. We will.   *Exeunt.*

Gib. Well, my dear Bonny, you assure me that
Scrub is a coward.   160

Bon. A chicken, as the saying is. You'll have no
creature to deal with but the ladies.

Gib. And I can assure you, friend, there's a great
deal of address and good manners in robbing a lady. I
am the most a gentleman that way that ever traveled   165
the road. But, my dear Bonny, this prize will be a
galleon, a Vigo business. I warrant you we shall bring
off three or four thousand pound.

Bon. In plate, jewels, and money, as the saying is,
you may.   170

Gib. Why then, Tyburn, I defy thee! I'll get up to
town, sell off my horse and arms, buy myself some
pretty employment in the Household, and be as snug
and as honest as any courtier of 'um all.

Bon. And what think you then of my daughter   175
Cherry for a wife?

Gib. Look'ee, my dear Bonny—Cherry "is the goddess I adore," as the song goes; but it is a maxim that
man and wife should never have it in their power to
hang one another, for if they should, the Lord have 180
mercy on 'um both!

                                              Exeunt.

---

167. VIGO: the British admiral, Sir George Rooke, seized part of the
Spanish treasure fleet at Vigo Bay in 1702.
173. HOUSEHOLD: i.e., the royal entourage.

ACT V

Scene I. Scene continues.

Knocking without. Enter Bonniface.

Bon. Coming! Coming!—A coach and six foaming horses at this time o' night! Some great man, as the saying is, for he scorns to travel with other people.

Enter Sir Charles Freeman.

Sir Chas. What, fellow! a public house, and abed when other people sleep?   5
Bon. Sir, I an't abed, as the saying is.
Sir Chas. Is Mr. Sullen's family abed, think'ee?
Bon. All but the squire himself, sir, as the saying is; he's in the house.
Sir Chas. What company has he?   10
Bon. Why, sir, there's the constable, Mr. Gage the exciseman, the hunchbacked barber, and two or three other gentlemen.
Sir Chas. I find my sister's letters gave me the true picture of her spouse.   15

Enter Sullen, drunk.

Bon. Sir, here's the squire.
Sul. The puppies left me asleep.—Sir!
Sir Chas. Well, sir.

451

Sul. Sir, I'm an unfortunate man. I have three thousand pound a year, and I can't get a man to drink a   20
cup of ale with me.

Sir Chas. That's very hard.

Sul. Ay, sir; and unless you have pity upon me and
smoke one pipe with me, I must e'en go home to my
wife; and I had rather go to the Devil by half.   25

Sir Chas. But I presume, sir, you won't see your
wife tonight; she'll be gone to bed—you don't use to
lie with your wife in that pickle?

Sul. What! not lie with my wife! Why, sir, do you
take me for an atheist or a rake?   30

Sir Chas. If you hate her, sir, I think you had better
lie from her.

Sul. I think so too, friend. But I'm a justice of peace
and must do nothing against the law.

Sir Chas. Law! As I take it, Mr. Justice, nobody ob-   35
serves law for law's sake, only for the good of those
for whom it was made.

Sul. But if the law orders me to send you to jail,
you must lie there, my friend.

Sir Chas. Not unless I commit a crime to deserve it.   40

Sul. A crime? Oons, an't I married?

Sir Chas. Nay, sir, if you call marriage a crime, you
must disown it for a law.

Sul. Eh!—I must be acquainted with you, sir. But,
sir, I should be very glad to know the truth of this   45
matter.

Sir Chas. Truth, sir, is a profound sea, and few
there be that dare wade deep enough to find out the
bottom on't. Besides, sir, I'm afraid the line of your
understanding mayn't be long enough.   50

Sul. Look'ee, sir, I have nothing to say to your sea
of truth, but if a good parcel of land can entitle a man

(V.i.)
28. PICKLE: intoxicated state.

to a little truth, I have as much as any he in the country.

Bon. I never heard your Worship, as the saying is, 55
talk so much before.

Sul. Because I never met with a man that I liked
before.

Bon. Pray, sir, as the saying is, let me ask you one
question: are not man and wife one flesh? 60

Sir Chas. You and your wife, Mr. Guts, may be one
flesh, because ye are nothing else; but rational creatures have minds that must be united.

Sul. Minds!

Sir Chas. Ay, minds, sir; don't you think that the 65
mind takes place of the body?

Sul. In some people.

Sir Chas. Then the interest of the master must be
consulted before that of his servant.

Sul. Sir, you shall dine with me tomorrow!—Oons, 70
I always thought that we were naturally one.

Sir Chas. Sir, I know that my two hands are
naturally one, because they love one another, kiss one
another, help one another in all the actions of life; but
I could not say so much if they were always at cuffs. 75

Sul. Then 'tis plain that we are two.

Sir Chas. Why don't you part with her, sir?

Sul. Will you take her, sir?

Sir Chas. With all my heart.

Sul. You shall have her tomorrow morning, and a 80
venison pasty into the bargain.

Sir Chas. You'll let me have her fortune too?

Sul. Fortune! Why, sir, I have no quarrel at her fortune. I only hate the woman, sir, and none but the
woman shall go. 85

Sir Chas. But her fortune, sir—

Sul. Can you play at whisk, sir?

Sir Chas. No, truly, sir.

Sul. Nor at all-fours?

Sir Chas. Neither! 90

Sul. (*Aside*) Oons! where was this man bred?—
Burn me, sir! I can't go home; 'tis but two o'clock.

Sir Chas. For half an hour, sir, if you please. But
you must consider 'tis late.

Sul. Late! that's the reason I can't go to bed. Come, 95
sir! *Exeunt.*

*Enter Cherry, runs across the stage and knocks at
Aimwell's chamber door. Enter Aimwell in his
nightcap and gown.*

Aim. What's the matter? You tremble, child; you're
frighted.

Cher. No wonder, sir. But, in short, sir, this very
minute a gang of rogues are gone to rob My Lady 100
Bountiful's house.

Aim. How!

Cher. I dogged 'em to the very door and left 'em
breaking in.

Aim. Have you alarmed anybody else with the 105
news?

Cher. No, no, sir, I wanted to have discovered the
whole plot, and twenty other things, to your man
Martin; but I have searched the whole house and
can't find him. Where is he? 110

Aim. No matter, child; will you guide me immediately to the house?

Cher. With all my heart, sir; My Lady Bountiful
is my godmother, and I love Mrs. Dorinda so well—

Aim. Dorinda! The name inspires me, the glory and 115
the danger shall be all my own.—Come, my life, let me
but get my sword.

Exeunt.

[Scene II.] Scene changes to a bedchamber in
Lady Bountiful's house.

*Enter Mrs. Sullen, Dorinda, undressed; a table and
lights.*

Dor. 'Tis very late, sister. No news of your spouse
yet?

Mrs. Sul. No, I'm condemned to be alone till towards four, and then perhaps I may be executed with
his company.   5

Dor. Well, my dear, I'll leave you to your rest; you'll
go directly to bed, I suppose?

Mrs. Sul. I don't know what to do. Heigh-ho!

Dor. That's a desiring sigh, sister.

Mrs. Sul. This is a languishing hour, sister.   10

Dor. And might prove a critical minute, if the pretty
fellow were here.

Mrs. Sul. Here! What, in my bedchamber at two
o'clock o' the morning, I undressed, the family asleep,
my hated husband abroad, and my lovely fellow at my   15
feet!—O 'gad, sister!

Dor. Thoughts are free, sister, and them I allow
you. So, my dear, good night.

Mrs. Sul. A good rest to my dear Dorinda!
                      Exit Dorinda.

Thoughts free! Are they so? Why, then suppose him   20
here, dressed like a youthful, gay, and burning bridegroom, (*Here Archer steals out of the closet.*) with
tongue enchanting, eyes bewitching, knees implor-
ing.—(*Turns a little o' one side and sees Archer in the
posture she describes.*)—Ah! (*Shrieks and runs to the*   25
other side of the stage.) Have my thoughts raised a
spirit?—What are you, sir, a man or a devil?

Arch. (*Rising*) A man, a man, madam.

Mrs. Sul. How shall I be sure of it?

Arch. Madam, I'll give you demonstration this 30
minute.   *Takes her hand.*

Mrs. Sul. What, sir! do you intend to be rude?

Arch. Yes, madam, if you please.

Mrs. Sul. In the name of wonder, whence came ye?

Arch. From the skies, madam. I'm a Jupiter in love, 35
and you shall be my Alcmene.

Mrs. Sul. How came you in?

Arch. I flew in at the window, madam; your cousin
Cupid lent me his wings, and your sister Venus
opened the casement. 40

Mrs. Sul. I'm struck dumb with admiration!

Arch. And I with wonder!

          Looks passionately at her.

Mrs. Sul. What will become of me?

Arch. How beautiful she looks! The teeming, jolly
spring smiles in her blooming face, and when she was 45
conceived, her mother smelt to roses, looked on lilies—

  Lilies unfold their white, their fragrant charms,
  When the warm sun thus darts into their arms.

          Runs to her.

Mrs. Sul. (*Shrieks*) Ah!

Arch. Oons, madam, what d'ye mean? you'll raise 50
the house.

Mrs. Sul. Sir, I'll wake the dead before I bear this!
What! approach me with the freedoms of a keeper!
I'm glad on't, your impudence has cured me.

Arch. If this be impudence—(*Kneels*) I leave to 55
your partial self; no panting pilgrim, after a tedious,
painful voyage, e'er bowed before his saint with more
devotion.

Mrs. Sul. (*Aside*) Now, now, I'm ruined if he

36. ALCMENE: one of the god's mistresses, later mother of Hercules.

kneels!—Rise, thou prostrate engineer, not all thy un- 60
dermining skill shall reach my heart. Rise, and know
I am a woman without my sex; I can love to all the
tenderness of wishes, sighs, and tears—but go no
farther. Still, to convince you that I'm more than
woman, I can speak my frailty, confess my weakness 65
even for you—but—

Arch. (*Going to lay hold on her*) For me!

Mrs. Sul. Hold, sir! build not upon that; for my most
mortal hatred follows if you disobey what I command
you now. Leave me this minute.—(*Aside*) If he 70
denies, I'm lost.

Arch. Then you'll promise—

Mrs. Sul. Anything another time.

Arch. When shall I come?

Mrs. Sul. Tomorrow when you will. 75

Arch. Your lips must seal the promise.

Mrs. Sul. Pshaw!

Arch. They must! they must!—(*Kisses her*) Raptures and Paradise!—And why not now, my angel?
The time, the place, silence, and secrecy, all conspire. 80
And the now conscious stars have preordained this
moment for my happiness.   *Takes her in his arms.*

Mrs. Sul. You will not, cannot, sure!

Arch. If the sun rides fast, and disappoints not mor-
tals of tomorrow's dawn, this night shall crown my 85
joys.

Mrs. Sul. My sex's pride assist me!

Arch. My sex's strength help me!

Mrs. Sul. You shall kill me first!

Arch. I'll die with you.   *Carrying her off.* 90

Mrs. Sul. Thieves! thieves! murder!—

Enter Scrub in his breeches and one shoe.

Scrub. Thieves! thieves! murder! popery!

Arch. Ha! the very timorous stag will kill in rutting
time.　　　　　　　　　*Draws, and offers to stab Scrub.*

Scrub. (*Kneeling*) O, pray, sir, spare all I have, and　95
take my life!

Mrs. Sul. (*Holding Archer's hand*) What does the
fellow mean?

Scrub. O madam, down upon your knees, your mar-
rowbones! He's one of 'em.　　　　　　　　　　100

Arch. Of whom?

Scrub. One of the rogues—I beg your pardon, sir,
one of the honest gentlemen that just now are broke
into the house.

Arch. How!　　　　　　　　　　　　105

Mrs. Sul. I hope you did not come to rob me?

Arch. Indeed I did, madam, but I would have taken
nothing but what you might ha' spared; but your crying "Thieves" has waked this dreaming fool, and so
he takes 'em for granted.　　　　　　　110

Scrub. Granted! 'tis granted, sir; take all we have.

Mrs. Sul. The fellow looks as if he were broke out of
Bedlam.

Scrub. Oons, madam, they're broke into the house
with fire and sword; I saw them, heard them; they'll　115
be here this minute.

Arch. What, thieves?

Scrub. Under favor, sir, I think so.

Mrs. Sul. What shall we do, sir?

Arch. Madam, I wish your Ladyship a good night.　120

Mrs. Sul. Will you leave me?

Arch. Leave you! Lord, madam, did not you command me to be gone just now, upon pain of your immortal hatred?

Mrs. Sul. Nay, but pray, sir—　　*Takes hold of him.*　125

Arch. Ha, ha, ha! now comes my turn to be ravished.
You see now, madam, you must use men one way or
other; but take this by the way, good madam, that

none but a fool will give you the benefit of his courage
unless you'll take his love along with it.—How are 130
they armed, friend?

Scrub. With sword and pistol, sir.

Arch. Hush!—I see a dark lantern coming through
the gallery.—Madam, be assured I will protect you
or lose my life. 135

Mrs. Sul. Your life! No, sir, they can rob me of nothing that I value half so much; therefore, now, sir, let
me entreat you to be gone.

Arch. No, madam, I'll consult my own safety for the
sake of yours; I'll work by stratagem. Have you 140
courage enough to stand the appearance of 'em?

Mrs. Sul. Yes, yes, since I have 'scaped your hands,
I can face anything.

Arch. Come hither, Brother Scrub! don't you know
me? 145

Scrub. Eh! my dear brother, let me kiss thee.
                                    Kisses Archer.

Arch. This way—here—
            Archer and Scrub hide behind the bed.

*Enter Gibbet, with a dark lantern in one hand, and
            a pistol in t'other.*

Gib. Ay, ay, this is the chamber, and the lady alone.

Mrs. Sul. Who are you, sir? What would you have?
D'ye come to rob me? 150

Gib. Rob you! Alackaday, madam, I'm only a
younger brother, madam; and so, madam, if you make
a noise, I'll shoot you through the head; but don't be
afraid, madam.—(*Laying his lantern and pistol upon
the table.*) These rings, madam—don't be concerned, 155
madam, I have a profound respect for you, madam;
your keys, madam—don't be frighted, madam, I'm the

most of a gentleman.—(*Searching her pockets.*) This
necklace, madam—I never was rude to a lady;—I have
a veneration—for this necklace— 160

> Here Archer, having come round and seized the
> pistol, takes Gibbet by the collar, trips up his
> heels, and claps the pistol to his breast.

Arch. Hold, profane villain, and take the reward of
thy sacrilege!

Gib. O, pray, sir, don't kill me; I an't prepared!

Arch. How many is there of 'em, Scrub?

Scrub. Five-and-forty, sir. 165

Arch. Then I must kill the villain, to have him out
of the way.

Gib. Hold, hold, sir, we are but three, upon my
honor.

Arch. Scrub, will you undertake to secure him? 170

Scrub. Not I, sir; kill him, kill him!

Arch. Run to Gypsy's chamber; there you'll find the
doctor; bring him hither presently.—(*Exit Scrub, running.*) Come, rogue, if you have a short prayer, say it.

Gib. Sir, I have no prayer at all; the government has 175
provided a chaplain to say prayers for us on these
occasions.

Mrs. Sul. Pray, sir, don't kill him. You fright me as
much as him.

Arch. The dog shall die, madam, for being the 180
occasion of my disappointment.—Sirrah, this moment
is your last.

Gib. Sir, I'll give you two hundred pound to spare
my life.

Arch. Have you no more, rascal? 185

Gib. Yes, sir, I can command four hundred, but I
must reserve two of 'em to save my life at the sessions.

> *Enter Scrub and Foigard.*

Arch. Here, Doctor, I suppose Scrub and you between you may manage him. Lay hold of him, Doctor.

                     [Foigard lays hold of Gibbet.]

Gib. What! turned over to the priest already!— 190
Look ye, Doctor, you come before your time; I an't condemned yet, I thank ye.

Foi. Come, my dear joy, I vill secure your body and your shoul too; I vill make you a good Catholic and give you an absolution.   195

Gib. Absolution! Can you procure me a pardon, Doctor?

Foi. No, joy.

Gib. Then you and your absolution may go to the Devil!   200

Arch. Convey him into the cellar; there bind him. Take the pistol, and if he offers to resist, shoot him through the head—and come back to us with all the speed you can.

Scrub. Ay, ay; come, Doctor, do you hold him fast, 205
and I'll guard him.

         Exit Foigard and Scrub with Gibbet.

Mrs. Sul. But how came the doctor—

Arch. In short, madam—*(Shrieking without.)*
'Sdeath! the rogues are at work with the other ladies. I'm vexed I parted with the pistol; but I must fly to 210
their assistance. Will you stay here, madam, or venture yourself with me?

Mrs. Sul. O, with you, dear sir, with you.

         Takes him by the arm and exeunt.

[Scene III.] Scene changes to another apartment in
the same house.

*Enter Hounslow, dragging in Lady Bountiful, and
Bagshot, hauling in Dorinda; the rogues with swords
drawn.*

Bag. Come, come, your jewels, mistress!
Houn. Your keys, your keys, old gentlewoman!

Enter Aimwell and Cherry.

Aim. Turn this way, villains! I durst engage an army
in such a cause.   *He engages 'em both.*
Dor. O madam, had I but a sword to help the brave   5
man!
Lady Boun. There's three or four hanging up in the
hall; but they won't draw. I'll go fetch one, however.
                                        Exit.

Enter Archer and Mrs. Sullen.

Arch. Hold, hold, My Lord! every man his bird,
pray.   10
*They engage man to man; the rogues are thrown
                                        and disarmed.*
Cher. What! the rogues taken! then they'll impeach
my father; I must give him timely notice.   *Runs out.*
Arch. Shall we kill the rogues?
Aim. No, no, we'll bind them.
Arch. Ay, ay.—(*To Mrs. Sullen, who stands by*   15
him.) Here, madam, lend me your garter.

Mrs. Sul. (*Aside*) The Devil's in this fellow! He fights, loves, and banters, all in a breath.—Here's a cord that the rogues brought with 'em, I suppose.

Arch. Right, right, the rogue's destiny, a rope to 20 hang himself.—Come, My Lord.—This is but a scandalous sort of an office (*Binding the rogues together.*) if our adventures should end in this sort of hangman-work; but I hope there is something in prospect that— 25

Enter Scrub.

Well, Scrub, have you secured your Tartar?

Scrub. Yes, sir; I left the priest and him disputing about religion.

Aim. And pray carry these gentlemen to reap the benefit of the controversy. 30

Delivers the prisoners to Scrub, who leads 'em out.

Mrs. Sul. Pray, sister, how came My Lord here?

Dor. And pray, how came the gentleman here?

Mrs. Sul. I'll tell you the greatest piece of villainy—
They talk in dumb show.

Aim. I fancy, Archer, you have been more success-ful in your adventures than the housebreakers. 35

Arch. No matter for my adventure, yours is the principal. Press her this minute to marry you—now while she's hurried between the palpitation of her fear and the joy of her deliverance, now while the tide of her spirits are at high flood. Throw yourself 40 at her feet, speak some romantic nonsense or other—address her like Alexander in the height of his vic-tory, confound her senses, bear down her reason, and away with her. The priest is now in the cellar and dare not refuse to do the work. 45

Enter Lady Bountiful.

Aim. But how shall I get off without being observed?

Arch. You a lover, and not find a way to get off!— Let me see—

Aim. You bleed, Archer. 50

Arch. 'Sdeath, I'm glad on't; this wound will do the business. I'll amuse the old lady and Mrs. Sullen about dressing my wound while you carry off Dorinda.

Lady Boun. Gentlemen, could we understand how 55 you would be gratified for the services—

Arch. Come, come, My Lady, this is no time for compliments; I'm wounded, madam.

Lady Boun., Mrs. Sul. How! wounded!

Dor. I hope, sir, you have received no hurt? 60

Aim. None but what you may cure—

> *Makes love in dumb show.*

Lady Boun. Let me see your arm, sir.—I must have some powder-sugar to stop the blood.—O me! an ugly gash, upon my word, sir! You must go into bed.

Arch. Ay, My Lady, a bed would do very well.— 65 (*To Mrs. Sullen.*) Madam, will you do me the favor to conduct me to a chamber.

Lady Boun. Do, do, daughter, while I get the lint and the probe and the plaster ready.

> *Runs out one way; Aimwell carries off Dorinda another.*

Arch. Come, madam, why don't you obey your 70 mother's commands?

Mrs. Sul. How can you, after what is passed, have the confidence to ask me?

Arch. And if you go to that, how can you, after what is passed, have the confidence to deny me? Was 75

(V.iii.)
100. MACHINE: device; scheme.
101. EDDYSTONE: the lighthouse on Eddystone Rock, destroyed in a storm in 1703.

not this blood shed in your defense, and my life exposed for your protection? Look ye, madam, I'm none
of your romantic fools, that fight giants and monsters
for nothing; my valor is downright Swiss; I'm a soldier of fortune and must be paid.   80

Mrs. Sul. 'Tis ungenerous in you, sir, to upbraid
me with your services!

Arch. 'Tis ungenerous in you, madam, not to reward 'em.

Mrs. Sul. How! at the expense of my honor?   85

Arch. Honor! can honor consist with ingratitude?
If you would deal like a woman of honor, do like a
man of honor. D'ye think I would deny you in such a
case?

Enter a Servant.

Serv. Madam, My Lady ordered me to tell you that   90
your brother is below at the gate.   *Exit.*

Mrs. Sul. My brother! Heavens be praised!—Sir, he
shall thank you for your services; he has it in his
power.

Arch. Who is your brother, madam?   95

Mrs. Sul. Sir Charles Freeman. You'll excuse me,
sir; I must go and receive him.   *Exit.*

Arch. Sir Charles Freeman! 'Sdeath and hell! my
old acquaintance. Now unless Aimwell has made
good use of his time, all our fair machine goes souse   100
into the sea like the Eddystone.

Exit.

[Scene IV.] Scene changes to the gallery in the same
house.

Enter Aimwell and Dorinda.

Dor. Well, well, My Lord, you have conquered;
your late generous action will, I hope, plead for my
easy yielding; though I must own your Lordship had
a friend in the fort before.

Aim. The sweets of Hybla dwell upon her tongue!—   5
Here, Doctor—

Enter Foigard, with a book.

Foi. Are you prepared, boat?

Dor. I'm ready. But first, My Lord, one word. I have
a frightful example of a hasty marriage in my own
family; when I reflect upon't, it shocks me. Pray, My   10
Lord, consider a little—

Aim. Consider! Do you doubt my honor or my
love?

Dor. Neither. I do believe you equally just as
brave; and were your whole sex drawn out for me to   15
choose, I should not cast a look upon the multitude
if you were absent. But, My Lord, I'm a woman;
colors, concealments may hide a thousand faults in
me—therefore, know me better first. I hardly dare
affirm I know myself in anything except my love.   20

Aim. (*Aside*) Such goodness who could injure! I
find myself unequal to the task of villain; she has
gained my soul and made it honest like her own. I
cannot, cannot hurt her.—Doctor, retire.—(*Exit Foi-*

gard.) Madam, behold your lover and your proselyte, 25
and judge of my passion by my conversion! I'm all a
lie, nor dare I give a fiction to your arms; I'm all
counterfeit, except my passion.

Dor. Forbid it, Heaven! a counterfeit!

Aim. I am no lord but a poor needy man, come with 30
a mean, a scandalous design to prey upon your fortune. But the beauties of your mind and person have
so won me from myself that, like a trusty servant, I
prefer the interest of my mistress to my own.

Dor. Sure I have had the dream of some poor mari- 35
ner, a sleepy image of a welcome port, and wake in-
volved in storms! Pray, sir, who are you?

Aim. Brother to the man whose title I usurped, but
stranger to his honor or his fortune.

Dor. Matchless honesty! Once I was proud, sir, of 40
your wealth and title, but now am prouder that you
want it; now I can show my love was justly leveled
and had no aim but love.—Doctor, come in.

*Enter Foigard at one door, Gypsy at another,
who whispers Dorinda.*

—Your pardon, sir, we sha'not want you now.—Sir,
you must excuse me. I'll wait on you presently. 45
                               Exit with Gypsy.

Foi. Upon my shoul, now, dis is foolish.   *Exit.*

Aim. Gone! and bid the priest depart!—It has an
ominous look.

Enter Archer.

Arch. Courage, Tom! Shall I wish you joy?

Aim. No. 50

Arch. Oons, man, what ha' you been doing?

Aim. O Archer! my honesty, I fear, has ruined me.

Arch. How?

Aim. I have discovered myself.

Arch. Discovered! and without my consent? What! 55
have I embarked my small remains in the same bottom with yours, and you dispose of all without my
partnership?

Aim. O Archer! I own my fault.

Arch. After conviction—'tis then too late for pardon. 60
You may remember, Mr. Aimwell, that you proposed
this folly. As you begun, so end it. Henceforth I'll
hunt my fortune single. So, farewell!

Aim. Stay, my dear Archer, but a minute.

Arch. Stay! what, to be despised, exposed, and 65
laughed at? No, I would sooner change conditions
with the worst of the rogues we just now bound than
bear one scornful smile from the proud knight that
once I treated as my equal.

Aim. What knight? 70

Arch. Sir Charles Freeman, brother to the lady that
I had almost—but no matter for that; 'tis a cursed
night's work, and so I leave you to make your best
on't. *Going.*

Aim. Freeman!—One word, Archer. Still I have 75
hopes; methought she received my confession with
pleasure.

Arch. 'Sdeath! who doubts it?

Aim. She consented after to the match; and still I
dare believe she will be just. 80

Arch. To herself, I warrant her, as you should have
been.

Aim. By all my hopes, she comes, and smiling
comes!

Enter Dorinda, mighty gay.

Dor. Come, my dear Lord—I fly with impatience to 85

your arms. The minutes of my absence was a tedious
year. Where's this tedious priest?

Enter Foigard.

Arch. Oons, a brave girl!

Dor. I suppose, My Lord, this gentleman is privy to
our affairs?   90

Arch. Yes, yes, madam, I'm to be your father.

Dor. Come, priest, do your office.

Arch. Make haste, make haste, couple 'em any
way.—(*Takes Aimwell's hand.*) Come, madam, I'm to
give you—   95

Dor. My mind's altered; I won't.

Arch. Eh!—

Aim. I'm confounded!

Foi. Upon my shoul, and sho is myshelf.

Arch. What's the matter now, madam?   100

Dor. Look ye, sir, one generous action deserves another. This gentleman's honor obliged him to hide
nothing from me; my justice engages me to conceal
nothing from him. In short, sir, you are the person
that you thought you counterfeited; you are the true   105
Lord Viscount Aimwell, and I wish your Lordship
joy.—Now, priest, you may be gone; if My Lord is
pleased now with the match, let His Lordship marry
me in the face of the world.

Aim., Arch. What does she mean?   110

Dor. Here's a witness for my truth.

Enter Sir Charles Freeman and Mrs. Sullen.

Sir Chas. My dear Lord Aimwell, I wish you joy.

Aim. Of what?

Sir Chas. Of your honor and estate. Your brother died the day before I left London; and all your friends have writ after you to Brussels; among the rest I did myself the honor.

Arch. Hark ye, Sir Knight, don't you banter now?

Sir Chas. 'Tis truth, upon my honor.

Aim. Thanks to the pregnant stars that formed this accident!

Arch. Thanks to the womb of time that brought it forth!—away with it!

Aim. Thanks to my guardian angel that led me to the prize! *Taking Dorinda's hand.*

Arch. And double thanks to the noble Sir Charles Freeman.—My Lord, I wish you joy.—My Lady, I wish you joy.—Egad, Sir Freeman, you're the honestest fellow living!—'Sdeath, I'm grown strange airy upon this matter!—My Lord, how d'ye? A word, My Lord; don't you remember something of a previous agreement that entitles me to the moiety of this lady's fortune, which, I think, will amount to five thousand pound?

Aim. Not a penny, Archer; you would ha' cut my throat just now, because I would not deceive this lady.

Arch. Ay, and I'll cut your throat again, if you should deceive her now.

Aim. That's what I expected; and to end the dispute, the lady's fortune is ten thousand pound. We'll divide stakes: take the ten thousand pound or the lady.

Dor. How! is your Lordship so indifferent?

Arch. No, no, no, madam; His Lordship knows very well that I'll take the money; I leave you to His Lordship, and so we're both provided for.

Enter Count Bellair.

Count Bel. Mesdames et messieurs, I am your servant trice humble! I hear you be rob here.

Aim. The ladies have been in some danger, sir.   150

Count Bel. And, begar, our inn be rob too!

Aim. Our inn! by whom?

Count Bel. By the landlord, begar! Garzoon, he has
rob himself and run away!

Arch. Robbed himself!   155

Count Bel. Ay, begar, and me too of a hundre
pound.

Arch. A hundred pound?

Count Bel. Yes, that I owed him.

Aim. Our money's gone, Frank.   160

Arch. Rot the money! my wench is gone.—*Savez-
vous quelque chose de Mademoiselle Cherry?*

Enter a Fellow with a strongbox and a letter.

Fell. Is there one Martin here?

Arch. Ay, ay—who wants him?

Fell. I have a box here and letter for him.   165

Arch. (*Taking the box*) Ha, ha, ha! what's here?
Legerdemain!—By this light, My Lord, our money
again!—But this unfolds the riddle.—(*Opening the
letter, reads.*) Hum, hum, hum!—O, 'tis for the public good, and must be communicated to the company.   170

Mr. Martin,

My father, being afraid of an impeachment by the
rogues that are taken tonight, is gone off; but if you
can procure him a pardon he will make great discoveries that may be useful to the country. Could I   175
have met you instead of your master tonight, I
would have delivered myself into your hands, with
a sum that much exceeds that in your strongbox,
which I have sent you, with an assurance to my

dear Martin that I shall ever be his most faithful 180
friend till death.   *Cherry Bonniface.*

There's a billet-doux for you! As for the father, I
think he ought to be encouraged; and for the daughter—pray, My Lord, persuade your bride to take her
into her service instead of Gypsy.   185

Aim. I can assure you, madam, your deliverance
was owing to her discovery.

Dor. Your command, My Lord, will do without the
obligation. I'll take care of her.

Sir Chas. This good company meets opportunely in 190
favor of a design I have in behalf of my unfortunate
sister. I intend to part her from her husband. Gentlemen, will you assist me?

Arch. Assist you! 'Sdeath, who would not?

Count Bel. Assist! Garzoon, we all assest!   195

Enter Sullen.

Sul. What's all this?—They tell me, spouse, that you
had like to have been robbed.

Mrs. Sul. Truly, spouse, I was pretty near it, had
not these two gentlemen interposed.

Sul. How came these gentlemen here?   200

Mrs. Sul. That's his way of returning thanks, you
must know.

Count Bel. Garzoon, the question be apropos for
all dat.

Sir Chas. You promised last night, sir, that you 205
would deliver your lady to me this morning.

Sul. Humph!

Arch. Humph! what do you mean by humph? Sir,
you shall deliver her! In short, sir, we have saved you
and your family; and if you are not civil, we'll unbind 210

the rogues, join with 'um, and set fire to your house.—
What does the man mean? not part with his wife!

Count Bel. Ay, garzoon, de man no understan common justice.

Mrs. Sul. Hold, gentlemen, all things here must 215
move by consent; compulsion would spoil us. Let my
dear and I talk the matter over, and you shall judge
it between us.

Sul. Let me know first who are to be our judges.—
Pray, sir, who are you? 220

Sir Chas. I am Sir Charles Freeman, come to take
away your wife.

Sul. And you, good sir?

Aim. Thomas, Viscount Aimwell, come to take away
your sister. 225

Sul. And you, pray, sir?

Arch. Francis Archer, Esquire, come—

Sul. To take away my mother, I hope.—Gentlemen,
you're heartily welcome; I never met with three more
obliging people since I was born!—And now, my 230
dear, if you please, you shall have the first word.

Arch. And the last, for five pound!

Mrs. Sul. Spouse!

Sul. Rib!

Mrs. Sul. How long have we been married? 235

Sul. By the almanac, fourteen months—but by my
account, fourteen years.

Mrs. Sul. 'Tis thereabout by my reckoning.

Count Bel. Garzoon, their account will agree.

Mrs. Sul. Pray, spouse, what did you marry for? 240

Sul. To get an heir to my estate.

Sir Chas. And have you succeeded?

Sul. No.

Arch. The condition fails of his side.—Pray, madam,
what did you marry for? 245

Mrs. Sul. To support the weakness of my sex by the

strength of his, and to enjoy the pleasures of an agreeable society.

Sir Chas. Are your expectations answered?

Mrs. Sul. No.   250

Count Bel. A clear case! a clear case!

Sir Chas. What are the bars to your mutual contentment?

Mrs. Sul. In the first place, I can't drink ale with him.   255

Sul. Nor can I drink tea with her.

Mrs. Sul. I can't hunt with you.

Sul. Nor can I dance with you.

Mrs. Sul. I hate cocking and racing.

Sul. And I abhor ombre and piquet.   260

Mrs. Sul. Your silence is intolerable.

Sul. Your prating is worse.

Mrs. Sul. Have we not been a perpetual offense to each other? a gnawing vulture at the heart?

Sul. A frightful goblin to the sight?   265

Mrs. Sul. A porcupine to the feeling?

Sul. Perpetual wormwood to the taste?

Mrs. Sul. Is there on earth a thing we could agree in?

Sul. Yes—to part.   270

Mrs. Sul. With all my heart.

Sul. Your hand.

Mrs. Sul. Here.

Sul. These hands joined us, these shall part us. Away!   275

Mrs. Sul. North.

Sul. South.

Mrs. Sul. East.

Sul. West—far as the poles asunder.

Count Bel. Begar, the ceremony be vera pretty!   280

Sir Chas. Now, Mr. Sullen, there wants only my sister's fortune to make us easy.

Sul. Sir Charles, you love your sister, and I love her fortune; every one to his fancy.

Arch. Then you won't refund—   285

Sul. Not a stiver.

Arch. Then I find, madam, you must e'en go to your prison again.

Count Bel. What is the portion?

Sir Chas. Ten thousand pound, sir.   290

Count Bel. Garzoon, I'll pay it, and she shall go home wid me.

Arch. Ha, ha, ha! French all over.—Do you know, sir, what ten thousand pound English is?

Count Bel. No, begar, not *justement.*   295

Arch. Why, sir, 'tis a hundred thousand livres.

Count Bel. A hundre tousand livres! Ah, garzoon! me canno' do't; your beauties and their fortunes are both too much for me.

Arch. Then I will. This night's adventure has   300 proved strangely lucky to us all, for Captain Gibbet in his walk had made bold, Mr. Sullen, with your study and escritoire, and had taken out all the writings of your estate, all the articles of marriage with your lady, bills, bonds, leases, receipts to an infinite   305 value. I took 'em from him, and I deliver them to Sir Charles.

Gives him a parcel of papers and parchments.

Sul. How, my writings!—my head aches consumedly.—Well, gentlemen, you shall have her fortune, but I can't talk. If you have a mind, Sir Charles, to be   310 merry and celebrate my sister's wedding and my divorce, you may command my house—but my head aches consumedly.—Scrub, bring me a dram.

Arch. (*To Mrs. Sullen*) Madam, there's a country dance to the trifle that I sung today; your hand, and   315 we'll lead it up.   *Here a dance.*

Arch. 'Twould be hard to guess which of these

parties is the better pleased, the couple joined or the
couple parted; the one rejoicing in hopes of an un-
tasted happiness, and the other in their deliverance 320
from an experienced misery.

> Both happy in their several states we find,
> Those parted by consent, and those conjoined.
> Consent, if mutual, saves the lawyer's fee,
> Consent is law enough to set you free. 325

(Epilogue)

9. LEUCTRA: site of a battle in 371 B.C. at which Thebes, under
Epaminondas, defeated the Spartans.

14. SERGEANT KITE: the hero of Farquhar's *The Recruiting Officer*
(1706).

16. BAYS: victorious wreaths; honors.

AN EPILOGUE

Designed to be spoke in "The Beaux' Stratagem"

If to our play your judgment can't be kind,
Let its expiring author pity find.
Survey his mournful case with melting eyes,
Nor let the bard be damned before he dies.
Forbear, you fair, on his last scene to frown,   5
But his true exit with a plaudit crown;
Then shall the dying poet cease to fear
The dreadful knell, while your applause he hears.
At Leuctra so the conqu'ring Theban died,
Claimed his friends' praises, but their tears denied;   10
Pleased in the pangs of death, he greatly thought
Conquest with loss of life but cheaply bought.
The difference this: the Greek was one would fight
As brave, though not as gay, as Sergeant Kite.
Ye sons of Will's, what's that to those who write?   15
To Thebes alone the Grecian owed his bays;
You may the bard above the hero raise,
Since yours is greater than Athenian praise.

A new and growing series presenting distinguished
literary works in an inexpensive, well-designed format

• • • • • • • • • • • • • •

Anthologies of Short Stories, Poetry and Essays Now in Washington Square Press Editions

CHAUCER, GEOFFREY, *The Canterbury Tales*. Translated by R. M. Lumiansky, Preface by Mark Van Doren. Illustrated. W 567 (60¢)

CRANE, STEPHEN, *Maggie and Other Stories*. Selected and with an Introduction by Austin McC. Fox. W 133 (45¢)

FROST, ROBERT, *New Enlarged Anthology of Poems*. Edited by Louis Untermeyer. Illustrated. W 556 (60¢)

HAWTHORNE, NATHANIEL, *Twice-Told Tales and Other Short Stories*. Introduction by Quentin Anderson. W 580 (60¢)

MILLAY, EDNA ST. VINCENT, *Collected Lyrics*. Introduction by Norma Millay. W 550 (60¢)

MILLAY, EDNA ST. VINCENT, *Collected Sonnets*. Introduction by Norma Millay. W 551 (60¢)

PETERSON, HOUSTON, ed., *Great Essays*. W 598 (60¢)

POE, EDGAR ALLAN, *Great Tales and Poems*. W 246 (45¢)

SHAKESPEARE, WILLIAM, *The Complete Sonnets, Songs and Poems*. Edited by Henry W. Simon. W 131 (45¢)

SPEARE, M. EDMUND, ed., *A Pocket Book of Short Stories*. W 255 (45¢)

SPEARE, M. EDMUND, ed., *The Pocket Book of Verse*. W 241 (45¢)

WILLIAMS, OSCAR, ed., *Immortal Poems of the English Language*. W 553 (60¢)

WILLIAMS, OSCAR, ed., *The Pocket Book of Modern Verse*. W 554 (60¢)

• • • • • • • • • • • • • •

If your bookseller does not have the titles you want, you may order them by sending retail price, plus 10¢ per book for postage and handling, to: Mail Service Department, Washington Square Press, Inc., 1 West 39th Street, New York 18, N.Y. Please enclose check or money order—not responsible for orders containing cash.